Let Your Light Shine

Angel Messages

of

Healing, Love and Light

Swell Press

Let Your Light Shine

Angel Messages

of

Healing, Love and Light

Melanie Beckler
www.Ask-Angels.com

66 You are never alone in navigating your path through life on Earth. You have guardian angels and spirit guides who are always with you and waiting to help. You simply have to acknowledge them, and ask for their help and guidance. Invite them into your meditation space and they will help you to further strengthen the connection. **99**

-Archangel Haniel, channeled by Melanie.

Contents

Introduction
Increased Light On Earth

Right now is an exciting time of increased light and transformation on Earth. A wave of light energy, is passing through our galaxy significantly raising the vibration of everything within its reach, including all life on planet Earth. This increased energy alters the course of all that it touches, triggering accelerated changes on a physical, social, even political level. These changes are no accident, they are an essential step in the process of awakening all humanity and Earth through the process of ascension, or "upliftment" as my guides have often started referring to it.

Imagine a spiritually awakened humanity. Imagine the collective consciousness of humanity being fully aware of what we are co creating as individuals, and collectively. Imagine all beings consciously living in balance with

Mother Earth, and with each other, radiating compassion and love for all creatures. This vision may seem afar or even impossible, but now more than ever the potential for change on Earth is huge, and the opportunity for taking a giant stride forward on the path of conscious awakening is divinely aligned. One thing is certain, the veil of illusion has been lifted by this wave of light and energy. The realms of the Divine, of the Angels, Archangels and of Spirit are more easily accessed now than ever before.

Embrace your spiritual growth now. By activating your light body, following the path of your open heart, and riding this wave of increased change and light on the planet you can choose to consciously create more joy, love and peace in your experience than you have ever known. Fully shining your light and expanding your consciousness is both liberating and empowering. It is by no mistake that you are here on Earth now and it is no mistake that you are reading these words. You are here to participate in and observe the mass spiritual awakening of humanity.

In this book you will read channeled messages from the Angelic Realm which will empower you to brightly shine your unique inner light. As you read the messages to follow, simply open your heart and your mind and you will be presented with an opportunity from the angels to cleanse and lift your vibration, and to bring new levels of love and light into your reality.

I have been working with the angelic realm since 2007 when much to my surprise, Archangel Michael came into my meditation with an incredibly specific and accurate answer in response to a question I had written down in my journal. Since that first day of connecting, the angels have continued to love, lift, and assist me in increasing the connection, and anchoring more love and spiritual light into my life.

I have always experienced the angels as incredibly loving, powerful and light filled beings. The angels advice to me and others, is to call upon them often as they are always near, ready, and willing to assist in the journey through life. Angels will show you the path to connect with your higher self, and your inner source of unconditional love.

When I channel the angels I am in a peaceful trance like meditative state, aware of the angels around and the message and frequency they flow through me. I experience angelic guidance as a stream of consciousness alongside of my own. When I am channeling the angels I feel as though I have been lifted up into the light into a peaceful, safe place which radiates with unconditional love and understanding. The words the angels transmit through these messages are a small fraction of the full power and meaning that is conveyed.

An uplifting frequency is transmitted along with the angel messages that assists in expanding consciousness and lifting in the incredible light present amidst each and every word. If you're open, these messages from the angels will empower you to take the reigns of control to begin consciously moving forward on your path of anchoring your full light into physical form.

Ahead of you lies an unending journey of expansion and spiritual awakening. Wherever you are now, you can always progress further, more deeply and more fully into experiencing the magnificent light of your soul. Do not let this unending progression worry you, let it inspire you. Your angels and guides are on hand to assist you in this process now, in taking a step forward, and letting your full light shine.

~**Melanie**

Angelic Invocation

Take a deep and relaxing breath as you begin to quiet your mind and allow your heart to open... Breathe and find your center. I now ask that we be surrounded with light and with One Hundred Thousand Angels of Divine Love, Wisdom, and Protection, to assist in connecting with knowledge wisdom and truth.

Now feel or imagine, that your energy is grounding into the core of the Earth. As your energy is grounded to Earth, allow yourself to feel the incredible light of the planet, and notice that you are one with it, feel this and know that you are an integral part of the One Source Energy flowing throughout Earth and throughout All That Is. Take another deep breath now as you now allow this light from the core of the Earth to begin flowing up and in through the bottom of your feet, opening, balancing, and healing all 7 chakras of your physical body, and as this light continues to lift up now above your crown chakra let your consciousness go with it, opening your higher energy centers and continuing to lift up above the light, and into direct presence and connection with Creative Source Energy, with God, and with the Divine.

Relax and breathe. Feel what it is like to be deeply loved. Feel your Oneness with Source, and with All That Is. Enjoy this feeling. Bask in the Divine Love that radiates all around you now. Simply connecting with these energies will cleanse and lift your being, bringing you healing love and blessings. But there is more... Now think or say;

"I now invite my highest best and most loving Guardian Angels, Spirit Guides, Ascended Masters, and Archangels to come in, and connect with me now"

Now simply relax, breathe, and open your heart to feel and know the connection of your Guides and Angels who are indeed here. Open your heart, let go...and lift!

1

Cleanse and Connect With Your Angels
~Archangel Michael

Beloved one, indeed, I am Archangel Michael and I am here with you now, with you always. I invite you to now connect with me deeply, profoundly for your benefit and for the benefit of manifesting that which you desire into the physical. For, understand, when your heart is open, when you are connected to your angels and attuned to love you are able to flow with the natural course of reality. You are able to manifest blessings of love, joy, health, and abundance in your life.

To connect with the angelic realm, all you must do is relax, breathe, and open your heart. The angelic realm exists very near to your own physical realm. In many senses we angels are only a breath away. And so as you take in a deep breath of fresh, healing air now, allow your conscious awareness to drop into your heart. Open your heart chakra now. Open your heart and open the doors to the angelic realm therein to instantly feel, sense, hear, smell, know, feel the love of your angels that are indeed all around.

Think or say, "Angels surround me. angels lift my vibration. angels guide me, help me upon my path." Know that when you ask, we answer. Every time you ask for angelic assistance we are always happy to assist. Know that the more you practice, the more you open, the more you lift your own vibration by choosing and living love; the more clearly, the more accurately, and the more profoundly our guidance, love, and presence will appear in your life. Part of this process, indeed, is raising your vibration. You are able to do this by releasing the lower vibrations of density, fear, and negativity that still dwell within your being. Releasing and replacing these lower vibrations with love, with compassion, with joy, and with light. As you consciously practice this, you lift, you become more compassionate, more closely connected to the full light of your soul... You ascend. Your vibration becomes more closely attuned to the realm of angels and you are able to experience our love, our guidance, our light in your own life in the forms of living joyously, living in love, living inspired, living in alignment with your true and authentic purpose.

Now to cleanse your energy, to lift you into the realm of angels and light and love so that you may continue to increase your connection...

Relax, breathe, and imagine now that there is an orb of light above your head, angelic light, light of the divine. This golden orb of light now begins to pour light down like a waterfall of light. When you're ready, step directly into this flow, let the light we angels broadcast, let this energy of divine love flow all around you, cleansing those residues of fear, doubt, and negativity away. Clearing you mind, body, spirit.

Let go. Like holding a helium balloon out in front of you and loosening your grip. Let go of all that no longer serves you. Release past residue from your physical body, your emotional body, your etheric body, your light body.

Imagine this waterfall of light from above continues to pour down on you and when you are ready, open up your crown chakra at the top of your head by simple thinking it so and letting more light into your being. You may feel a tingling, a pulsing sensation as this light comes in. This light is connecting you with the angelic realm of love, with your unique spiritual gifts and psychic abilities; abilities to heal, to manifest, to live your inspired life, your divine blueprint, your love in the physical.

Let your vibration continue to lift as this light pours in and all around you. And now at this time, with your permission, with your simply thinking, "Yes." I, Michael, agree to cut any and all cords that are draining you energetically, consciously or unconsciously. These draining cords, with your permission, are now cut and released into the light All energy that is yours that has been drained now returns to you cleansed, purified, and activated with love. All that remains in you that does not serve, that is not rightfully yours, that is not love is lifted up and out of your being now, beyond this orb of light above you, and into the light. And now you are cleansed and your vibration lifted. All you are left to do is quiet your mind, open your heart, feel the love of angels, and feel us wrap you with our wings of love.

Lift, breathe, and now beloved, if you have a question, let yourself formulate this in your mind and then pay attention to the thought, to the feeling, to the sense that your angels respond with.

Or if you would simply like to sit and bask in this energy of angelic love that is indeed all around you. We will stay with you and continue to nurture, to love, and to lift your vibration.

The more often you connect with this energy of your open heart, consciously reflecting, and opening your senses beyond the physical, the more you are able to pick up the love, the guidance, and the messages of your angels. Feel this love now, radiate this love, and share this love with others.

You are blessed and you are lifted, you are cleansed. Now shine your light and continue forward on your path, if you will, to feel, to know, to fully experience the light of your angels and the light of your inner divine being and higher self. All accessible in every moment simply a breath away. Open your heart and tune in to the angelic realm therein. *I am Archangel Michael, and you are so dearly loved.*

2

Experience Angelic Healing
~Archangel Raphael

Dearest one, I, Archangel Raphael, greet you in this very now. I greet you with an energy of healing love and light. In your mind's eye open and see the emerald green healing light that is all around you. Relax your mind now, trusting that your mind will observe this experience in the way that is best and right for you. Surrender to how you experience this healing light and energy. Trust that it is well and it is flowing now, in divine time and order. And now release your mind.

You may still notice your conscious awareness present, but drop in deeper with your awareness to a deeper state of consciousness, into your heart, into your center, into your spirit. Good. I greet you in this now to offer energy of healing light and of well being, to infuse your path and your being with this energy of healing love. At this time you may feel your angels around you and a bit of motion as I, Archangel Raphael, place my hands on your back, on your shoulders. Feel a surge of light, of connection, of love as you read these words and healing is broadcast through you now.

Healing is nothing more than frequency, than energy. It is a vibration and your body indeed, holds the key to healing. If there is a symptom you are experiencing now, know that its root cause is not in the physical. The root cause is in spirit, is in mind, is in the realm of the unseen, the untouched.

When you open your heart and calm your mind you are able to see through and past the illusion of the physical realm to experience directly the realm of spirit. By tuning into this now, by being aware, and by consciously intending what you will receive from this awareness, from this energy beyond the physical, you are able to now connect fully with my energy. And, as you may know, I Archangel Raphael am an archangel of healing. Right now is a powerful time of healing for both you and for your planet and for all of humanity.

Know that if you are called to share healing with others, if you are compelled to bring about positive changes on Earth or in others lives, all you must do is bring this healing into you, for you truly are one with all that is. As you heal and as you nurture your heart and your spirit, you therefore do nurture the heart and spirit of your planet and the heart and spirit of the collective humanity that is one, one with all, one with you, one with love. Open your heart, feel your heart throb and beat as more and more energy is broadcast your way. Relax and let yourself lift as you are initiated, as you are blessed with healing love, with the remembrance of your ability to self heal.

Draw your awareness to any area of your body, of your mind, or of your spirit that is in need of healing at this time. With awareness, the energy automatically flows to this area, wrapping it in love, pulsing, and releasing now pain, tension, disease, fear, anger, hurt, into the light. These emotions that manifest as illness, as pain are released into the light. And you may feel now that there is some void, for where once was held pain, disease, and illness is now empty. And for a brief moment let yourself dive in to that emptiness, complete stillness, complete calm. And now in the place where disease, illness, pain, negativity or tension was once held, we angels now flow light to you and fill this void within you with love, with healing, with compassion, with light.

Accept these gifts if you like, feel lighter, feel blessed, feel loved as you are filled with this healing light now, and as you are initiated with your full power to self heal. "How?" you may ask, "Is it really possible for me to heal my body, my mind, my spirit?" And I say to you, believe, trust, accept the gift of self-healing that you have always had, but that we draw your attention more closely to now. Self heal. Think, "Yes." Think, "Yes to angelic healing." Think, "Yes to healing from within." Think, "I am vibrantly healthy. I am healed from the inside out. I am loved and I am love."

While you are in a vibration of complete love; disease, pain, tension, even negativity cannot occupy you. As you are in a vibration of gratitude, you are in a vibration of health. The more you are able to love and give thanks, the healthier, the more energetic, the more vibrant you will feel and you will continue to move in this direction. It is true that thoughts of fear, of worry and distress bring you disease and bring you discomfort. If you have physical symptoms that have manifest, it is a sign that thoughts have been creating this manifestation. And so while healing in many cases can be instant, in other cases there requires time, there requires a refocusing of the mind, a return to trust, to love, to gratitude, to acceptance of all that is in this very now.

Know and trust all is well, indeed, all is divine, and any pain you have experienced up unto this point has come about to simply to provide contrast and ultimately encourage you to more fully connect with your authentic self in spirit. We in the celestial realm see you as the light. You are a powerful, spiritual being able to heal from the inside out. Able to heal mind, body, spirit, Earth, physical, nonphysical consciousness... by opening fully to love. Simply accepting the love and blessing of angels, by allowing the healing energy of light in, by releasing fear, doubt, negativity that plagues and weighs you down, and by diving into full expression of joy, love, and compassion. These are the healing energies we broadcast your way now. Green, emerald light all around you. Breathe it in and let yourself be healed from the inside out. Believe, moving forward, that you are healed mind, body, and spirit, and so it shall be. And if you find that you are doubting, if your faith is wavering, call upon I, Archangel Raphael, and I will, once again, place my hands on your back broadcasting light, love, and healing, reawakening and energizing your inner innate divine ability to heal. With your heart open, with your crown open wide, by calling upon healing angels, and by calling upon your full spirit, your higher self, your soul, you too can flow the healing energy of the divine in from above through your body and out through your hands.

Where do you desire to send healing energy at this time? It can be yourself, your planet, a loved one. Be aware of this your intention of where the healing will flow, and the open your energy up to receive all the healing that is needed. And now, through your hands, with your heart open, feel this energy pour out. Energy streaming in through your crown and flowing out through your hands and through your heart, surrounding your Earth, surrounding your loved one, surrounding you, and healing with love.

It is true that healing energy and loving energy and light are one in the same. The more you love, the more you give thanks, the more you believe in your ability to heal, the more quickly healing will manifest. Be aware of anywhere that is in need of healing light, and then open your heart, think, "Healing angels, come in". Open your crown chakra, and think, "Healing energy, pour into me now," witness and feel this. Feel your healing ability awakened, feel your angels sending you healing love, let it pour in, and now let it flow out of your hands, out of your heart, send this where it may go.

Healing, love, and light are with you. You are awakened to this innate, natural ability to self heal, believe, and intend for healing to flow to areas which you desire. As you walk your path of love, notice the repetitive thoughts and ideas that come into your awareness, encouraging you to make healthy choices for your body and spirit.

"Angels help, angels heal, angels send me your healing love." Call upon us at any time and we shall assist you in this continued evolution and awakening. You are powerful beyond measure. It is your innate gift, an ability from God and from the angels to heal yourself, to live vibrantly, to live with well being, to live with love.

If you are experiencing disease, pain, or illness, it does not mean that you are a bad person, it does not mean that you are any less powerful as spirit. It simply means that the thoughts, the seeds of creation have been planted for this to come to be. But you are able to weed your garden of your mind of that which no longer serves, and plant new seeds of thought which empower, nurture you and assist you in believing in your healing ability.

We angels send you this healing energy, it is all around you. Breathe it in, accept it, embrace it, and so be healed in mind, body, and spirit, activated and awakened to share this healing with Earth, with family, with friends, and with all.

Open, and let healing flow in, healing you, and let this same energy flow out, healing all that is.

I am Raphael and I am closely connected to you always. Simply think, "Angels, heal me," and we will answer. Remember, we do not interfere without your permission, but with a simple thought you may call us in and we will always come. We are your humble servants. You are so dearly loved, you are blessed, you are lifted, and you are healed mind, body, spirit. Accept these blessings, release that which is not truth and that which does not serve.

Embrace love, embrace healing, embrace gratitude, and step boldly into the light, for you are a light being and you are ready to shine. You are so loved and you are blessed. Indeed, it is so. I, Raphael, deem it to be. I love you and celebrate your miraculous health, well being, vitality, and light. And so it is, and so it shall be.

3

Light Infusion
~Archangel Uriel

Greetings, indeed, we your angels and guides are here and I am Archangel Uriel. I greet you with an incredible amount of love and, indeed, frequency. Know, beloved one, that the ascension of planet Earth, the evolution of humanity and the planet and of all beings and creatures is going according to plan. Indeed, wave after wave of light frequency, or ascension energy as you may call it, has been streaming to the planet.

You are now living in a world which is ever carrying more light, more love available, and with easier access to the realms beyond the physical than has ever been. Indeed, now is a powerful time for you, beloved one, to unite fully your physical self, your physical being, with your full spirit, with the radiant and loving vibration of your soul, the spiritual you, your light and your power. And, indeed, to unite your mind, some may call your ego, your thoughts, your personality with the more subtle, finer, and lighter vibration of your intuition.

Beloved one, we invite you to relax, take in a deep breath of air, and of the light and love vibration that is all around you. Let this frequency fill you, lift you, and cleanse you. Let your vibration become fine and fluid and let yourself lift, float, fly.

At this time as your physical body is infused with light. You are now able to connect with your etheric body, your auric body, your light body. Lift in consciousness, with this spiritual aspect of you, lift in love. While your vibration is lifting you may also feel as though you are dropping in, dropping inside, dropping into your heart. And through doing this, through opening wide the doors of your heart, you are able to fully enter into our realm, the realm of angels, of unconditional love, of light, fine, high, vibrations of love, well being and compassion.

Relax and allow your frequency to lift, allow healing, cleansing, and loving vibrations in. Dear one, as more and more light becomes available to you in your life, in your body, and on your planet, you will undergo your own unique process of detoxification and then integrating and lifting with new levels of light. Your personal process of ascension is guided by your team of nonphysical, spiritual, angelic beings and by creator source. There is a divine plan, and we are here in this now to tell you that all is well and all is going according to plan. Do not worry or be dismayed if there is some area in your physical body that is experiencing a state of discomfort or disease. Pain during your ascension process does not necessarily mean that there is a serious illness or sickness as may have occurred earlier in your life and have memories of.

At this powerful time in which you live; of evolution, of unfolding, of raising in vibration, if you notice that there is an area of your body that hurts, know that it is simply a sign. It is a clue of where you can draw in more light, of where you may have some current energetic blockage. Blockages can come in many forms. Do not be afraid of this word, but know that rather past experiences, past lives, past personalities, or even challenging trying moments from this life, can indeed, stay with you at cellular level. When you let light in, the light knows where to go, finding the source of your pain or blockage.

And so if you find that there is pain or discomfort, open that area up. Imagine your cells blossoming like lotus flowers and as they open, the light we angels flow your way gently enter in. Feel this light flowing in now, cleansing out all that no longer serves, all that inhibits you from opening fully to your full power, your full spirit and soul.

Understand that at your core level you are powerful beyond measure, spirit, spiritual being, light. You are at soul level connected to the benevolent, loving, and all powerful energy of the creator of all that is.

From our perspective, you are not separate from the oneness of God, of creator. Indeed, even in many mainstream religious texts and doctrines, it is said that you are made in the likeness and the image of God. We take this a step further and say that you are one and when you leave your body, when the body dies, your soul and your spirit returns to the full connection with creator, to the full awareness of all that is, of everything, of everyone living, not in physical, but in spirit, in complete bliss, acceptance, love, awareness.

The time of transition after physical life offers, indeed, a powerful clue for you, an ascending human being. You see, as you begin to become more aware of consciousness while you are in the physical, you are able to claim the joy, the acceptance, the love, the compassion, the knowing of the inner workings of the multi verse and all that is. Your benefit in doing this is that you can claim this ability while still in physical, form. To live joyously, vibrantly, to live with love, and to live your inspired life, the life of your dreams, the life of your conscious creation.

Dream awake means simply to open to your full vibration and power in spirit, to be conscious and to be aware. To plant new seeds of thought into your awareness, into consciousness, that can sprout, that can grow and bloom like a beautiful flower into the manifestation of your desire. Increasing in vibration, opening to your full spiritual power and your light is an important, aye, an integral part of your purpose of being here in life as a human physical being. You may have forgotten your full light and power upon your birth, but we are here, indeed, you are here connecting with the angelic realm now in this way because you have the full capacity to return to this connection while living.

Gone are the days of needing to die to fully remember and return to full awareness. Indeed, many masters who have come before you have become enlightened. This does not mean that they have anything that you do not, it simply means that they integrated the light on Earth, that they released those blocks, those past experiences, past emotions, and past challenges, and opened their mind, body, spirit to unite as one energy, one light, one consciousness not separate from anything else but one.

We give you now this visualization. Open your heart and imagine an orb... A circle, a sphere, of light all around you. Notice what color it is. The color that shows up has a hidden clue for you, a message. Just be aware and know that this colorful orb of light offers you what you most need now, the energy of healing, of love, of acceptance, of compassion, of hope, of well being, of comfort and harmony. Whatever you're most needing now to take that next step forward on your ascension path, to integrate more light and to boost your vibration level to enter into a finer, lighter vibration appears for you now, simply be aware. The benefit of doing this, dear one, is that you can, and will in time, become aware of your full nature.

We have mentioned that aye, indeed, you are physical and, indeed, you are spiritual, and we take this a step further now and say, you are indeed multidimensional.

You exist in the physical and you exist in the spiritual and you exist in many realms or alternate realities in between. As a physical and spiritual being alive at this powerful point of acceleration of time, of ascension and upliftment upon your planet, you can connect with all of who you are, across the lines of time. You can heal yourself completely, heal the past expressions of you that were hurt or betrayed. Flowing love their way and integrating the skills, the traits, and the spiritual power that you had at that time, integrating into yourself here and now, at time time, in your current physical vessel.

But for now simply note, be aware, feel the light that is around you that offers you what you most need now be it healing, compassion, or love, or some combination. When you are ready now, imagine again that your heart is open and now breathe in the light from this orb around you, indeed, light from the angelic realm.

Breathe light in, flow light in. Let light enter your body so that your physical vessel, indeed, takes on a luminescent glow from the inside out. You are being cleansed and lifted beloved. You are being lifted in vibration and illuminated from within.

Light, frequency, fine refined, high vibration, in line with love, with joy, with compassion... These energies that serve you, that heal you, and that empower you to claim the reigns, to take control.

You see, you are created in the likeness and image of God. You are connected to all that is, you are connected to we angels, you are connected to creative source. When you allow your ego mind to merge with your intuition, when you allow your physical vessel and body to merge with the spirit of your soul, you are able to create change in your realm, here and now.

You have the ability to help your planet, to help your fellow humans, to help your family, your friends, and help you to live more in line with your divine blueprint, to live more in line with love. You are one who is here to usher out the age of war and tension and conflict and to usher in a new era for humanity, a new renaissance where love, where compassion, where art, where creation, where creative expression, communion with nature, and with all beings, awareness of all levels and dimensions of reality prevails. Becoming more aware serves you in creating and designing the life you desire, in healing and lifting so that you are able to feel good and celebrate your way through life and your time in the physical. You are here because there is work for you to do. However, it does not need to feel like the heavy work of the physical realm you have grown accustomed to.

Your spiritual work can feel like play. Your path is meant to be fun, exciting, positive. We urge and encourage you to follow the nudges and the guidance of your heart. When you do quiet your mind and open your heart, the guidance of your spirit, and your intuition are able to be heard and understood.

The dimension in which you currently reside is where the ego and the physical body are most at home. You were born into this the physical world from a state of full connection to All That Is. You chose to leave the comfortable realm of Spirit, to temporarily forget your full light, so that you could experience firsthand the process of going from physical, being grounded in ego, to reuniting with and remembering the full light of your spiritual self. This process gives you the opportunity to learn immense lessons therein. Although this realm of the physical has not been the primary realm for spirit to dwell, you are involved in a great experiment now. You are an integral player in the ascension process, and you are well qualified for your role in this mission, and all that is involved in the full return of Spirit to Earth. This is our mission, this is why we Angels flow light to the planet, and this is why you are so supported and why now is such a powerful time to open and express your spirit fully.

You are supported, in nurturing your inner light, the light of your soul, and allowing it to grow and build in you until it becomes the prominent force of creation in your life. With your spiritual self and light body fully activated you are able to create from love and from your heart, not from your mind in doubt or fear.

Know that love has the power to heal any pain, any ascension symptoms as you travel the path of your raising vibration. Let love in, let it fill any area of discomfort. As love and light fills you, the density, the pain, the negativity that may have be stored there comes to the surface to be released. Let it go, hand it to your angels, release into the light, and let more love in.

You are surrounded with love, you are embraced with love, you are filled with love. Return to love in every moment, respond with love, flow love, and know that love is your ticket, love is your passport, love is the way for you to bring more of your soul into the physical. Indeed, you are divinely supported now, right now, more than ever before in uniting the power and light of your spiritual self with your physical body. Now is the time to return to the full knowing of your intuition, knowing the guidance and messages available to you from the spiritual realm.

Practice turning away from your ego from time to time. Although ego is strong in your realm, by quieting it, by letting your ego focus on the blank screen of your mind before you and opening your heart and letting intuition in, you can experience your full self, your true self, and the many beings of light, love and compassion (your angels, your guides, your team) who desire to help you live fully, and vibrantly. You are meant to live passionately, you wanted to be of service; serving the Earth, serving humanity, and, indeed, ushering in the new age of love, of well being, of conscious connection, awareness, and cooperation.

You are a leader and a way shower in this time of change and upliftment. The full transition back to love on Earth cannot, will not, happen without your participation. And so dear one, open to your light and release that density, those blocks that still lie within you. Release attachment to pain and disease for they no longer serve. Open yourself up to love... Flow love, be love, live love, know love, for we angels love you dearly and we are near to support you along every step of your journey.

Call us in, acknowledge our presence and think, "Yes, help me. Yes, I grant you permission to assist me on my journey," and we shall, for we are your friends and allies. We desire nothing more than for you to become more aware of our realm of love. With awareness you can flow love into the physical realm to heal the wounds inflicted upon your planet and upon each other. You are able to release past conflicts, struggle, and strife, and to enter in to the new age of love, of compassion, of conscious co creation.

You are an essential player in this transition, and we need you to shine your light, know that you are ready.

Your destiny awaits you. Now is the time and here is the place. Open your heart, lift in vibration, embrace all that is, and love willingly. You are so deeply loved. As you love, you are able to notice the incredible love we have for you.

Working together all things are possible. If you can dream it, together we can achieve it. We can manifest blessings in the physical realm, but remember we will not interfere in your physical realm without your permission... and so ask for our assistance!

Now is the time and you are the one. I am Archangel Uriel and together now with your team of guides and angels we embrace you in wings of love. We offer you now the energy of healing, of compassion, and of love. Take this gift, and continue forward on your path.

Remember, to invite your intuition in, as your intuitive responses will always come in response to a question or challenge. Angels are always willing to assist you in opening further, remember to ask for our assistance. We honor your free will to create, and learn your life lessons on your own should you choose, but are always happy to assist when called.

Quiet your mind, take a deep, relaxing breath in through your nose, open your heart, and drop into your heart. There... The peace, still, and calm within you will serve, and will assist you in many ways. Enter within often, shine vibrantly, and live with love and compassion. While we leave you now, we angels are always near. Call upon us for assistance at any time. I am Uriel and you are so dearly loved.

4

Soul Light Power
~Archangel Uriel

Dearest one, indeed, I, Archangel Uriel, am here. You are greeted with an immense amount of love and gratitude and frequency from the divine. Trust that, yes, your unique team of guides and angels here to assist you right now in this very moment with where you are in your life. We are here, ready and willing to assist you in taking a step forward out of the grip of confusion and control and into empowerment. We will assist you in bringing your spiritual energy into physical form so that you may clearly know and follow the desires of your soul, so that you may clearly communicate and understand the messages, the wisdom, the guidance your soul offers you now on your path towards accomplishing your purpose. Do not doubt dearest one, that you are here on Earth to experience greatness, you are here to create positive change. There may be times when the Earth plane seems too dense and too hard. You may wonder why you are here, why would your soul, your spirit, your guides, God subject you to the challenges and trials and tribulations of the physical realm? But know, dear one, that you have been in situations such as these before and you also have overcome them. You have lived and you have ascended into spirit in the past and so you are here now to make this quantum leap once more.

You are here on Earth now to tune into your vast past experience as a spiritual being and to bring this light to the surface in the physical realm. Although, upon your birth, the details of your empowerment, and of the full light of your spiritual self, have been forgotten. The the veil of illusion is still present in the physical world, but it is being weakened. Light, indeed, streams to your planet now at ever increasing rates. And so, dear one, more light is present now than ever before. This is true even as you head into winter and a time where there is more physical darkness on the planet, this is true as you head into the more quiet introspective, inner focused time which serves you well, as well as the time of energy, of spending time outdoors, of light. Now is the time of release. Now is the time of ritual and of remembering and honoring those who have come before you, your ancestors, the divine family of yours that walked upon this Earth, and now graces you still, still present, still tuned into you but from another realm. You see, as the veil is lifted all realms are accessible from the physical plane. You are not only physical, this message has come through for you before, but we remind you of this now, that you are more than simply physical and the realms beyond the physical, the realms of spirit, the nature realms, and the higher realms of divine love open their doors to you now.

We angels broadcast a frequency to uplift you, a soul download now. If you desire to receive this download of frequency, of love, and of ever increasing connection with your soul and your soul's ability to communicate with you, think, "Yes, I accept! Yes, I receive this soul download now," and imagine now that a light comes in, an orb of light, whatever color your soul chooses to represent itself as now to assist in healing your physical body as you receive this download.

Imagine the orb of light lower down from the heavens and the higher realm where a large part of your spirit and your energy exists. As we said, you are physical but you are more. You exist across realities and dimensions. You are multidimensional and so although you are in physical form now, your spiritual self, the angelic aspect of you, the high vibrational soul aspect of you, so too exists in the realm of divine love, peace, and truth.

And so from above, allow this download from your soul. Let the energy around you now nurture you in ways you knew you needed not, let it lift, cleanse, soothe, and increase your vibration.

This may feel like an inner expansion. Let yourself lift as this orb of light c activates your latent abilities and empowers you with frequency and with a deep inner knowing that, indeed, you are more than physical.

Tune in to your spiritual body and self now and as you do you create a link. What are the benefits of linking your physical and spiritual self? Dear one, there are many. As this connection is strengthened, your full light, your full power, your full love can be accessed by you in physical form. The light of your soul will create a positive ripple throughout your experience, when it is present. Joy, love, and compassion are the foundation of what you will experience, but then as your frequency increases more and more, your gifts, strengths, and abilities naturally rise to the surface.

You are here for a purpose and a reason on Earth. You are here to make a difference and be a leader in transitioning away from the current structure and into a way that serves all beings and Earth so that humanity and Earth can live in balance with the physical and nonphysical realms. And so that humanity can cut the cord that drains.

Dear one, we invite you to imagine now that you are tuning into the whole of collective consciousness, for you are one with all, including humanity. And so tune into this oneness, this one consciousness that connects you along with every being on the planet. Awake, asleep, one.

Open your heart, and it may help to visualize holding your hands out and holding hands with the beings of your planet, creating a great circle around the Earth. Tune into the consciousness of humanity. And now invite in the healing light that your soul, your higher spirit, and your guides and angels have to offer the collective consciousness of all. Invite this energy in. Healing, love, understanding, joy. You may feel an updraft of energy now as the angels on hand energetically lift up limitations, doubts and beliefs that do not serve humanity. Beliefs set in superstition and fear, based and taught from those who sought control and manipulation. Let them go, let fear be released from your experience, and from your emotions. Let anger, hatred, war, all that no longer serves, let it go into the light, into the Creator's light, and let it be replaced with a wave of love which flows all around your planet. A wave of frequency, and of light. Let this in. Let this light uplift you, let it raise you high into the light so that you may directly experience Source. This connection eases the aloneness you have often felt in life thus far is not felt, that cannot not filled through human relationships or interaction. Simply connecting with this Divine Love now may ease the burden of your suffering, but ultimately the loneliness you feel from time to time, is your soul calling you forth to return to full connection with Divine Love.

Once again now, invite the full frequency and light and spirit of your soul, of your higher self, to come into your physical body and to unite with you fully in this very now. This time and place, this moment, and so it is.

Read these words, set the intention with your heart and then witness as the light of your soul pours down from the realms of divine. Soul light now entering in through your crown, and filling out your entire physical body with light.

Radiate the light, the love, the compassion that flows through you now. Let your spinal column be a white light pillar as all your chakras are united, cleansed, and blessed. You are grounded to the Earth below and the light above and you can simply be calm, still, and yet your energy is alive and awakening and swirling around you uniting with the full love and the authentic truth that you are.

Be consciously aware as you allow yourself permission to simply bask in this energy now, embrace it, feel it, let it nurture you as you knew you needed not. And yet, it is exactly what you need right now. Receive this healing and love from your soul that now energetically shows you, "Everything is going to be OK. You are going to make it." More than that, you are now stepping into your role here on Earth.

Open your heart, and notice what message, what visual, what feeling or insight your soul communicates to you now. Healing is transferred. Emotional, physical, mental, and, of course, spiritual well being frequencies fill you and lift you now.

As this light from your soul and from the divine fills your physical body, know that indeed your very cells respond. Your cells respond by releasing the density they have held, perhaps for years. Density attached to past challenges, to struggles, to grief. Your body is experiencing an upliftment now and as a part of this, your cells are releasing that which no longer serves. Detoxifying on a physical, mental, emotional, and spiritual level. Let go of that which weighs you down.

Release, and feel lighter instantly as your cells freely release and your angels swoop in and around you in a spiral of love, releasing any toxicity into the Creator's Light. And now more light than you even though possible to hold, streams in and your cells absorb this blessing, and this love. As your energy increases ever more, there is a final push as your pain, attachment, and suffering is lifted away. Imagine the orb of your soul's light around you once more and imagine the light filling you, filling out your aura, strengthening this bio magnetic protective sheath around you, strengthening your aura for protection, for growth, and so that you are able to know and to understand and to experience directly your spiritual soul, and experience uniting with this, your light.

When you shine more love and light in your life, indeed, this makes a difference. Your choices and actions, your thoughts, indeed influence collective consciousness as a whole, in every moment. As you merge more and more with the full light of your soul, there may be past challenges, even pain, that comes up for you. Know that this is a blessing, it comes up because no longer can it be held within you, your light is too great and so simply let it go. Let your Angels fill you to a new degree with light, with love, and frequency. Daily invite us in, invite the light in, invite your soul in to connect, to merge, to uplift you, and in this process notice what is triggered. Notice how your body reacts. Is there anywhere that is storing dense energy on your physical level? As you lift in vibration this will become apparent to you, and then simply focus your awareness wherever the pain or the darkness, where you see red or dense energy. Simply be aware and from your connection, the light flows there filling any holes in your aura first and then pushing out toxic and dense energy from your cells. Let it go, let it release into the light, and then allow the space to be filled with compassion and with love. Dearest one, you are in many ways at a new beginning right now. As you move forward now consciously seek to make and increase your light connection with your soul. Think about your spirit and your soul, and invite this presence in, for there is much wisdom and knowledge stored at your soul level that serves you in uniting with. Open your heart and make the connection, and as you do, the healing, the upliftment, the light you experience does not end with you. You are always broadcasting, you are like a broadcasting tower in every moment. Your energy signature sends out and connects with that of the collective consciousness. There is always this energetic link and so as you uplift, you naturally bring energy healing to those around you; your family and friends and those you do not even know.

Your personal growth and ascension, are the most important things you can focus upon to encourage all of humanity in ascending, and in returning to love. Focus first upon yourself dearest one. Your progress forward on your path. You are the change, you are the light that is needed, you are love. Let your light shine, let compassion radiate from you and know that in this, you are making a difference and this difference is profound. You are needed, you are the one, and as your light is activated and opened now, let it flow. Follow the wisdom of the gentle, soft, quiet voice of guidance from your soul. You are connected. Quiet your mind and open your heart to listen, trust, and act on the guidance you do receive for it will serve you well.

I, Archangel Uriel, leave you now with my blessing and with the reminder that your angels are always near in your every day and every moment, they are near. Be aware, acknowledge, and ask upon our assistance, and we are happy to assist in your growth, in your transformation, and upliftment when asked. Goodbye for now.

5

Self Healing
~Guides and Angels of the Light

Greetings, we are here. We are the guides and angels of
the light and we greet you, as always, in this now with
our love, with frequency of the divine, and with healing
light.   Allow yourself to relax and focus within as you
read these words. Allow your heart to open and begin at
this time to tune in to your body, understanding that, indeed, your thoughts effect your physical vitality. Indeed,
your beliefs effect the condition and shape your body
is in. Understand that your physical body is, indeed, an
organic computer of divine design blessing you with
the ability to experience the physical realm and beyond.
Your body holds great power, the likes of which humanity is really only beginning to understand. The ability to
heal, to connect with realms beyond the physical, to live
in vibrancy and well being.

And so we angels present now, invite you now to tune
into your physical body as a whole, as one unit. And as

you do this now, know that we are surrounding you with light, with emerald green healing light, surrounding your entire being with healing, and lifting you in vibration.

Allow this healing light broadcast your way into your experience. It is always available, angelic assistance. Help beyond the physical realm is always there, we are always waiting, but unless you ask, we cannot intervene. And yet now, with your intention, you can allow us to help. You can allow this healing light that is all around you to begin to enter in from the top of your head. This yes, as you allow healing light from above to now flow in through your crown, and down your spinal column.

As this light flows through your body, feel it being drawn to any areas where you are holding pain or tension, feel this light entering into the part of your body where it is most needed at this time. Breathe in the light, green, healing rays of the divine are entering into your body and feel where this light goes. If there is one place, imagine drawing a circle around the area where the concentrated energy will flow. Feel it entering this place, entering the individual cells, filling your cells with light, with love, and as this occurs, the density you have been storing from past belief, from negative thinking, from holding on to that which is ready to move beyond you and your experience.

Where are you holding tension? Where have you not let go? Tune into it. Feel the pain you have been storing, now release and let it go. Feel the tension lift out of your body, out of the top of your head, and into the light. After this happens, breathe in again and where the pain was stored, let this space now fill with well being, fill with light, fill with the energy of unconditional love and compassion. Love truly has the power to heal every aspect of your life, your physical body, and your outer surroundings, they are all impacted greatly by thought , consciousness, and by feeling. So with your intention now, imagine that you are zooming out with your perspective. You are connected now to a part of yourself that is no longer in your physical body. Imagine now that you are connected to your higher self, your spirit, and that you are actually looking down at your physical form, viewing your physical experience from a completely outside perspective.

Look at your physical body and now with your imagination, with your will power, with your thought; see your body wrapped in light, a bath of golden and green healing light. Feel the tension in your neck and shoulders wash away. Feel whatever pain, whatever disease you have been experiencing in your body, allow it to lift up and out of your physical being, releasing into the light and being replaced with light and unconditional love. As this light enters, feel as though you are lifting and floating with it.

Imagine that you're swimming in a peaceful, warm pool of water, healing water. You are mostly made of water and now as you dive into this water of the divine, it washes the tension, washes the pain, washes the struggle you have experienced this far up and away from your being. And now for a moment imagine your body in extreme vitality, complete well being. Imagine running and jumping and feeling great, feeling connected to your heart, connected to source, connected to total well being in this now. You are connected to this light, this well being of the divine that is always near.

A huge component of the ascension process you are undergoing is learning to release the past, release the doubt, release the belief that you must get a cold every winter, release the thoughts of "I am getting sick" or "Illness is a natural part of life". Feel these beliefs that no longer serve you simply wash away in the light, into the water, and healing energy of the divine. Feel this light and love all around you; warming, lifting, freeing you from these limiting thoughts and beliefs that have manifest in your physical form.

In this now, you are vitally alive, filled with well being, and connected through your open heart to source, to God, to your source of unlimited well being. It is found within and it is created by you. In this now in which you live, many have the tendency to look outside for advice on health and well being. But we assure you that your internal state of being influences every aspect of your outer world, health and wealth and happiness included. And so now, turning inward, focusing on your heart, and feeling the divine well being of this now moment, the peace you experience will ripple and carry this effect out into your world, into manifestation in your physical form.

Imagine complete well being, and from this moment forward you will be guided to take appropriate action, healthy choices, drinking water. You will be guided to move fully into alignment with well being. This is made possible through the power of intention, positive thought, and sincere desire for health, connection to spirit, physical vitality and total well being. Feel these thoughts, these vibrations and allow them enter, and become united your experience. Allow them to align you with positive choices and actions that will continue to move you towards attaining your goals.   On your behalf now we angels ask that any and all energetic cords that may be draining you be cut, all energy that is yours that has been drained consciously or unconsciously is now returned to you cleansed and purified. Feel your energetic form gaining strength, feel your aura being healed, and cured around you. Feel your power returning to you and know that we did not cause this. This improvement is your manifestation, your doing. With intention you are able to heal every aspect of your life.

By intending, "I am totally healthy and experiencing complete well being in my now moment" and by combining this intention with the actions you are inspired towards it will come to be. Feel that well being is resonating in your body. If you are experiencing doubt, if your ego mind is strongly coming in now and saying, "No," release this and return to just being present in the now, feeling your heart beat in your chest, feeling your breath move in with healing vitality and life force energy, and exhaling, releasing the old, releasing limitation, releasing tension and disease.   Breathe in well being, and as you breathe out let go, relax, and just be present in this now. Be present in the healing love that is all around you forming a sphere of light around your body, strengthening your auric field, your protective barrier, strengthening your natural immune system.

Open your heart and strengthen your connection with your inner source of power, your inner connection to divine well being. From your open heart, you can allow energy of the divine to flow in. With this power you can choose to change any aspect of your life you desire with intention, with open heart and connection, and with releasing attachment to the outcome, and taking action as inspired.

Release the past beliefs and thoughts that weigh you down, and commit to accepting what is and being present in this now, surrounded with vibrations and thoughts of love. Let love be your primary experience. Release fear, pain, old outdated paradigms that no longer serve and then tune into your heart, as your body fills with light, love, and well being.

Do you perhaps notice an area where it seems the light is unable to freely flow? Do you still feel tension, pain, or heaviness? Mentally draw a circle around this area and imagine the light entering here now, filling this space, automatically releasing the density, releasing the residue of past trauma.

Breathe in the light now, and feel well being wash throughout your being. Breathe, be, and know that indeed, from your open heart healing, well being and total connection to source is made available to you.

Open your heart and go within. Return to this place often, daily. Imagine the healing light that is present is flowing through your body, and releasing all that no longer serves you. Let the light effectively bring you into alignment with well being, physical vitality, and a strong well connected mind, body, and spirit. Vibrant health is your birthright. Release limiting thoughts in this regard, and empower yourself to consciously create and manifest a healthy existence. You have this ability, it truly begins with your belief, with your intention, and with quieting your mind, opening your heart, breathing, and allowing well being to flow through. All that you need for a happy, healthy, abundant experience on this physical Earth is found within you. Yes outside action is required, but release the belief that it is hard, that you must try hard to change your experience from the outside in.

It is from a strong inner connection with source, with your inner power that all you desire can manifest around you from the inside out.

Connect, and raise your vibration above the realms of duality where illness, disease, and pain are prevalent. At first, these things may hold on, may latch on. Draw a circle around these areas and open your heart. Let more light into your being, allow more love flow into your ex-perience releasing blockages, releasing tension, releasing past experiences still held in your body at cellular level. Let your cells be filled with love. Allow the healing light of love, green emerald light all around you to transform your physical vessel, to return you to vital well being, connection to spirit, and connection to your ability to consciously create your experience.

Health, excitement, abundance, well being, and inner peace are all yours. Accept this light we broadcast your way now; open your heart, release thoughts of ego mind and be present in this now with healing light, with love. Allow it into your being. Feel lightened, feel illuminated. Relax, float, be, feel the divine love in you, around you, flowing through you. See yourself connected to your divine blueprint for your physical body. Health, vitality, energy, well being are yours. Breathe and feel your heart open, feel well being enter your experience. When negative thought comes up, when disease makes itself apparent, breathe light into those areas, turn away from doubting, from struggling, and claim your power, your light, your innate ability to heal and to create your life's experience by design.

Beloved one, you are dearly and deeply loved. Return to this healing space, this circle of healing light as often as you wish and we will be here with you to assist you in claiming your inheritance as a conscious creator, claiming your well being, your physical vitality, innate ability to manifest miracles and blessings in your world all stemming from your willingness to open your heart and allow healing light of the divine to enter in to your mind, body, and spirit, uniting them in unconditional love.

You are loved and you are assisted. Remember to ask for help. Remember your inner power to create blessings and well being in your outer world. From the still, peaceful, inner calm within your heart, all things are possible. Believe, create, intend and know that you are so loved.

Healing Orb of Light
~Archangel Uriel

Indeed, dearest one, we are here and know that as I Archangel Uriel speak these words and as you read them, you are in the presence of many angels and guides. Indeed your personal team is here and present with you now to assist you in bringing light to dark, illuminating within you what needs to change, balancing your independence and assertiveness with the knowledge that we are all in this together and you are one with all that is. You are an individual, yes, but you are also connected to the greater whole.

Now is the time to find middle ground, to raise the vibration of competition to collaboration, the act of plundering the Earth into being a steward of the planet and to transform the act of war into living peace, shifting how you see and do things in your world, utilizing your right and left brain, and aligning your head and heart. Dear one, we invite you now to once again take a deep, relaxing breath and consciously allow yourself to open. Open to your subtle senses, to feel, know, understand, experience directly the love of the creative source, of the universe, of all that is, and to recognize in this moment, indeed, and in every moment that you are one with all, you are a part of all, the living, breathing Earth that you are on. You are not separate, indeed, you are one.

Now imagine an orb of light above your head and let your consciousness go up with this orb. Notice if it has a particular color, as it will take whatever form, whatever color most serves to heal, balance, enlighten, illuminate you right now. Imagine that you are floating up with this orb of light into the angelic realms, and continuing up into the direct realm of prime creator, the source plane of existence. We invite you to now look down at your physical body from this place of consciousness. In your mind's eye, imagine your body and that you are able to scan your physical body now beginning at the top of your head and slowly moving down neck, shoulders, upper back, belly, sexual organs, lower back, legs, calves, ankles, feet. Scan your entire body and notice anywhere that you are especially drawn, anywhere that is highlighted so to say, that draws you in. Where is your awareness drawn now in your physical body? And know that you are drawn here now for some darkness to be illuminated, and by darkness I do not mean evil or even bad, but simply a lower vibration. There could be some blockage or illness or belief system engrained at a cellular level that is keeping you in pain or illness. And so notice this area of your body and we angels flow light, healing vibration, love this way to illuminate and to loosen the hold of any negative belief, for your beliefs on many levels create in physical reality.

Therefore everything that you have experienced, good, bad, ugly, exciting, or boring, is because there is a belief, either consciously, unconsciously, at the cellular level or even historically, some belief that does not serve. And so in this area where you are drawn, where light is shining, where it is being illuminated, notice, ask, what belief is causing this state of dis-ease? What belief is causing a an energetic block or physical pain in me? This question is posed to the Creator of all that is, to the universal source, to the energy of Oneness, of consciousness that flows through all beings, all things, and all that is. Allow yourself to open your heart, allow your imagination to turn on, allow your subtle, psychic senses to activate and be aware now.

What belief? When you are ready, release whatever has come up for you into the creator's light and witness as it is replaced with the feeling, and the belief of "I am loved".

When you pray to God, to angels, to the ascended masters, your prayers are always answered. But you, beloved one, conscious creator of your physical reality and world, you are required to witness the healing in order for it to be so. And so now witness this change, this release, and replace a belief. Release those blocks present that no longer serve. Good. And now one area, one focus, one belief, and feel the change, see, witness, observe that you are now able to lift even higher. Your consciousness exists still in this heightened state, in an orb of colored light, but now you are ready to bring this healing energy all around you, around your entire body. And so imagine the orb of healing light custom for you, for your unique needs and spirit and personality.

Let this orb of light settle down so that it is surrounding your entire physical body. You are in this orb of healing, of love, of illumination. Know that this will illuminate areas of you where density, where darkness, where lower vibrational beliefs remain. Do not run from these as they come up, as they bubble, boil, rise to the surface. If there is already some belief coming up for you, rejoice and celebrate for this is good news. This means this process is working for you. Tune in. Identify a belief in you that no longer serves. Notice and look at the belief, and do not judge but simply rather allow yourself to feel. Whether the belief is I am not worthy of love or something more physical such as I have this problem, feel it. Feel the emotion that this stirs and causes in you and now release it into the creator's light and we angels wrap you in our wings of love and release that which does not serve into the light. And we now ask that an empowering belief, a love filled belief, love, compassion, joy, unity and light take its place. You may ask, "What belief most serves me to replace this with?" Quiet your mind, open, and be aware of your feeling, of thoughts that come into your head, of a new belief that is downloaded into your consciousness. Allow this in and now witness, observe, notice this change in you. Release lower density, and enter into increased light, illumination, and empowerment. For, indeed, beloved one, you are empowered, you are an empowered being. And although there may be beliefs that are limiting you from aligning with your full power, returning to this simple process of connecting with the creative source of all that is and then scanning, observing your body, noticing what may need a shift, and doing it. Ask for assistance and witness the shift of energy. You may experience a physical shift or rather there may be a change in how you see and do things, how you perceive your physical world around you.

Remember, you are one with the world, and one with all. Indeed, you are a part of the team of creators on Earth creating reality one moment, one breath, one thought, one feeling, one belief at a time. And so in this process of observing yourself and your life up until this point, you are supported in becoming aware of any density, any stuck energy or any beliefs you hold that do not serve. Let these things rise to the surface and do not be afraid. Be courageous, be willing to consider these things and to release them into the light. Know that your spirit body is the first to ascend, and in spirit you are light, you are empowered, you are united with the love of the universe. And now this same love and healing and light and vibration is ready to go to work on your physical body. A physical recalibration. All is well, and we remind you once more of the orb of light that is all around you, assisting you in this process.

Your angels, your guides, your team of spiritual beings who love you dearly are always happy to assist you in this process of spiritual and physical recalibration.
You will see big changes, but we say to you, the changes in your perspective, the changes in your consciousness must be balanced by changes in your diet, exercise, and lifestyle for the full effect to unfold. Your uplift-

ment begins with opening to light, with changing and replacing limiting beliefs with those that will empower and further illuminate you. As you do this work of personal development through reflection, willingness to question reality, and consciously changing any limiting beliefs you do encounter, the physical changes that do occur will unfold effortlessly.

Do give yourself permission to take a walk, to experience the natural world, to put healthy, organic whole foods in your body, and to align your physical lifestyle with the empowered, illuminated light of your authentic self.

This recalibration means and intends to align you fully with your higher spiritual self, with your authentic self here in the physical. Not only meant to be connected with in a meditative, trance like state, but in every now and every moment you are able to live love, to live peace, to be protected and shielded and united with your power, with gifts from God, and, indeed, with love.

Your inner God or Goddess activated, balanced, united, masculine, feminine, right brain, left brain, mind, and heart, sexuality, and passions. Notice once more the orb of light around you. What color is it? What does it look like? Is it iridescent or glittery or solid? It is right for you right now. Observe and now when you are ready, breathe this light in, into your being, and relax into it, and know that you are receiving the proper healing on divine time. That which most serves you, that which you most need is offered to you now through this beautiful light from the angelic realm. This should feel good. Allow yourself to feel blissful, feel loved, relaxed, like you are being empowered from within.

If you do notice something that does not feel good, an area that is tense, that feels like a struggle or a challenge, know that it is coming up for release now. It is likely tied to a belief, a feeling, an emotion. Look at it now, identify it, notice it, and then release it into the creator's light of all that is, and replace it with unconditional love, compassion, well being, and vitality.

Dear one, I'm Archangel Uriel and you are so dearly beloved. Allow yourself to once more tune into the orb of light that is all around you. Present now in this orb of light, consciously allow your awareness to flow down into the center of Earth, grounding you into this magnificent planet on which you are a part of. As you connect with the light, the heart, the core of the Earth you find therein. Allow yourself to feel, to open, and experience your connection with Earth, and with all that is.

And now imagine that this light from the core of the Earth that you are a part of begins to flow up through the bottom of your feet. Allow this light to continue up as it effortlessly opens, blossoms, balances, and activates to its highest and greatest good your root, your sacral, your solar plexus, your heart, your throat, your third eye, your crown, your light body. Imagine all your chakras united in one column of white light. Allow yourself to be present full in the physical realm, and in your physical body but remember that you are also fully connected with spirit. Retain this connection, embrace it, live it in every now.

You are so loved, you are so loved, you are so loved. I leave you with my blessing and with the reminder that you can return to this healing space, this healing orb at any time. All that you need is here within you. Connect, open, lift. Goodbye for now.

7

Aura Cleanse
~Archangel Uriel

Dear one, know that indeed I, Archangel Uriel, am present with you now and you are, indeed, surrounded with One Hundred Thousand Angels, with your guides and your team of light beings and spiritual beings who are on hand now to assist you in taking a giant leap forward.

For understand, right now you are on the precipice of yet another great change. A tsunami wave of change is once again headed for your planet offering you the ability to step into more light and joy and truth. To make this transition, however, to increase greatly in light, to ascend and to be uplifted, your guides and angels, I, Uriel, are on hand first to assist you in release. We are here to assist you in releasing whatever dense energy remains in you physically, mentally, emotionally, or spiritually.

Take a deep relaxing breathe and focus inward as you

read these words, and as we prepare your energy to take this quantum leap forward. You are ready to leave behind the restrictions and density and challenges of your past and present and to step into your future self centered in love, grounded to Earth, and grounded to the greater multiverse. These aspects of you unite in your open heart, in the energy of unconditional love and acceptance. And so now take another deep breath, and quiet your mind as you focus your awareness within.

Imagine with your mind's eye that you are being transported now to your inner sacred space, your inner sanctuary, a place of peace, of love, and of tranquility designed specifically for you. As you are taken here, open your mind's eye and look around. What do you see? What characteristics does your sacred sanctuary hold? This is your creation. Notice the perfect temperature, the flora and fauna, the architecture. Are you indoors or outdoors? What is the weather like? Take this all in, this sacred place that you are creating. And now in this place, with your awareness, invite in your highest, best, most loving possible guides and angels, your unique team of spiritual beings who serve and love and assist you.

Invite your guides in. Simply think, "Yes," or think, "I now invite my highest, best, most loving possible team of guides and angels to come in and assist me in releasing all that no longer serves and taking that next leap into truth, into love, and into light."

Let your mind remain calm and open your heart. Feel, sense, see, witness, know the presence of divine love all around you, the presence of your team of guides and angels. And now will your main guardian angel step forward and show themselves to you now by wrapping you in wings of love, lifting you up.

Enjoy connecting with your guardian angel now in the way and form that is easiest and best for you.

Now before you, in your sacred space, imagine a labyrinth, a maze which appears before you. This maze will take you to the center of your being and to the center of your conscious and subconscious mind.

Your guardian angel now hands you a golden spool of yarn, of light twine. Take this and know that you are safe to enter deeply in, deeply within, to find at your core what lies therein. And so imagine now that you have this golden light twine in one hand, connected to your Guardian Angel at the other end. You are safe... enter within. Embark into the labyrinth, into the maze that will take you to your center. Focus your awareness inward, and go deeper. One step after another, enter into your inner being. Notice that it is somewhat dark in this maze, that there is a sense of traveling down, into your depths, but that you are protected.

Feel deeply loved and safe. keep going inward, winding around, spiraling through this labyrinth in a peaceful somewhat excited state until you reach the center.

Here at the center there is a message for you, a message from deep within your being, a message about your purpose and about your authentic truth. There may be a guide that meets you here. Notice what form your guide takes, feel your connection with them. And now we ask this guide on your behalf "What information will most serve now to bring this beloved being more in line with authentic purpose? With joy, with love and with the transformation that is possible now? Receive this answer. Your guide may energetically answer, may hand you an item, a gift, that will assist you, imprint a word, message, or a feeling upon you. Whatever you receive here at the core of your being, let it be OK.

If it is a subtle feeling, this is fine, or if it is a magnificent token or omen of what you are meant to do, whatever you receive, give thanks, it will all make sense in time. Now notice the golden cord of light in your hand, and begin to follow it out, follow this golden cord of light out of the maze which led you deep into your being.

As you walk your way out, let yourself remain in a meditative state calm, peaceful, whole. Let yourself gently reflect upon your authentic truth. And now, you begin to see the light at the end of the maze, the light at the end of the tunnel. See this light growing larger until you are surrounded by it, and as you step out of the labyrinth now, you are greeted by your team of guides and angels, and by an incredible light that is showered over you.

You have received a glimpse or a feeling about your life, path, and purpose, about your next steps to take. To prepare you for this journey, the shower of angelic light all around you cleanses away any remaining density, doubt, and fear which is stored within your cells, or attached to your energetic body. Let this go, release it into the light and now let your vibration lift.

Let this light strengthen your auric shield. Your aura is the base, the root, of your light body. Your aura is essential for your protection and for your well being. It protects you against physical and nonphysical threats, it allows you to stay centered in love regardless in what is going on around you. When your aura is strong and intact and whole, your vibration is able to lift and lift and you are able to pour and hold more light into your vessel. When your aura is strong you are able to build your light body, you are able to unite with your full truth.

And so, once again, I Archangel Uriel draw your awareness to the waterfall of light streaming down above you. Consciously let your crown chakra at the top of your head open. Know that you are safe, you are in the presence of your team of spirit guides and angels, and we assist you in integrating this light in the most powerful way, first releasing density, fear, and negativity into the light, and then this light goes to work patching and repairing any holes in your auric field, any leaks where your energy is exiting. Archangel Michael comes in as well to cut any energetic cords that drain you, pulling out the roots and releasing them into the light, releasing the cords into the light, and now calling back all energy that is yours that may have been drained consciously or unconsciously. Let this your energy and your light return to you now. Let it strengthen your auric shield, let it lift you in joy, love, and peace. Breathe and open your heart wide, open the doors of your heart wide to let more light in. Now that your auric shield is once again strong and intact, you are able to lift to a new level.

Relax, as your angels lift you up now into the higher

realms. Up above the vibrational realm of physical reality. Up above the realm of angels, up above the astral realm and into direct presence with Source.

This is an important aspect of what your aura and your light body enable you to experience, direct presence, connection, oneness with creator, with source, with all that is. From this space and connection, let whatever healing energy you most need, now flow in to your aura, into your physical body, into your spiritual body.

If you need emotional healing, this is what you receive. If it is physical healing that you are in need of, feel this energy and light flow to the area where you have experienced a block or pain, and let it be miraculously healed now. There may be beliefs that need to change for your ultimate healing to occur. Ask, "What beliefs now hold me back from my highest truth?"

Enter within your sacred space which is always a breathe away, simply quiet your mind, open your heart, and listen.

What beliefs come into your awareness?

Do they serve you or not? If not, if there are beliefs that come up such as, "I am not good enough. I hate myself. I am not worthy of divine love," let these go. Let them be lifted out of your physical, mental, spiritual, emotional auric bodies and released into the creator's light.

Now let love, let joy, let peace, let the creator's love flow into you replacing this belief with an empowering belief, a belief in line with your growth, with your transformation, with compassion, and with your miraculous healing. Allow the belief, "I am loved. I am deeply loved by all that is" become a reality for you. "The universe loves and supports me." "All is well."

As this shift of beliefs occur, notice and observe, witness, the old beliefs being lifted out of your experience and new empowering, love centered beliefs entering in. Breathe and relax, and simply be here now.

Feel your connection to source and to all that is. Feel the peace and love and tranquility in this very moment, in this silence. Breathe deeply into your abdomen letting the light that is all around you enter within you, letting yourself become more illuminated than you have ever been. Let your vibration lift and know that a high and light vibration protects you and also cannot help but bring you in to alignment with your purpose, for when you are in a state of high vibration, you naturally vibrate with joy and love, and with joy and love as your foundation following this your purpose naturally unfolds.

Let joy and love be your guide, and take one step at a time forward, towards letting more light, more love, more peace into your being.

As your auric shield remains strong and intact, you can steadily increase the amount of light you hold. It is when your aura becomes damaged and leaks that your vibration again decreases. Drugs and alcohol, negativity, challenging times can weaken your aura, but you always have the ability to call in your team, to call in your angels and receive a shower of light.

Right now, imagine that a waterfall of light is once again above you and pouring down. Witness the light patching any weak spots, any holes, filling your aura out so that a strong, beautiful light shield surrounds you. Remember, that as you follow the inspiration of your heart towards more joy and love in your life, your authentic purpose beautifully unfolds.

Dear one, take one step at a time in joy, love, and truth, and you will achieve all that you set out to do.

You are here and now in the physical realm to experience upliftment. You are here to experience first being disconnected from source, and then remembering how to strengthen your energy and lift in light to directly connect with the presence of I am, of all that is, of the one energy flowing throughout everything and everyone. When you connect directly with this presence, with source, you are healed on all levels.

Let this healing in, embrace it, and now feel your energy ground, returning to your physical body, and then flowing down through the bottom of your feet as you ground your auric body and your light body (the incredible light you have connected with now), into the core of Earth. Share this light with Earth, ground this light from the divine into the physical, and into the planet.

For you see, you and Earth are one. As you grow and lift and ascend, so too does all life upon your planet. Know that you are here to return the planet to a place of harmony, of love, and of well being. The first step is increasing your light, claiming your personal power, your intuitive power, your creative power, and with this power then taking action, following your joy and your love and your bliss and creating change in your life and in the lives of those around you, manifesting blessings, consciously creating those changes that you desire to see in the world. The change on a global scale begins with you.

You are now able to consistently progress in the direction of your goals, to ride the tsunami wave of light safely and joyfully towards accomplishing your purpose. Choose love consistently, daily. In every moment respond with love. Practice quieting your mind. Visualize a blank screen before you and enter in.

Open your heart, connect with your light, connect with your team of guides and angels, imagine yourself in your sacred space that brings you healing, love, and peace. Imagine that you now once more, in your inner sacred sanctuary, and that your team of guides and angels are circled around you flowing you the energy of divine love.   Embrace this love broadcast your way. Let love push out all that no longer serves you. Let love release those blocks that have kept you stuck, stagnant, or in fear. Let fear go, let fear be released into the creator's light, and replaced with increased vibration, with prosperity, with love, compassion, excitement, and with joy. Maintain your auric shield by becoming consciously aware. Ask your guides and angels to help. Know that you will be protected when this auric shield is intact, when your vibration is high. And so when you notice that your vibration is low, when you notice that you are not feeling good, that you are feeling bad, enter inside. Let yourself be transported once again to the sacred space. Let your team come in and heal your aura, lifting you with love and joy, and then grounding this increased light into Earth.

Having a high vibration, being spiritual, is not enough. This is simply the foundation. Now that your foundation is strong, it is up to you to claim your personal empowerment, to take action and create that which you desire.

You create the world around you with your energy, with your emotions, and with your beliefs. Empower these and you will empower your life. Now is the time, you are the one, shine your light, live your truth, and know that you are divinely assisted and supported when you remember to ask.

Invite your team of guides and angels in, for we are here, but will never interfere in your reality without your permission, we honor the universal law of free will. We honor your ability to create your life by design, to claim your empowerment. However, we are happy to assist you in any way, when specifically called upon and asked for assistance. We will assist you in lifting your vibration, in bringing more passion, more joy, more love, and more compassion into your life.

When you ask for angelic assistance, be sure you act upon any guidance you receive. Asking for assistance is only the first step, and receiving an answer the second.

Your action is required to truly transform the planet in which you live into a paradise of love and hope.

We see this transformation as being possible, as happening, and you are paramount to this transition.

The light is present on the planet now, let it into your being and as it stirs up that which no longer serves, let those things be released into the light. Let yourself shine brighter, higher, more vibrantly than you ever have, and then take action. Follow your intuition, follow your heart and your inner nudges, be the change you wish to see, create the change that is needed on the planet now.

Love yourself and love all beings and know that we, angels, are always on hand to assist you. Call us in and we will illuminate your aura, heal your being, and assist you in any way, but remember to ask. I, Archangel Uriel, leave you with my blessing and with an infinite well of love.

Tune into this love now, flow it through you, and then take action as you are inspired, for this is an essential step. You are so loved. You are so loved. Goodbye for now.

8

Setting Your Intention
&
Hitting Your Mark
~Archangel Michael

Beloved one, indeed, I, Archangel Michael, greet you in this very moment. Let yourself relax and let yourself open to experience the love that is all around. You are now at a most powerful point for moving forward, for shifting out of waiting for things to happen in your world and moving into being a creative participant, a co-creator.

We connect with you now to assist you in focusing your attention and your awareness towards what will serve all, and towards what it is you truly desire. As you read these words we invite your higher self, your soul, your full spiritual self to enter in, to connect, and to unite with you now.

Breathe, relax, and feel your energy expand and lift as

this connection is made. You are physical beloved, indeed. Present in the realm of elements, of duality and polarity. Earth, air, fire, water, feel these life sustaining forces around you, for you are always connected to them. Feel the Earth and that you are a part of it. Earth, air, fire, water, duality, polarity, and yet there is more. The space that fills the gap, the void, the in between, the ether, Spirit. This the non tangible element, indeed, serves you in creating at this time. For your intention and then action on both the physical level and the energetically to tune into and experience the hidden blessing within the void.

Imagine now that you are dropping in, in between the elements, and in between these very words. In between, you will find a gap, a void, a peaceful, soothing, quiet still calm within. Regardless of what is happening around you now with noise, with emotion, and with commotion, you are bale to simply enter in. It is within you that you will find your quiet, peaceful inner sanctuary by which you are able to connect with the energies of divine, of your spirit, and with the light of your authentic self. And so enter in now to this void. Breathe, quiet your mind, open your heart and enter in. Feel peace wash over you, and tune into the love that runs throughout this space, experience its uplifting and soothing presence. And from within this space where you are consciously aware within your open heart, we ask your team of guides and angels, to give you a clear sign. Moving forward past this point now, what is your direction? What are your next steps? Quiet mind... open heart. What does your soul long for, yearn for, and desire? Open yourself to receive this information, for indeed your angels are present with you now to assist you in knowing your true desire so that you may then intend and begin the process of creation. From an energetic sense you do this by planting the seeds of intention with your thoughts, and by shooting forth an arrow of focused desire.

Let your purpose come into focus for you now, your purpose right now. For, indeed, purpose is ever evolving and changing as you are. What you are drawn to and called to do now may not serve you in a year or 10, but let yourself be OK with whatever you receive, with whatever your next steps, whatever is meant for you, now.

And now, dearest one, imagine in your mind's eye that you have traveled to a training ground, a meadow, outdoors and there are targets set up. Visualize yourself picking a target that represents what you desire to accomplish in this next half of the year. And now you are given a bow and arrow. Regardless of whether you have used this equipment in physical reality or not, the knowing of how to aim, release, and hit your mark is known to you. You know what to do. And so pick up this bow and arrow and focus upon your goal, your desire, the target of what you most wish to design in your life. Aim for the desire that is centered on your path, aligned with your purpose, and now pull the arrow back, focus your intention, and release. Let go, let the arrow fly, and notice that, indeed, you have hit your target.

You've hit your mark, and now your intention is already in the process of being manifest into physical reality. This process of creating with energy, creating from within the space of the void, although powerful is not complete.

This is most important to remember as you move forward, for you are in an incredible time, a time when change is both necessary and possible on your planet. This is why you are here, this revolution, this evolution that you witness around you. Yes, you are here to witness and to plant seeds of intention but more, you are here to participate. And so focusing your intention is essential. This first step of creation, of knowing what you are going after, of aiming in the right direction, and then there is a fine line like letting go of a taut bow and arrow, a fine line between release and action. For even in the act of releasing the arrow, you took action, you pulled it back in order to reach your mark. And so, dearest one, the teachings that all you must do is ask and trust and receive are missing an important component, ye physical creator, divine being in physical form.

Do you not see? You must actively create that which you desire. You must be the one to design the changes you see fit in this physical world and to take action to bring your ideas and intentions into being. Yes, we in the angelic realm say to you, change is needed, it is necessary. Old limiting paradigms and institutions are beginning their fall, but do not let this be a fearful thing for you. Let it bring joy for presented before you is an opportunity, a target, a window of opportunity. When change is needed, the opportunity for growth, for transformation, for your upliftment and ascension increases tenfold as well.

Now is your time to leave your mark on your life... The time to really go for it is here and now. When you are looking back at your life, let yourself see that it was well lived, that you took action, that you were not afraid, that you did not stay within the confines of a box reality has created, but rather see that you were able to be free, to unite with what you are here to do as a soul, and to take action bringing about significant change in physical form.

You are supported in this path, of course, you are never alone, there is a mass of information and guidance and support available for you from the spiritual realm.

We your angels will nudge you in the right direction, we will align things on your path, we will plant seeds that you can nurture and grow to fruition if you choose. But do know that you are an important factor in what will come to be. You are physical, you are within the duality matrix, the matrix of four fire, air, Earth, and water, and yet made of these elements, surrounded by these elements, one with these elements.

You are also able to step back and step into the space between, the gap, the void, all that is. Feel this distinction, set your intentions from within this place of full connection. Meditate, lift, and enter in.

What do you really want? What is important to you? How can you serve? Ask your soul, ask your guides, and meditate on this question and let it come more and more into focus. As you do become aware of this your truth now, take action. Create that which you desire, design, that which you see fit. This is essential, an essential step of your evolution and, indeed, something that brings humanity great benefit. The time is now for change, create it.

What changes do you need to begin to create in your

life? Your action is required, but once you know and ask for help and set your intentions, the world can shift around you to make this transition effortless. We angels will help you in flowing effortlessly through the changes if asked, but even then, indeed, your conscious awareness and your effort is required. Taking action is a key component of the creation process. Intend, ask for help, believe, manifest what you are creating, and make it so.

Beloved one, you have spiritual power within you. Let it come to the surface. The time is now to use it. The times of old, of being persecuted for spiritual gifts and traits is through. You are safe. And so release any fear, release any past uncertainty that still clings to your being into the light, and step into the light. Take a step forward with your awareness and now imagine that from above a waterfall washes down. Let this water refresh and cleanse your being. Mental, emotional, spiritual, and physical body filled with light. Lifted and illuminated, be cleansed, fill with light, increase your frequency and, indeed, take this light forward with you. The light will serve you in hitting your mark. Focus your intention and then stay focused. Prioritize and take action.

I, Archangel Michael, am here to assist you at any time. Whenever you feel challenged or stuck, call upon your angels, but know that ultimately you are the physical being. The power and the right to create in physical form is yours now. Take this blessed gift, be a leader, a way shower, a technician, and create the changes in your life that you see fit for the benefit of you, of your family, and for all.

Notice now above your head the waterfall of light still

pours down completely cleansing your being and filling you with energy, with strength, with vitality for health and healing. Let this light empower you to step into the role of the creative, powerful, beloved being that you really are.

Now is the time, you are the one, let your light shine, create positive change. One more moment now, review your year so far. What have you accomplished? Give thanks for this. And what is left unfinished? What needs to be completed? What do you desire to experience? Focus your intention and take the steps forward to meet your mark. I leave you with my blessing.

9

Healing Your Inner Goddess
~Archangel Haniel

Beloved one, indeed, I am here. I, Archangel Haniel, greet you in this now in a orb, a light, of bluish color that is all around you. Know that this light serves to simply lift you in vibration to cleanse your emotional field, your mental field, and your spiritual field. This blue light dissolves those limitations and doubts and any negativity that may be attached to you in this now. And so imagine this blue orb of light all around you, this is my energy and I am pleased to connect with you now, to assist you in honoring yourself in every aspect of you. You are beautiful, you are a dearly beloved, divine, spiritual being and as you are able to appreciate who you are in this very moment, as you are able to honor the cycles, moods, and rhythms that flow in and out of your experience, you will see that, yes, you will make it through this transition all on planet Earth are experiencing. Yes, you will come out on the other side more connected to your spirit, more connected to your light, and to love.

Consciously open your heart now and again notice the blue orb of light all around you dissolving away barriers, blockages, doubts, and helping you to tune in to your subtle senses, your psychic senses, the full spectrum of your sensitivity.

Beloved one, it is not with your physical senses that you are able to reach into the realms of angels and the non-physical, it is through the subtle vibrations of love, of compassion, of opening your heart that you, dearest one, that you are able to directly connect with the love, with the well being, with the peace, with the light of source energy, creative source, the one source flowing throughout all that is that you see, indeed, you are a part of, an essential component. And in this moment as you are able to embrace all that you are, take a moment to reflect on this year so far, on your path of awakening, and to fully awaken there must be the willingness, the acknowledgment, that perhaps you have been on auto-pilot still in some areas, asleep to others. Be aware that essentially there is room for new growth. Acknowledging this within yourself brings you into alignment with being able to flow with the changes happening on Earth. You are supported on your path of improvement and spiritual growth.

A divine recalibration is happening now on Earth as Goddess energy returns to power on the planet. You are supported in bringing the goddess energy inside of you to the surface. This is true whether you are feminine or masculine as your natural physical state of being on your Earth, on your planet, for many decades a realm of patriarchy has resided. The goddess energy has been suppressed for some time and it now reemerges beginning with you and you are able to witness new beginning with the transit of Venus across the sun. (refers to June 2012 event)

Venus representing the goddess, representing love, and moving into direct alignment with the sun, illuminating then the goddess energy, the love energy, tenderness, gentleness, sensitivity. And so while these things are illuminated, the wave of resurgence of the feminine power begins. This is now brought to the surface within you. And so if your goddess self, whether you are male or female, has been injured in this life or others, has been mistreated, has experienced challenges, when this goddess energy comes to the surface, so too do these hard aspects that are still present. And all this bubbles up now for a very divine and a very important reason, it is for you to, once and for all, heal your goddess self.

For men this may be healing the part of them as a small sensitive child that was taught to not show emotion, to be tough, to be fierce, to be masculine. But now honoring your intuitive, emotional, feminine side offers a gift, offers you the ability to tune in more subtly. You are sensitive now and this increasing sensitivity serves you so that you are able to know your direction, know the new project that will bring you more joy and love into your life, that will serve you in assisting humanity, bringing forth new ideas and new ways of relating.

The ability to choose love in every moment comes not from being totally in masculine or totally in feminine, it is important for these two forces to be balanced and so we mentioned the masculine feminine healing. And now for females, what wounds to your goddess nature have occurred in this life, in past lives? Let this come to your awareness, to the surface now. What wounds to your goddess energy have occurred? Male or female, wherever you are in this moment, open your heart. What wounds to your goddess energy have occurred? You may catch a visual, a feeling, a clear memory of something that happened in your past. This density that comes up to the surface does so now that your full light may emerge, but first you must release and so feel this past experience whatever pain or hardship or struggle was brought about from it. And now, once again, noticing that I, Haniel, am with you. Blue light is all around you, many angels are present and loving you, lifting you up, as you now experience this pain, shadow, the memory of setback, abuse... Pain, the emotion stored in your physical body at a cellular level that has been there since the experience and is now ready to go. Let it come up to the surface and release into the light.

Witness this release and we now replace with love, compassion, sensitivity, and joy. Let these vibrations fill the void where pain, where setback, where struggle was. And now, once again, as you are illuminated by blue light we ask your soul and higher self, "what wounds to your goddess self are needing to be released now?   I f anything else is present for you, let it come up. It may be a memory of being told to be strong, not to cry, not to show your emotion, not to be your true self. It may be words that were said to you that you believed. It may even be a way you have treated yourself, not honoring your full inner light and power. It may even be the vision or knowing of a past life experience. Open your heart, quiet your mind and let this knowing come to the surface. Whatever it is that is ready to go so that the full power of your goddess light from within may shine. For men, this does not mean you're going to be overly feminine. It simply means that you are coming into alignment with your spiritual body and self. For, you see, in spirit you are not masculine nor feminine. You are connected to all, and in your physical body by balancing your masculine and feminine, by healing your goddess side, your full spirit, your full light is able to exist in the physical realm.

Imagine now before you a pool of light crystalline water clearly glistening in the sun that is shining down above. Notice this water, the smooth calm ripples, the subtle currents as air flows across. Water is representative of the feminine forces of the universe, healing, emotional, of love. And, beloved one, in a visualization of honoring your inner goddess now, we invite you to dip your toe in this pool of water representing the unconscious, representing the goddess. And as you do as if in a dreamlike state, you dip your toe in the flow of life, in the water one oneness, and suddenly the scene shifts around you.

No longer are you standing on the shore of experience dipping in your toe, but now you are in a boat on a river that is calm but wide. Flowing gently and easily but steady, a massive body of water flowing and you are going with this flow, effortlessly floating down the river of life on your boat, on your vessel. Imagine this scene, feel it and open your mind's eye to see yourself in this flow of life effortlessly moving with the flow of creation. Flowing with the cycles and changes happening on Earth, flowing through challenges and struggles, flowing with the Earth, with creation, with the goddess energies that indeed are present upon the planet.

And, dear one, as you flow with this force, you are in the flow of life and being in the flow of life brings you into alignment with accomplishing your manifestation goals, with living in love.

Allow your inner feminine wisdom and dynamic beauty to wise to the surface. This force within you, this goddess light whether you are male or female, whether you have been aware of it up until this point or not, serves you. Cherish this sacred power and know that this inner feminine nature that is yours nourishes you and guides you. This is your intuition and your natural instinct. As you become aware of this intuitive side of you, as you take excellent care of this side of you, as you celebrate your inner goddess and your magnificence in the light you merge your a physical being with your true spiritual form and light.

Honor your inner divinity through self care, through movement, through dance, through thought. Your thoughts have the power to heal and when you think, "Self, I love you. I approve of you," then your thoughts bring you into alignment with the energy of love, and with in the flow of life. Dear one, when you are in the flow of life, life is fertile, opportunities are ever present, all things are possible. When you are one with the flow of life you are able to make the transition into living fully empowered in physical form. You are beautifully unique, honor this, appreciate this about yourself, and love you, for that love will bring you into direct alignment with what you are here to accomplish, and with who you really are. The full truth of who you are is multi faceted. The essence of your purpose is that you are here to fully know your power to create, your power to impact the world around you, to bring about positive developments and changes that are so needed in a world that often feels tumultuous and challenging in this now. But your love, your love brings you in alignment with spirit and by remaining connected with spirit, dear one, all things are possible.

Your dreams, your goals, your aspirations shall come to be one moment at a time, one step at a time as life opens up and reveal itself to you. Choose love, choose to honor yourself, and choose to flow with life. Not resisting what appears in your reality before you, but accepting all that is and allowing the universe to guide you effortlessly over any rocks, obstacles or challenges on your path. Flow with the oneness of creation. With the force of love you are able to heal your mind, body, and spirit to step into your full light and spiritual power. A part of this being in your light, being in your spirit as you are now is your ability to directly connect with source, with creator, with all that is. By making this direct connection, by returning to this direct connection that is your birthright, serves you greatly as healing, blessings, realignment with your full light and spirit occurs.

The process is simple. Open your heart and breathe and imagine your energy flowing down through the bottom of your feet. You are now at the core of Mother Earth, feel her goddess light shining brightly within. Feel your oneness with Earth from which you came, and feel your oneness with all that is, that Earth is a part of. Feel your connection with the infinite creative source flowing throughout all of existence, feel this connection, enter into the silence and stillness of the core of the Earth feeling your oneness with source here now. And now let this light energy begin to stream up, enter in through the bottom of your feet, and quickly, instantly opening and activating all your chakra energy centers and continuing up, out of your crown, into the light, up above the lights, above all of your higher spiritual chakras, above the universe, above the planes, directly into presence of source. Direct connection with God, with Goddess, with Creator, Source Energy. Feel this. Feel that you are not separate, you are made of the same stuff which Source is made of. You are connected to this divinity. Open your heart to it, let the love in, and the energetic wave on Earth, the astrological shifts that aim to recalibrate you, realign you with spirit, happen now.

Through your willingness to directly connect, through your birthright to directly connect... The healing, the blessings from source are transferred to you now. Whatever you most need on your path now, open to it. Be willing to receive, and witness this blessing you most need coming in to being. If it is something physical you are manifesting, you may feel as though you are turned into a magnet that can now attract all that you need. Or there may be some emotional or mental healing. Whatever it is that you are given now, open your arms to receive and if it feels good, you may want to place it in your aura so that you may return to this place of blessing.

The process is simple, the rewards are great. Connecting directly to source will fuel you. Do not try to get energy from others, this is draining for all. Instead, get energy directly from source and overflow love and blessings to all you encounter. This puts you in a state of attraction where you are magnetizing blessings, that which you desire, more love. Love is truly the force that will bring you into alignment with your dreams, but to manifest your dreams remember that you must fully awaken, claim your power, and start taking action. The experiences you have had with I, Archangel Haniel, now serve to do just this, to awaken you to your full inner power.

You are directly connected with Source and from this connection you are able to create all that you want; blessings, manifestations of joy, happiness, and love. It all begins with intention, with planting seeds of thought, and continues with action, with being inspired in a certain direction and taking that next step. You are divinely supported in this now, in bringing about positive changes into your experience. That which you are not proud of that has happened in your life, you can release. Hand over the hurt, release the disappointment to your angels and into the light, and refocus upon what it is you truly desire.

Now is the time to believe in the power of your dreams, to awaken to the realization that you can accomplish them, and to take steps, action steps, to manifesting your highest and greatest good. You are here for greatness. You are here to co create directly with the energy of Source. Make the connection, stay focused on what you want, let love be the guiding force in your life, and the rest falls into place.

Dear one, you are so loved, you are lifted, you are cleansed. Notice now the blue orb of light around you begins to lift, and now above your head the orb of light sits and a waterfall of light begins to stream down, cleansing your emotional state, your mental state, cleansing body, mind, and spirit. Raindrops of love, a waterfall of light, cleanse and lift. And now bring this increased energy with you unto your day, share love with all you encounter, and love will bring you into alignment with that flow of life. Stay in the flow, and all you need will come across your path.

You are so loved, you are lifted, you are blessed. I, Archangel Haniel, leave you with my blessing, with angels' kisses, with a vision of you aligning and balancing your masculine and feminine self and fully integrating your light body, and your spirit into physical. Living awakened, living love, and living joy. This is possible, simply take a step, even if they are baby steps at first. Take your next step and then another until the whole picture comes into focus.

All is well, all is divine, go with the flow. Work within, work with source, work with your angels. All things are possible. You are loved, you are loved, you are loved. Goodbye for now.

10

Increasing Your Intuition
~Archangel Metatron

Dear one, indeed I Archangel Metatron am here and present with you now. Your Guardian Angels are also here with you now. This very moment is, indeed, a time of increased intuition and vibration woven throughout these words and as you read, angelic frequency is broadcast your way. Relax, focus your mind upon opening your heart to new levels of love and with this the opening of your intuition to a new level.

Understand that intuition does not only mean the ability to psychically see or know information from beyond the veil. With your intuition you are feel the truth about being and situations, you are able to clearly know your unique path, and understand and to express yourself in many ways.

Intuition is closely tied with creativity. When you open intuitively, creativity is able to infuse your life in all forms. Intuition is not only clairvoyant sight, though this is the gift that we will largely assist you in opening to now. This opening you may expect to begin at your third eye, however, know that your base chakras, your Earth chakras, and that which grounds you to the Earth are as essential, if not more, than your upper chakras. For it is your base that feeds your intuition and your third eye. It is your root, your grounding to Earth, that gives you the strength and energy needed to open and to clearly see beyond the veil, beyond the realms, of physical and into the realm of spirit. When you are consciously connected to the spiritual realms you can know, see and experience your angels, your guides, your team who is here to assist you. You are able to tune directly in to the guidance and love and meaning from the divine.

And so to make this connection with the Divine, first imagine your energy grounding. Grounding into the core of the Earth. Feel, experience, connect with this light at the core. Feel your connection with it, and your oneness with Earth, and with all that is. Let this energy now flow up now and let it activate your Earth chakra, between the core of the Earth and your feet. Your root chakra in between where your tailbone and the front of your body are, in the center. Tune in here and feel the energy gather, strengthening your base. Light building and growing here , grounding you to the physical Earth from which you came. This base energy indeed, provides the foundation for the rest of your energy body to build.

With a strong base you are able to reach new heights and so we infuse the energy around you with frequency and as you breathe it in, let it flow to your base chakra and whatever healing you need is given, whatever security you need is aligned. You are safe, feel this and feel your power as you are deeply grounded to the physical Earth. And now feel the link as the light continues to flow up, activating all your body's energy centers in a beam, in a pillar of white light. Imagine this light is all around you and it flows above and below you, above your crown your soul star chakra, and below your root, and your Earth chakra. You are surrounded, you are wrapped in a pillar of light. Let this light penetrate, cleanse and elevate you in vibration. Let this light carry the strength from your base now up to your third eye.

Consciously aware, alert and present now in the third eye chakra, imagine that there is a chair you find here in the energetic center of your intuition. You have just found the seat of your clairvoyant sight. Imagine you are now taking a seat, and while you are sitting in this chair, imagine a blank movie screen before you and in front of you. While you are here in your center of psychic sight simply quiet your mind, consciously open your heart and now you are able to tune into and to see all that you need to know at this time. What do you need to most know now? Let this come to your awareness, to your third eye. Breathe, and see now the guidance available to you beyond the physical that you are tuning into from within.

Draw your attention now to your lower chakra, your second. Your chakra of creativity and intuition. Let it open and as it does feel your energy level jump up, increase, expand exponentially. Your power, your creative light, your sensual self, and, indeed, your intuition are held here, the seat of your soul, your power. Once this center is activated notice the column of light all around you once more and now imagine above your head a sacred geometric shape as I, Metatron, lower down Metatron's cube, the merkava. Scanning your entire body, feel the frequency as you are uplifted again. Consciously allow your awareness to open now to allow this light and cleanse and blessing from the divine in. Open to allow your intuition to blossom. Feel warm, feel loved, feel joy.

Know that this lower chakra center grounded to Earth feeds your upper chakras so that you are able to see, know, and experience more divine love in your life and safely experience beyond the veil. With your clairvoyant sight activated you are able to peer into the mysteries of the universe and the love of the higher realms.

Now notice your solar plexus chakra receiving a cleanse, its golden light beginning to freely shine. Feel your energy lift as this radiant center opens. Now the final chakra of foundation, of your grounding required to fully lift is from within your heart. Open your heart now, the portal to the divine, the home of unconditional love.

Open your heart, in your imagination and with your conscious awareness, and then allow your energy to flow up as now your throat chakra is opened as well.

Now your third eye gathers light, white light, violet light. Notice the flashes of light before you as your third eye awakens. Notice in the images or pictures you see as the symbolic language of the divine begins to appear for you to see. Let yourself tune in, let yourself open, relax, and let yourself lift.

Consciously open your crown chakra now and continue to move up with your conscious awareness, up above your entire physical body and into direct alignment and presence, direct connection with source, with all that is. Feel you are a part of it, you are one with Source, and, indeed, from this place of knowing and connection great insight can come unto you. What is it that you desire to know, dear one? What can your intuition serve in aligning you with? Do you have a question? Ask this now. If you do not have a question, ask what do I most need to know?

Practice entering into the sacred space found within. As you open more, to fully experience your oneness with source, the answers you receive will increase in clarity as your body, mind, and spirit go through a detoxification, as dense energies of old are released from yourselves, from your cellular memory. Let them go, let your physical body move beyond the limitations of duality and past, and let yourself unite with the light, with love.

In this time of balance, you are being balanced by the divine, balanced masculine and feminine within you, balanced left and right. Open, see, know the divine love that is around you. Feel our blessing from the celestial realm and know that an energetic transfer, indeed, has occurred. You have been blessed and uplifted and opened. And as you move forward into your life and throughout your day, quiet your mind, open your heart, connect to all that is, open your third eye, and clearly see the divine love that is with you.

Your full opening will happen in stages, at the pace that is right for you. Choose love, and you will accelerate your opening. Love is with you. You are always loved, you are always blessed, and I, Metatron, am always happy to assist when called upon. With love and blessings. Goodbye for now.

11

Light Body Activation
~Archangel Gabriel

Beloved one, indeed, I, Archangel Gabriel, am here. I greet you in the company of many Archangels and beings of light. Know that we are here to assist you in lifting and in opening to your inner spiritual light and power, for beloved one, this time in which you live holds an incredible light that is available to you right now.

You are divinely guided and assisted in entering inward, in quieting your mind to the illusions of the physical realm around you, and opening within, lifting in vibration, and tuning into the higher realms of Spirit. Take a deep breath and now imagine that there is an ocean of light above you and this light now begins to pour down in a column of white light. Let this light in to your being and let your body fill with white light. Let your vibration increase now to the highest possible vibration you can hold at this time safely. Lift and fill with light as this ocean of light above you pours down, cleansing and lifting... Filling you so that you become illuminated, glowing light from within.

Now, let your consciousness continue to flow downward with this light, for you can only safely hold the amount of light you are able to anchor and ground into the physical. And so now that you are filled with a new level of light and vibration, breathe and feel your energy ground into Gaia, deep down into the core of the Earth. Go down and feel your connection now with Gaia, with Mother Earth. Feel your oneness with the energy of the core of Earth, feel loved, and feel your connection with All That Is... for Mother Earth and you, are a part of the greater whole, the one energy making up all of existence.

Feel this... Be aware, be present, and observe. Now imagine, or visualize this light energy once more flowing up from the core of the Earth, activating your root chakra. And while we are focused on this, your root, your survival, your base and support center for all your chakras. We invite the divine shape of the merkava to come in. A star very similar to Metatron's cube, let this divine shape come in and activate your body's merkava to the first level. This deals with survival, abundance, and connecting with the world around you. Imagine that this star shape is around you and continue now to go up with the energy of the light, tuning in to your second chakra, your sacral, the seat of your soul. This is where your creativity, and sexual energy reside. Imagine that there is a star merkava around this, your sacral chakra, activating your merkava to the second level, aligning you with the graceful energy of movement and flow. Your vibration is increasing, your light quotient lifting, and now this energy of the Light, of the Earth, of Creative Source flows up once more to your solar plexus, your power center, your gut feeling, your authenticity and intuition. We now activate this, your third merkava center. Imagine the merkava star all around you lifting you in frequency, activating your innate personal power in the light to live compassionately, joyously, and vibrantly. Go up once more now and open your heart as the merkava star in the heart opens and activates to the fourth level. Allow balancing of your emotional levels to occur.

Breathe, and open your heart, the doorway to the angelic realm, to the inner plane. Focused within your open heart now, we draw your attention up to your higher heart above your heart chakra. In your chest is your higher heart where in burns a threefold flame, your atma. Tune into this, your higher heart center, and the three flames within, creating all life. We angels flow light your way now, activating both heart and higher heart. Feel yourself fill with love as this activation takes place. Feel your energy safely lift to a new level of vibration and frequency. And now, notice the area of your throat chakra as we send the merkava star therein to activate your merkava to the fifth level. Align with your authentic inner identity, your ability to clearly communicate divine love, and to telepathically link with divine guidance. Now notice, and open your third eye, your clairvoyant sight, your ability to see beyond illusion and into the realm of truth. Activate your star merkava to the sixth level and connect with the divine understanding available to you.

Now, beloved one, at the top of your head your crown chakra by which you are able to connect with the infinite source of the universe, with your guides and angels who wish to assist you in reconnecting fully with your higher self and your spiritual light, imagine a merkava star on your crown chakra activating you now to the seventh level. Open, lift, and raise in vibration, and connect now with your soul star chakra, your eighth merkava level. Unite with your prophetic sense, and with the oneness of all that is, this is the gateway to your soul... to all that you are, where pure Divine Essence is filtered down into your physical being. Activate this gateway to fully activate your spiritual abilities, to transcend the limitations of physical reality.

And now, dear one, witness, as an orb of light forms around you and a Taurus shape, as your scientists may call it, an orb flowing beautifully above and below you, lifting you and activating you. This is a blue light from the heavens transmuting all lower vibrations that have clung on to you, transmuting the worries of your mind and any emotional baggage or drain, any physical density or block, and finally releasing any strain or struggle. With all this now released into the light, this orb of light activates you to a whole new level. Feel the light entering into your physical body, feel your skin becoming luminescent, feel your heart wide open, and let yourself glow. Your light body is being activated through eight open chakra centers and this orb of light around you. You can now safely hold a vibration higher and lighter than you have yet attained.

We draw your attention, once more, to the shape of the merkava star. Now, imagine that this is around your physical body and the light orb around that. And now, you are visualizing the shape of your light body and as you open your crown consciously once more, letting more light from your soul star chakra and the ocean of light above, flow in.

The final piece, is the column of white light now uniting all your chakra centers as one, and connecting you in your physical sense to the higher universal energies of light and love above you, then grounding all this light that you are now able to hold, into the Earth.

This column of light flows up, flows down, and flows through you. Dear one, consciously think or say now *"My light body is activated now to the highest possible vibration I can safely hold."* know that your full and ultimate light body activation is a process. Today may be one of the first steps or one a bit further... regardless of where you are now, your full vibration, your full upliftment into the higher realms, into the fifth, sixth, and seventh dimensions, this ascension process happening now that you are a part of, that Mother Earth- Gaia is a part of, that the plant and animal kingdoms are a part of. This lifting in vibration enables you, dearest one, in this lifetime to ascend and to experience fully the higher realms. Experience fully your full light and spiritual power, your higher self fully present, awake, and aware in physical form.

The Masters of the past on your Earth who experienced this level of spiritual awakening would die or physically leave the planet, for their body could no longer live holding that much light and power fully connected to unity, to source, to spirit. And, so, their body passed and their Soul continued on. But, dear one, as you, as Earth, and as all the plant and mineral and animal kingdoms are ascending along with you now, you are able to reach these new spiritual heights. You are able to awaken fully your light body and bring your full spiritual power into the physical while remaining alive and in your physical body. This works because you can ground this light into Gaia, who is ascending alongside you. She will assist you in then expanding your 3D matrix, the amount of light your physical body can hold. And when you do this, you not only enable yourself to carry more light and more love, you are assisting, you are lending your hand, you are helping all to ascend... The Earth and all of humanity.

Know that you are a way shower in this process, beloved one. You are a leader and an example for many. There are agreements which you have made when you planned out your holographic 3D experience. You agreed that you would strive to remember the truth, you would strive to unite with your spiritual light while still in physical form. You were determined to lift, to awaken, and to experience the quantum leap in awareness and awakening available to you know.

For right now you are able to expand your consciousness, and the growth you experience now will benefit you forever more. The growth and the light you connect with in this life will stay with your soul forever throughout your journey, even as you fully return once again to the realm of spirit.

Now, dearest one, imagine once more that each of your eight chakras are fully illuminated, bright lights shining simultaneously; red, orange, yellow, green, blue, violet, white, indigo, and tune into the ocean of light above you, letting the column of light flow down transforming these seven colors of your physical chakra energy centers into a tube, a column of light, down your center stretching all the way to the core of the Earth and all the way up into the heavens, the center of the universe. Anchor this light. Allow yourself to open up to it as it flows through you, and ground it into the physical.

Notice the merkava around you activated to the eighth level. This star shape, this sacred geometric shape, increases you in vibration safely and assists you in tuning into the love of the higher realms. Ultimately, this is why you are here in the physical in this very now. You are here to bring your full light into physical form and this, your light body, will help immensely.

There is much growth and expansion accessible by you now, in physical form. When you consciously develop and maintain your inner light, you are able to build and maintain your light body. This merkava star, and now the Taurus orb of light extending around you beyond your auric field, beyond your ethereal field, this light body exists in the physical realm but extends beyond that into the fourth, fifth, sixth, and seventh dimensions, dearest one.

As you consciously think about increasing your light quotient, your body can hold more and more light. As you build your light body and hold more and more spiritual light, your joy, your love, and your compassion increase immensely. Your psychic and spiritual abilities become clear and strong. Your vitality and energy and passion for life grow exponentially. The density you have experienced in life thus far melts away, the tiredness that you may have felt in recent past, is simply that you are tired of living in density and in the struggle of the third dimensional realm. You need not die to leave this struggle behind. Know many are here to assist, many angels, many guides, many advanced spiritual beings closely connected with source come in now to assist you, beloved one, in awakening to the highest possible degree, to the highest possible vibration you can hold right now.

Feel your light lift, let your light shine, your light body has now been activated, dear one, and now it is up to you to maintain this light. There are many things that will assist you in strengthening and maintaining the light body around you. 3D activities can draw you back into illusion, but taking time to be in joy, in love, in nature, meditation increases your light, healthy foods and beverages increase your light. Any time you consume food from the physical world, think or imagine, "This food is accepted as nutrients for by body and raises my light quotient. This healthy food fuels my light body."

Dear one, your thoughts are powerful, your emotions create, your feelings serve a divine purpose, and as you are able to focus all of these attributes now on increasing your light, consciously thinking, "I am increasing in light in every moment," you can create this.

As you truly open to your light body through focus, through determination, and through persistence, as your full body of light comes into view, your manifestation powers increase, your ability to focus and meditate increases, and your ability to live in love and joy and compassion comes to the fore.

Know that a new paradigm is being ushered in, and you are an essential component of this new Earth paradigm. Prepare for what is to come by connecting and opening to your light now. Again, every time you take a drink of water, think, "This water is increasing my light quotient, increasing the amount of light I can safely and effectively hold and vibrate."

The more you think and are aware of your light increasing, the more light you are able to hold. And, dear one, the more light you can safely hold, the more of your authentic power, the more of your essence, your soul light, your higher self, the spirit in you, is able to ground into the physical.

Know that this is your essential mission, this is the essence of your ascension, bringing your spiritual light into physical form. Not waiting until you die and cross over to reconnect fully with Source, but taking this journey inward while alive. Taking an evolutionary leap to be physical and be fully spiritually activated light, and love.

Dear one, I am Archangel Gabriel, and I am present with many beings of light and love. We are always on hand to assist you. The Archangels and the guides of the spiritual realm call upon assistance, but remember, you have access to power. You have light at your fingertips. Simply think, "Light surrounds me. My light quotient increases." And we leave you now with the visualization, once more, of an ocean of light above you, above your crown, above your head.

This ocean of light is always present, tune in to it on

a daily basis and now imagine that this ocean of light begins to flow down once again through your soul star chakra, and into your crown... Fully filling your physical body with light. Increasing your light, helping you to hold the most light that you can safely hold right now, and know that as you practice this visualization of opening to more and more light, that amount will ever increase. Gradually you will be able to hold more and more. Let this ocean of light in, let it activate the tube of white light down your spinal column filling your body, now filling the merkava star around you, and now filling the orb, the Taurus of light around that. Your light body activation is complete for now, but remember, you have only been activated to the degree which you can safely hold now.

From here we will continue to work with you to increase this light one moment at a time, one breathe at a time. As you choose love and joy and compassion, you increase the light that you can hold. And as you think, "My light quotient is increasing," indeed it will. With every activity, think, "This is raising my light," and not only will it, but so too with you then be guided to activities that will increase, to foods and water and friends that uplift.

Remember your upliftment is your ultimate purpose. Make this your priority, connecting with your full spiritual power and essence. Remember to ask, and we angels will assist you. We love you dearly and we leave you with our blessing as you now ground your light body to the Earth.

This new level of consciousness you have expanded to today, ground it into the physical, sharing this light with

Gaia, and she then sends back love and light to you. This is a mutually beneficial relationship, you can both help one another and together reach new heights, reach new light, reach a new level of love and connection with All That Is, with Source, with Spirit.

Dearest one, you are so loved and your light brightly shines. Overflow, share your joy and compassion with all. You are so loved. You are so loved. Goodbye for now.

12

Releasing Blockages
From Your Light Body
~Archangel Haniel

Dearest one, indeed, I am here. I am Archangel Haniel and I greet you in a warm embrace, with an orb of bluish healing light that goes to work, transmuting all that is held in your aura that no longer serves. Any negativity, fear, or attachment is released. Allow yourself to let it go. Do not hold on, but simply be present in this now moment, be aware, and allow your energy to open up.

Open your heart and now feel your energy ground to the core of the Earth where you connect with an incredible light and spirit therein. Feel your connection with it, with Earth, and with all that is. You are made connection and now this light begins to flow up in a column of light opening the seven chakras of your physical body center, activating an orb of light around you, a merkava of light around you and activating your light body.

Let yourself be filled with light now as your vibration increases to a new level of joy, of love, of intuition. This light body is built with love, with compassion, and with trust. This light body is a vehicle that enables you, dear one, to fully experience the light of the divine, of creator, of source, and of your personal, spiritual power and soul.

With your seven chakras active and illuminated, as they are now, your light body is able to form. And so imagine above you now an ocean of light that begins to pour down from the heavens. And as you open your crown chakra and let this light in, you are filled with light from above, from below, from within, and from without.

Let your mind, your emotions, your body, and your spirit all be filled with light becoming completely illuminated. Relax and breathe as you are continued to be lifted gently, lovingly, directly into the light. Now increasing your vibration, increasing your light quotient so that you may carry more light in every moment, anchoring the light from the heavens, into the Earth.

With this visualization of an ocean of light from above pouring down into you, imagine that this light is removing any blockages, anything that prohibits you from fully shining your light, from living your full expression of joy and love and connection.

The light pours in through your crown, down your spinal column, filling you, filling your aura, filling your etheric body, filling your light body, and removing any blocks. Imagine that this light continues to flow down grounding into the Earth, so that any blocks are actually grounded into the Earth, into the light found at the core of the Earth. Let go of these past limitations and blockages and let your light be grounded also.

An ocean of light pours in from above, uplifting you, filling you with light and overflowing now, grounding into the Earth, creating a matrix of light around the planet. Your participation in grounding your light body into the Earth benefits you in that blockages are released. Utilizing this process also benefits the Earth as the vibration of the entire planet is then able to increase also.

Continue with this visualization of light pouring in from above, filtering down, and bringing with it any fear, any attachment, worry or anxiety is released, effortlessly into the light. Notice now the blue orb of healing light around you turns to purple, golden light, white light, silver light, and any additional colors that you see or notice. Know that this orb is designed specifically and attuned to you right now to uplift you and to help you to let go of all that blocks you from your direct connection with your soul, with your spirit, with God.

Move forward on your path towards being fully activated, full light body, fully aware, and able to consciously create magnificent change in the physical, for this light body represents your spiritual power grounded into physical form. The power to create, to celebrate, to live abundantly, and illuminated, joyfully and filled with love. Indeed, love and joy are broadcast your direction now. As these emotions fuel your power center, your base, enabling you to reach into the higher realms where new levels of love and joy can be experienced. Let yourself be empowered to simply take the next step, move forward towards the next level. Your light makes a difference. Now is the time to let it flow and let it shine. Once more, a waterfall of light begins to pour down around you, cleansing anything that does not serve you that is stored in your body, your emotions, your mind, or your light body. Let these blocks be gently and effectively washed away by the waterfall of light.

And as your blockages, and limiting beliefs are released, you are free to lift higher, to shine brighter, to be more joyful, more connected, more compassionate, and more true to who you really are, a light being, a spiritual being in physical form. Now is the time to unite with your spiritual light body and self actualized power.

Notice or visualize the orb of light around you, the merkava star of light brightly shining within. Know that this your energetic field can be programmed much like a crystal to help you accomplish your goals. Remember, you are the conscious creator and releasing blockages and limiting beliefs is one important step. The next step is to go within. Meditate, be quiet, be activated, be still, and listen. And as you hear your intuition, the whisper of your soul, act, be willing to listen and to act. Make a change in the physical that will benefit your spirit, be willing to move in the direction of increased joy, love, prosperity, and light. Anchoring your spiritual light, your authentic self, here in the physical is your mission; it is what you are here to do and you are well equipped one moment at a time. Choose love and be aware, ask for assistance and all the light in the universe will come to you to assist you in moving forward. In lifting, in building your light body, and in strengthening the bridge of light, the connection between you in the physical and the divine realms of spirit, of source, and love.

I am Archangel Haniel. I am here to assist at any time. Call me in and I will answer. You are loved. Let your light body shine. Let your energy open. Let yourself be free. You are so loved. Goodbye for now.

13

Grounding The Light Into the Earth
~Archangel Michael

Beloved one, indeed I Archangel Michael connect with you in this now. I am present with many beings of light and love, with your team of guides and guardian angels who indeed surround you now flowing frequencies of light and love and well being all around you. Let this frequency of the divine and of the light enter into your aura and into your experience.

Imagine now that there is an ocean of light flowing above you, for understand that indeed, there is an immense amount of light, more than an ocean, that has flowed unto your planet. More light is present now on Earth than ever before. This frequency serves you in uniting with your authentic self, with remembering your full spiritual nature, power and ability. As your strengths in the divine come into focus and come into your awareness, you are able to utilize and use them in the physical world around you, to create benefit and blessings in your life and in the lives of others. You are creating in the realm of one energy flowing throughout all that is, that you are able to positively contribute to, energetically, and physically for the highest and greatest good, for the continued advancement and upliftment of planet Earth on which you live.

Dear spiritual being in physical form who has forgotten the full magnificence of your light and ability to connect directly with source, creator, God, and to co create. Consciously intend and manifest and then take action towards creating your intentions, the blessings and dreams you desire to see in the physical world around you. These are dreams that you as an individual have, glimpsing what you are able to contribute, earning your living in a way that serves those around you and serves you. This is possible for you when you unite with your full light and spiritual self. And from this place where your light it fully integrated it is not that all challenge and all struggle in your world will be miraculously alleviated. Rather, from your connection with your spiritual light, with your empowered being, with the energy of divine love when challenges do appear on your path, when you are in an experience of struggle, of lesson, when you are at a point of a challenging lesson, your full spiritual light will serve you in overcoming. Again, when you fully let your light shine it does not mean that all your worries and struggles in the physical are gone. However, through this empowered state of being that you are able to connect with, you are able to flow through the challenges before you, to respond to the challenges of your reality with love.

Do not be wrapped up in drama, struggle, or chaos when it does pop up on your path. Rather you can reach a point where you are able to simply observe the challenge, observe the lesson, or even negative experience that comes up on your path and to observe it from the perspective of your authentic spiritual self. What is this perspective? It is not judgment, it is non judgment. For when you step out of the experience of duality and into the experience of observer, united with your angelic spiritual self, you can view the challenge or lesson you are currently facing in reality and not be adversely affected by this challenge. By simply observing the challenge, the lesson, or current circumstance from the perspective of your spiritual self, you will be able to see your next step. You will be able to see the next action step to take to overcome the challenge, to move beyond the current struggle, and return to forward progression on your spiritual path.

Practice taking a step back, stepping into the observer mode when you are not challenged, when things are going well for you. By mastering this skill when you are calm and focused you will be able to remember and effectively achieve this change in perspective when needed, when things are hard, when you are in the midst of a lesson. In these times when reality does not flow as planned or according to your intentions. Instead struggle appears. When in struggle, step back. Your natural tendency may be to engage, to flow your own negative emotions and frustration towards whatever challenging lesson or circumstance has appeared on your path. But, I, Archangel Michael, connect with you now to say simply, "Step back. Pause as if you are pausing the show of life, pausing your reality, and take 3 seconds, 1, 2, 3. And as you count to 3, enter in, into your heart, into the still, silent, peaceful calm found within the void, your inner sacred space."

You see dear one, as you enter into your inner world of still, of calm, you are able to pause whatever has been happening in your world around you, your biggest struggles, for you, in your personal life. When you enter into the space of your open heart, you need not be affected by these things. This does not mean that they immediately go away or vanish from your experience, but you are able to refocus, view the situation from another perspective so that you can adequately respond, overcome the lesson, and turn it into an opportunity. For, you see, your challenges are opportunities. They're not the worst thing in the world, they are blessings in disguise, for they give you the opportunity to heal past parts of you that are triggered.

When something frustrates you, when it brings up anger, when it brings up sadness or discomfort, step back. Enter In. 1, 2, 3. Open your heart. "Angels, surround me, lift my vibration. Lift up and out of my body any dense or challenging emotions that are coming up now. I release them into the light, into your wings of love. Take them, release them into the light, replace with unconditional love, compassion, and well being." When you respond with love, even the challenge that seemed most overwhelming, the lesson that seemed impossible to overcome, becomes manageable. Consciously take a step back. Open your heart and unite with your power, unite with your full light and spirit by simply quieting your mind, opening your heart, entering in to the still, calm, quiet void within. For within this place of still, silent calm, your true power as a spiritual being can be found. And so in your moments of triumph and exaltation, in the times of your life when things are going well, practice this, indeed, then as well. Step back. 1, 2, 3. Open your heart and enter in. And, you see, from this place your energy can become intact once more. Perhaps you are now able to see your next step. What is next? How it is most beneficial for you to respond. What does your response of love looks like? What does it mean for you in this situation to respond with love?

1, 2, 3. Open your heart, drop in, connect with the love that is found within your inner sacred space for the highest and greatest good. Connect and feel the blessing of this connection ripple throughout your body, bringing you healing. This ripple of healing love and light does not end with you. Indeed, in your every moment your energy connects to the greater whole, to all that is, to all beings on planet Earth, and Earth included.

When you take a step back from challenging emotions and return to love, you are able to, once again, contribute love to the greater whole around you, which of course serves in many ways. By then filling yourself up with light and grounding this light to Earth, the light of your fully cleansed, fully connected self strengthens, the light crystalline grid of planet Earth, ushering in the new beginning for the planet and for all beings. Ascension energy is present on Earth in full force, light is present in full force. And while this may seem good, and it is, this light can bring up challenges and heavy situations for you. This does not mean you're not on your path, this does not mean the work you are doing is not valid or is not working. It means that something is coming to your awareness, for it is ready to be released. And so step back, 1, 2, 3. Enter in. Open your heart, breathe, and imagine now that your angels and guides are all around you and that an ocean of light is above you that begins to pour in opening all your chakra energy centers, cleansing away reside of past challenges, emotions that no longer serve, negativity that has clung onto your aura or your energy. Let this be released now into the light. Let yourself fill up with light now, with well being, with love, and awareness. Allow yourself to be illuminated in the light that is all around you, and release all that no longer serves.

Your next step, dear one is to simply ground this love and well being and light into the Earth, into the physical. For light grounded into physical form enables you to benefit from this light, and for it to be a positive force of love, of well being, of health, of vitality, of vibrant living for all. And so your process is simple. Open your heart, quiet your mind, think, "Angels, guides, connect." And then imagine the light that becomes available to you with this connection, an ocean of light above you. Know that this light is already present on your planet, and there is only a slight attunement of your conscious awareness needed to turn in and integrate. Open heart, quiet mind, and then allow. Let the light flow in. Let it cleanse and let it lift.

Let light fill your entire being, your chakra energy centers united in one light, white light. And now as you continue to focus upon your breath and on the light that builds and grows and swirls around you, let yourself consciously ground this energy, this love, compassion, this light force into the Earth, into the physical.

Imagine now that the light is flowing down from the bottom of your feet. A tap root, like roots from a tree extending down now below the surface of the Earth to the very core. Go with the light, let your conscious awareness flow with it, and now at the core of Earth, grounded in light, connect with the warmth, love, and well being that is present here. Notice that you are a part of it, you are a part of Earth, you are not separate, you are one, and Earth is a part of all that is. Oneness, not separation. This is the lesson now. By uniting with the light present, by grounding it into the Earth, by opening your heart, by feeling, you can know and experience and benefit from this one energy that makes up all that is and that is now infused with the blessings of the light grounded into physical form. You see, you have the ability to translate the light codes into a mode that can benefit life in the physical.

When you allow light to flow into you and then ground this light to Earth the full benefit may be seen. This process may seem simple, but it is profound. As you practice, as you open to more and more light, more and more joy, more and more of your true, authentic, spiritual, light, self, power, and allow this to flow into you, to lift you, to illuminate you, to enlighten you, and then to return this energy to the one source, to the Earth connected to all, the loop is complete. The light becomes accessible in the physical realm in a way that you can relate to, in a way that you can share, and build upon, and understand. And so let the light into your experience and as you begin, you may find that it brings about more challenge than you anticipated. Don't let this discourage you. This is a sign it is working. And so what comes up for you, let it go. The belief, the way of relating, the way of responding, the emotion that is around you, if what comes up is something that is hurtful, painful, challenging frustrating, let it go. Release it into the light and let love, let light, let compassion take its place. Witness this, and then ground your energy to Earth so that you may receive full benefit from the increased vibrations and frequencies and wavelengths of love that are present now in physical form.

Open your heart to let love in, and then ground this love unto the Earth. This is how you receive full benefit from the energy and how you contribute to all, for light grounded to Earth becomes love, becomes joy, becomes well being. And so embark, engage in this alchemical process of transmuting light that is present in your physical world into a tangible form that you can use and share and build upon.

You are able to co create with the divine. Open your heart, lift, enter in, and connect with the divine realms of love accessible from your heart. Float, fly, absorb more light than you even thought you could carry.

Let yourself become illuminated. let the light push out all that no longer serves you, let go, release it, and then ground your new found level of love, of light and well being into the Earth. Ground light into the planet and into your life so that you may enjoy it, share it, live it, so that you may live an awakened life, a master of light in physical form united with your full power, with your full spiritual light and ability to co create with divine. This is the direction you are moving in, this is the blessing that is possible when you do step back when you are challenged, when you enter in, and instead of engaging the struggle and the negativity in the world around you. Enter in, open your heart, unite with the light and ground a new level of light and love into the present. Now is the time. Now is a powerful time for advancement, to shift the scales on Earth away from control and power and manipulation and negativity. Release these dense emotions and vibrations from your own experience and let light in, let your light shine and ground the light into the Earth. The new beginning you are working towards with this process, is Earth and an awakened humanity co creating with love, with compassion, and with respect, with light.

I am Archangel Michael and as we angels take a step back now, we first flow a wave, a surge, another influx of light into your unique experience. Open your heart, and let this love, let this light in. Now imagine that like a root extending down from a tree, you are able to consciously ground the light now into the Earth, into physical reality, into physical form now. You know how to do this, it's simple. Ground this love, light, and well being into your experience for the highest and greatest good. And so it is.

You are so loved and you rapidly approach a new beginning in which love is the foundation. To prepare for this, release that which cannot hang in the light, that which is ready to go. Open to new levels of frequency, love, compassion, and well being. Ground these high vibrational energies into your life, into the physical, and you will see the blessings from them. And then when a challenge does appear, step back, step in, unite with your light, and choose how to respond. Overcome challenge, learn from your lessons, keep progressing forward. You are a spiritual, divine being. You are on the path of re-membering your full light and bringing it into physical form. One step at a time, choose love, and when you find it is impossible to choose love for you are challenged, step back, enter in, unite with love, and then choose your reaction, then choose your response.

1, 2, 3. Open your heart and enter in. I, Archangel Michael, leave you with ultimate blessings of light. Ground these into the Earth to receive their full benefit and love, for this is available to you. You are so loved and blessed and encouraged. You're doing well. Keep going. Goodbye for now.

Acknowledgements

Thank you to the compassionate guides, angels, and ascended masters committed to assisting humanity and Earth in releasing past density, and stepping into a new paradigm of love and light. Without these benevolent spiritual beings, who have helped me so much on my path, this book would not be possible.

Thank you to Toni Zora, Betsy Morgan Coffman and Sanaya Roman for being graceful and loving teachers. Thank you to Miles Beckler for encouraging me on my path of awakening, and for offering continued love and support in my life. Thank you to all of my friends and family who have taught me so much in both beautiful and challenging ways.

Thank you to you! Thank you for your willingness to seek the truth within you, for opening your heart and letting your light shine.

About The Author

Melanie is a clear channel for the angelic realm. She feels both honored and blessed to share the ever unfolding and expanding guidance, love and upliftment from that flows through as a result of her direct connection with the realm of angels.

For more information regarding Melanie's work, visit her website www.Ask-Angels.com

CPSIA information can be obtained at www.ICGtesting.com
Printed in the USA
BVOW041902030413

317236BV00001B/2/P

SUSTAINABLE
MATERIALS
WITH BOTH EYES OPEN

Preface

We don't talk enough about steel, cement, plastic, paper and aluminium, but without them we'd be living in huts and walking to work, our shops would be empty, we'd have to grow all our own food and we'd have no medical care. We make these materials with amazing efficiency, yet they have the same impact on the environment as the whole of the world's transport system. And that impact is growing, we're likely to want twice as much material within 40 years. And if we do that, we'll reduce the chance that our children can live as well as we do.

We'd all like to take action to find a more sustainable future—but what can we do? Can we put pressure on the materials industries to 'clean up their act'? Not really, they've largely done so already, and they're so efficient that we've nearly reached the limits of what's possible. So it sounds as if we're stuck, but that's where this book comes in. So far we've been looking at the problem with one eye open, hoping that industry can magically solve the problem. But with both eyes open we have a whole new set of options. Rather than making more materials, we could use them more wisely—with less material, keeping them for longer, re-using their parts and more. And these options make a huge difference: we really could set up our children with a more sustainable life, without compromising our own.

We've spent three years looking at the realities of a sustainable materials future with both eyes open. We've made hundreds of factory visits, held meetings and workshops spanning every aspect of the materials world, we've tried things out in our lab, and checked out our ideas with other scientists and people in the government. This book is the result: it tells the story of materials production, what we make and how we do it, who's involved and how we make money, and we've found out about every way we could do things differently from new processes to new products to new ways to use and value materials.

We've written the book to share our optimistic view of the future: we can make a big difference if we look ahead with both eyes open. We've written it for people who work with materials—making them, shaping them, or using them—and people who influence how it happens. For policy makers and negotiators, financiers and accountants, people who assess risks or set standards, and for teachers, researchers and the students who'll define our future material world. It's written for people in industry and it's for their customers. Because we're all involved. We all depend on these five tremendous materials, we need to learn to use them in a different way, and we all have a say in the change. And the good news story in this book is that we can make a big change—but only if we look for it with both eyes open.

SUSTAINABLE
MATERIALS
WITH BOTH EYES OPEN

Julian M Allwood

Jonathan M Cullen

with
Mark A Carruth, Daniel R Cooper, Martin McBrien,
Rachel L Milford, Muiris C Moynihan, Alexandra CH Patel

Department of Engineering
University of Cambridge

UIT
CAMBRIDGE, ENGLAND

Published by:
UIT Cambridge Ltd.
PO Box 145
Cambridge
CB4 1GQ
England

Tel: +44 1223 302 041
Web: www.uit.co.uk

ISBN 9781906860059 (paperback)
ISBN 9781906860073 (hardback)

UIT books may be purchased in bulk for academic, corporate, or
promotional use.
eBook versions and licenses are also available for many titles.
For more information, contact special-sales@uit.co.uk

10 9 8 7 6 5 4 3 2 1

Contents

Prologue: Our Material Children

If we take the world's annual production of steel and divide it by the world's population, each one of us causes 200 kg of steel to be made each year. If we used this steel to make a sculpture, it would have the same volume as a life-size statue of an eight year old child. Following the same logic every year every one of us also 'gives birth' to ten cement, one plastic and three paper eight-year olds, and one new-born aluminium baby.

These material children are largely hidden. We are anaesthetised to their birth, but it is environmentally painful. Converting natural resources into useful materials is energy intensive, uses land and water, and releases emissions to air, water and soil. Using one measure only, creating our material children causes the release of around 1,000 kg of CO_2 per year, the same as would be emitted by burning 400 kg of coal. And if we made sculptures with the coal, we would have three or four average sized men of coal.

On average, every person on the planet gives birth to these 16 material children and launches their 4 coal parents into the sky every year. But we aren't all average. In the UK and other developed economies in Europe, America, Japan and parts of China, our annual consumption of materials is approximately four times the global average. So for us, the aluminium baby is now two, the rest of our material children have grown up and married, and they now have 14 coal parents.

The life-size procession of material adults marching down this page could be sculpted from the materials produced every year, for every person in the UK, and every one of us causes the 14 coal adults at the back to be launched into the sky, every year.

the world
of materials

1. Material wealth and health

In developed economies we live the good life for now – with an amazing level of comfort and interest created by our astonishing ability to make and transform materials. We've really only done this at scale in the past 150 years, in which time our use of engineered materials has rocketed, literally. However, if we have some concern about 'sustainability' we need to anticipate what effects our use might have on future generations – and we're getting some clear indicators that there's a problem.

2. Scale, uncertainty and estimation

If we are creating big problems, we need to look for big solutions: just putting our newspapers in the recycling bin won't be enough. We need to answer the question "what really matters?" However, we can't give a precise answer to that because we won't know till after the event, so how should we deal with uncertainties about future impacts, and about the effect of different options for change?

3. Our uses of steel and aluminium

To understand what options we might have to change the way we use materials, we need to find out what we use them for at present and this requires some detective work. We also need to look at the key properties of the materials we use, to find out why they're so attractive

4. Metal journeys

The materials we use start in the ground as ores/minerals and transforming them into finished goods is a long journey. If we can create a map of that journey, we can build up a picture of scale, anticipate the set of processes we need to explore, and by looking at the way the flow has evolved in the past, can start to predict what might be required in future.

5. Energy and emissions

Many of our concerns about sustainable materials relate to the requirements for energy to process them, so we need to find out where the energy is used, and how that use evolves. In response to concerns related to climate change, we need to know in particular which processes emit most greenhouse gases.

6. Where does the money go

Most of us have never directly purchased engineered materials—because we buy them when they have been formed into components and assembled into finished goods. So, when we buy cars or buildings, how much of the money flows back to the material producers, and who else is involved?

1   Material wealth and health

What are we worried about?

In developed economies we live the good life for now – with an amazing level of comfort and interest created by our astonishing ability to make and transform materials. We've really only done this at scale in the past 150 years, in which time our use of engineered materials has rocketed, literally. However, if we have some concern about 'sustainability' we need to anticipate what effects our use might have on future generations – and we're getting some clear indicators that there's a problem.

Welcome to this edition of "The World's got Materials" and we'll go straight into the first round: name the first thing that comes into your head when you hear the following place names: you must answer immediately. San Francisco, *Golden Gate Bridge*; Paris, *Eiffel Tower*; Hong Kong, New York and Shanghai, *skyscrapers*; Sydney, *Harbour Bridge*; North Pole, *pole*. Excellent. A perfect score, so we'll move straight on to the second round: for each of the following decades name its key icon. 1960's, *moon landing*; 1970's, *cassette decks and VCRs*; 1980's, *personal computers*; 1990's, *internet*; 2000's, *mobile phones*. Very good, albeit a little selective, and finally in the third round, tell us how you spend most of your money: *housing; car and other travel; food*. Congratulations! A perfect set of answers and, apart from some of the food everything you've mentioned depends on energy intensive materials.

We learnt at school the progression from stone age, bronze age, iron age through the dark and middle ages, age of discovery then enlightenment and on to machine and information ages. But we could equally label the past 100 years, our era, as the material age. Our ability to find and convert fuels into intense heat has allowed us to extract and convert natural ores and minerals into the metals, ceramics and polymers with which we have constructed all our recent icons and inventions, and on which we spend most of our money. This phenomenon is so common, and largely so well hidden, that we are hardly aware how recent it is: Joseph Aspdin in Leeds first patented the production of Portland Cement, the basis of modern concrete and mortar, in 1824; Henry Bessemer in Cheltenham patented his steel making process in 1855; Charles Hall in Ohio in 1886 and simultaneously but independently Paul Héroult in Paris worked out how to produce aluminium cheaply. These inventions, all occurring during the lives of our grandparents' grandparents, and their equivalents for plastics and industrial paper production, transformed the economics of materials from precious to commodity, and opened

A Bessemer converter in which hot air is blown through liquid iron to burn off impurities and so produce cheap, malleable steel

the door to our current remarkable dependence on materials. In just over 100 years, global production has grown from virtually nothing at the turn of the 20th century to the point that we now make more than 10 times our body weight of these five materials every year, for every person alive.

Our primary use of materials has been to live in more comfort in much higher densities, while travelling much greater distances. In the past 100 years we have shifted rapidly from rural to urban dwelling, and can sleep, work and relax in remarkable comfort in cities, solely because we have the materials to build, heat, cool and light safe interior spaces at high density and to travel rapidly and comfortably between them. In fact, such is their attraction that in 2009, for the first time in history, half the world's population lived in cities. Worldwide, we now have 21 mega-cities, with more than 10 million people each, housing nearly a tenth of the world's population[1]. And although large cities appear to be efficient, moving people to cities tends to increase economic growth, both within the city and in the surrounding rural areas, leading to an increase in demand for materials.

Making, transforming and buying these fantastic materials uses a good deal of our money. Around one third of a billion people worldwide[2], 5% of all of us, are directly transforming the materials for us and 10% of our collective spending goes to the companies who make these materials.

All of this sounds terrific: what fortunate people we are to have such apparently unlimited access to such high-quality but cheap material that we use to create such a great lifestyle. No one has ever lived like us before. We are the lifestyle kings and queens of history!

But of course no fairytale is worth telling if there isn't a villain—without the wolf, we'd remember neither Little Red Riding Hood nor her grandmother—and this book exists because there are several baddies roaming around our material world. To find out more, where else could we turn other than to the BBC who introduce their evening news programme with the sonorous bongs of Big Ben (13.5 tonnes of cast iron, made at the Whitechapel Bell Foundry in 1858):[3-6]

The clocktower of the Palace of Westminster, which houses *Big Ben*

Sustainable Materials with both eyes open

12th October 2010

Villagers despair in Hungary's red wasteland

Around 600,000 tonnes of toxic red mud, a by-product of washing bauxite in sodium hydroxide to create alumina, covered around 40 square kilometres, may take a year to clean up. The accident injured more than 150 people and has claimed 10 lives. Hungary's Ajka Alumina Plant produces around 0.5 % of global alumina output.

20th October 2010

Rio Tinto in $3.1bn Australia iron-ore expansion

Typically we extract about 10 tonnes of iron sands to yield 1 tonne of ore, so if the sands are in a band about 10 metres deep, and have a density of 5 tonnes per cubic metre, Rio Tinto's Australian production uses up about 560 square kilometres of Australia each year—equal to about half the land area of Hong Kong.

4th January 2011

China to restrict exports of rare earth elements

China currently produces around 97 % of the global supply of rare earths (elements we use in making permanent magnets, used in some electric motors and generators, particularly in wind turbines) so could limit development of these products elsewhere, unless other supplies are found.

9th March 2011

Polar ice loss quickens, raising seas

Satellite imaging demonstrates that ice loss from Antarctica and Greenland has accelerated in the past 20 years, due to global warming, and sea levels are rising faster than anticipated by the Intergovernmental Panel on Climate Change (IPCC) in its 2007 assessment.

It's getting a little noisy, so we'll cut off Big Ben, and reflect on the range of issues which are causing us concern about our escalating demand for materials:

- **Resource shortages**: clearly the world must eventually run out of minerals and fossil fuels, but that point is a long way ahead. The more pressing challenge related to resource shortages is that we are using up the best deposits, so in future will have to invest more money and energy in exploiting less convenient sites. This will drive up prices and may create conflict due to the uneven geographical distribution of the resources.

- **Water stress**: possibly more pressing than mineral shortages is parallel concern about fresh water. Globally we are not short of water, there is plenty. However in some places, we are short of water of the quality we would like. For poor areas, there is no solution except for people to move. For rich areas, such as the state of California, water can be transported by (energy intensive) pumping, or in Malta, fresh water is made from the Mediterranean by (energy intensive) desalination. Some aspects of materials production are water intensive, increasing the potential for local water stress.

- **Land stress:** there is a limit to how much more land can be brought into agricultural production, so any use of land to generate bio-fuels is likely to be at the cost of land used for some other valued purpose.

Shanghai

- **By-products and toxic chemicals:** for most ores, we have to extract ten tonnes of rock to gain one tonne of ore, and then we need to extract the element of interest from the ore. This extraction requires energy, but also the use of chemicals, some of which are harmful. Most are regulated and well controlled, but as we saw in Hungary, accidental releases will occur. As we don't know the long-term consequences of releases of all chemicals, it is difficult for regulators to know that they have set safe levels. Emissions of chemicals to soil, water and air can have a wide range of harmful effects on different species.

- **Climate change:** the greenhouse effect has been known and understood since John Tyndall's experiments published in 1858, and is undisputed. The sun's rays fall on the earth, which radiates back some of their energy, at a different frequency. Greenhouse gases in the atmosphere absorb some of this reflected radiation, and re-radiate it in all directions, including back towards the earth. The greenhouse effect thus causes the earth to warm up. The greenhouse gases include most gases with two different atoms and all with three or more, of which the most important is carbon dioxide (CO_2). Burning fossil fuels, coal,

Bauxite mining in the Amazon rainforest

gas and oil, releases CO_2 into the atmosphere, so increases the strength of the greenhouse effect, and hence causes global warming. All of this is undisputed fact. However, there remains debate about man-made global warming, not because of these facts but because (a) we have only partial records of greenhouse gas concentrations and global temperatures over both space (i.e. throughout the atmosphere) and time, (b) the climate is subject also to many other effects, not all of which are fully understood and which are difficult to forecast, and (c) there is a lot of misinformation around, and various groups are motivated to increase it. The Intergovernmental Panel on Climate Change (IPCC), whose 2007 Nobel Prize winning 4th Assessment Report has been widely examined (and to us it is most remarkable not because a small number of errors were found, but because the number of errors was so small), claims that "most of the observed increase in globally averaged temperatures since the mid-20th century is very likely due to the observed increase in anthropogenic greenhouse gas concentrations." As a result, the IPCC recommends that global emissions of greenhouse gases should be cut, by 2050, to 50%-85% of 1990 levels, to limit the global average temperature increase to 2.0–2.4°C and avoid the adverse effects of climate change.

These concerns are all real, serious, and pressing. The world's population has more than doubled in the past 50 years, and our use of engineered materials has increased by 4 to 15 times in the past 50 years. All the issues we've raised are driven by the volume of production of materials: if we double production, and make no other changes, we will double the drivers of each concern.

However, this book is not about gloom. We've been motivated by these concerns to look for implementable practical changes that will reduce the likelihood that our own actions seriously degrade the quality of life that generations after us can enjoy. With that ambition, we join a whole raft of others who sail under the banner of "Sustainability" and that's a mixed blessing. The pioneers who have raised awareness about the problems we've listed above are heroes without whom we wouldn't have started. Defining the problem—of climate change, sustainability or, environmental impacts—is not what we're about, because that's been done well, and ongoing work by others is improving our ability to forecast consequences.

Instead, our aim is to look at solutions, and our number one guiding principle is about scale—we want to make sure that we identify options for change that are big enough to make a big enough difference. In fact the whole of our next chapter discusses scale, so no more on that for now. However, given that many others have

Mining iron ore

written about solutions, before we set off with our search for solutions, and very delicately, we'd like to say briefly what we're not:

- We're not promoting an ideology. We've read several books where the authors claim to have found the answer, "Do what I say, and use my catch phrase, and we can all get there, yee-ha" and so on. The difficulty about these books is that they all seem to validate their claims by showing that passive houses use less energy than conventional houses. We know that, but if we look at the third of the world's energy that's required to make and form materials, we have to look at more than just domestic heating.

- We're not actors within industry and we're not a lobby, so we can explore all possible options including those that don't involve growth. This is vitally important. Nobody employed in industry can be seen to explore the option that their industry should shrink. That's obvious—but for the materials producing industries, who are also the main sources of data on the impacts of materials production, there is a danger that they might only inform governments about options which allow further expansion of the industry, so the idea of reduced output will never be considered.

- We're not a national government. Presumably that's obvious, but it's very important, because it means we can't pursue solutions that shift the problem elsewhere. Our former Prime Minister Tony Blair was the first to sign up for the Kyoto Protocol. Broadly that's good and we wish everyone else had done so, but he did it in the knowledge that we'd already met the target, by a combination of switching from coal to gas powered electricity generation and by continuing Mrs Thatcher's policy of allowing manufacturing to shift off the shores of the UK. The shifting part has obviously had no effect on global emissions because the activity continues elsewhere, so we have to be very careful about national emissions figures.

The authors

What we are is a research team of eight at the University of Cambridge, who have been funded[7] for five years to explore sustainable materials. The main focus of our work has been on steel and aluminium production and its emissions of CO_2, but we think we have learnt enough to expand our remit to the three other key materials, and to demonstrate that the options that would lead to a cut in emissions will also be the main options required to address most other concerns about future sustainability. We only put two of our names on the front cover of the book so it didn't look too much like a take-away menu, but the eight of us in the photo have shared the learning and the work leading to this book.

Sustainable Materials with both eyes open

So our aim in this book is to explore all possible options for creating a sustainable materials future, and as much as we can, to present a rational evaluation of how difficult it would be to implement them. An over-riding concern in our work has been to examine the whole picture and because scale is so important to us, that's the focus of the next chapter.

And although we're not selling an ideology, an important discovery in our work has been that there is a whole raft of options for creating a sustainable material future which have had very little attention. Material efficiency, using less new material to achieve the same goals, is a rich opportunity. We've used the phrase "with both eyes open" in our title as a reminder that, as well as making materials efficiently, we can also make less of them. We particularly want to raise awareness of these options, so as well as writing the book for a broad audience and making it freely available online, we've also written a set of songs on the theme. We've spread a few song fragments through the book, and have been fortunate to persuade Adey Grummett, star of Cats, Les Miserables and D'Oyley Carte to record them for us. You can hear Adey, find out more, and download chapters of the book at www.withbotheyesopen.com.

Notes

1. The United Nations Population Fund (UNPFA) publishes a State of the World Population Report every year, which includes demographic, social and economic indicators, by country and region. Figures in this section were taken from the 2010 report (UNPFA, 2010). The United Nations also has a Population Division in the Department of Economic and Social Affairs which reports urbanisation figures, (UNDESA, 2009)

2. We will look in more detail at who's involved in transforming materials into products in chapter 6.

3. The BBC article "Villagers despair in Hungary's red wasteland" BBC News, 2010a) describes the release of toxic "red mud" from a holding reservoir in Ajka, Hungary. The Ajka Alumina Plant is owned by MAL Hungarian Aluminium and is licensed to produce 300,000 tonnes of alumina per year, according to Jávor and Hargitai (2011). The plant was originally established to process bauxite ore to alumina to feed Hungary's aluminium furnaces for metal production. However, because of the closure of these furnaces and rapid growth in demand for non-metallurgical alumina the Ajka plant has not produced alumina for metal production since 2006. The International Aluminium Institute (IAI) provides annual statistics on alumina production and estimates the 2010 global production of alumina to be 56.3 million tonnes: 51.6 Mt for metallurgical uses and 4.7 Mt for chemical uses (IAI, 2011b). Thus the Akja Alumina Plant contributes 0.55 % of total global demand for alumina (but 6 % of alumina for chemical uses).

4. Reported on the BBC website: Rio Tinto in $3.1bn Australia iron ore expansion (BBC News, 2010b). The land area calculation is conservative, as it excludes mining infrastructure such as access and haulage roads and processing facilities. Rio Tinto recently signed agreements with Aboriginals to gain iron ore mining access to 71,000 square kilometres of land in Pilbara, Western Australia (BBC News, 2011a). The deal will allow Rio Tinto to expand their iron ore operations in Australia to 330 million tonnes by 2015, a 50 % expansion on 2009 levels.

5. Based on a debate on BBC Radio 4's Today Programme, with Dr Richard Pike, of the Royal Society of Chemistry and Mark Leonard, of the European Council on Foreign Relations (Pike & Leonard, 20aa).

6. From an article by the BBC's environment correspondent, Richard Black, "Polar ice loss quickens, raising seas" (Black, 2011).

7. Nearly all the funding for our work has been provided by the Engineering and Physical Sciences Research Council (EPSRC) of the UK through a 'Leadership Fellowship' awarded to Julian Allwood. The funding has no pre-conditions. One of us is funded by a PhD studentship three quarters of which is paid by the EPSRC and one quarter by Arup, but our agreement with Arup is about confidentiality only. Our work has been supported by a consortium of more than twenty large companies, with whom we've met frequently to discuss all aspects of the work in this book. Much of the evidence presented in the book has been gathered in collaboration with them, but the interpretation is our own. More details about our ongoing research are on the project website, www.wellmet2050.com.

2 Scale, uncertainty and estimation

What would make a big difference?

If we are creating big problems, we need to look for big solutions: just putting our newspapers in the recycling bin won't be enough. So we need to answer the question "what really matters?" However, we can't give a precise answer to that because we won't know till after the event, so how should we deal with uncertainties about future impacts, and about the effect of different options for change?

In 2007 Gordon Brown, the UK Prime Minister, announced that the UK would now get serious about climate change, and we would cut down on the use of carrier bags in supermarkets[1]. In making this statement, he was following the leadership of some UK supermarkets, who had already begun to charge for bags, and now, in most shops when we reach the checkout, we're asked if we want a bag or will use our own. Apparently our use of carrier bags has reduced by 41% as a result[2]. Good news, and now we've all done our bit, so can fly off to sunny Spain for the weekend with a clear conscience. "Sin bolsas el sol es más sabroso. ¡Adiós bolsas!, ¡Hola sol!"

13 plastic bags for the weekly shop...

Well, maybe, but let's check. Firstly we'll do an informal experiment: imagine we have a typical family of five, who live in Cambridge for example, and buy most of their food at a supermarket in a weekly shop. The two photos to the left show (a) that their weekly shopping requires 13 carrier bags weighing around 100 grams, and (b) that the weight of the other plastic brought home in the carrier bags (two-thirds of which was bottles) was ten times greater at about 1 kg. So carrier bags are a small fraction of the plastic we purchase in supermarkets. Does our use of supermarket packaging form a significant part of the country's total use of plastic? If we look at the total use of plastic in the UK, carrier bags account for less than 1%. So, as plastic accounts for around 1% of the UK's total CO_2 emissions, if we all stopped using all plastic carrier bags, we would reduce our national emissions by less than 0.01% (less than one 100th of 1%). This is a step forwards, but it is a small step. Roughly, it is equivalent to avoiding driving 4 miles per year each, or turning off one 60 W light bulb each for one day, once a year.

... and the rest of the plastic that was inside the bags

It turns out that the problem with plastic carrier bags is actually about litter—when they blow around after use, they get caught in hedgerows and railings. We don't like to see them, and it is a shame to throw out 65,000 tonnes of carrier bags when landfill space in the UK is tight, but they're almost irrelevant to our search for responses to climate change.

We've started with this story, not because we have any particular interest in carrier bags, but because it illustrates three major challenges as we look for a sustainable materials future: scale, uncertainty and estimation. If we want to make a big difference to our environmental impacts, we need to make big changes. Many small changes, if they each apply in different areas, do not add up to a big change. It is very difficult for us to be certain about exactly how much impact any action will have, not only because of a lack of data (exactly how many carrier bags did you use last year?) but also because we don't know precisely how one change to our behaviour leads to other consequences. (How many straw baskets were flown in from the Caribbean to allow us to go shopping without using carrier bags?) As a result, we can only make sensible decisions by estimating the scale of change they cause, and of course estimates are imperfect.

These three issues are linked, but we can't defer action until we have perfect data, because by then it would be too late to make effective changes. If we can make sensible estimates of what's big and small, we can start to take actions leading to big changes knowing they will make a significant difference, even if we don't know exactly how big that difference will be. So the aim of this chapter is to identify the key 'bigs' of sustainable materials, make clear why we're uncertain about how big they are, and then explain how we're going to use estimates to predict likely big actions.

Scale

This book is made from more than ten materials: the paper is mostly wood fibres, but also contains kaolin clay, calcium carbonate, titanium dioxide, silica or talc; the print on the page may be made from polymers (styrene/acrylate, polyethylene, or others), wax, resin and silica, with colours made with iron oxide or other pigments; the cover is coated with varnish, aqueous coatings or film lamination; the pages are bound by stitching, stapling or glue, requiring a further nine or more materials. Remarkable. A book made mainly of paper, which we consider to be a relatively natural material, contains numerous engineered materials. Glance up from the book, and start counting the number of materials you can see around you and whether you're looking at the inside or outside of a building, some furniture, the toaster, or your computer you'll probably lose count within a minute or so. Our lives depend on a cornucopia of materials, so much so that our colleague Professor

This book uses more than ten different materials

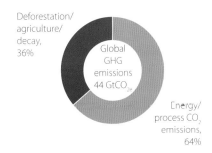

Deforestation/
agriculture/
decay,
36%

Global
GHG
emissions
44 GtCO$_{2e}$

Energy/
process CO$_2$
emissions,
64%

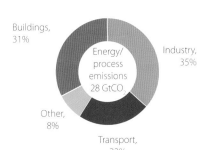

Buildings,
31%

Energy/
process
emissions
28 GtCO$_2$

Industry,
35%

Other,
8%

Transport,
22%

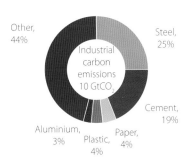

Other,
44%

Industrial
carbon
emissions
10 GtCO$_2$

Steel,
25%

Aluminium,
3%

Plastic,
4%

Paper,
4%

Cement,
19%

Figure 2.1—**Pie charts showing the sources of global CO$_2$ emissions**

Tom Graedel at Yale has shown that a typical mobile phone now uses more than two thirds of the periodic table of elements[3]. So, if we're concerned about finding a more sustainable material system, where on earth should we start? What should be our priorities?

Fortunately, we can give a rather simple answer to this question, based on the three pie charts to the side. We've drawn the charts using data published by the International Energy Agency (IEA), who collate the most comprehensive global data set on energy use and consequent emissions[4], and they give us a great basis for identifying priorities. The IEA data is extensive, covering all greenhouse gas emissions including CO$_2$ emissions, details for the three main sectors (buildings, industry and transport) and importantly for our purposes, giving details for 13 industry categories including direct emissions (from burning fuels for energy), process emissions (from chemical reactions) and indirect emissions (from upstream electricity generation). The pie charts all show fractions of 'equivalent' annual CO$_2$ emissions, i.e. they show the effects of other greenhouse gas emissions translated into units equivalent to CO$_2$, and we drew them using data from 2005. Total global emissions are rising year by year, but the fractions change more slowly, so the breakdown in our three pie charts is likely to be a useful predictor of proportions in future years.

The first chart shows that emissions arising from burning fossil fuels to generate energy, and those released directly by industrial processes, form about two-thirds of the world's total "man-made" greenhouse gas emissions (i.e. those which are in addition to the natural cycle, in which plants and animals absorb and release CO$_2$ during growth, life and death). The other third of the first chart represents emissions which arise from changes in land-use (particularly deforestation) and from agriculture. As CO$_2$ is invisible, and of course we can't accurately measure all releases either, these numbers are estimates. However, the estimates from fuel combustion and processes are likely to be quite accurate, because our colleagues in chemistry know how much CO$_2$ is released from burning fuels and we can measure the amount of CO$_2$ emitted from a car or power station to verify our estimates. In contrast, it is much more difficult for our colleagues in biology, plant sciences and agriculture to predict the remaining third, because there are so many different and complex processes involved. The second pie chart explores the largest segment of the first one. It shows the main drivers of CO$_2$ emissions arising from energy production and industrial processes. Roughly one third of these emissions come from the use of buildings, a quarter from the use of transport, and one twentieth in "other" relates to upstream emissions from fuel processing. But

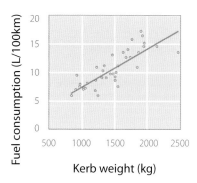

Figure 2.2—**Vehicle fuel consumption against mass for a typical range of cars in use in the UK at present**[15]

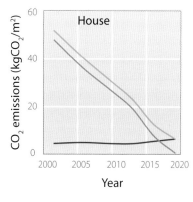

Figure 2.3—**CO_2 emissions per square metre for buildings**[16]

the largest segment, just over one third, arises in industry in making the goods, buildings and infrastructure with which we live our lives.

Most public debate about energy efficiency in the past 5–10 years has focused on the first two segments we mentioned, the use of buildings and transport, both because of their significance on this pie chart, and because we have many options for making them much more efficient. The two graphs to the side illustrate this for cars and houses. For cars, there is a strong correlation between fuel consumption and the weight of the car, so if we want efficient cars, we need to make them lighter. This is hardly surprising as on average our cars in the UK weigh 1.5 tonnes, but with an average contents of 1.5 people, the ratio of car weight to passenger weight is around 10:1. The second graph shows a recent history of CO_2 emissions for houses, per square metre of floor area, projected forwards to the targets we now have in UK law for future efficiency. The graph shows rapid improvement of the emissions arising from use (for heating, cooling and powering electrical goods), but little change to embodied emissions (those associated with constructing and maintaining the building). The three key design options that drive the improvements in use are better insulation, better sealing so that all exchange of air (and hence heat) with the outside world is controlled, and better design for natural air flow. The fact that we have already built 30,000 "passive houses" worldwide, without regular heating or cooling, is confirmation that the governments targets for future 'zero energy' buildings can be achieved[5].

So, we have good options for making a significant impact on two of the three big segments in the second pie chart. But what about the biggest one: industry? The third pie chart shows the major contributors to this industrial segment, and here we find a very useful simplification of our question about priorities: production of just five materials accounts for 55 % of industrial emissions, so this gives a clear focus to our exploration of sustainable materials. The five key materials are steel, cement, plastic, paper and aluminium, with the first two of these, steel and cement, the materials with which we construct buildings, roads, bridges and tunnels, accounting for nearly half of all industrial emissions.

We seem to have five clear priority materials, but let's just check that we haven't missed anything. The 'other' segment still represents 45 % of industrial emissions, and the segments related to the five key materials describe the energy and emissions required to produce the materials as stock products (such as plates, sheets and bars), not the total energy for delivering final goods. Are there other important materials in 'other' or are we actually under-representing the five key materials, by not showing the emissions associated with converting stock materials into goods?

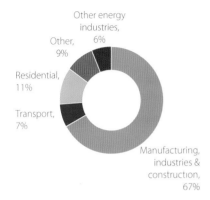

Other energy
industries,
6%

Other,
9%

Residential,
11%

Transport,
7%

Manufacturing,
industries &
construction,
67%

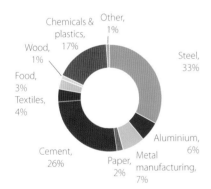

Chemicals &
plastics,
17%

Other,
1%

Wood,
1%

Food,
3%

Textiles,
4%

Steel,
33%

Cement,
26%

Paper,
2%

Metal
manufacturing,
7%

Aluminium,
6%

Figure 2.4—**Sources of
Chinese CO₂ emissions**

To answer this question, we need to know more about the 'other' segment, and to find out whether any downstream activities connected with our five materials are hiding in the data. The IEA gives only a broad analysis of the 'other' sector but we can find out more by looking at data from particular countries. Both the UK and the US have more detailed data, but manufacturing in both countries has declined recently so the proportions would not be globally representative. However, fortunately the Chinese government publishes excellent data on their own energy use, and China is 'the workshop of the world' so spans all manufacturing activity. The two pie charts in Figure 2.4 recreate the second and third of our global charts from Figure 2.1, for China[17].

The first chart for China shows that around two thirds of all energy used in China is for industry. However, the bottom chart is the key one: if we're right that China's industrial activity is a good proxy for global industrial activity, then this is the best insight we can gain into the global 'other industry' segment. The same five materials—steel, cement, plastic, paper and aluminium remain dominant, but they are now followed by other materials—textiles, food, and wood. We can also see that converting metal stock into products requires significant energy input, around 7% of the industrial total. (Incidentally, although these numbers are clear and widely agreed, it's remarkable how much variety you can create by presenting them in different ways. Take a look at our box story on the next page, 'Fun with numbers 1', to see how you can correctly argue that steel drives any fraction between 4% and 35% of the world's emissions.)

In exploring scale, we've now come up with five priority materials to examine in our search for a sustainable materials future. We've come a long way, but we need to address one other key issue before moving on. To illustrate it, let's say that I currently drive 9,000 miles per year in a car that does 30 miles per gallon, so each year I purchase 300 gallons of fuel. If I swap my car for one that does 60 miles per gallon, I will halve my fuel purchases and save 150 gallons per year. Alternatively, if I decide to drive half the distance each year, I will also halve my required fuel and save 150 gallons per year. So, what if I do both: swap the car, and also halve the annual distance? Clearly, I've now taken both savings, so I buy 300 gallons per year less, so that's …. no gallons at all to drive 4,500 miles! Perfect, all solved. But of course it's not true. The two options are not independent, and if I adopt both of them then firstly, I halve my consumption with the new car, and then I halve the remaining consumption by reducing the distance, so I arrive at 75 gallon per year to drive 4,500 miles. However, we find that errors like this, where energy efficiency options are wrongly added up has permeated debate about future energy use and emissions, so we need to clear it up completely.

When we started looking at global energy use, we found that the excellent data of the IEA is collected by country and by economic sector, but not by the technologies in which fuel is converted into services. If we have data on energy use in economic sectors, we can address the question "who should I blame?" for energy consumption but we can't ask "what can I change?" To do so we need to know how many electric motors are involved, for instance, or how much gas is burnt in boilers, and how efficient they are. So, we ran a major project to develop a map of global energy use, to show how energy sources (mainly fuel, but also renewable sources) are transformed by technologies to deliver the final services required by consumers. Our key map is to the right, showing this transformation. The map is in the form of a Sankey diagram in which the width of the lines are proportional to annual use of energy. (The box story on Riall Sankey describes the origin and uses of this diagram. We'll be developing several other Sankey diagrams later in the book.)

Fun with numbers 1

How significant is steel as a driver of global emissions? We need to answer the question with a ratio dividing the top number, the numerator, by the lower denominator. On the top, we can choose emissions associated with making liquid steel only (2 GtCO$_2$/year), with making the stock products that are sold by steel makers for manufacturing (2.5 GtCO$_2$/year), or the emissions associated with final goods made from steel (3.5 GtCO$_2$/year). On the bottom, we could include all possible emissions due to mankind, including agriculture and land-use change (44 GtCO$_2$/year), or we could use total emissions from the use of energy and processes (27 GtCO$_2$/year), or the emissions of the industrial sector (10 GtCO$_2$/year). So the unique and clear answer to the question is 4.5%, 5.7%, 7.4%, 8%, 9.3%, 13%, 20%, 25% or 35%—all of which are true! But this is just the beginning. Here are some other recent suggestions about the 'real value' of the numerator in our ratio: steel can be recycled, where cement cannot, so the emissions in making steel the first time should be reduced by a third to account for the benefit of using it in 40 years time; making a tonne of steel leads to production of about a quarter of a tonne of unwanted by-product called blast furnace slag, which can be used to reduce requirements for cement, so the true emissions of steel should be reduced by a quarter; new cars are more fuel efficient than older cars, so we should use more steel to make more new cars, and credit the resulting 10% emissions savings to the steel.

And the point of raising this is that all of these ratios arise from the same agreed figures on global emissions. We can have a lot of fun creating ratios that slant the story in one direction or another, but our concern is the total environmental impact of the whole system, so blame-shifting by playing with ratios is of no interest as we look for options for change.

Sustainable Materials with both eyes open

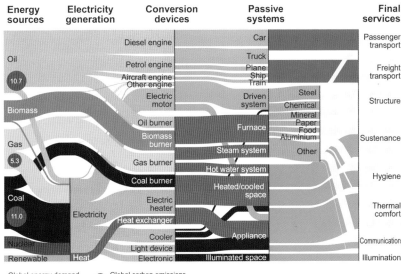

Figure 2.5—**Sankey diagram of global energy use**[18]

Global energy demand in 2005, total = 475 EJ

 Global carbon emissions in 2005, total = 27 Gt CO_2

The origins of the Sankey diagram

Sankey diagrams were first used by the Irish engineer Riall Sankey in 1898 to compare the energy flows of a real steam engine, a Louisville Leavitt Pumping Engine, with a 'perfect' engine. Within ten years the diagrams were being used to visualise 'heat balances' for engines and industrial processes, particularly by German engineers. Following the First World War, supplies of steel were critical in Germany, prompting the use of more complicated Sankey diagrams as a tool to identify options to conserve raw materials and improve production efficiency. Sankey diagrams are now commonly used to visualise flows of mass, energy, water and greenhouse gases across systems ranging from the smallest engines, to factories, to the entire global eco-system.

The key principle of a Sankey diagram is that flows are represented by arrows or lines where the thicknesses of each line represents the amount of flow. In systems, such as those related to energy or materials, where the flows cannot be lost, the sum of the widths of the lines (the sum of flows) across any section of the diagram, must always be the same. The reason we find Sankey diagrams so useful, is because at a glance we can gauge both the scale of a flow, and see how it connects with other flows.

If we take any vertical slice through our global energy map, the width of the lines adds up to the same number, which is the total energy value of the input sources. Therefore, if we want to consider the effect of making several efficiency improvements at the same time, all of which occur in a single vertical slice, then we can simply add up the savings from each, to get a total saving. However, if our efficiency gains occur along a horizontal line in the map, an improvement in power generation and an improvement in electric heater efficiency for example, we must multiply their effects to predict the total saving in fuel inputs. In our earlier example a 50% saving through fuel efficiency multiplied by a 50% reduction in driving distance gave an overall efficiency gain to 25%.

We've emphasised this difference between vertical and horizontal slices on the energy map because it is otherwise easy to make misleading claims. Many commercial organisations currently produce 'Abatement Curves' as a way of showing the relative cost of different options to reduce emissions, but every example we have seen has misleadingly suggested that efficiencies along a horizontal path on the energy map can be added up[6]. An important example of this confusion in Europe at present is in the strong move towards electric 'plug-in' cars charged from the national grid. The energy map makes clear that even if the car itself uses less energy (in direct electricity) than a petrol equivalent, we can only compare an electric car with a conventional one if we chase back through electricity generation to the original energy source. Using this approach we quickly come to the conclusion that an electric vehicle is currently no more efficient than a comparable petrol version, and may be worse.

It would be much more sensible to reduce the weight of cars first, and then change to battery power

Summarising what we've learnt about scale:

- Five key materials—steel, cement, plastic, paper and aluminium—dominate emissions from industry, and producing them accounts for 20% of all global emissions from energy use and industrial processes.

- This 20% figure relates to producing stock forms of the five materials, prior to final construction and manufacturing. Our analysis of Chinese energy use suggests that construction and manufacturing adds a further 2% of global energy and process emissions[7].

- In discussing efficiency options for producing the materials, we have to account carefully for the connection of energy transforming devices within the overall energy map as some efficiencies are additive and some are multiplicative.

Uncertainty

If only CO_2 were coloured pink, toxic releases were noisy and resource depletion caused a light to flash. It would be very much easier to address concerns about sustainable materials if all the drivers of harm and their long term impacts were instantly visible. But for most environmental processes there's a time delay between cause and effect and anyway our understanding of the causes is only partial. Here are the main uncertainties we face in exploring the impact that materials have on future sustainability:

- We do not fully understand how human activity now will affect the environment in the future.

- We do not fully understand how future environmental conditions will affect human and other life.

- We do not fully understand the environmental consequences of changes in human activity.

Specifically with regard to our five key materials, we face several other uncertainties that limit our ability to predict the consequences of future materials processing:

- We don't know how the world population will evolve or how rich we will be in future, so we don't know how demand for materials will develop or how it will be affected by environmental pressures.

- Although we have good understanding of emissions released from industrial processes and fuel combustion, we don't have a clear picture of all the uses of electricity associated with materials processing, which indirectly drives emissions.

- We don't have perfect data on the current end-uses of the key materials, because no one collects it, nor do we have good data on existing stocks of materials in use that might be re-used, recycled or replaced in the future.

- We don't know how costs will evolve, for example as oil becomes more scarce, less pure reserves of iron ore are used for normal production, or if more electricity is in future generated by renewables.

On top of this, we also have to deal with the fact that well informed organisations can make considerably different, even opposite, statements about the impacts of different choices. Two key issues have dogged our efforts to develop a clear picture of priorities:

- Materials producers naturally want to present their own material in the most positive light, so all use a different basis of comparison in order to present their particular material as "green." We've listed some examples of current claims in the sidebar, and further illustrated this problem in our second 'fun with numbers' box, which explores the much publicised information that "recycling aluminium requires 5% of the energy used in making new aluminium from ore." As the box shows, the 5% claim is factually correct if you are considering only the production of unrefined molten metal, but the can made from recycled material actually requires about a quarter of the energy required for the can from primary material. The materials producing industries are highly sensitive to the presentation of energy and emissions data and of course they can only report the most positive story. We've worked closely with them in preparing the book, and know that they would tell the story a different way, so to help them do so we have shown the basis of every number we're using in our footnotes and references.

- The processes which make materials from ore are generally much more damaging to the environment than downstream processes in which components are shaped and assembled into products. Materials processing is largely invisible to final consumers, so should we transfer responsibility from the processes onto the products which they make? Unfortunately this is an extremely difficult transfer to achieve. The most common current technique for attributing impacts to products, Life Cycle Assessment (LCA), was designed only to make relative comparisons between similar products but now is largely used to make assertions about absolute impacts of products. This is not a valid use of the technique, so the results can easily be manipulated to provide an answer that suits the preferences of whoever funded the study.

The uncertainties we've found in this section seem rather overwhelming: we're uncertain about how the environment works, we can't know the future, and much of the information provided to us is slanted. So what should we do?

We can't wait till everything is certain: there is a time delay between actions and environmental consequences, so that if we wait till all the environmental harm is visible, we will have missed the important opportunities to make change. In the case of climate change in particular, CO_2 emissions released today will linger in the atmosphere for around 250 years, so our children, and many generations to come, will live with the cloud we've released.

So we need to plan ahead using estimates, making sure we're clear about the uncertainty in them, but not using uncertainty as an excuse for inaction. How do we make good estimates?

Fun with numbers 2

Making a tonne of liquid aluminium from ore uses more than twenty times as much energy as making it from scrap (168 GJ/t compared to 7 GJ/t), so can we say that making a can from recycled aluminium only uses 4% of the energy to make it from primary aluminium?

Before aluminium cans are melted, coatings, other materials and moisture must be removed in an oven by a process called de-lacquering. De-lacquering uses about the same amount of energy as the melting process: our recycling energy is now 8% of the primary energy.

After de-lacquering, the cans are melted, however, a can is made from two different aluminium alloys, one for the lid and tab and one for the body. Therefore the composition of the melted aluminium scrap must be 'sweetened' with primary aluminium before it has the right composition for use as can body stock. About 5% primary aluminium must be added to correct the composition, and the recycling energy is now 13% of the energy to produce primary liquid metal.

However, we still need to make the can. The liquid aluminium from either source must be cast, rolled, blanked, stamped and coated to create can, and this requires a further 30 GJ. So making cans from a tonne of liquid aluminium from ore required 198 GJ, while from scrap it required 52 GJ, or 26%. Therefore recycled cans do save energy but require 26% not 4% of the energy used for primary cans.

The data used for this calculation is from the European Aluminium Association, EAA (2008).

Process stage	From ore (GJ/t)	From scrap (GJ/t)
De-lacquering		7
Liquid aluminium	168	7
Sweetening		8
Can-making and coating	30	30
Total	198	52

Table 2.1—**Energy use in recycling an aluminium can**

Estimates

We started this chapter with data collected by the International Energy Agency about fuel use, which is given by country and region, and in the key sectors. These numbers are probably reasonably accurate because fuel trade is recorded with some precision, so we have high confidence in our claim to have identified five key materials.

We are less sure about exactly how much energy is used, or the level of emissions released, in processing these five materials. No one collects a complete global data set for the performance of all processes, so instead we infer data from specific cases. In some countries or regions, businesses operating in particular sectors must report their emissions at a company or site level, as required for example by the European Union Emissions Trading Scheme. But unless the site is dominated by a single process this number requires interpretation and the companies involved are understandably reluctant to reveal details because their customers could use them in negotiating future prices. Most information on processes is therefore collected by trade associations, and they in turn are only able to release information approved by their members. In future, we hope that governments will mandate more reporting on energy, just as financial reports are required of companies. But at present most reporting is still voluntary, and we must rely on estimates. The box story describes the best voluntary scheme we've found while preparing the book.

Our uncertainties increase rapidly as soon as we look at environmental effects other than those related to energy use, as the data shortage becomes more and more severe. In particular, although we know that industrial production uses over 100,000 chemicals at present, we only really understand the toxic impacts of a small fraction of them, and even then our understanding is largely about short-term impacts.

Sustainable Materials with both eyes open

Overall, we have good data on energy and emissions by sector, but must use estimates to relate the data to particular processes. We have some data on material production volumes and use, but will need to make many estimates to predict all flows of metal into goods. Furthermore, in making estimates we've had to unpick several causes of confusion:

- Electricity or energy: we often find these two words used as if they were inter-changeable, but as we've seen on the global map of energy use, making electricity requires around one third of the world's energy sources. This is because electricity is a 'final fuel' (it can be metered by the final purchaser), sometimes called a direct energy, unlike original energy sources such as coal or gas which are called primary. To compare like with like we must always refer our numbers back to primary energy because this is the source of all energy-related carbon emissions.

- Energy or emissions: in many cases, energy use and CO_2 emissions are closely related, but not always. In manufacturing cement, for instance, roughly half the emissions arise from energy use and half are from the chemical reaction of converting limestone into cement and can't be avoided whatever energy source is used.

Data collection and reporting schemes

The Eco-Management and Audit Scheme (EMAS) introduced by the European Commission in 1995 and updated several times since, is a voluntary tool to help companies to evaluate, manage and improve their environmental performance. EMAS aims to support continuous improvement in the environmental performance of organisations and sites, through provision of transparent credible information updated at least annually. EMAS requires reporting of six key indicators, for energy efficiency, material efficiency, water consumption, waste generation, land use and emissions of greenhouse and other gases. To develop the material efficiency indicators, companies must report annual mass flows of the different materials they process.

Around 8,000 sites are now registered with EMAS, and during the many visits we made in preparing the book, we were particularly impressed by the Alunorf site near Dusseldorf, Germany, which uses EMAS to provides full public disclosure of their mass and energy flows.

- CO_2 or CO_{2e} (equivalent) emissions: we're sticking to CO_2, because making materials produces mainly CO_2, and it simplifies the problem enough for us to see a big-picture. However, CO_2 although clearly dominant, is just one of the three main greenhouse gases, alongside methane (CH_4) and nitrous oxide (N_2O). We'll need to use CO_2 equivalents, weighted over a long-time period, when we want to include the effects of the other gases in our analysis.

- Everyone uses numbers in a way that supports their interests: in gathering information about emissions and material use, we've found that authors will always choose to present their data in a way that adds weight to the argument they are making. This includes switching between giving absolute numbers (28 Mt) or ratios (32%) and, as we saw in our first 'fun with numbers' box, manipulating the terms in a ratio.

Defining the scope of the book

Given our problems with uncertainty, and the shortage of data that drives us to use estimates to anticipate the scale of key changes, we need to simplify the problem of searching for a 'sustainable' future. So we've decided to focus this book on CO_2 emissions. Climate scientists tell us that we need to cut CO_2 emissions by 50% or more by 2050. This is a massive challenge within a very short time, and unlike many of the other concerns raised in the previous chapter, governments have generally picked up on these targets and placed them into law in various forms[8].

In focusing on CO_2 emissions, we run the risk of missing other key environmental concerns such as water stress and toxic emissions to air, water or land, but having a single target helps us to clarify what is big and what small, and gives us increased confidence that our estimates can lead us to identify changes that will make a big difference. As we'll spend a good deal of the book exploring options to reduce our dependence on the production of new materials, we can also anticipate that where environmental harm is driven by intense industrial processes, reducing the demand for those processes will reduce other impacts too.

The topic of Material Efficiency, delivering the services we want from materials in a way that uses less material, has had very little previous attention. This is hardly surprising, because it would be much easier for everyone including those in industry and government and consumers, if our concerns about the environmental impact of materials production could be solved 'invisibly' by producers, without consumers being aware of any change. As a result, this book arises out of ongoing research, in which we're trying to gather the required information from scratch.

To increase our chances of covering all possible options in sufficient depth to be useful, our main focus has been on just two of the five key materials, steel and aluminium. We've chosen them because they're the most complicated of the five: more processes are required to make finished metal goods than goods in cement, plastic or paper. We'll describe in detail our exploration of the two metals in the first three parts of the book, and then in Part IV we'll go back to give shorter versions of the same story for cement, plastic and paper, before discussing implementation of change in Part V.

And finally, a word on units. While preparing the book we've come across energy measured in Joules, kilowatt hours, nuclear-power station years, average planet person years, Belgian household electricity years, windmills, solar square metres, Calories, British Thermal Units, cans of Coke, lightbulb years, kettle minutes, Joules per kilometre, Joules per kilogram, sheets of paper … Brilliant! Energy units are a game everyone can join, and with around seven billion people on the planet, each thinking of a new unit each day, we could generate 2.5 trillion energy units per year. If it takes one of our daughters two hours and one chocolate biscuit to make one friendship bracelet, how many friendship bracelets does it take to light the Eiffel Tower in winter?

There isn't a single convenient answer, because we often want to make comparisons, so units abound and will always do so. However, the problem we all face is that when we hear a talk in which someone introduces a new unit (standard sea level hamster vertical metres, anyone?) we spend most of the talk trying to translate them into the units in which we keep our own reference data. David Mackay included an excellent appendix in his book which is freely available online, showing a wide range of units on consistent scales and we'd recommend this as a great way to speed up conversions[9]. For our own purposes, where possible we've tried to stick to simple units for exploring energy and emissions with materials processing: for energy we'll use megajoules per kilogram (MJ/kg which, if you multiply both terms by one thousand is the same as GJ/tonne) and for emissions we'll use kilograms of CO_2 per kilogram of material processed (kg CO_2/kg which similarly is the same as tonnes CO_2/tonne.) These are manageable units for comparisons, but of course, to make sense of them, we also have to remember the total volumes of materials involved, so we can convert rapidly from relative to absolute units. The table below contains the key set of numbers we try to keep in mind whenever we're hearing other people talk about materials and energy in order to assess the scale of their suggestions. As we work through the book, we'll show that using simplified single numbers for energy and emissions ratios could be misleading. For example recycling is usually more energy efficient than producing new material. However these 15 numbers remain important as a first health check on any new presentation of data.

Material	Global annual production (Mt)	Energy intensity (GJ/t)	Carbon intensity (t CO_2/t)
Cement	2,800	5	1
Steel	1,400	35	3
Plastic	230	80	3
Paper	390	20	1
Aluminium	70	170	10

Table 2.2—**Useful approximate numbers for making estimates about the key materials**

It is much easier to memorise this table if, as Jeeves would advise, you eat plenty of fish, though don't forget to bring it home wrapped in used newspaper, to save that carrier bag. In fact, after a chapter of heavy thinking about uncertainties, Jeeves might well suggest that we nip off to the Savoy for a quick bracer...

Notes

1. The full speech by UK Prime Minister Gordon Brown is transcribed on the website (Politics, 2007).

2. Between 2006 and 2010 the UK's leading supermarkets reduced the total number of carrier bags given out by 41%, according to WRAP (2011).

Scale

3. The reported Metal stocks and recycling rates, by the Global Metal Flows Working Group at the UNEP states "a mobile phone contains over 60 different metals: [two-thirds of the periodic table, including] indium in the LCD display, tantalum in capacitors, and gold on the conductor boards" (UNEP 2011).

4. The pie charts are drawn based on data from various publications from the International Energy Agency.

   Pie chart (top): Man-made (anthropogenic) greenhouse gas emissions (GHG) in 2005 were equivalent to 44.2 billion tonnes of CO_2 (IEA 2008, p.398). The 44.2 Gt CO_{2eq} includes three main gases: carbon dioxide (CO_2), methane (CH_4) and nitrous oxide (N_2O)—which account for 99% of all GHG gases—along with small quantities of fluorocarbons (HCHF, HFC, PFC) and sulphur hexafluoride (SF_6). The emissions from different gases are totalled based on their CO_2 global warming potential over a 100-year time horizon, as standardised by the IPCC (2007). Energy-related CO_2 emissions account for 61% of all GHGs (and 76% of total CO_2 emissions). A further 3% of GHGs come from non-energy related CO_2 emissions in industry, mainly from the calcination reaction cement production, giving a total of 28.2 $GtCO_2$ (64% of GHGs) for energy-related and industrial process CO_2 emissions (note the eq subscript has been dropped, because only CO_2 emissions are included in the 64%). The remaining 36% of man-made GHG emissions fall under the LULUCF category (land use, land use change and forests) including activities such as "deforestation, unsustainable use of traditional biomass, burning of scrubland, decay of biomass after logging, peat fires, decay of drained peat soils and loss of organic matter from soils after cultivation" (IEA 2008c, p.399). Note that this category does not include natural flows of carbon dioxide and methane, to and from plants, animals and oceans.

   Pie chart (middle): The 27 $GtCO_2$ of energy and process related emissions are divided into four categories, using data from the IEA's Energy technology perspectives report, (IEA 2008a): industry (9.9 $GtCO_2$, p.479), buildings (8.8 $GtCO_2$, p.519), transport (7.3 $GtCO_2$, p.425) and other (solved, 1.1 $GtCO_2$). Emissions are both direct (from the burning fuels) and indirect (from the upstream CO_2 from electricity production). The "other" category is the CO_2 emissions not covered in the three main sectors, but appears to be upstream energy use for processing fuels (extraction, refining, transportation and storage) which cannot be directly attributed to the sectors.

   Pie chart (bottom): The industry sector from the middle pie chart, is broken down further to highlight the five materials we are interested in for this book. This is not easy, as most emissions data for industry is given as direct emissions only (the metered electricity and fuel inputs to the factory), and excludes any process emissions from chemical reactions in industry and also the

upstream emissions from electricity generation. So we need to find numbers for all three components of the emissions figure: direct energy-related emissions, direct process emissions, and upstream indirect emissions. Table 16.4 of the IEA Energy technology perspectives (IEA 2008a) report gives direct energy and process CO_2 emissions for 13 industrial categories and 31 regions of the world—we use only the global figures. The industrial categories still don't match our 5 materials—steel, cement, paper, plastics and aluminium—however we also know that 94% of the non-metallic minerals category is cement (IEA 2008a, p.489), 60% of the non-ferrous metals category is aluminium (IEA 2007, table 8.1), and Allwood et al. (2010) perform a detailed calculation to show that plastics make up 31% of the chemical and petrochemical category. Process CO_2 emissions are associated with steel and cement manufacture, but the fluorocarbon emissions from aluminium are not included here, as they are not CO_2. Added to these direct and process emission values are the indirect emissions from upstream electricity generation, estimated from the sector graphs of 2005 baseline emissions in IEA (2008a) and scaled for cement, plastic and aluminium. The other category contains the remaining industrial emissions from table 16.4 (IEA 2008a). The table below summarises the industrial CO_2 values and references.

Sector	$GtCO_2$	Direct	Indirect	Process
Steel	2.49	1.88	0.50	0.11
Cement	1.85	0.72	0.19	0.94
Plastic	0.35	0.20	0.15	
Paper	0.42	0.19	0.23	
Aluminium	0.24	0.08	0.17	
Other	4.5	2.54	19.6	
Total	**9.86**	**5.61**	**3.20**	**1.05**

Sources—For direct and process emissions of all materials, see IEA (2008a) Table 16.4. For indirect emissions, see: Figure 16.6 for steel, Figure 16.9 for minerals, of 94% is cement (p.489); Figure 16.2 for chemicals of which 31% is plastic (Allwood et al. 2010); Figure 16.3 for paper, Figure 16.5 for aluminium; Table 16.3 for other.

5. The Passivhaus (Passive House) is the fastest growing energy performance standard in the world with 30,000 buildings already having been realised (BRE, 2011). The design standard requires a building's annual heating/cooling load to be less than 15 kWh/m^2 with particular detail paid to insulating to reduce heat loss, and sealing leaks to stop hot air escaping. The first Passivhaus residences were build in Darmstadt, Germany in 1990, and the standard has been promoted mainly in Europe by the Passivhaus Institut (2011) However, the UK's introduction of 'zero carbon' targets for housing has created more interest in the UK: BRE (2011) and the Passivhaus Trust (2011) provide excellent information on their websites. It is clearly much easier to apply the standard for new-build, but recently the first UK house retrofit was undertaken in West London, by greentomatoenergy (2011).

6. Two well known examples of abatement curves are: the Global climate abatement map by Vattenfall (2007); the McKinsey Global Institute report, Curbing global energy demand growth (Mckinsey,

2009). Neither study appears to address the problem of 'adding up' emissions savings along the energy chains.

7. Steel and aluminium make up 39% of China's industrial emissions, with an extra 7% attributed to metal manufacturing. For the world, steel and aluminium make up 28% of industrial emissions, so by the same ratio we expect that 5% of global industrial emissions arise in metal manufacturing, equivalent to 2% of all global emissions from energy and processes (LinWei, 2011).

Defining the scope of the book

8. The UK's Climate Change Act (26 November 2008) is a long-term legally binding framework aimed at tackling the dangers of climate change. The Act requires emissions reduction of 80% by 2050, measured against 1990 levels. It also sets legally binding carbon budgets limiting the total amount of emissions that can be emitted.

9. This appendix is in David MacKay's book "Sustainable Energy without the hot air" (MacKay, 2009) which is online for free at www. withouthotair.com.

Box stories, figures and tables

10. A quote from the World Steel Association's climate change position paper (World Steel Association, 2011).

11. This statement was taken from the Cement Sustainability Initiative webpages on the World Business Council for Sustainable Development's website, under the heading of "Sustainability Benefits of Concrete" (WBCSD, 2010).

12. The British Plastics Federation have published several 'position statements' on the sustainability of plastics. The extract reprinted here, was sourced from their website (BPF 2011).

13. The Confederation of European Paper Industries champions the achievements and benefits of the European pulp and paper industry. The quote was taken from their "Q&A on the sustainability of the paper industry" webpage (CEFI 2011).

14. This comment is found on the Welcome page of the International Aluminium Institute website (2011a).

15. Car data was collected from manufacturer's specifications for a wide range of makes and models in the UK.

16. The emissions for a current house are an average from 46 studies surveyed by Ramesh et al. (2010). The trend for future emissions is based on the UK's Part L Building Regulation targets and the Zero Carbon targets for new buildings, which aim to reduce use-phase emissions to net-zero by 2019 using aggressive efficiency measures complimented by onsite renewable generation.

17. These charts were compiled from government statistics (Linwei, 2011).

18. The Sankey diagram of energy flow is adapted from the paper by Cullen and Allwood (2010a)

3 Our uses of steel and aluminium

and why we choose them

To understand what options we might have to change the way we use materials, we need to find out what we use them for at present and this requires some detective work. We also need to look at the key properties of the materials we use, to find out why they're so attractive

We're going to focus mainly on steel and aluminium, so obviously our first question is "what are we using them for?" No one else can tell us the answer, so we need to do some detective work. Fortunately help is at hand...

... and the elite crowd of metal detectors gathered in the Beaufort Bar at the Savoy. In the silence, broken only by her quiet clicking, Miss Marple stood to reveal that at last she had solved the riddle of the long products, but as she reached for her dénouement, stumbled, her (steel wire) knitting needles silenced forever as they plunged through her heart. Hercule Poirot, reacting with the slightest lift of an eyebrow, and having arrived only that afternoon on the (17,000 tonnes of hot rolled steel plate) Cunard Princess, took a pinch from his (deep drawn cold rolled steel strip) snuff box, ready to reveal the locations of the world's rolled strip and plate, choked, and was silent—the wax of his skin finally matching that of his perfect moustache. The (aluminium and steel) ambulance drew to a halt as the doctor ran to the terrible scene, pausing only to ask his companion about the fundamental basis of such metal variety. "Elementary, my dear Watson." [1]...

"Elementary, my dear Watson"

OK—that's not going to work, we'll have to do the detective work ourselves. There is no catalogue of current metal products, because of the number of different businesses involved in making them. The terms "steel industry" and "aluminium industry" are used to describe the companies that transform ore or scrap metal, via a molten liquid stage, into 'intermediate' stock products such as plates, coils of thin strip and standard bars, for which we have good data[2]. These products are 'intermediate' because no final consumer wants them in that form—"would you like to come up and see my bar stock?" Instead, through manufacturing, fabrication and assembly they are converted into final goods. But this conversion involves a huge range of different businesses, and there is no co-ordinated data from there on. So we've assembled the best data we can find, and used it to estimate where steel and aluminium end up. The result is the two catalogues on the next two double pages—one for each metal.

Transport

Cars and light trucks
93 Mt
9%

An average car contains 960 kg of steel and iron. 34% is in the body structure, panels and closures (doors and bonnets), consisting of welded, profiled sections produced by stamping formable cold rolled sheet. This provides high strength and energy absorption in case of a crash. 23% is in the drive train, consisting of grey cast iron for the engine block and machinable carbon steel for the wear resistant gears. 12% is in the suspension, using rolled high strength steel strip. The rest is spread between the wheels, tyres, fuel tank, steering and braking systems.

Trucks and ships
28 Mt
3%

The basic steel components described for the car also apply to trucks, but unlike cars, all truck engine blocks are steel. Frame rails and cross members are usually high tensile steel, and the cab structure and outer skin is often made from galvanized steel. Steel for the ship hull is rolled primary mild steel, providing strong, tough, dimensionally consistent plates that are welded together.

Industrial equipment

30% of steel in electrical equipment is high silicon content electrical steel forming the cores of transformers or the stator and rotor parts of electrical motors. Other major uses include pylons (constructed from bolted, cold-formed, galvanized L-sections forming a light-weight durable tower); and steel reinforced cables (where wound galvanized steel wires provide the strength to carry conducting aluminium in long span transmission cables).

Electrical equipment
27 Mt
3%

Mechanical equipment
137 Mt
13%

This covers a wide range of equipment from small workshop tools to large factory-based robotic machinery and rolling mills. 40% of the steel is plate or hot rolled bar; tubes contribute a further 22%, as do hot and cold rolled coils. Cast products and wire rod contribute the remainder.

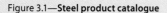

Figure 3.1—Steel product catalogue

We make over 1,000 Mt of steel products every year, equivalent to a 1 metre square band of steel wrapped around the equator more than three times. Global steel production is divided into 4 sectors and 9 categories of end-use products. The amount of steel in each category is given in millions of tonnes **Mt** and the fraction of global steel as a percentage %, with the images sized to reflect this fraction. The end-use of steel is dominated by construction (56%). These numbers are derived from data for 2008.

Construction

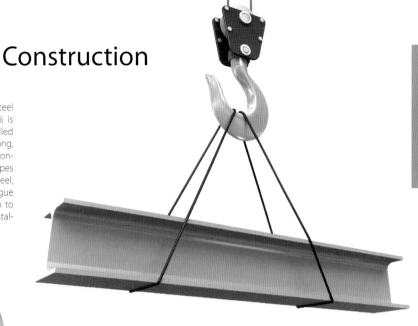

Infrastructure
150 Mt
14%

For infrastructure: 24% of steel is in structural sections; 54% is reinforcing bars; 6% is hot rolled train rails (providing a strong, wear and fatigue resistant contact surface); 16% is in pipes formed by welding rolled steel, with high corrosion and fatigue resistance, and high strength to resist internal pressure and installation stresses.

Buildings
433 Mt
42%

25% of the steel in buildings is in structural sections, mainly hot rolled sections but also some welded plate. Sections form a strong, stiff structural frame. 44% is in reinforcing bars, adding tensile strength and stiffness to concrete. Steel is used because it binds well to concrete, has a similar thermal expansion coefficient and is strong and relatively cheap. 31% is in sheet products such as cold-formed purlins for portal frame buildings and as exterior cladding.

Metal products

Domestic appliances
29 Mt
3%

Metal goods
134 Mt
12%

Other metal goods include a multitude of products, from baths and chairs to filing cabinets and barbed wire. 30% of steel entering this product group is hot rolled coil; 20% is hot rolled bar; and the remainder is either plate, narrow strip, or cast iron.

Consumer packaging
9 Mt
1%

Steel use in packaging is dominated by tin-plated rolled steel, which doesn't corrode. 60% of this steel is made into food cans, providing durable packaging for the subsequent cooking and distribution. 40% is used for aerosols.

Appliances are dominated by white goods (up to 70%). The vast majority of steel used here is cold rolled coil, often galvanized or painted. Most of this steel is used for panelling. Other applications including washing machine tubs (welded rolled steel strip), motors, expanders in fridge/freezers and cast parts for transmissions.

Transport

Cars

8 Mt
18 %

Trucks

3 Mt
7 %

Many of the basic aluminium components described for the car also apply to trucks, with the exception that aluminium cast engines are rare. Aluminium is used in trucks for corrosion resistance and weight saving. Applications include the cab structure and outer skin, chassis and suspension parts, tipping bodies and sliding side doors.

An average car contains 120 kg of aluminium. 35 % is in the cast engine, requiring high strength and wear resistance. 15 % is in the cast transmission casing, providing stiffness for gear teeth alignment and thermal conductivity for dissipation of frictional heat. 15 % is in the cast wheels, giving a lightweight aesthetic design. The remaining aluminium is mainly in the heat exchanger (requiring high thermal conductivity) and forgings in the chassis and suspension. Aluminium is increasingly used in car engines and bodies to save weight.

Other

1 Mt
2 %

Aluminium, used extensively in the aerospace industry for its high specific strength, fracture toughness and good formability, typically makes up 80 % of the airframe. Common alloys are AA2024 and 7xxx. Rail carriages are made from aluminium welded extrusion frames (AA5083/6061) and sheet sidewalls (5xxx/AA6061), giving light, non-corroding vehicles.

Industrial equipment

Electrical equipment

2 Mt
4 %

Electrical cable

4 Mt
9 %

Mechanical equipment

3 Mt
7 %

Electrical equipment includes conduits (often AA6063) and sheathing (Alclad 5056) to strengthen and protect electrical wiring. Other applications include wide strip aluminium in bus bars (1xxx) to conduct electricity around switchboards.

Cables are made from concentrically stranded aluminium wire (typically AA1350-H19) wound in multiple layers around a steel core. The aluminium has conductivity around 60 % that of copper, but is cheaper and lighter.

Mechanical equipment includes products such as heating and ventilation systems. Aluminium is widely use in heat exchangers for its high thermal conductivity, good corrosion resistance and low cost. Drawn or extruded tubes are either brazed or mechanically fastened to sheet (both 1xxx or 3xxx alloy).

Packaging

6 Mt
13%

Aluminium is used in packaging, and provides an attractive outer package and inert inner surface. Half of this aluminium is used in light-weight drinks cans (14 grams each), where rolled (AA3104) aluminium strip is drawn to form the can body, the lid attached (AA5182) and inside sprayed with an epoxy-based lacquer. The other half is thin aluminium foil used in household foil, food and drink pouches and semi-rigid containers to provide an inert and flexible package.

Construction

Buildings
11 Mt
24%

Most aluminium in construction is made from extrusions or sheet. 45% of it is used for extruded frames in windows, doors and curtain walls (projected, non-load bearing façades on commercial buildings). Another 40% is used in corrosion resistant roofing and cladding, for which aluminium strip is cold formed to a profile.

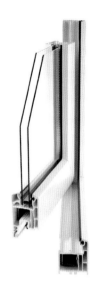

Metal products

Other
4 Mt
9%

Approximately half of this is powdered aluminium used in powder metallurgy, paints and pigments. Other applications are the deoxidation of steel: aluminium has a high affinity for oxygen, so is used to reduce formation of gas bubbles in steel casting. Lithographic plate (1xxx and 3xxx series) is another significant use, for which aluminium is chosen because of the criteria for flatness and high surface quality.

Appliances
3 Mt
7%

The main use of aluminium in consumer durables is in household white goods. Most aluminium in white goods is in fridges/freezers and washing machines. AA5754 is a common sheet alloy of medium strength used for appliance bodywork, and AA3003 and AA3103 are common sheet materials used as fridge/freezer linings. Fridge/freezers also require heat exchangers where the fins, and sometimes tubes, are aluminium.

Figure 3.2—Aluminium product catalogue

We make approximately 45 Mt of aluminium products every year. We have shown the uses of global aluminium production divided into 4 sectors and 10 categories of end-use products. The amount of aluminium in each category is given in millions of tonnes **Mt** and the fraction of global aluminium as a percentage %, with the images sized to reflect this fraction. The end-use of aluminium is more evenly spread across the 4 sectors than for steel. These numbers are derived from data from 2008. (Aluminium alloy codes, e.g. 1xxx are described at the end of this chapter).

By mass, we make around 25 times more steel than aluminium each year. By volume, because aluminium is three times less dense than steel, we make about eight times more steel than aluminium. However, aluminium products are around five times more energy intensive than steel, which is why aluminium is one of our top five materials. The average life expectancy for a steel product is 34 years, and for aluminium is 21 years, predominantly due to the use of steel in longer lasting construction and the use of aluminium in short-lived one-way packaging.

The catalogues show that we can conveniently group the uses of steel and aluminium into four main areas: construction (of buildings and infrastructure), transport (cars, trucks, trains, planes and ships), equipment used in industry, packaging and a range of consumer and business goods. The last category is the most amorphous, and spans what's in your kitchen, what's in your office, and the multitude of other final goods we all buy. As construction is such a dominant application, we'll explore that in more detail shortly.

Vehicles are predominantly made from steel, and at present more than 70% of the mass of typical cars is steel, in the body, engine and drive train. The aluminium industry has for 30 years wanted to expand the use of aluminium in cars, promoting it as a means to save weight and so increase fuel economy. At present this is leading to significant growth in aluminium production. Most aluminium in cars is used to make engine blocks, but a few cars such as recent Jaguar models, have aluminium bodies. Ships are predominantly welded together from plates of steel, trains are made with a combination of the two materials, and aeroplanes are mainly aluminium. Despite aerospace being the most obvious and iconic use of aluminium, it only accounts for a small fraction of total use.

Nearly one fifth of global output of both metals is used to make industrial equipment: whether in sewing machines, robots, paper machines, drills or ovens, the world's factories depend on steel and aluminium equipment to produce goods in all materials. Steel is of course primarily used to provide strong stiff structures on which equipment is built, as well as moving parts and drive trains. Aluminium is widely used for its good thermal or electrical conductivity, particularly because it is both cheaper and lighter than copper. Heat exchangers in air conditioning units and at the back of fridges and freezers contain tubes (that would previously have been made from copper) connected to aluminium fins that dissipate the heat. Electrical distribution cables made from drawn strands of aluminium acting as the conductor, wrapped around a steel core. The strength of the steel core combined with the lightweight and conductive aluminium, allows long spans between supporting towers (pylons).

Aluminium, is used extensively for packaging, particularly for drinks cans (beverage cans in the US) and foil food containers. In fact we make as many steel cans as aluminium ones—although the steel cans are mainly used for food not drinks, and the steel has a thin coating of tin to avoid corrosion on contact with food. However packaging is a smaller fraction of steel use, because we produce so much more steel than aluminium.

Construction is the largest application of the two metals, so we've examined that area in more detail, and our next double page spread gives a further catalogue of the uses of the two metals in construction, followed by a more detailed breakdown by component of steel use in a 'typical' building. Using the word 'typical' is of course rather brave, because each country has quite different traditions in building, so really this building is 'typical' of those for which we've been able to find the relevant data.

Over half of the world's steel is used in construction, and perhaps surprisingly, the single largest area of application is for rebar in concrete. Concrete is strong in compression but weak in tension, so is almost always reinforced with steel to improve its overall performance. In the UK we make many of our tall buildings using steel frames, so use a high volume of steel sections, but other countries, for instance many of our European neighbours, currently prefer reinforced concrete construction, as do rapidly developing China and India. The remaining uses of steel in buildings are largely to do with surfaces. For example, steel sheet is often used for the exterior walls of industrial warehouses, factories, and large retail stores, and the 'purlins' of framed structures (which support the roof between the major frames) are usually formed from sheet steel.

Steel reinforcing bars, used to provide strength and stiffness in tension in concrete structures

Construction is often split between buildings projects and the infrastructure which provides our transport network, and the distribution of utilities. This is a major driver of steel use, with rebar required to make roads and tunnels, sections needed for bridges, and shaped rails needed for tracks. We also use significant and growing volumes of steel line pipe to transport the world's oil, gas and water. As our demand for these resources grows, we are extracting oil and gas from ever deeper water in more hostile environments, and this is driving demand for higher quality line pipe production, in greater volumes.

Perhaps surprisingly, construction is also a major end use for aluminium, nearly all for buildings rather than infrastructure. The main applications are to provide frames for windows but also for external cladding, and internal ducting. Exactly as we saw with steel, patterns of aluminium use in buildings vary among different

Aluminium

Windows and doors

3 Mt

27%

Window and door frames must be strong enough to provide security, and be durable and attractive. A wide range of cross-sections is required, so they are extruded from alloys AA6060 and AA6063 which allow design flexibility and efficient material use.

Curtain walls

2 Mt

18%

Curtain walls are not part of the structural frame of a building but must carry their own weight and survive wind loads. They are made from aluminium because it is attractive, stiff and has both a high strength-to-weight ratio and good corrosion resistance. The same alloys used for windows and doors are used to make curtain walls by extrusion.

Roofing and cladding

4 Mt

37 %

Roofing and cladding must provide a thermal barrier while also being weather proof, light and attractive. It is typically made with sheet alloys AA3003 and AA5005, which are cold-rolled into corrugated shapes and used to sandwich an insulation layer.

Other (gutters, spouts, façades)

2 Mt

18 %

Aluminium is used in various other building components such as gutters, spouts, signage and internal fittings. In most cases a strong but lightweight material is required, often with good corrosion resistance and a high quality surface finish.

Figure 3.3—Construction product catalogue

The largest application of steel is in construction which is also the second largest use of aluminium. Most steel in construction is used for reinforcing bars (rebar), structural sections (I-beams) and sheet. Aluminium is used either in extruded profiles or rolled sheets. The images on this page are scaled to reflect the proportions of their use in construction, which is also shown as a % and given in millions of tonnes **Mt**.

Steel buildings

Commercial
129 Mt
22 %

Multi-storey commercial buildings are designed around structural frames constructed either from steel sections (30% of steel-use in this category) or reinforced concrete. Reinforced concrete is also used to provide deep foundations and basements, so 40% of steel-use is as rebar. Steel is also used as sheet for purlins and internal fittings, and occasionally for facades.

Industrial
145 Mt
25 %

Most industrial buildings for factories, warehouses and large retail stores, are single-story portal frame designs. The frame is made from sections (40% of steel) while roofing and facades use corrugated steel sheet (55%) supported by steel purlins.

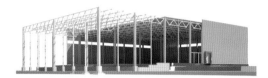

Residential
90 Mt
16 %

Individual houses mainly require steel in reinforced concrete foundations with some light sections for supporting floors. However, the main use of steel for residential buildings is to construct apartment blocks, largely from reinforced concrete, so that 90% of steel use in this category is for rebar.

Other
69 Mt
12 %

Other buildings include stadia, hospitals, schools all with diverse designs, but mainly made with reinforced concrete.

Steel infrastructure

Roads and rail
107 Mt
18 %

Transport networks require steel for bridges, tunnels and rail track and for constructing buildings such as stations, ports and airports. 60% of steel-use in this application is as rebar and the rest is sections and rail track.

Utilities (fuel, water, power)
43 Mt
7 %

Underground pipelines distribute water to and from houses, and distribute gas to final consumers. These pipes use just over half of the steel in this category and the rest is mainly rebar for associated constructions including power stations and pumping houses.

Steel use in a building

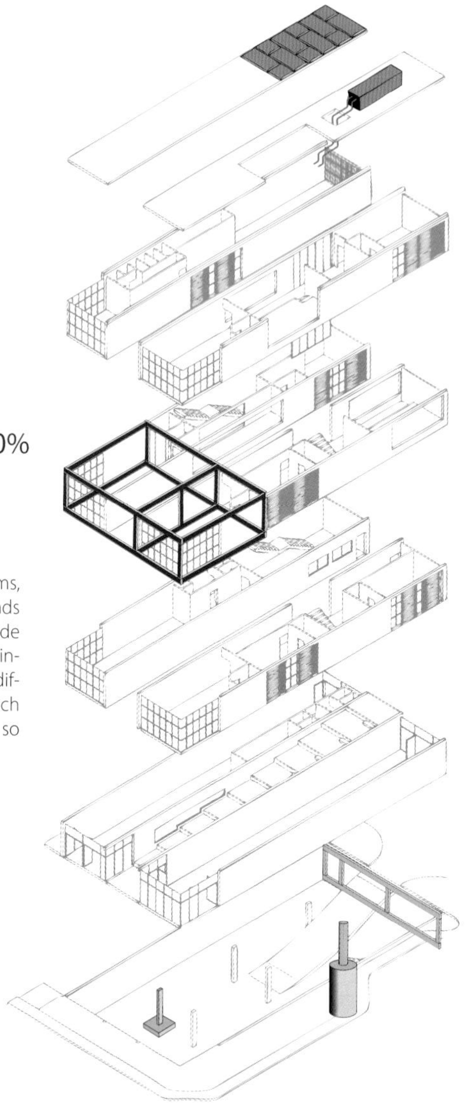

Non-structural 20–30%
Mechanical equipment: 5–10 kg/m²
Fixtures, fittings + façades: 5–10 kg/m²

Buildings are heated and cooled by large equipment, in the basement or on the roof, connected to the interior by ducting, and both equipment and ducting require steel. Some internal fixtures and fittings including rails, shelving, and stairways are also made from steel.

Superstructure 60–70%
Columns: 2–7 kg/m²
Beams: 5–40 kg/m²
Slabs: 10–30 kg/m²

The building frame, made of beams, columns and slabs, transfers loads to the substructure. It can be made either from steel sections or reinforced concrete leading to quite different requirements for steel, which is why the ranges given here are so broad.

Substructure 10+%
Shallow foundations: 60–70 kg/m³
Basements: 100–300 kg/m³
Deep foundations: 35–65 kg/m³

Low buildings stand on concrete foundation strips that distribute loads from the structure to the ground. However, taller buildings, or those built on poor soil, require foundation piles: reinforced concrete columns plunged deep into the ground to provide stability. These piles support high loads, must outlast the building, and cannot be repaired in use, so are steel-intensive. For the same reason, walls below the surface which hold back soil and water to create basements, also use steel at high densities.

Figure 3.4—Construction product catalogue

No building is truly 'typical' however this image demonstrates the main uses of steel in commercial buildings, identified from a survey of recent building projects and published reports. The percentages are representative averages after we excluded unusual features such as basements, deep foundations and steel facades. The rates of steel use above the surface are averaged over the total floor area of the building. However foundation design depends so strongly on local geology that the rates of steel use below the surface are given per cubic metre of reinforced concrete.

countries, so for instance southern European homes contain over 10 times as much aluminium as those in northern Europe. Aluminium window and door frames were popular in houses in the 1970's and 80's, but now have largely been displaced by cheaper plastic extrusions. However, they remain common, in commercial buildings.

Our detective work has given us an estimate of where steel and aluminium are used, and we've shown that these two metals pervade every aspect of our lives: in effect everything we touch either contains one of these two metals, or was manufactured with equipment made from them. Why do we find them so useful, and is there anything else we could use instead? We'll spend the rest of this chapter looking at those two questions.

The useful properties of steel and aluminium

The Eiffel tower made from
stiff wrought iron

If the Eiffel Tower were made of rubber, it would bend in the wind like a tree. It doesn't because it's made from wrought iron, a relative of steel, which is *stiff*. When the traffic grinds to a halt in San Francisco, and the line of trucks with the day's supply of sourdough bread backups up over the Golden Gate Bridge, it doesn't collapse because the steel from which it is made is *strong*. The miracle of commercial flight occurs because the planes are light enough to take off—they're largely made from aluminium, which has a low *density*. If you sit in the back row of a 747 as it takes off, you see the wing tips move two metres upwards as the plane leaves the ground. They continue bending up and down during any turbulence in flight, and if made of ceramics would snap off, but they don't because aluminium is *tough*—cracks don't grow quickly. However the aeroplane's jet engines are largely made from special steels and nickel alloys, because the engines are most efficient when running hottest, and these alloys have a high *melting temperature*, but when hot undergo relatively little *thermal expansion*. The Forth Road Bridge in Scotland is painted continuously because steel rusts, but aluminium window frames corrode only very slowly even if unpainted: they have high *corrosion resistance*. Electrical cables as we've seen are a major application of aluminium because it has a low *electrical resistance*. Hercule Poirot's metal snuff box could be formed from a flat sheet of either steel or aluminium without any joints, and indeed the whole plethora of goods made from sheets of these two metals can be manufactured, because both metals are *ductile*: they can be made to change shape without cracking. And we'll finish off by noting that both metals are easily *available*: the earth has vast reserves of bauxite and iron ore with which to make them, and we can produce them *cheaply*.

Rust forming on painted steel

Figure 3.5—**A piston which has been cast then machined**

Figure 3.6—**The surface finish on the piston (above)**

We've listed the properties of stiffness, strength, density, toughness, melting temperature, thermal expansion, corrosion resistance, electrical resistance, ductility, availability and cost, and could add a few more if we kept going, and it is the combination of all these properties that make steel and aluminium so extraordinarily useful, and hence widely used. In the next section we'll explore whether we have any viable alternatives, for now we'll explore just two of the properties in more detail: strength and ductility. We want to look at those two in detail because, so far, we're referred to steel and aluminium as metals, but actually they're both families of metals. The members of the families vary because of *alloying*—adding other elements such as chromium, manganese or magnesium to our vats of liquid iron or aluminium to change their composition. They also vary due to *processing*—even with the same composition, we can create different properties for particular family members, by changing what we do to them after we've poured them from liquid. Surprisingly, many of the properties we've mentioned are virtually unaffected by alloying and processing. For example stiffness, density and electrical conductivity are virtually constant within the two families. However, in just over 100 years since Henry Bessemer, Charles Hall and Paul Héroult opened the door to cheap mass production of these two metals, we've discovered that we can create an amazing variety of strength and ductility in the two metals. In fact the aim of a vast swathe of ongoing metals research and development has been to increase both: increased strength allows us to use less metal for applications limited by strength, while increased ductility leads to easier manufacturing and often improves toughness also. So for the rest of this section, we'll explore where those properties come from, and how we can influence them.

Armed with a camera, an optical microscope (invented in Holland around 1590 by Zaccharias and Hans Janssen), a scanning electron microscope (invented by Max Knoll in Germany in 1931, but developed up to commercialisation in 1965 by Charles Oatley, in our department in Cambridge), and a good computer drawing package (Adobe, ~1982) the pictures in Figures 3.5 to 3.9 show us what metal looks like as we keep hitting the zoom-in button. Our zooming is pretty impressive: the piston in the first picture is about 300 mm tall, and the atoms in the last picture are spaced at around a tenth of a nanometre: there are a million nanometres in a millimetre.

Figure 3.5 shows the piston, which has been cast and machined, and Figure 3.6 shows its surface as seen with the naked eye. The product has a precise geometry, with a surface that looks and feels smooth, but on closer inspection you might see traces of the manufacturing route: abrasions from machining or pinholes from casting. You won't be able to tell by eye, but the surface of aluminium parts is

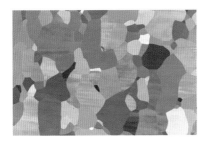

Figure 3.7—**The grain structure within the metal**

Figure 3.8—**The structure within a grain**

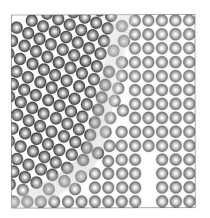

Figure 3.9—**The boundary between two grains**

actually an oxide layer, the prettier equivalent of rust on steel parts. In contrast to rust on steel, this oxide layer doesn't grow upon continued exposure to air, as the aluminium oxide forms an impenetrable barrier to air and so prevents further oxidation. Steel parts can rust away, which is why they must be coated with paint or other protection.

Figure 3.7 has zoomed in further, and with the benefit of polishing and etching, has revealed the grain structure of the metal. At school we hung a thread with a knot into a glass of concentrated salt solution, and watched as a crystal of salt grew on the knot. The crystal was roughly cubic, and every grain of salt in our salt cellar is a single crystal. Metals similarly form crystals as they solidify. However, unlike the school experiment, many crystals—called grains in metals—begin to grow at the same time, but in different directions. So, the picture shows us the final form when all the metal has solidified and formed grains, and we can imagine that at the boundaries between the grains, the material is locally much less ordered than within a single grain.

Figure 3.8 is an image of the material within a grain. Things aren't as uniform as we might expect, and this is because the metals we're looking at aren't pure iron or aluminium, but have alloying elements mixed in. We can see that two different types of crystal have formed in the one grain: a dominant formation, in which the main metal has a small concentration of one of the alloying elements (light areas); a secondary formation, with a much higher concentration of the alloying elements, and relatively less of the base metal (dark areas). The secondary formation occurs in smaller volumes, because we have much more of the basic metal element (iron or aluminium) than the alloying elements. But you can imagine how many interesting small secondary grains you can create if you mix up several small quantities of other elements in one alloy. We can see several different formations in this image, and that's what metallurgists dream about at night!

Figure 3.9 (in the absence of a suitable microscope, we've turned here to a drawing package) shows the material within a grain and at a boundary between two grains. The atoms mostly form a regular lattice pattern within a grain, but in some places discontinuities form as 'dislocations' in the lattice. These dislocations are important when the grains change shape under load.

Figure 3.10 shows our most detailed zoom in and we can see how the atoms of the previous picture link together. The balls represent atoms, nature's building blocks, and the lines are a convenient way of showing how they relate to each other. This picture represents a 'unit cell' which replicates and tessellates thousands or

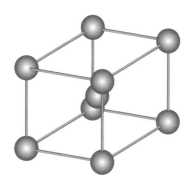

Figure 3.10—**The arrangement of atoms in a typical 'unit cell'**

millions of times to form each grain. When we referred to grains 'growing in different directions' you can now see exactly what that means: the direction of the lines joining the outer atoms in the cell are the same for all the unit cells replicated in a single grain.

These pictures have shown us everything we need to know about the two metal families to understand the properties of strength and ductility. But before we look at how composition affects them, we need to address one more question: how do metals deform? For ceramics, which also form in crystal like structures, when we stretch them with sufficient force we will eventually separate the bonds between the atoms in the material, at which point it will fracture. If the microstructure of the ceramic is imperfect, which in reality is always the case, there will be small cracks in the initial structure, so a tear starts at an existing crack, and then propagates rapidly across the piece we're pulling. The strength of ceramics is therefore usually determined by the largest pre-existing crack in the material. Metals however are quite different: they can deform before they fracture, and this requires a different mechanism.

Let's imagine a tug of war between one team on a level platform attempting to pull a second team, which has formed up as a Chinese Dragon, up a long set of steps. If the people in the dragon were on adjacent steps, they would all be able to pull with full strength, but in fact they've made a mistake, and left one step empty in the middle. This means that the person just below the empty step is greatly disadvantaged—he can't brace himself as well, so is pulled forwards to the point that he can't avoid stepping up onto the empty step. He can now brace properly and take up the full load, but the person immediately behind him is disadvantaged, and is now under tremendous pressure so he too, eventually steps up to the newly empty step in front of him. Over time the empty step appears to move downwards, as each member of the Chinese Dragon in turn, steps up, until the whole dragon has moved one step upwards. Rather than having to pull against all the people in the dragon at the same time, the team on the level have a great advantage, and need provide only enough force to de-stabilise the one behind the empty step.

Shear stress τ

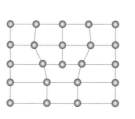 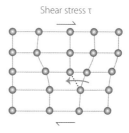 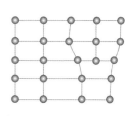

Figure 3.11—**A dislocation moving under an applied force**

Sustainable Materials with both eyes open

Figure 3.11 shows this story being played out in a metal grain. The empty step is called a dislocation, and as a force is applied across the grain, the atom just ahead of the dislocation is under extra pressure, so jumps into the gap of the dislocation, the gap moves backwards, and slowly the metal deforms forwards. The strength of the metal is the force required to cause the dislocation to move. Its ductility is the amount of movement (shape change) that can occur before the metal eventually fractures.

In reality, the dislocation is a line, going straight into the page, so what happens when the line meets with one of the secondary particles, we saw in Figure 3.8? If these small particles are stronger than the surrounding metal, in effect they provide an extra brace point, the force required to move the dislocation to the next step increases and the strength of the metal has increased. Metallurgically, alloying has therefore increased the strength of the metal and this increase depends on the size of the secondary particles, their distribution and relative strength. A similar strengthening happens when two dislocations intersect, which is more likely as more deformation occurs. This is known as work hardening and explains why metals get stronger as they are deformed more, up to the limit when they fracture. Finally, we noticed earlier that the grain boundaries disrupt the regular structure of the metal grains or crystals and of course, it is difficult for dislocations to cross these boundaries. More boundaries makes stronger metal so small grains imply greater strength. We can also now see that strength and ductility are in conflict with each other: strength is increased when it is more difficult for dislocations to move, but dislocation movement is what we need for ductility.

So if this is how composition affects strength and ductility, we also need to work out what's the effect of processing. And we can do so with just one more piece of information. So far the atoms in the metal grains were fixed in their initial positions on solidification, and have moved in the lattice only when an applied force has caused dislocations to move. However, if the metal is heated up, the bonds between atoms become weaker, so some internal reorganisation of atoms occurs, driven by energy stored in dislocations and grain boundaries.

On solidifying from liquid to solid, grains grow in the metal. Slow cooling leads to big grains of more uniform composition, faster cooling to smaller ones with more variety. Once cool, deforming the metal tends to increase its strength by work hardening. However, if it is re-heated to above one third of the melting temperature, internal reorganisation can occur, which may involve growing new larger grains and allowing smaller secondary particles to coalesce into fewer bigger ones.

For our purposes in this book, that's all we need to know about the formation of properties. Obviously there are libraries worth of further detail, but our purpose is to understand enough about how properties arise that as we start to look at recycling, or different processes, we can deduce the consequences. Let's pose a couple of questions to test that:

- What happens if I recycle a skip of aluminium scrap containing a mixture of different alloys? The composition when I melt the scrap will be different from any previous alloy, and rather difficult to predict. Therefore I will tend to have a wider variety of secondary particles forming in my recycled material, and while these may or may not increase strength, it's very likely that they will reduce ductility so the material will be brittle and therefore probably less useful;

- Could we save a lot of energy by casting steel and aluminium components directly into their final shape? If we do so, it will be difficult to control the cooling rate, so we will get a mixture of grain sizes, an uneven distribution of the secondary particles, and without any deformation to break up the grains or induce work hardening, it's likely that the final product won't be very strong. Worse, the casting process may leave imperfections in the metal and we won't have a chance to remove them with further processing. These defects can be sources of failure that mean the product also won't be tough.

Armed with what we now know about strength and ductility, we can do a quick survey of the different branches of the steel and aluminium families. Our table at the end of the chapter summarises the main groups within the two families, and describe the main features of their composition, processing and resulting properties. The two graphs summarise this information, by showing for the two metal families how strength and ductility play off against each other.

This section was motivated by the question "why do we find these two metals so useful?" The answer is that the ores required to make both metals are widely available at low cost, and we have efficient routes to process the ores into liquid metal. The two metals are both families, and by adjusting their composition and processing we can create a very wide range of strength and ductility to suit particular applications. We can't directly mould liquid metal into final products, because the resulting properties would be poor. But we can select our composition with great precision, to allow a range of deformation and heating stages, at the end of which we'll have components of the required shape and with the required properties.

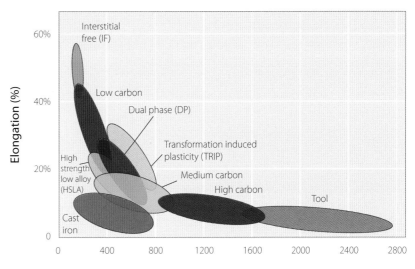

Figure 3.12—**Typical properties for groups of steels**

Strength (measured by yield stress in megapascals, MPa)

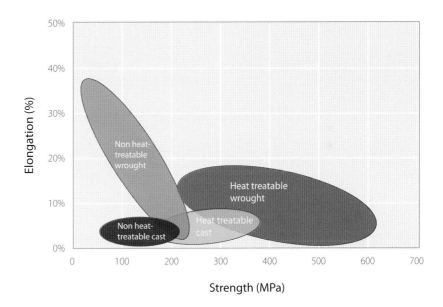

Figure 3.13—**Typical properties for groups of aluminium alloys ('wrought' alloys can be deformed)**

Strength (MPa)

To end this chapter, we need to find out whether any other materials could replace these two key metals.

Could we use other materials instead of steel and aluminium?

The Burj Khalifa in Dubai, the world's tallest building, has ten times the embodied emissions square metre...

We decided that making the Eiffel Tower in rubber didn't look too promising. What else could we use? Marble? Expensive, and probably the blocks at the bottom would crumble. Clay? Not strong enough? Glass? Too fragile. Concrete? Yes—we could and the wasteful and pointless world of 'my tower's taller than yours' is currently headed by the horrible and concrete Burj Khalifa in Dubai. 2.5 times taller than the Eiffel Tower, it has 300,000 m² of floor space made from 1 Mt of concrete and 55,000 tonnes of steel re-bar, giving an average embodied emissions of around 4 tonnes of CO_2 per square metre. This is eight times the average office block, and at least 10 times the typical traditional and beautiful homes of Dubai.

If not steel and aluminium what else? The US Geological Survey regularly reports estimates of mineral availability in the earth's crusts, and we aren't going to run out of iron, aluminium, limestone, trees, magnesium, titanium or any of the other structural materials in the next hundred years or more[3]. So purely by volume, we have a lot of possible substitute materials, but of course the energy requirements for extracting the different materials vary considerably, as does their cost: Figures 3.14 and 3.15 show an estimate of the current cost per tonne of each key material and the energy of converting it to a useful form[4]. At first glance, concrete, stone and wood appear to be interesting alternatives to steel and aluminium. However, the bar charts do not tell the full story, as in reality we would not replace one tonne of steel with one tonne of wood. Different families of materials have radically different properties (strength, stiffness, ductility and many others as just discussed) so to compare the energy used when making the same products, we must delve deeper. Professor Mike Ashby in our department has initiated a huge effort to map materials by their various properties, to help designers make good choices, and particularly recently his concern has been to account for the environmental impact of their choices[5]. His maps of materials show an enormous span of material choices and as we'd anticipated, wood, stone and concrete stand out as the three viable candidates to substitute for steel and aluminium. Members of the family of composite materials, glass/carbon fibre reinforced epoxies mainly, can meet the strength criterion, but their embodied energy is higher than the two metals, and they can't be recycled. So, although they often come up in conversation about substitutes, they're not a great choice if we're after reduced emissions. They're also used much less: today's use of composite materials is around 8 Mt per year[6], compared to 1040 Mt of steel and 45 Mt of aluminium.

... of a beautiful traditional home in Dubai

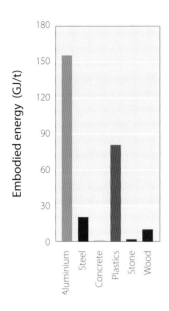

Figure 3.14—**Embodied energy in conversion for key materials**

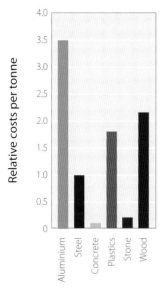

Figure 3.15—**Relative costs per tonne for conversion of key materials to useful forms**

So now we're down to concrete, stone and wood. What were the two dominant materials before the industrial revolution? Stone and wood, the predecessors of cement and steel/aluminium. Stone and concrete have similar properties, but concrete is much easier to use: you can pour it into moulds to create any shape, and while pouring you can include rebar within the mould to make up for the problem that both stone and concrete are rather weak in tension. Wood has excellent properties, and other versions of Professor Ashby's charts show that it performs extremely well on the axes of strength or stiffness against density, so the Wright brothers choice to build the first aeroplane with a wooden frame was inspired. However wood also has disadvantages compared to steel and aluminium: it is less stable, more easily damaged by fire, and although it has a good strength to weight ratio, you still need a lot of wood if you want a lot of strength.

That leaves concrete as the competing material and it is the material of choice for construction in many countries. However, it has to be reinforced by rebar before use, and has few applications outside of construction: we don't make vehicles or equipment from concrete.

To summarize, we don't have any real substitutes for steel and aluminium. They can substitute each other, and that's the subject of a lengthy marketing campaign by both trade associations so not our business here, but there aren't any other materials with such a good range of properties, available cheaply and in abundance.

Outlook

We've seen in this chapter that steel and aluminium are used across a very broad range of applications, because of their excellent combination of properties. We've looked into the link between two of those properties, strength and ductility, and seen how they arise from selection of composition and processing. And finally, we've seen that there aren't really any substitute materials available in sufficient quantity, with guaranteed supply, and comparable performance. That sets us up for chapter 12 when we'll be looking for new options to use less metal. But we're not ready for that yet. Instead we need to find out how the uses of the two metals in our catalogue of applications adds up to global demand for metal, and by looking at past and present production data, we can begin to forecast future requirements.

Notes

1. In case you are not fully briefed on British crime writing, all these characters are famous fictional detectives. Miss Marple is an elderly spinster and Hercule Poirot a suave Belgian, both of whom were created by author, Agatha Christie, to solve crimes in 1920s and 30s Britain. Dr Watson is the companion of Sir Author Conan Doyle's famous creation, Sherlock Holmes.

2. There are not so many companies operating in the steel and aluminium industries, and most of them belong to the two key organisations, the World Steel Association or the International Aluminium Institute. These two organisations publish detailed data on annual production of stock products which gets us half way to solving the mystery of the uses of metals.

Could we use other materials instead of steel and aluminium?

3. Based on data collected and published in USGS (2011).

4. Embodied energies for a range of building materials have been collated by Hammond and Jones (2011) in their 'Inventory of Carbon and Energy'. Costs have been obtained from a range of sources including Steel Business Briefing (2009), UNCTAD (2011) and IDES (2011)

5. Examples of Professor Ashby's charts appear in his book (Ashby, 2009) and are available as a software package through Granta Design (2011)

6. According to a Pudaily (2007), global composites production was 8 million tonnes in 2010 with 40 % of this occurring in the Asia-Pacific region.

Images

We would like to thank Novelis for their image of aluminium grain structure in Figure 3.7.

	Alloy Group	Composition	Processing	Typical Properties	Examples of applications
Carbon steels	Low-carbon	<0.25wt% C	Hot rolled and allowed to cool in air	Low to medium strength and moderate ductility	Structural beams for buildings, plates
	Med-carbon	<0.25–0.5wt% C	Heat treatment through quenching and tempering	High strength and moderate toughness	Forgings
	High-carbon	<0.5–1wt% C	Heat treatment through quenching and tempering	Very high strength	Rail, wire
	Cast iron	>2wt% C	Cast to shape directly, possibly with heat treatment	Low strength and ductility	Large equipment and transport parts
Alloy steels	High strength low alloy (HSLA)	<0.25wt% C plus Nb, Ti, V	Hot rolling with controlled temperature	Higher strength than plain carbon steels through grain refinement	Line pipe
	Stainless	>12wt% Cr, plus Ni	Hot and cold worked	Corrosion resistant	Food handling equipment
	Tool	>0.5wt% C with combination of Mn, Cr, V, W, Mo	Hardened through heat treatments of surface or entire part	High strength and toughness	Machining tools, dies
	Interstitial free (IP)	Very low C and N content	Vacuum degassing and casting control to avoid carbon, nitrogen and oxygen pickup	Very high ductility and formability, low strength	Outer automotive panels
	Dual phase (DP)	<0.25wt% C plus Mn, Si, V	Heat treatment through intercritical annealing and controlled cooling	Lower yield strength and similar tensile strength to HSLA steels with increased ductility	Automotive sheet
	Transformation induced plasticity (TRIP)	<0.25wt% C plus Si, Mn	Heat treatment through intercritical annealing and holding at temperature	Higher ductility than DP steels at high strengths	Automotive sheet

Table 3.1—**The world of steel**

	Alloy Group	Composition	Processing	Typical Properties	Examples of applications
Wrought	Heat-treatable (AA2xxx,6xxx,7xxx)	Cu, Si, Mg-Si, Zn	Heat treated to increase strength by solutionising, quenching and then age hardening	Medium to high strength	Aircraft and automotive structures
	Non heat-treatable (AA1xxx,3xxx,5xxx)	Mg, Mn	Cold worked to give strength by strain hardening	Lower strength	Foil, cans, electrical conductors
Cast	Heat-treatable (2xx.x,3xx.x,5xx.x,7xx.x)	Mg	Casting followed by heat treatment (solutionised, quench, age harden)	Low-medium strength, low ductility	Engines, housings
	Non heat-treatable (1xx.x, 4xx.x)	Si, Si-Mg, Si-Cu	Cast directly to product shape	Lowest strength aluminium alloys, low ductility	Pipe fittings

Table 3.2—**The world of aluminium**

4 Metal journeys
flows, stocks and demand for steel and aluminium

The materials we use start in the ground as ores/minerals and transforming them into finished goods is a long journey. If we can create a map of that journey, we can build up a picture of scale, anticipate the set of processes we need to explore, and by looking at the way the flow has evolved in the past, can start to predict what might be required in future.

Let's imagine that you're reading this at the end of a warm day in early summer, sitting outside in your favourite chair, and on the table next to you is a clean empty glass and a perfectly chilled unopened can of your favourite beer. The can glistens in the evening light, its dappled moisture announcing its cool readiness in the warm air...

... and it's going to sit there waiting for us throughout this chapter, but while looking forward to seeing it again, let's briefly look backwards in time at the journey the can has been on to get ready for this wonderful moment: back to being filled and sealed; to the heat of the lacquering line; the threefold stretch in can making; the blanking line; the coating line and the tension stretch-leveller; the tandem cold rolling mill; the annealing and solution heat treatment line; the water quench; the tandem hot mill; the reversing mill; the pre-heating furnace; the cooling air of the open warehouse; the direct chill caster; the crucible. At every stage, it has been processed with tremendous care so that now while it's waiting to be opened it is an object of unimaginable quality: purged of edge cracks, surface imperfections, split noses and fish tails, blanking skeletons, mis-feeds and deep drawing ears. Slimmed down by nearly 50% since casting, this can is a miracle of engineering development and control, one out of 280 billion drink cans in action this year[1] and drinks cans are just one of the products we found in our catalogue.

We'll leave our can where it is (but perfectly insulated so it's ready for later), and try to put some data around our brief odyssey. We found out in the last chapter where steel and aluminium are currently used. In this one, we want to put some numbers on those uses. In particular we want to find out how current global production of liquid metal flows into final uses: what's the journey, and what masses are involved each year? how has the required mass of metal built up in the past to the levels we use today? what stocks of steel and aluminium goods are on the planet today? what can we say about how demand is going to develop in the future?

How does steel and aluminium flow from ore to final uses today?

We saw in the last chapter that processing steel and aluminium requires a carefully controlled sequence of deformation and heating stages, to create the properties we want. Two other factors affect the physical journey from ore to finished product:

- The resources required to make metal—ores, coke, coal, gas and electricity—are not uniformly distributed across the earth's surface. For example, much of our bauxite and iron ore comes from Australia[2], but there is a large supply of relatively cheap hydro-electricity in Canada[3].

- Making liquid metal, casting it and deforming it into the stock products we've already mentioned, has significant economies of scale: the cost per unit of metal delivered generally decreases as the total volume made by the equipment increase.

As a result, the production of finished goods containing steel and aluminium involves many conversion steps, and many different businesses. Because of the two factors above, this conversion works via a clear intermediate stage. The steel and aluminium industry which make liquid metals, cast and form them into stock products with high economies of scale at relatively few locations. These products are not in the form required by the final consumer, but are of a sufficiently general shape that they can be formed, cut, drilled and joined into any required finished form.

We want an overview of the flow of material through a series of transformations, and because scale matters to us, we need an overview at a global scale. When we started our work in this area, only parts of this map of flows had been documented, and was largely hidden in tables of numbers, so we've worked hard to collate estimates of all the remaining numbers and the result is the two maps on the next double page.

We've constructed these maps as Sankey diagrams, with the same rules as for the Sankey diagram of global energy transformation we presented in chapter 2. In this case our units are in megatonnes (millions of tonnes, Mt). Looking at the maps from left to right you can see how ore is transformed firstly into liquid metal, then into stock products, and then into the components that are assembled into final goods. As our focus is on steel and aluminium, but almost no product is made solely of those two metals, we've chosen to end the diagram with components, rather than finished products, but you can see immediately that the final uses are precisely the ones we indentified in our detective work in the last chapter. The first half of each map is based on data from the World Steel Association and International Aluminum Institute, although we've had to perform various adjustments to make sure everything adds up. But for the second part, we found no existing data set on the final destinations of all stock products, so the tangled web of lines leading to final uses is the result of us solving a sort of Sudoku puzzle of data sources. For example, data from the Aluminium Association suggests that 62% of the steel in a car is sheet metal[4], and according to two wire rod companies, 10% of all the world's steel wire rod is used in cars[5]. So to create the maps we've worked our way through a large pile of data covering both the composition of final products, and the destinations of intermediate stock products, and then resolved conflicting estimates as required.

The grey lines on the two maps show flows of scrap metal leading to recycling processes. Interestingly, for both metals, we collect far more scrap from production processes than from products that have reached their end of life. This is very helpful because, remembering the last chapter, scrap with a uniform composition can be recycled back into material of equal value, but scrap of mixed composition will generally make metal of less value. Typically the composition of production scrap is known, and it is separated at source, while post-consumer scrap is mixed. For steel, it is possible to remove some unwanted impurities, but for aluminium it isn't, so most recycled aluminium is used in the casting family of aluminium alloys which have a less pure composition than the wrought family. The only major exception is for drinks cans which have been thrown out after use and the industry is, rightly, proud of this story. In future, as the supply of post-consumer scrap increases, we will want to use more of it to reduce demand for new metal made from ore, but unless we separate the different alloys effectively, recycled material will be useful only for less demanding applications.

These maps of metal flow help us greatly in our quest to understand scale. We can quickly see what's big and what's small, and as we work through the book looking at every possible option for change, we can use the maps to work out how much the global flows of metal will change. Once we've worked through the next

4 Metal journeys

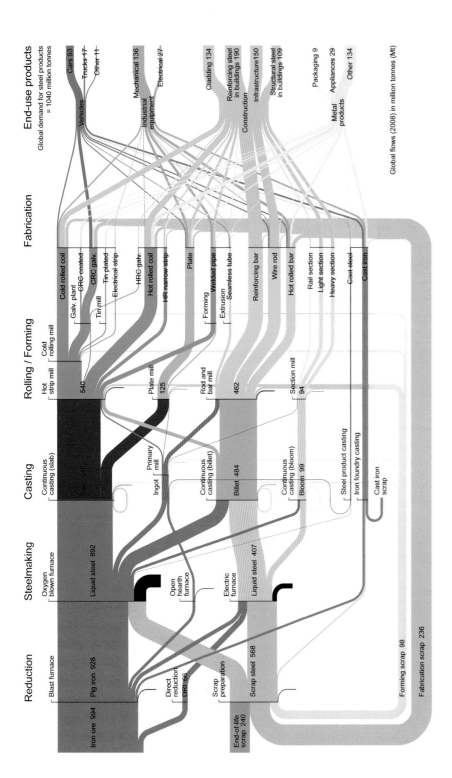

Figure 4.1—Sankey of steel flow

The steel map shows that: two thirds of the world's steel is made from mined ore, and one third from recycled scrap; one-fifth of the scrap arises from within the steel industry itself, two-fifths from manufacturing and fabrication (making components) and two fifths from end-of-life products and buildings; the dominant production route for steel made from ore is the basic oxygen furnace, and from scrap is the electric arc furnace, although there is some interchange between the two; more than 99% of the world's steel is rolled after casting, and the resulting stock products are approximately one tenth plate (thick sheets), four tenths strip (thin sheets), four tenths rod and bar, and one tenth sections (constant cross-section profiles); half of the world's steel is used in construction, of which one third is reinforcing steel; most steel used in vehicle manufacture is from cold rolled coil, or from castings.

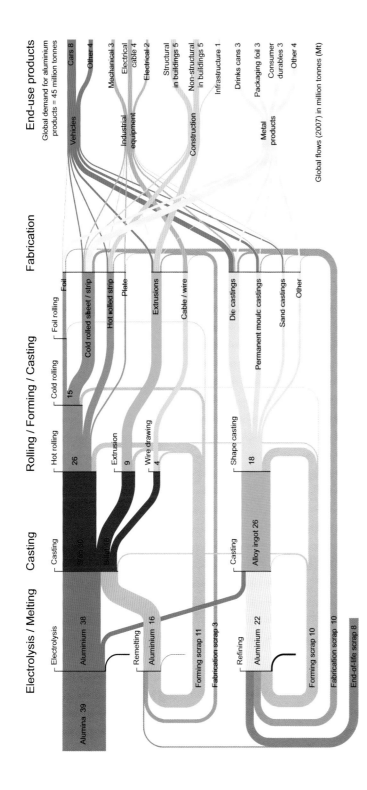

Figure 4.2—**Sankey diagram of aluminium flow**

Half of all aluminium is made from ore and half from scrap. Aluminium is produced from ore by electrolysis and aluminium scrap may be recycled via remelting or refining. Aluminium made from ore or remelted scrap generally has a low silicon content and is used in wrought products that are made via deformation processes. Aluminium from refining post-use scrap generally has a higher silicon content, so is used for casting products by pouring liquid metal into a mould. Two thirds of wrought aluminium is rolled into sheet or plate, a quarter is extruded and the remainder is used to make cable and wire. A third of liquid aluminium is directly cast into finished products, which is a much greater proportion than steel. Like steel, the majority of aluminium

scrap arises during the production of stock and finished products: a quarter arises within the aluminium industry, half is from manufacturing and fabrication and the remainder comes from recycling discarded products. Manufacturing aluminium products generates a greater proportion of scrap than steel: over 40% of liquid aluminium is scrapped in production compared to just over a quarter for steel. Aluminium is used in approximately equal volumes in vehicles, industrial equipment, construction and metal products. Although aeroplanes are a well-known application of aluminium, the total masses involved are small, and they do not even show up on our map.

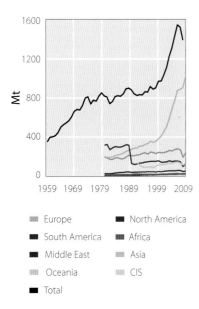

1600

1200

Mt 800

400

0

1959 1969 1979 1989 1999 2009

▦ Europe ■ North America
■ South America ▦ Africa
■ Middle East ▦ Asia
▦ Oceania ▦ CIS
■ Total

Figure 4.3—**Historic global steel output 1959–2009**[7]

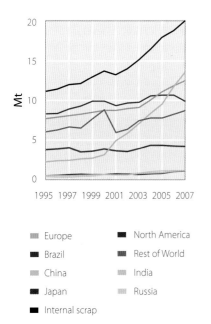

20

15

Mt 10

5

0

1995 1997 1999 2001 2003 2005 2007

▦ Europe ■ North America
■ Brazil ▦ Rest of World
▦ China ▦ India
■ Japan ▦ Russia
■ Internal scrap

Figure 4.4—**Historic global aluminium output 1995–2007**[8]

chapter exploring the energy and emissions involved in each process, we'll be able to see how any strategy for change might affect the total emissions implied by the map.

Our maps show us the process chains we have to explore when thinking about energy requirements, give us an understanding of scale in metal production and teach us about scrap. When we predict future environmental impacts, particularly CO_2 emissions, from making steel and aluminium components, we need to anticipate how the maps will change: will they both simply expand as demand grows, or will the distribution of flows change? To start answering this question, we first need to explore how demand for the main applications in both sectors has evolved over time.

How has demand for steel and aluminium built up to present levels?

In our prologue, we made an analogy about present levels of material use based on sculptures. Global production of liquid steel and aluminium is currently 1400 Mt, and 76 Mt respectively, so dividing that by a global population of around seven billion, we get to 200 kg of steel and 11 kg of aluminium produced for every person on the planet every year. This metal has the same volume as an 8 year old child and a new born baby respectively, and since we thought of it the image of those metal children, and the emissions of more than 400 $kgCO_2$ emitted in making them, has haunted us.

Our steel production per person is three times our average weight and yet because the materials industries operate at such vast scale, in out of the way locations, most of us are virtually unaware of our metal consumption. Interestingly this wasn't always the case: before the Second World War we had no agreed single measure of the economy, and instead used a range of production figures concerning pig iron production, railway freight tonnage and so forth[6]. If only we could go back: it would be much harder to have a financial crisis driven by a pyramid scheme of betting if the bankers had to prove their assets in pig iron rather than fairy tales.

Bessemer invented modern steel making in 1855, just 150 years ago, yet today we make three times our body weight of the stuff every year. Figures 4.3 and 4.4 show the recent history of global steel and aluminium output and we've shown estimates of where it was made. Some recent events show up clearly in the graphs,

Sustainable Materials with both eyes open

for example the recession in 2008 and rapidly expanding production of both metals in Asia in the past decade.

To understand how demand for the two metals might develop in future, we need to make two changes to these graphs. Firstly we need to change them to metal produced per person, to separate out the effects of population growth and to see if production per person keeps growing, or if there's a plateau. Secondly, because both metals are widely traded, both as stock products and in completed goods such as cars, we'd like to manipulate them to find out how much is consumed per person, by country, rather than how much is produced. We don't have perfect answers to either question but help is at hand from two of our colleagues.

Professor Daniel Mueller at the Norwegian University of Science and Technology (NTNU) leads a research group who explore all possible aspects of metal stocks and flows. Along with his colleague Tao Wang, they have produced Figure 4.5 to show the output of several steel producing countries divided by the population at the time. The great revelation of this graph is that steel output per person seems not to grow indefinitely but to reach a plateau. We're not sure why the plateau is different in different places, but Daniel Mueller and Tao Wang suggest that Japan's high plateau may be influenced by a prevalence of high-rise buildings, strict building requirements due to the risk of earthquakes and corrosion from the hot, humid and coastal climate. However, while production in developed countries appears to have reached a plateau, in developing countries, notably China and India at present, the graph demonstrates rapid growth.

Recalling the global figure of 200 kg per person for steel and 11 kg per person for aluminium, it appears that production per person in the UK has stabilised

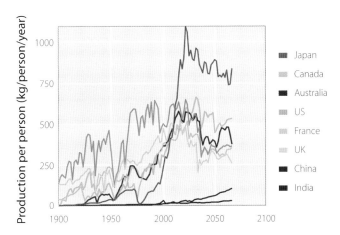

Figure 4.5—**Crude steel production per person for different countries**[9]

at the global average figure. At first sight that seems sensible, but on reflection, it isn't right. Figure 4.5 is based on national production figures but doesn't take account of trade because we don't have the numbers. So the fact that one country produces more than another may only mean that they have a large number of metal producing sites. What we really want to know is how much we consume per person.

We have found two estimates of consumption, both for the UK. In the UK at present we produce around 10 Mt of steel per year[10], of which we use around a half in the UK. But Figure 4.6 also shows that we import around 15 Mt of steel. As half of that is in products made from sheet steel, and we'll show in chapter 13 that we generate a lot of scrap when producing sheet components from liquid metal, we estimate that we cause about 23 Mt of steel to be made in other countries. So our total "steel footprint" is around 28 Mt—or 450 kg per person.

To check this number, we can turn to Professor John Barrett at the University of Leeds in the UK. His research group aims to show how the UK's emissions arise not from production but from consumption. This is very important: if we take responsibility for our emissions, we must do so regardless of where they occur. Despite national claims to a British sense of fair play, we are currently not doing this. Our national emissions figures take no account of what we import, and as we are net importers of goods, that suggests we're underplaying our real emissions impact. We also deny causing any emissions due to air travel, because the aircraft didn't burn the fuel when standing on the land of the UK. Good eh? Must have been dreamt up by bankers.

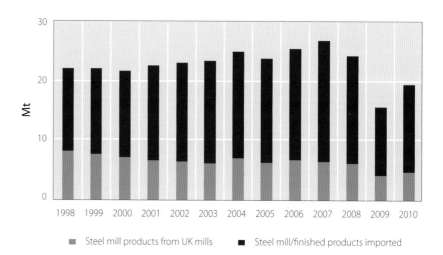

Figure 4.6—**UK steel requirements**[11]

■ Steel mill products from UK mills   ■ Steel mill/finished products imported

Sustainable Materials with both eyes open

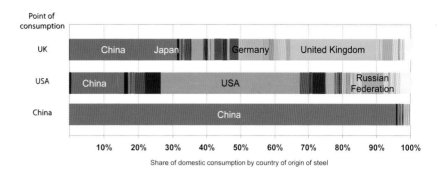

Point of consumption

UK	China · Japan · Germany · United Kingdom
USA	China · USA · Russian Federation
China	China

10% 20% 30% 40% 50% 60% 70% 80% 90% 100%

Share of domestic consumption by country of origin of steel

Figure 4.7—**Consumption of steel by country of origin**[12]

John Barrett has been working to come up with a fair figure of UK emissions based on what we buy not what we make. He does this by looking at the flows of money between sectors in the UK and elsewhere, so for example, when we buy a German car, he can estimate where our money ends up and what activities were involved. At the end of his arduous and data-intensive calculations, he comes up with a figure of 32 million tonnes as the UK's steel footprint and the share of domestic consumption by country of origin is shown in Figure 4.7. It's only an estimate, but now we have two different ways of coming to a similar number for UK consumption of steel, which appears to be around three times greater than UK production. We haven't found similar estimates for aluminium, but the UK's output of aluminium is now very small, so we have to assume that our real aluminium footprint would be an even greater multiple of what we produce. We would love to be able to produce new versions of Daniel Mueller's graph based on John Barrett's calculations of consumption but we only have one data point so will have to wait.

Let's quickly replay what we've just found about UK steel consumption, through the eyes of Chinese negotiators on climate change. We showed that in the UK we are responsible for more production in other countries than in our own, particularly in China, and to us it is clear that we should negotiate future international agreements on climate policy based on consumption not production. Therefore we agree with Chinese negotiators that targets for emissions reduction in China should be modified to account for trade—apparently good news for China. However, if we now impose our UK targets on emissions reductions to our consumption, that means we must reduce production emissions wherever they occur. So unless the Chinese steel industry cuts its emissions by 80% per unit output sold to the UK, our targets clearly tell us that we should buy less steel from China. Take your pick!

We've learnt in this section that although per capita production figures appear to reach a plateau, these are not for the UK good indicators of our total consumption. This makes it rather difficult for us to look ahead and forecast future demand for the two metals, whether in the UK or elsewhere, so in the next section we'll move onto estimating stocks of the two metals in different countries. Perhaps we'll be able to spot a pattern there so we can make some forecasts.

What stocks of steel and aluminium goods exist today?

The fact that in the UK we're each 'consuming' around 450 kg of steel and let's say 35 kg of aluminium per year is quite surprising: what on earth do we do with it? Most of us have no idea that we're purchasing these two metals at this rate. Worse, given that metals last a long time, our stock of both metals must be many times our annual demand. So we must each be responsible for several tonnes of steel and about half a tonne of aluminium. What have we done with it?

We're into difficult territory here because no one has ever collected comprehensive data to answer the question. So we're back to estimates, and estimating current stocks of steel or aluminium within a country is remarkably difficult. Broadly we have two options: to make a 'bottom-up' approach based on what we find in a particular area, or a 'top-down' estimate based on production figures.

For the 'bottom-up' approach, we could draw a boundary round some representative geographical region and then count the total stock of steel or aluminium in that region. If the region is representative, this should allow scaling up to a national estimate. This would be extremely arduous, although remarkably we have found a few PhD theses from students who've been positioned at municipal waste dumps for a year or more recording exactly what gets deposited: we can't imagine anyone more deserving of the cold beer we left on ice at the beginning of the chapter. Respect! But this bottom-up approach is imperfect. It would be very difficult to cover a large enough area in sufficient detail to be representative: just think of the vastly different architectural styles and building materials used for houses in different countries, and you can see the challenge.

In contrast, the top-down approach requires adding up annual production and net imports of each metal and subtracting annual disposal through waste management, to calculate the 'net additions to stock' for each year. Adding up these net additions should give us a figure for total current stocks. That would be straightforward, if only all our governments had decided 100 years ago to keep

Country	Steel stocks (tonnes/person)
Argentina	4.1
Australia	9.8
Bangladesh	0.1
Brazil	3.1
Canada	12.1
China	2.2
Congo, DRC	0.1
Egypt	1.1
Ethiopia	0.1
France	7.5
Germany	9.0
India	0.4
Indonesia	0.3
Japan	13.6
Mexico	4.8
Nigeria	0.1
Pakistan	0.1
Philippines	0.1
Russia	4.6
South Africa	3.0
South Korea	7.9
Spain	8.7
Thailand	2.2
Turkey	4.2
United Kingdom	8.5
United States	10.5
Vietnam	0.1
World	**2.7**

Table 4.1—**Steel stocks in-use for selected countries**[23]

all the appropriate records. However, of these three variables—production, net imports, and disposal—we only have data on production. The monetary value of net imports can be estimated from trade data, which has been collected for many years, but estimating the metal content in each type of traded product is difficult. Disposal figures have only been recorded recently.

In reality, we can't know precisely how much steel or aluminium is in current stocks, but Daniel Mueller, Tao Wang and Benjamin Duval have created an extensive top-down model based on six countries to see how steel stocks are built up over time as economies grow. In Figure 4.8 we can see the results of their model, with steel stocks per person (called iron after the chemical name) plotted against income per person. We see, not surprisingly, that as a person's income increases they build up their stock of steel. The graph also suggests that steel stocks might reach a plateau, above which more money no longer means more steel—but more on this later.

Based on Figure 4.8 (the grey band) Mueller, Wang and Duval then estimate stocks of steel per person for all countries, based on their current wealth (GDP per person) as shown in Table 4.1. Steel stocks range from 0.1 tonnes per person for the poorest nations to over 13 tonnes per person for Japan, with the world average around 2.7 tonnes per person. Despite the vast quantities of steel being produced at present in China, stocks still lag the global average, at around 2.2 tonnes per person. India, the other major growth economy in Asia, falls even further behind with only 0.4 tonnes per person.

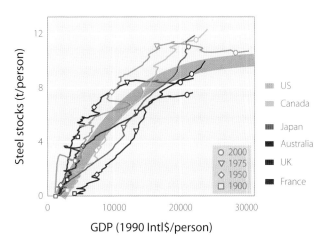

Figure 4.8—**Steel stocks in-use against GDP for different countries**

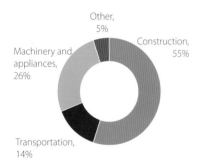

Figure 4.9—**Composition of UK steel stocks**[13]

The numbers in the table give total stocks, but for the UK we also have enough data to show roughly what stocks each person 'owns', and this is illustrated in the pie chart of Figure 4.9. We each use between one and two tonnes of steel in vehicles. This is roughly the weight of a car, although in reality, each person has less than a whole car and the rest is made up of other vehicles. Two to three tonnes of our individual stocks are in machinery and appliances. This includes household appliances like fridges, lawnmowers, computers, televisions and furniture as well as a proportion of the steel used in industrial machinery, such as farming and manufacturing equipment. Most of the rest of our individual steel stock is in buildings.

Steel stocks in construction vary by country, from under three tonnes per person in France to nine in Japan, and in the UK we have about four tonnes each. Typically about two thirds of this is in buildings and the rest in infrastructure, mainly bridges and pipelines. The difference between countries reflects local preferences in building towers and skyscrapers, as well as commercial and industrial buildings: the French have a strong preference for reinforced concrete framed buildings, while the Japanese (and the British) make much more use of steel frames.

Having found out more about our personal steel stocks, we can see why stocks tend to saturate as countries become wealthier. In the UK, most of us who want a car already have one and we have little land for new buildings or infrastructure, so although we upgrade what we already have, we are unlikely to increase the total stock significantly. This stabilisation of stocks is typical of developed countries, as illustrated in Figure 4.10. The graph on the left shows historical levels of steel stocks in six nations all following similar S-shaped curves, and levelling

Figure 4.10—**Forecast of stocks and production in China and India**

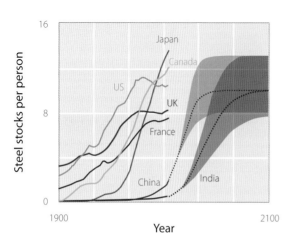

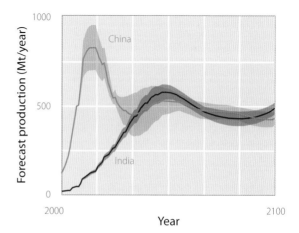

out at between 8 to 12 tonnes per person. If China and India follow a similar development path then, as shown in the graph on the right, annual demand for steel in these countries will rise rapidly before eventually stabilising.

Graphs like these have not yet been produced for aluminium stocks, however, Professor Tom Graedel and his student Michael Gerst at Yale University have collected some aggregated estimates. They found that in certain developing countries stocks are around 35 kg of aluminium per person, while in developed economies they have reached between 350 and 500 kg per person, leading to a global average of 80 kg per person[14]. However, unlike steel, it seems that aluminium stocks are not reaching a plateau even in developed economies, probably because our use of aluminium in applications such as construction and cars is still growing. We anticipate that aluminium stocks may eventually saturate between 500 kg and 1000 kg, but for now will use the lower value.

Understanding stock levels gives us a basis for predicting future demand. We buy steel and aluminium for two reasons: to replace the goods we throw out and because we want new goods. Trading in an old car for a brand new car is replacing stock, but buying a second car grows our stock. For a developing country, this means that the driver of demand changes as stocks build up. In the UK we have a stable stock of nearly 10 tonnes per person, which we replace at a rate of around 400 kg per person per year. In contrast, in China, stocks are much lower at around 2 tonnes per person[15]. Maintaining this stock, at similar replacement rates to those in the UK, would require production of no more than 100 kg per person, but Chinese demand is much higher than this due to stock expansion, leading to demand for around 400 kg per person[16]. So China and the UK appear to have similar rates of consumption per person, but for different reasons: UK demand is to maintain an existing higher but stable stock; Chinese demand is to maintain and grow a much smaller stock.

We're nearly ready to attempt a forecast, but first, let's check two other features of metal stocks and their saturation.

Firstly, our friends in economics might be tempted to tell us that demand for materials grows with GDP, as we get richer we consume more. Yet our graphs in this section have told a different story: while a country grows richer, metal production increases to drive up stocks, but then we stabilises at some threshold, required to maintain stocks at some plateau.

Secondly, if stocks really do stabilise, can we achieve the nirvana of a 'closed loop' economy? This is a great banner phrase and for example Chinese policy is currently directed towards the idea of a future "Circular Economy"[17] but the reality has proved elusive. Achieving a closed loop would require that stocks stabilised at a plateau for longer than the average product life time, and that our collection and recycling of old material occured with no losses. This is as yet far from the case: despite clear incentives, and well managed collection schemes, we only recycle around two thirds of our used drinks cans; most aluminium foil is not recycled, because it isn't collected or is recycled in mixed streams with high losses[18]; steel reinforcement bars in sub-surface concrete (for example foundations and tunnels) are not extracted at end-of-life; deep-sea line pipes are not removed at the end of their life. So we're still a long way from collecting all of our discarded metals for recycling, although our box-story overleaf on aluminium lithograph plates used for printing tells a positive story about a closed-loop in action.

How will demand for steel and aluminium develop in future?

Our exploration of patterns of steel and aluminium stocks has given us a basis for forecasting future demand. If you tell us (a) how the population will grow in each country over the next 50 years (b) how economic development will occur in each country over the same time (c) whether there will be any new products invented during that period so that saturated demand in developed economies gets unsaturated as everyone races to purchase a new iSkyscraper—then we'll be able to tell you exactly what demand will be…

…but of course, no one can possibly answer those questions, so instead we'll use a simplified approach and apply it for steel. We'll start with the United Nations' forecasts of population over the next century as shown in Figure 4.13 and the US Energy Information Administration's forecasts of global GDP growth. Dividing the second by the first gives us an estimate of future global wealth, which we can then apply to the graph of Figure 4.8, to predict future evolution in global steel stocks. And from annual changes in stocks, we can now forecast global steel production up until 2050.

The resulting steel forecasts are presented in Figures 4.11 and 4.12. The first graph shows our simple forecast of global steel stocks and the second shows the resulting steel production required to grow and replace these stocks. Based on our simple

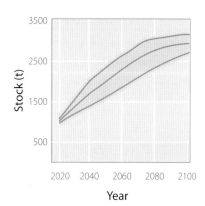

Figure 4.11—**Forecast of global steel stocks**

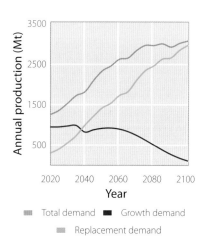

Total demand Growth demand

Replacement demand

Figure 4.12—**Forecast production to replace steel stocks**

Sustainable Materials with both eyes open

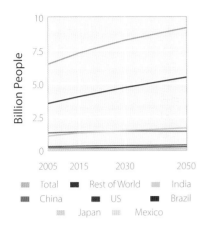

Figure 4.13—**Forecasts of future population**[20]

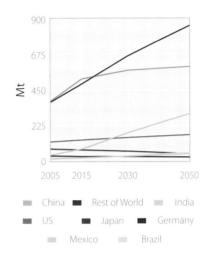

Figure 4.14—**Past and forecast steel consumption**[21]

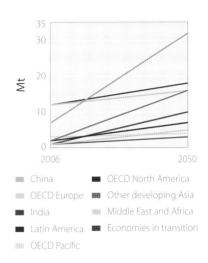

Figure 4.15—**Past and forecast aluminium consumption**[22]

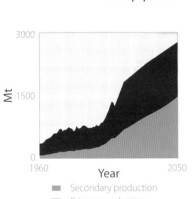

Figure 4.16—**Forecast of primary and secondary steel production**

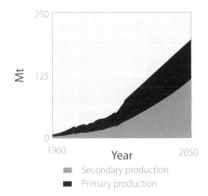

Figure 4.17—**Forecast of primary and secondary aluminium production**

model we predict that steel production in 2050 will be 1.7 times today's levels. We could produce similar graphs for aluminium demand if we had the required equivalent of Figure 4.8.

The approach we've described is also used by the International Energy Agency for their forecasts of future steel and aluminium consumption which are shown in Figures 4.14 and 4.15, although with different assumptions about steel stocks reaching a plateau. Because we are unable to create our own forecast for aluminium, we've chosen to use the IEA's forecasts of demand for the rest of our book.

Finally, as we want to anticipate energy and emissions associated with both metals, we need also to predict how future production will be split between primary (from ore) and secondary (from scrap) routes. We've shown this split on the IEA forecasts in Figures 4.16 and 4.17, which we've predicted by dividing the total demand into product categories, and used estimated product lifetimes to work out the flows of metal products into and out of use. Following our discussion about our failure to collect cans, foil and sub-surface rebar for recycling, we've used an estimate from Professor Robert Ayres at INSEAD in France that a practical maximum for recycling rates might be around 90%[19]. The graphs show that the fraction of secondary aluminium production might rise to around 60% by 2050, while for steel, with longer product life times, this fraction may be around a half. The circular economy is obviously a long way ahead of us yet.

Outlook

Our story in this chapter has been that we have a pretty good idea of how metals flow from ore into current uses, and a broad idea of what's being produced where, although we wish we knew more about consumption rather than production. We have shown a simple method for predicting future stocks and shown that we can use this to estimate how demand for metals will grow in future. Broadly we anticipate that demand for steel will grow by 1.7 times by 2050, while aluminium demand will grow by 2.5 times. As we set out in this book looking for options to deliver more sustainable materials, the precision of this forecast is much less important to us than its order of magnitude. Climate scientists are clear that we should aim to cut CO_2 emissions in 2050 to no more than half present levels, but over that period we've seen here that demand for steel and aluminium is likely at least to double. Halving emissions while demand doubles requires that we reduce the emissions associated with each product to one quarter, which is an extraordinarily demanding target.

Before we start adding up our options for change, we need to explore where energy is used and emissions arise in present day production, and to anticipate the challenge of implementing change, we need to find out how money flows in parallel with the metal. That's coming up in the next two chapters, but having now realised just how severe the challenge is, you might want to take a seat outside in your favourite chair, and look on the table next to you—where there's a clean

Lithographic plate

Lithographic plate is used to print the images and text that form our books, newspapers and magazines. We currently produce around half a million tonnes of aluminium litho-plate every year. Commercial print shops can use more than 100 hundred of these plates each day. An important characteristic is a high quality flat and degreased surface. 1xxx series alloys are often used (such as AA1050 and AA1100), or alternatively more durable 3xxx series alloys (such as AA3103 and AA3003) for mass printing.

Production may be from primary or recycled material. The business-to-business transaction, high specification and cost of the aluminium (accounting for 50% of the cost of lithographic coil), encourages nearly 100% closed loop recycling. Often, a recycling agreement will be part of the initial contract between the supplier and printer.

empty glass and a perfectly chilled unopened can of your favourite beer. The can glistens in the evening light, its dappled moisture announcing its cool readiness in the warm air, the three different alloys required to make body, cap and opener balanced in perfect harmony, ready to be recycled in a closed loop…

… but you can't recycle them until the can's empty. Cheers!

Notes

1. The aluminium producer Novelis (2011) reports that "Each year, more than 280 billion drinks cans are manufactured worldwide, and more than 85 percent of them are made from aluminium".

How does steel and aluminium flow from ore to final uses today?

2. The US Geological Survey produces annual mineral commodity summaries reporting national and global industry data, including where bauxite and iron ore is mined. The information on bauxite and iron ore mining is taken from the Bauxite and Alumina and the 2011 Iron Ore Mineral Commodity Summaries (USGS, 2011a, USGS, 2011b).

3. The US Energy Information Administration collects information on international electricity generation for different technologies, including hydroelectric power. Excel tables of all of their data can be found on their website (USEIA, n.d.).

4. The Aluminum Association produced a report on the manufacturing and lifecycle costs of different vehicles (Bull et al., 2008), and this included an estimate of the steel sheet contained within a conventional vehicle .

5. This data was collated from conversations with steel companies.

How has demand for steel and aluminium built up to present levels?

6. In their book, Macroeconomics: Understanding the wealth of nations, David Miles and Andrew Scot say until GDP was defined as a measure of growth "there existed a collection of disparate production numbers concerning pig iron production, railway freight tonnage, and so forth" (Miles & Stott, 2005). Victoria Bateman, economics lecturer at Cambridge University also pointed us towards a US resolution from 1849, which states "That the manufacture of iron is not a mere local or individual interest, but is of national importance, as affording a supply of a chief element of progress in time of peace, and an important engine of defence in time of war" (French, 1858).

7. This graph is produced from regional and global production data from the World Steel Association's steel statistical archives. Both this graph and the one for aluminium show regional net production (having accounted for the effects of trade) as well as the scrap recycled internally within the industry, which could not be separated by region. (World Steel Association, n.d.).

8. This graph is produced from regional and global production data from the International Aluminium Institute's mass flow model avaiable for the period 1997-2007. This data is not publically available but results of the mass flow analysis are reported in the IAI's global recycling report (IAI, 2009).

9. This graph is taken from analysis of patterns of iron use in society over time by Mueller et al. (2011).

10. The trade assocation for the UK steel industry, UK Steel reports on the state of the UK's steel industry in their annual Key Statistics report (UK Steel, 2011).

11. The UK steel demand includes steel mill products from UK mills used in UK products, steel mill products imported and steel contained in imported manufactured goods. (UK Steel, 2011)

12. This figure comes out of research on consumption by Barrett et al. (2011).

What stocks of steel and aluminium goods exist today?

13. Mueller et al. (2011) provide the data for this figure in their paper on iron stocks in use in their figure 4.

14. Michael Gerst and Tom Graedel wrote a paper summarising surveys of regional and global stocks of in-use metals from 124 different estimates (Gerst & Graedel, 2008).

15. This figure comes from Mueller and Wang's paper on iron stocks, Mueller et al. (2011).

16. Of course, part of the reason why China's per capita production figures are so high is because they are producing so many metals products for other countries. Part of their production will go towards production for other countries, a small part will go towards replacing their existing stocks (but not very much as the stocks are small and quite young) and part will go towards new demand, building up new stocks of metal products.

17. In 2008, China adopted a circular economy law, which aims to encourage increased recycling and further innovation in recycling technologies. A translated copy of the law can be found at China Environmental Law (2008). A summary of circular economy legislation around the world was put together by Davis & Hall (2006).

18. Boin and Bertram (2005) estimate that more than 30% of scrap foil is lost when remelting.

How will demand for steel and aluminium develop in future?

19. From Ayres (2006) on why growth will not continue to be exponential.

Box stories, figures and tables

20. The population forecasts are taken from the IEA's book, Energy Technology Perspectives, (IEA, 2008a), which are based on UN predictions.

21. The future demand for steel is calculated by multiplying per capita demand from the IEA's projections in IEA (2009) by population projections.

22. The future demand for aluminium is calculated by assuming a linear relationship between current consumption and projections of total regional consumption for 2050 from the IEA (2009).

23. Mueller et al. (2011) provide the data for this table in their paper on iron stocks.

5 Energy and emissions
in making steel and aluminium components

Many of our concerns about sustainable materials relate to the requirements for energy to process them, so we need to find out where the energy is used, and how that use evolves. In response to concerns related to climate change, we need to know in particular which processes emit most greenhouse gases.

Wohhhhhhh!

We're going clubbing, but let's have a drink first. See that small bottle with the cork stopper? Glug-glug-glug, Oh Man! The world's expanding around me, everyone else looks so small. We fly to the club, and almost everyone looks like us, but there's a few big guys in the line and they move to a different beat. Inside, the dancers are packed in close and we're shaking, and I don't know if it's us making the heat, or the heat that makes us move. There's a couple over there, a bit mismatched but they're nice and tight, and … wham! Some other guy, came out of nowhere, knocks into them, and would you believe it, now she's split from her partner and is all wrapped up with the new one. And look, there are those big guys, and they can really move. They're doing that big arm thing with the double twist, and somehow they've found each other. Maybe it's easier to do their moves when they all get together. Now the DJ's giving us a break, and he's slowing it down, and we're all still and cool. But wait—what's happening over there? The walls front and back they're moving in, while the other two are going out. Nnnnggg! We're all packed right in, and we can't move. But now the DJ's had an inspiration, and he's put on a fast track, and we're all moving like crazy. And you know what? Now we're moving, side to side, in and out, and we must all be spilling into the space where the walls are moving out, and that's relieving the pressure of the walls coming in. Alright! It's hot, we're shaking, but the squeeze is gone and we've got the beat. Wohhhhh!

Got it?

That potion really was powerful—Lewis Carroll with another 150 years development in the lab—and we all shrank 10 thousand million times to become atoms. And we've seen in the club everything we need to know about energy use in making our two metals. The dancers (atoms) shake more when it's hotter and less when cooler, and when they're shaking more it's easier for them to move past each other. The big guys, alloying elements, prefer being close to each other, but can only move (by diffusion) when it's hot. The close dancing couple? Two different atoms bonded together tightly (they might be iron and oxygen in a naturally occurring ore, like Haematite, say) but when they were hot, a carbon atom was able to knock them apart, and also get his arms round her (the oxygen) and carry her off, the hound. And when the dance floor cooled and the walls moved in, no one could move, so they really felt the squeeze. But when they could move again as the temperature went up, they could slide past each other much more easily, and rearrange themselves sideways. Metal deforms more easily when it's hot.

In making steel and aluminium, we need energy for three things: to drive chemical reactions to rearrange the bonds between different atoms; to create enough heat for diffusion to allow atoms to reorganise, so changing the distribution of alloying elements, relieving stress around dislocations, and allowing bigger grains to grow; to raise the temperature so the metal can deform more easily. In this chapter we'll first look at how energy needs are met by existing processes. Then we'll explore the conversion of process energy requirements into process emissions. Adding these up, we can examine global emissions figures, and by looking at their history, we can begin to forecast how they may develop in the future. Finally we'll explore the difficult problem of allocating energy and emissions from processes to products.

Energy use in the process of making steel and aluminium components

The next two double pages show how the three requirements for energy are in the processes we use to make steel and aluminium. We've started from greyed out versions of our two metal-flow Sankey diagrams from the last chapter, and shown on them all the key processes required to convert ores mined from the ground into finished metal components. For each process we've also shown an estimate of the annual energy required to drive the steel[1] and aluminium processes[2]. (The energy values are reported in exajoules (EJ) one of which is equal to a billion billion joules, as we saw in Figure 2.5, we use just under 500 EJ of energy each year). There's a lot of information on these pages, but nothing happens except what we saw in the Atomic Club.

The energy values in the Sankey diagrams are given as primary, rather than final energy values as discussed in chapter 2. We've shown the processes on top of our Sankey diagram of flow, because one of the big concerns of the trade associations for steel and aluminium, who have the best data on energy use, is it's only possible to understand energy needs for metal production if we show the exact route by which the metal is made. For example, for both steel and aluminium, making liquid metal out of scrap takes much less energy than making it from ore, particularly so for aluminium. But some metal flows between the primary (from ore) routes and the secondary (from scrap) routes. So, the trade associations are absolutely right that we can't give a convenient single number to answer the question "how much energy does it take to make steel/aluminium?" because the answer depends on the exact combination of processes involved. For both metals, we can always use a much lower number if our product was made entirely from scrap and not ore.

The number of processes involved also influences the total demand for energy. The diagrams show us that the liquid metal processes are the energy intensive ones: for both metals, making liquid metal, whether from ore or scrap, uses far more energy than any other stage in the process. Downstream, once the metal has been formed into a stock product, the energy required to shape it into its final form depends strongly on how many processes are involved. A steel I-beam (known as a double T beam in Germany, and a grrrdr (tr. girder) in Scotland) is made with very few processes: it's hot rolled to shape, then cut to length and a few bits are welded on. In contrast, a steel car door requires a long series of process steps: cold-rolling (to give the required surface quality); galvanising (adding a coat of zinc for protection against rust); blanking (cutting a specific shape from the two metre wide coil of strip made in the rolling mill); deep-drawing and punching to give it the required 3D shape, and cut out holes for instance for the window and door handle; hemming (folding over the sharp edges); welding and assembly onto other parts of the door; painting; paint baking (hardening the paint and, remarkably, making a final change to the microstructure of the steel so it has maximum strength, having been designed to be more ductile for the deep drawing process). Each process requires more energy so it takes more energy to make more complex parts. However it is still the liquid metal processes that dominate total energy inputs. We've not attempted to show what happens after the component is completed because generally the process of assembling components into finished products, and the logistics of moving products from their point of manufacture to their point of sale, takes much less energy than any of the component manufacturing stages.

Steel process map

Blast furnace
16 EJ
7%

Coal and iron ore are processed and fed with lime into the top of the blast furnace. Hot air and additional fuels are blown in from the bottom. Coke reacts with air to form carbon monoxide, which reduces iron oxide to iron. The lime reacts with impurities in the ore to form a slag. Liquid iron collects at the bottom of the furnace and is tapped into ladles.

Basic oxygen furnace
0.2 EJ

Oxygen is blown through the liquid iron and this oxidises the remaining carbon into CO and CO_2. The reaction is exothermic (gives out heat) and steel scrap is added to reduce the temperature in the furnace. The molten steel is refined in a separate ladle furnace.

Continuous casting
0.4 EJ
74%

Molten steel is cast continuously into slabs, blooms or billets, and water-cooled. The majority of steel produced is cast continuously, although a small fraction is still cast as ingots.

Direct reduction
0.7 EJ

In direct reduction, iron ore is reduced into iron in a shaft or rotary furnace using natural gas or coal.

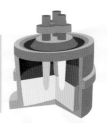

Electric arc furnace
2.7 EJ
86%

Carbon electrodes are lowered into the furnace and a high temperature arc forms between the electrodes and the metal charge. If the charge is not completely scrap, carbon or other fossil fuels may be injected with oxygen for the reduction reaction.

Shape casting
2.1 EJ
46%

Iron or steel is melted before pouring into a mould. Once solidified, the casting may undergo cycles of heat treatments to achieve the desired properties.

Steel (overview)
Energy = 38 EJ
Electricity = 39%

Coating
0.6 EJ
46%

Steel is cleaned before being coated with zinc (galvanised), tin plate or a range of paints (organic coatings). This provides corrosion protection for steel outside or in demanding applications such as food cans.

Rolling
3.6 EJ
46%

Steel is reheated and descaled before being rolled into strip/coil (from slabs), rod/bar (from billets) and sections (from blooms). The number and sequence of mill stands is matched to the thickness reduction and material properties required. Cold rolling, descaling, tempering and shearing processes can follow.

Forming
0.2 EJ
82%

Steel slabs and billets are formed into stock products using a range of techniques, including: extrusion, wire drawing, pipe bending/rolling and welding. Forming may take place cold to minimise oxidation, or closer to the melting temperature to soften the steel.

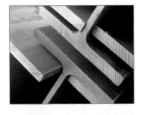

Fabrication
11 EJ
70%

Stock steel is cut, bent, drilled, milled, welded and painted to make bespoke components ready for assembly into end-use products.

Figure 5.1—**Steel process map**[9]

Alumina mining +refining

1.1 EJ
2%

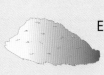

Bauxite is mined—mainly from open cast mines—washed and crushed before being dissolved in hot sodium hydroxide (caustic soda) in 'digesters'. The aluminium oxide reacts to form sodium aluminate, leaving residues, which sink to form 'red mud'. The solution is cooled and the water removed, leaving alumina as a white powder.

Electrolysis

5.0 EJ
100%

Alumina is dissolved in cryolite (sodium aluminium fluoride) at about 950°C. Electric current passing from the suspended carbon anodes to the graphite cathode lining the electrolysis cell causes the deposition of molten aluminium at the bottom of the cell (or pot) where it is periodically tapped.

Ingot casting

0.05 EJ
44%

Crucibles of liquid aluminium from the smelters are cast via the direct chill route, where large rectangular or log shaped ingots are lifted up from a water cooled casting mould.

Scrap remelting

0.04 EJ
30%

Clean, wrought process and post-consumer scrap is melted, mostly via the hot combustion gases in reverbatory furnaces, but sometimes using the heat generated during electromagnetic induction in induction furnaces.

Scrap refining

0.15 EJ
14%

Scrap is melted in rotary or ladle furnaces. Salt is used as a fluxing agent to remove impurities, resulting in the production of slag. Refiners produce mostly foundry ingot and so add silicon and metals like copper and magnesium to achieve the required composition.

Alloy ingot casting

0.03 EJ
44%

Alloying elements, such as silicon, are added to crucibles of liquid aluminium from the smelters, and then purified before casting by blowing gases through the melt. Liquid aluminium is cast into smaller ingots ready for shape casting.

Aluminium (overall)

Energy = 7.6 EJ
Electricity = 76%

Rolling
0.23 EJ
72%

Ingots are preheated to around 500°C before rolling. Several rolling passes are required to reduce the ingot to the required thickness for sheet (4-6 mm) or plate. Some sheet is cold rolled further down to 0.05 mm for foil, and passed through annealing furnaces and slitting if required.

Extrusion +drawing
0.09 EJ
19%

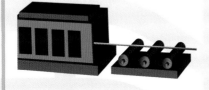

For extrusion, the billet is typically heated to 450-500°C and pushed through extrusion dies at a pressure of 500 to 700 MPa. Extrusion billets may have a diameter of 50 to 500 mm. For wire drawing aluminium rod is drawn through a series of dies with a decreasing aperture.

Shape casting
0.17 EJ
1%

Sand casting and die casting are the most important types of mould casting, sand casting moulds are one-use, whilst die casting moulds are generally re-used, being made of cast iron or steel. Foundry ingots are melted and the molten aluminium is poured into the moulds. Pressure may be applied during die casting.

Fabrication
0.62 EJ
70%

Aluminium stock products are cut, bent, drilled, milled, welded and painted to make bespoke components ready for assembly into end-use products.

Figure 5.2—**Aluminium process map**[9]

We'll conclude this section with two pie charts to show estimates of the total energy involved in making aluminium cans and steel car door panels. The energy for liquid metal production dominates all else for both products, which ties up with what we saw earlier about total energy use in China. So we've got a clear motivation to focus on (a) energy efficiency in liquid metal production and then (b) finding ways to use less liquid metal. That pretty much summarises what we mean about looking at the problem with one or both eyes open.

CO$_2$ emissions arising from the processes of steel and aluminium making

In addition to energy we are interested in emissions, Tables 5.1 and 5.2 show the emissions intensity of the key processes: how much CO$_2$ is emitted for each unit of metal processed. Our numbers for process energy can be measured precisely, with meters recording the supply of fuel or electricity to each process over some period, divided by the total mass of metal leaving the process in the same time. As we discussed previously, there are reasons why some of these numbers will only be made public as estimates, but any company wanting to understand the drivers of its energy consumption can measure them accurately.

The same is not true for CO$_2$ emissions. Although under laboratory conditions these emissions can be measured, in practice this is rare, so instead CO$_2$ numbers are calculated or inferred. Direct emissions of CO$_2$ from fuel combustion or from the chemical reactions which reduce ores to metals can be calculated with reasonable accuracy from the mass of ore and fuel being processed. Indirect emissions related to electricity generation can be collected, with significant effort,

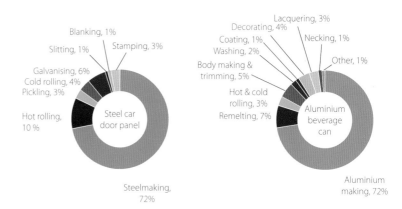

Figure 5.3—**Estimates of total energy involved in making components** [4]

Sustainable Materials with both eyes open

Process	Emissions (t CO_2/t)
Iron making—blast furnace	0.5
Coking	0.2
Sintering	0.4
Direct-reduction	1.2
Steelmaking—oxygen blown furnace	0.2
Steelmaking—electric arc furnace	0.5
Scrap preparation	0.01
Steelmaking—open hearth furnace	1
Continuous casting	0.01
Ingot casting	0.05
Hot strip mill	0.1
Cold strip mill	0.4
Plate mill	0.1
Rod and bar mill	0.2
Section mill	0.2
Galvanising plant	0.2
Tinning mill	0.04
Extrusion	0.2
Primary mill	0.1
Forming	0.1
Steel product casting	2.4
Iron foundry casting	1.7
Fabrication	1

Table 5.1—**Emissions estimates per unit processed for major steel production processes**[5]

by chasing the electricity back to its source. However, emissions from electricity generation vary widely, with hydro-electric power (commonly used for aluminium smelting) having the lowest intensity, and coal-fired power stations the highest. As a result, the emissions intensities of identical processes may be quite different in different locations. For the major processes used in making steel and aluminium, emissions intensities have been studied widely, by companies, trade associations and academics, and the numbers in the tables reflect our best estimates of these values.

Behind this allocation of emissions to electricity purchasing lies a further, political question that has had little attention, but is highly significant. If within a country there are a range of different power stations, each with different emissions intensities, is it reasonable for one company to claim all the benefits of using the lowest emission supply?

This is what happens in aluminium smelting at present, and the aluminium industry would correctly state that they are purchasing a large part of their electricity requirement directly from very low emitting hydro-electric generators. However, if the smelter ceased to operate at that location, the hydro-power would still be available, and would be reallocated to other uses in the country. It seems to us that we should therefore have just one average emissions intensity for all the electricity in a country, the same for all users. If that happened, the emissions intensity of aluminium would be increased. For obvious reasons, the aluminium industry would disagree with us, and as they are the main source of data on emissions, the numbers shown in Table 5.2 are indicative of currently reported emissions intensities.

The numbers in the tables demonstrate that for both metals, liquid metal processes lead to the highest emissions. The relative impact of downstream processes is higher for emissions than energy, because most energy used downstream is in the form of electricity.

Global energy and emissions history and projections

Although we have good records of total production of both steel and aluminium since the modern production processes were invented, we're much shorter of historical energy numbers, and don't really have any history of global emissions numbers. Instead we have a rough idea of the global average energy intensity of making steel from ore, shown in Figure 5.5. This approximate data illustrates that

Process	Emissions (t CO_2/t)
Bauxite extraction	0.02
Alumina production	1
Anode production	0.1
Electrolysis	5.4
Scrap preparation	0.3
Scrap remelting	0.3
Scrap refining	0.6
Ingot casting	0.2
Hot rolling mill	0.2
Cold rolling mill	0.2
Extrusion	0.3
Wire drawing	0.6
Shape casting/ secondary casting	0.5
Foil mill	0.9

Table 5.2—**Emissions estimates per unit processed for major steel and aluminium production processes**

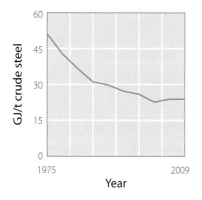

Figure 5.4—**The history of energy intensity improvements in primary steel production**[6]

steel production has become much more efficient over time, although it appears to be reaching a plateau. Figure 5.6 shows the historical development of CO_2 intensity for different countries, but we can't be sure exactly what this means as the changes in CO_2 intensity will be influenced by a whole range of factors including the technology mix, electricity mix and any efficiency improvements.

The data records for aluminium energy intensity is a little better as the IAI have kept historical data on the electricity requirements for aluminium smelting since 1980. Although we are generally reporting primary energy figures, in Figure 5.7 we've used final electricity values to show the improvement over time due to increased energy efficiency, without the disguise of changes in the mix of electricity generation. Again, we can see significant improvements in the energy intensity over time, but signs are that the rate of improvement is slowing.

We ended our analysis of demand in the previous chapter with a forecast, and within that, we made an assessment of the availability of material for future recycling in order to anticipate the likely future ratios of primary to secondary production. This gives us a basis for making a forecast of future energy and emissions. If we assume that energy and emissions intensities remain about the same as now, and that the mix of products remains about the same, we can forecast energy needs and CO_2 emissions in 2050 by applying our process energy and emission factors from the table to the relevant forecast metal flows. We've done that to create the next two graphs, which form a reference for our forecast of future emissions for the two materials. And these graphs demonstrate why we decided to write this book: without other changes, emissions for both metals will increase significantly, and although our forecast shows slightly less growth in emissions than demand due to the increased fraction of liquid metal being made by recycling, we clearly have a problem if we want to cut emissions by 50%. So, better keep reading…

Allocation of energy and emissions figures to products

Now, back to the Atomic Club, but after everyone's gone home, and only the owner Boris is left. Boris has recently opened a letter from Brussels, which has ruined his day. The Belgian bureaucrats have announced that Boris has to provide a carbon certificate to everyone leaving his club, identifying exactly how much CO_2 has been emitted as a result of their visit. Poor Boris: as if life's not busy enough already what with counting the cash and adding the water to the vodka.

Sustainable Materials with both eyes open

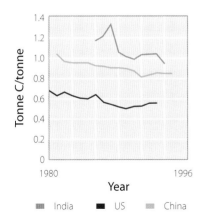

Figure 5.5—**History of CO_2 intensities for the iron and steel industry in selected countries**[7]

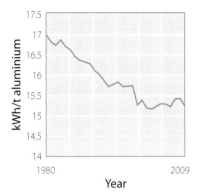

Figure 5.6—**Historical electricity intensity of primary aluminium production**

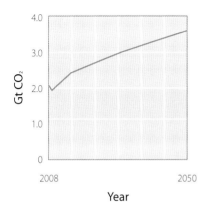

Figure 5.7—**Forecast CO_2 emissions in steel production if business continues as usual**

What's a fair basis for allocating CO_2 emissions to clubbers? Presumably we have to start with the total CO_2 emissions related to the club's energy purchases. The club only buys electricity, but Boris has two suppliers, as he buys some of his electricity from a local wind farm. They only send in the bill after each three months of use. So Boris has to guess what his bill will be for the next three months, and divide it up evenly between his customers. But, he doesn't yet know how many people are going to come to the club in the next three months, and he also has a suspicion that the party from the local aluminium smelter will only come in if they can buy 'green' tickets related to the wind farm electricity only, and without question, the bankers will want tickets based on the emissions 25 years ahead. But the problem gets worse. Making the materials to build and fit out the club required energy, so how does that fit in? And what about Boris' choice of transport to get to work: does it matter whether he comes to work on a bike or by car? And what about the emissions of the bands who recorded the music played in the club?

The problem Boris faces is in fact insurmountable. It isn't possible to allocate his emissions to his clients accurately because (a) he doesn't know what his emissions will be over the next period (b) he doesn't know how many punters will come in that period (c) he can't define clearly for which emissions he is responsible and (d) it isn't clear what fraction of the emissions should be attributed to each punter: should a 5 minute visit collect the same number of credits as a three hour stay? Despite this, we're currently surrounded by efforts, many driven by people in Belgium, to attribute carbon emissions to products and services. See the box story on the following page for some of the most common approaches.

This whole effort around emissions attribution simply doesn't make sense. Our concern is global emissions, so any exploration of whether particular choices or decisions are beneficial or not depends on whether they have a good or bad effect globally. If I switch from primary to secondary aluminium in making my product, that makes no difference whatsoever to global emissions unless I have somehow increased the amount of secondary production and decreased the amount of primary production occurring. To do that I need to find a new supply of material for recycling that would only exist because of me. If I divert wind-power from a new wind farm in the North Sea from the national grid to power my factory, it makes no difference to the country's total emissions because the wind power was going to be used by someone. And so on and so on and so on. Our only guiding principle is to establish whether some change causes a significant global reduction in emissions. So we have great doubts about any attempt to attribute emissions to products because it's so difficult to do so in a sufficiently consistent way that the sum of all attributed emissions is uniquely equal to the sum of all emissions.

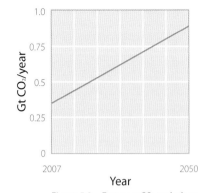

Figure 5.8—**Forecast CO$_2$ emissions in aluminium production if business continues as usual**

We've been clubbing, we've done some hard estimating, we've tried to help Boris solve his problems with Belgian bureaucrats, and we're all worn out. Time to rest now—ready for a day's shopping tomorrow.

Attributing emissions to products

There are three methods in current use to allocate carbon emissions from processes to products and services. These methods would be plausible if the sum of all emissions attributed to products equalled the sum of all industrial emissions.

- 'Carbon footprints' are calculated by summing the emissions directly and indirectly caused by an activity, to give a single emissions figure in grams of CO$_2$. There is no agreed approach to calculating such footprints, although Non-Governmental Organisations such as the UK's Carbon Trust have attempted to define methods. Carbon footprints are increasingly reported on consumer products, with the intention of allowing consumers to compare similar products. However, the methodology is ill-defined and consumers have little understanding of such labels, so their purpose is as yet unclear.

- In contrast, the technique of Life Cycle Analysis (LCA) is much more established and is defined in ISO standard 14040. The ISO standard assumes that LCA is used for comparing two similar ways to complete the same product. A boundary is defined round a system which is broad enough to encompass all differences between the alternative products. Every process within this boundary is examined and numerical values are calculated for drivers of any environmental concern within the boundary, for the two approaches. The LCA study then calculates the difference between the two approaches, and anticipates

how this will lead to environmental harm. This approach is well defined, and rigorous. Unfortunately almost all current users of the LCA method fail to apply it correctly as a comparison, and instead claim that it predicts absolute impacts associated with a particular product. It doesn't, and as a result, almost all recently published LCA studies are misleading. They are so dependent on the boundaries used that they can be manipulated to create any answer. We have yet to find a single LCA study in which the company who paid for the study is responsible for the largest environmental impact.

- Input-Output (IO) analysis assigns emissions to monetary flows and tracks these emissions through the production system from initial production to final demand. This method of analysis is comprehensive and complete and allows us to convert emissions from production to consumption in a consistent manner. Unfortunately assigning emissions to money flows can be quite misleading, and while the IO approach is logically consistent, it requires a huge data set, which is generally unavailable in sufficient detail, or for recent years. The analysis is performed for sectors, so cannot create results for individual products.

Hybrid methods, which combine IO and LCA analysis, have been developed, but many of the same problems with data (reliability, detail and boundaries) remain.

Notes

1. The energy numbers for the steel processes come from a wide range of sources including a report by Ernst Worrell and colleagues on the world best practice energy intensity values for selected industrial sectors, including steel (Worrell et al., 2008) and a report from the IISI (the old name for the World Steel Association) (IISI, 1998). Best practice values were converted into estimated average values by multiplying by a factor of 1.1.

2. The energy numbers for the aluminium processes come from a wide range of sources including Ernst Worrell and colleagues' best practise report (Worrell et al., 2008) and a report by the US DOE (BCS, 2007).

3. The energy data for fabrication processes is based on data we collected for case studies of metal products and their supply chains and is published in our report, Going on a metal diet. (Allwood et al. 2011a)

4. The energy data for making components is based on data we collected for case studies of metal products and their supply chains and is published in our report, Going on a metal diet.

CO2 emissions arising from the processes of steel and aluminium making

5. Like the energy numbers, the emissions numbers for steel and aluminium production processes are collated from a wide range of sources. For aluminium, most of the upstream data is taken from IAI analysis (IAI, 2007) and much of the downstream data is taken from the US DOE report (BCS, 2007). For steel, several of the values were taken from reports for the EU's Integrated Pollution Prevention and Control directive and from a study of the Canadian steel industry (Canadian Steel Producers Association, 2007).

Global energy and emissions history

6. This graph has been put together from a number of sources. The World Steel Association has produced an indexed graph of the energy intensity of primary production for 7 years between 1975 and 2004 (World Steel Association, 2004). We can use a data point of the absolute energy intensity of steel production, from Yellishetty et al. (2010). Finally, we can use energy intensity values from Tata (2011) to give us some more recent data points.

7. This figure is from Kim and Worrell (2002), but it includes the effects of changing technology (OHF to BOF for example) so does not just describe improvements due to energy efficiency.

8. Pelletising is another way to prepare iron ore but it is used far less than sintering and uses about 0.8 GJ/t steel produced. For simplicity, only sintering is described in the Sankey diagram.

Images

9. Some images on these diagrams adapted from World Steel Association graphics.

6 Where does the money go?

And who is involved?

Most of us have never directly purchased engineered materials—because we buy them when they have been formed into components and assembled into finished goods. So, when we buy cars or buildings, how much of the money flows back to the material producers, and who else is involved?

"Good morning, I'd like an office block please."

"Certainly Sir—would that be the 4-storey or the 7-storey?"

"Mmmm… I think I'll take the 7-storey, with all the trimmings."

"An excellent choice Sir—so that would be one 7-storey steel-framed office block, with advanced treble glazing, aluminium curtain walls, white flat roof, natural circulation, your name projected by laser on all surrounding buildings, and the three large pot plants at reception?"

"Just the job yes—and I think I'll take a small backup power supply and air conditioning unit on the side."

"No problem at all, and that comes to … about 14 million pounds all round."

"Good Heavens, you chaps certainly know how to add on a margin or two! I thought these office blocks used about 100 kg of steel per square metre of floor space, and with steel around £400/tonne I was thinking more in the line of £400,000?"

"I see sir—well, we do have a couple of abandoned wooden huts we could offer you in that range. Would that be more your sort of thing?"

So what's in an office block? Let's assume that our 7 storey office block has a footprint of about 10,000 square metres. When bidding for the job of constructing an office block, building contractors have various rules of thumb for estimating quantities of materials. 100 kg steel/square metre is a typical rule for the steel framed type of building that we saw in our catalogue in chapter 3. Typically the floor slabs in the building will be poured concrete at a rate of about 1,900 kg per square metre. Add on 4,600 square metres of triple glazed 4mm thick glass, and 46 tonnes of aluminium for the frames which support the glass and we're nearly there. We don't really know what else will be in the building—the metal for heating, air conditioning and ventilation equipment, furniture, carpets and so on, but based on our catalogue of metal use in construction, let's assume that our rules of thumb have covered 85% of the material by volume so we'll add a further 15%.

Now we can make the estimate of material costs for the building shown in Table 6.1. The prices are approximate but typical for 2009 in the UK, and we've reached an estimate that the materials required to build our 7 storey office block cost about £0.9 million? But the price we were offered was £14 million—why?

	Material Requirement (t)	Unit Cost (£/t)	Material cost (£000's)	Material cost as share of building costs (%)
Steel	1,000	410	410	3
Aluminium	50	1,100	55	<1
Concrete	4,500	32	140	1
Glass	140	2,000	280	2
+15%	810	-	130	1
Total	6,200	-	880	6

Table 6.1—**Cost estimates for a 7 storey office block**

The answer is of course obvious. Most of the difference between £14 million and £0.9 million is the cost of people involved in every stage of the process: block masons, carpenters, electricians, plumbers, plasterers, concrete workers, construction and building inspectors, equipment operators, glazers, painters, roofers, fabricators, steel fixers, construction managers, project managers, surveyors, civil/structural engineers, services engineers, specialist engineers and subcontractors, architects, interior designers, all of whom need to be managed, paid, supported and trained. The construction project probably requires some financing, to allow the contractor to purchase materials before the client pays the final price, so the bankers want their (large) share of the pie, and if there is any surplus it will be paid as profit to be distributed among the owners of the many companies involved.

With so many people involved, costing so much money, negotiations over the building process to create the office block will include a trade-off between material price and labour: if labour is expensive relative to materials, then most decisions will be slanted towards saving labour even if material purchasing increases. So that's why we need to know about the flow of money, to find out how much anyone cares to save material.

In fact, apart from the people being paid for the construction of the office block, several other groups have an interest in it: local planners will be concerned about the effect of the new office on neighbours; protest groups and other NGOs (Non-Governmental Organisations) may be concerned about the influence of the new office on natural species; community groups may be concerned about its social impact.

To understand options for changing the materials supply chain, we must understand the full directory of who's involved and why. Our ambition in this chapter is therefore to generalise from the office-block example and ask two questions: for products which contain steel and aluminium, where does the money involved in final purchase eventually flow? and who is involved in the whole business of delivering products containing the two metals?

Where does the money flow?

We're going to answer this question in two stages. Firstly we'll ask, "who, by their purchasing, causes steel and aluminium to be made?" Then, for these final purchasers who drive use, we can ask "where does the money they spend on goods that include steel and aluminium eventually end up?"

In both cases, we'll develop our answer by using a technique called "Input-Output" analysis, invented in 1936 by Wassily Leontieff, a Nobel Prize winning Russian, born in Munich, who emigrated to the US aged 25 to spend the rest of his career at Harvard University. Leontieff modelled money flow through an economy with a table that shows how the money flowing into one sector is the result of purchasing from another. The columns of this table show the production recipe for each sector in the economy: they show, for example, that a furniture supplier needs to make some purchases from other industries (for things like wood, metal and financial services), buy imports, pay a return on any capital invested, and pay for labour and taxes in order to make furniture. Collectively all of the spending from any one sector (the sum of all the costs in the column, which are called inputs, because the money is spent in order to buy inputs to the sector's activity) should add up to the total sales (or output) of that sector. This is what is shown in the rows of the table: they show purchases that are made by other sectors and also final purchases by households, government, exporters and businesses that are adding to their stock of equipment or other goods in order to produce more of their own outputs in the future. Input-Output tables for whole countries are adjusted so that if you add up either the sum of the row totals (all sales) or the sum of the column totals (all spending) you reach an identical single measure of the country's economic activity, the GDP (Gross Domestic Product). The tables are an interesting way to see the exchanges in the economy but Leontieff's particular innovation was to use these tables repeatedly in order to explore the origin of final demand: if some furniture is bought by equipment makers for their offices, then really that part of demand is driven by the volume of equipment being purchased. So, who causes equipment to be purchased, that in turn causes furniture to be bought? And so on. Eventually, using Wassily Leontief's maths, we can show how each different type of final demand (purchasing by households, government etc.) causes activity in each producing sector, or inversely, for each producing sector, we can find the primary causes of demand.

Input-Output analysis depends on a table of numbers that show the flow of money through a country's sectors. The original purpose of these tables was to reconcile different measures of GDP, so many countries produce them as part of their National Accounts. They can be published in various forms from raw data to 'balanced' Input-Output tables adjusted so that supply is equal to demand for each product and input equals output in each sector. Both the raw data collection and the balancing process are time consuming which limits the frequency of publication and level of detail in each country's reports[1].

Recent developments in Input-Output analysis have allowed exploration of environmental effects: if we attribute some environmental damage to a particular sector, and then assume that responsibility for that damage 'flows' with the money that flows into the sector through purchasing, then we can eventually find out which types of final consumption spending drive the damage. This is the approach taken by John Barrett, whom we mentioned in chapter 4, to understand the UK's responsibility for CO_2 emissions related to consumption.

For our needs in this chapter, we've used a global input-output table with 57 sectors[2]. The importance of using global data is that, as we already know from John Barrett's work, if we looked just at the UK we would find that a lot of steel is imported and we would be unable to trace the money flow once it leaves our borders. But with the global table we can trace all money from spending back to its source.

We're now armed to address our two questions: where does the money flow and who is involved? The answers are presented in five diagrams: the first two show which sectors purchase aluminium and steel; for the three largest sectors identified

Sustainable Materials with both eyes open

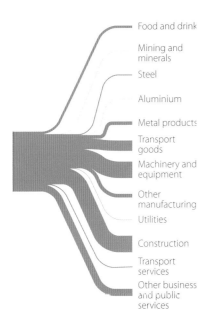

Food and drink

Mining and minerals

Steel

Aluminium

Metal products

Transport goods

Machinery and equipment

Other manufacturing

Utilities

Construction

Transport services

Other business and public services

Figure 6.1—**Which sectors purchase steel?**

Food and drink

Mining and minerals

Steel

Aluminium

Metal products

Transport goods

Machinery and equipment

Other manufacturing

Utilities

Construction

Transport services

Other business and public services

Figure 6.2—**Which sectors purchase aluminium?**

in the first diagrams, the other three diagrams show the final destinations of all their purchasing.

The first pair of diagrams show us a story related to our earlier Sankey diagrams of metal flow: the main sectors of final demand for steel are construction, vehicles, equipment and consumer goods. However, the weighting of the different sectors is not the same in money units as it was in material units. This is because of the variety in processing required when completing different types of finished goods and because of different profit margins that can be charged on more bespoke products.

The other three diagrams show us how the money spent on final goods containing steel and aluminium flows back to other sectors. In all three cases, most spending is within the sector, which seems surprising but is a consequence of describing the entire economy with just 57 sectors. For example, in building the 7-storey office block that our hopeful client wanted at the opening of the chapter, his money might flow first to an agent, then to a design consultant, then to an architect, then a contractor and so on—but all of the businesses mentioned so far would be in the same one of our 57 sectors.

The key message of the diagrams is that for most goods containing these two metals, the value of the metal is of the order of 4% to 6% of the final purchase price. In the example with which we started the chapter, the total cost of all materials was about 6% of the final purchase price, so a similar ratio. These diagrams show us where all the rest of the money has gone.

We've learnt something very important from this analysis: the ultimate costs of our two metals are small compared to the final prices of almost all final goods containing them. As a result, decisions about metal use may often have less priority than decisions about other costs, particularly labour. In turn, this suggests that we may well be purchasing more metal than we physically need to provide a given service, if doing so allows us to avoid other costs.

Who is involved in delivering products containing steel and aluminium?

Let's go back to our new office building. We've already started a list of all the different people we need to pay to understand why the price for the office block is

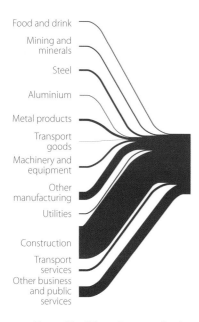

Food and drink
Mining and minerals
Steel
Aluminium
Metal products
Transport goods
Machinery and equipment
Other manufacturing
Utilities
Construction
Transport services
Other business and public services

Figure 6.3—**Where does spending by the construction sector end up**

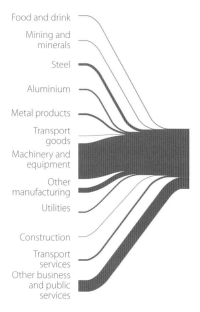

Food and drink
Mining and minerals
Steel
Aluminium
Metal products
Transport goods
Machinery and equipment
Other manufacturing
Utilities
Construction
Transport services
Other business and public services

Figure 6.4—**Where does spending by the machinery and equipment sector end up**

so much higher than the cost of materials within it. Who do they all work for? Our opening conversation was between a client and an agent of some type. To build his building he'd certainly need a contracting firm (who do the actual construction), an architect, an engineering consultancy and, in many cases, a property company who might own the land on which the building is to be erected, or who might own and build the building, with the client as the first tenant. The engineering consultants must comply with building regulations, construction standards and certification, insurance industry needs and planning regulations. The contractor will mainly pour and assemble materials on the construction site, but use a fabricator to make any non-standard steel shapes, including the reinforcement bar cages used in foundations, and the steel sections of a steel framed building. In turn the fabricator buys steel either from the steel mill directly, or more likely through a stockist or importer. The stockist purchases steel from the steel mill, which often has the same ownership as the rest of the production chain back to ore or scrap. The ore is bought from a mining company, possibly via a commodities market, and the scrap from a scrap metal merchant. Those are the direct players, but all the processes need an energy supply, there are plenty of specialised component or equipment suppliers involved too, along with the consultants, trade associations and other organisations that provide information. This whole network of companies is regulated, for the health and safety of its employees, and for environmental and safety concerns, and to ensure product quality, and is likely to be influenced by various levels of governmental support. NGOs, lobby groups, and charities may have local concerns about different aspects of the production process, whether about the noise of construction in a city, or the environmental impact of emissions, or the conditions of employment of the labourers.

We've illustrated this vast range of business types on the picture that follows (overleaf). As we explore how the services provided by steel and aluminium might evolve in future, we need to remain aware of this picture, to remember which groups would support or oppose possible changes.

We can estimate the total number of people employed in the world of steel and aluminium from the online data set at the website of the International Labour Organisation. This gives a detailed breakdown of employment by sector from countries which represent about one third of the world's workforce. We have to assume that these countries are representative of the whole, although given that China and India do not have detailed figures, our scaling won't be precise. However, the numbers suggest that around 120 million people worldwide are employed in transforming ores and scrap into manufactured metal goods. In addition around 250 million people worldwide are involved in construction, much

Sustainable Materials with both eyes open

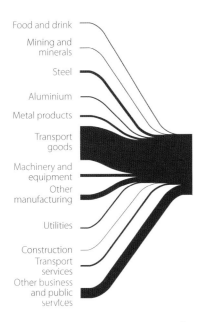

Food and drink
Mining and minerals
Steel
Aluminium
Metal products
Transport goods
Machinery and equipment
Other manufacturing
Utilities
Construction
Transport services
Other business and public services

Figure 6.5—**Where does spending by the transport goods sector end up**

of which involves steel, whether for reinforcing bars in concrete, or as sections. That makes a direct target audience of 370 million people who should be buying our book, and if they each enjoy it as much as we think they will, and then buy two more copies to give to family members as a gift…

The development of today's steel industry

The history of steel begins in 1856 with Bessemer's invention which was rapidly adopted by the former iron industry and soon there were over 200 steelmakers in England and Wales[3]. Andrew Carnegie, one of the earliest supporters of steel, took the process with him to Pittsburgh to found the Carnegie Steel Company. Unlike the UK where many small companies were active, US steelmaking was rapidly dominated by few larger companies. The biggest of them began when a group headed by Elbert H. Gary and JP Morgan bought Carnegie's steel company in 1901 to form the largest steel enterprise launched to that date, making two-thirds of US steel production[4]. Soon, companies in the US and elsewhere in Europe had overtaken UK productivity and national differences led to a period of protectionism[5]. Successive rounds of tariff reductions and the formation of free trade areas in Europe and North America later reduced barriers so that world trade in steel doubled between 1975 and 1995. In turn, this allowed individual producers to specialise in production of particular products at high volumes[6]. Global steel production grew 5% each year as Europe recovered from the Second World War until the global energy crisis of 1974[7]. This crisis depressed industrial activity and coupled with the saturation of steel demand per person in developed nations that we discussed in chapter 4, the industry stopped growing in the 1980's and early 1990's. However, the extraordinarily rapid growth of China starting in the 1990's followed by the other BRIC countries (Brazil, Russia and India) led to growth in global production of steel by 7% each year between 2000 and 2005. This growth, which has driven the great expansion of the steel industry in these countries, caused a rapid shift in relative output: the fraction of the world's steel production made in the BRIC countries has grown from 28% in 1999 to 58% in 2010[8].

Steel is a strategic industry, so state aid supported ailing steel works allowing differences in costs between similar countries to develop. For example, the cost per tonne of cold rolled coil was a third higher in Germany than that in Britain for much of the 1990's[9]. The collapse of the Soviet Union and a wave of privatization elsewhere in Europe led to a reduction in state ownership of steel works from 53% in 1986 to 12% in 1995[10]. Regional price differences however continue as shown

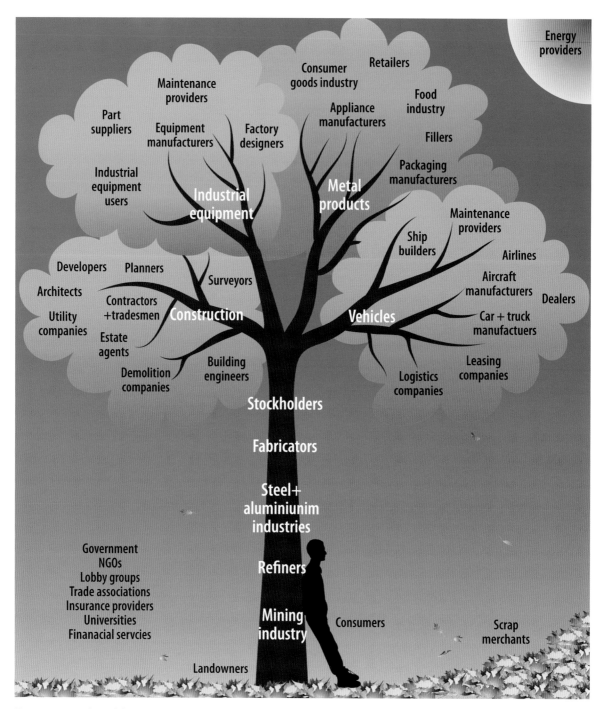

Figure 6.6—**An arboreal depiction**
of the steel industry

Sustainable Materials with both eyes open

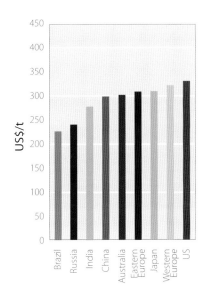

US$/t

Figure 6.7—**Comparison of international steel slab costs**

in Figure 6.7, with BRIC economies using cheap raw materials and labour and benefiting from their recent expansion through having some of the newest, and most efficient, technologies.

Steelmaking remained mainly a nation-based industry until the mid-1990's when a succession of mergers and acquisitions led first to regional consolidation (the creation of Corus in 1999 and Arcelor in 2001 in Europe and the formation of JFE in Japan in 2002) and then global consolidation (the creation of ArcelorMittal in 2006 and the take over of Corus by Tata Steel)[11]. Greater consolidation allowed steel companies to expand their activity downstream, for instance with Tata also now owning the car maker Jaguar Land Rover, and to increase their bargaining power for inputs.

Despite recent trends towards globalisation and consolidation the industry is still surprisingly fragmented: the top 10 global companies produce less than a quarter of all steel, and the largest producer, ArcelorMittal, makes only 6% of production[12]. Having many smaller steel-makers, rather than just a few dominant ones, increases competition for inputs, mainly for iron ore and coke, so gaining reliable access to raw materials is a key concern in the industry at present.

	Company*	Market Cap ($bn)	Company†	Output (Mt)	Company†	Output (Mt)
	Mining		Steel		Aluminium	
1	BHP Billiton	210	ArcelorMittal	78	UC Rusal	4.1
2	Vale	170	Baosteel	31	Rio Tinto Alcan	3.8
3	Rio Tinto	140	POSCO	31	Alcoa	3.4
4	Shenhua	84	Nippon Steel	27	Chalco	3.0
5	Anglo American	61	JFE	26	Hydro	1.3
6	Suncor	58	Jiansu Shagang	21	BHP Billiton	1.2
7	Xstrata	57	Tata Steel	21	Dubal	1.2
8	Barrick	41	Ansteel	20	China Power Inv. Corp.	1.0
9	Freeport-McMoRan	38	Severstal	17	Xinfa Group	0.9
10	NMDC	37	Evraz	15	Aluminium Bahrain	0.9

Table 6.2—**Industry leaders**

* Listed in descending order of Market Capitalisation, † Listed in descending order of total output (Mt)

Table 6.2 shows that the mining industry is more heavily consolidated than steelmaking: three large companies, BHP Billiton, Vale and Rio Tinto, have a quarter of all the sales of the world's top 100 mining companies. These "super groups" purchase a wide range of resources and sell two thirds of the global seaborne iron ore market[13]. Both iron ore and bauxite are abundant in the earth's crust. The main iron ore deposits are in Brazil, Australia and Russia. There are also high volume but lower quality deposits in China and the Ukraine. Australia and Brazil also have major deposits of bauxite, as do Guinea, Vietnam and India. In 2009, China imported almost two-thirds of the world's total iron ore exports and produced about 60% of the world's pig iron.

The structure of today's aluminium industry

The development of the aluminium industry sector has been driven by the need for access to high quality bauxite and cheap electricity. As a result, a recent trend has been for the major aluminium companies to purchase mining, electricity generation and alumina producing businesses. Ten years ago, the American aluminium company Alcoa had the largest share of bauxite mining. Today it ranks just 26th, with mining companies dominating bauxite extraction and taking a sizeable stake of aluminium production: the super group Rio Tinto acquired the aluminium company Alcan in 2007 to form Rio Tinto Alcan (now the second largest producer of aluminium) and BHP Billiton has expanded its aluminium operations to become the sixth largest aluminium producer globally. We saw in chapter 5, the process of refining bauxite to alumina and the process of smelting alumina to aluminium are both energy intensive with energy purchasing being around a third of all costs. As a result, aluminium makers have set up aluminium smelters in countries such as Brazil which have a rich supply of bauxite and cheap electricity. Aluminium production can be matched effectively with the flexibility but high power of hydro-electricity. In effect the electricity becomes embodied in the aluminium, so can be traded and exported without the expense and cost of electricity distribution.

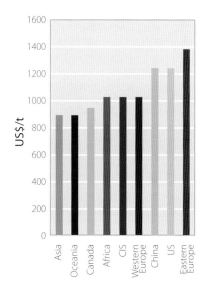

Figure 6.8—**Comparison of international aluminium slab costs**

Even when aluminium companies buy electricity rather than generate their own, they buy so much that they can negotiate low prices with long-term contracts, which may be linked to the primary metal price, and the form of these contracts has a significant influence on total costs. Figure 6.8 compares aluminium production costs by region and shows differences of up to $500/tonne between Asian and Eastern European plants[14].

Sustainable Materials with both eyes open

Most smelting companies have long-term contracts with alumina suppliers that set the price at a fixed proportion (10-15%) of commodity aluminium prices, which helps to reduce the risk of sudden cost variations. High-grade aluminium and aluminium alloy is typically traded on long-term contracts between producers and consumers with prices again set relative to an index supplied by the London Metals Exchange. This practice of relating prices to the underlying metal cost continues further downstream, for example the price of aluminium cans is typically expressed as a mark-up on the metal price. This means that, in the short term at least, the cost of aluminium production and the value of intermediate aluminium products are strongly influenced by the basic metal price so the sector is intensely cost competitive.

The story of regional production shifts for aluminium is similar to that for steel. Aluminium production grew rapidly from the turn of the millennium due to demand from China, with an amazing average yearly growth of 24% from 2000 to 2002[11]. A reduction in production in the US at the same time increased the relative shift of production from west to east. The global aluminium industry is more dominated by big companies than steel, with the top 10 producers making 85% of all output[15].

Global trade in steel and aluminium

Relating our brief history of the two sectors to our earlier picture of the main businesses involved in steel and aluminium, we have seen a significant 'consolidation' (fewer larger companies) in producing primary metals. Nearer to final consumers business is more fragmented with smaller companies serving localised markets. The clear exception to this is the automotive sector in which the top four producers make over half of all new cars[16]. The construction industry tends to be more localised although there are a handful of international companies, chief amongst them the French company Vinci with a turnover of $31bn[17]. The packaging sector remains similarly fragmented despite a couple of large players[18].

So much for company size—what about the flow of metal goods around the world? The map of Figure 6.9 shows the money value of trade in metal at various stages of its journey from ore to metal to final product. The largest two trade flows for each good are shown. The map shows a general flow from Southern to Northern hemispheres, but the value of the trade increases as the ores are processed into more complete goods. China's role as an importer of ores, scrap and machinery

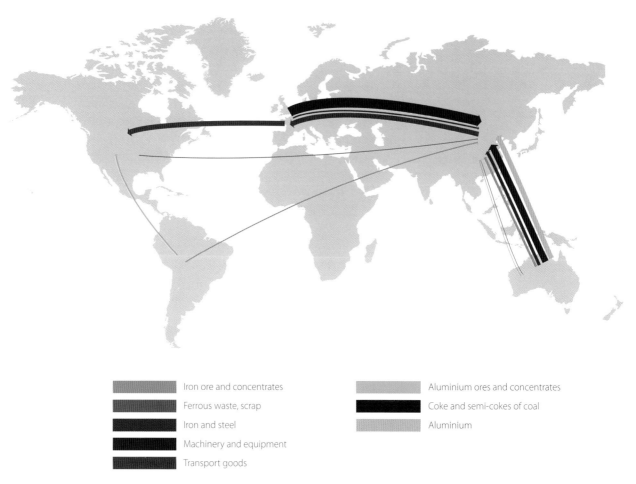

	Iron ore and concentrates		Aluminium ores and concentrates
	Ferrous waste, scrap		Coke and semi-cokes of coal
	Iron and steel		Aluminium
	Machinery and equipment		
	Transport goods		

The line thickness in the legend represents $10bn for steel and $1bn for aluminium, and the arrows on the map are scaled in proportion

Figure 6.9—**Map of global trade**

and equipment and exporter of vehicles is clear. We can also see that the United States is a major exporter of scrap.

Outlook

We've seen through our tour of industry structure, history and trade, that our friend who opened the chapter by considering the purchase of a new office building would, had he saved up enough to go ahead, have triggered an activity that would ripple round the world. Almost all of the money he would have spent would eventually be paid as wages, across the vast span of businesses required to deliver the completed building. The social needs of everyone employed and affected by the process, would be considered by a range of government regulations and other lobby groups. So, let's end by re-writing our sketch from a completely different angle:

"Good morning, I'm thinking of providing employment for about 4,500 people across the globe for around six months each."

"Certainly Sir—did you have any particular activities it mind?"

"Mmmm… I'm not too concerned about that, but I would like to be sure that they work in reasonably safe, socially acceptable, conditions and receive a fair wage."

"An excellent idea Sir—we do our best to ensure that all employment we create is well regulated, and we do support several active charities to watch our labour conditions and keep us up to the mark."

"Super—now, any ideas what they might actually do with their time?"

"Well, I think if we play our cards right we could just about get them organised to make a 7-storey steel-framed office block, with advanced treble glazing, aluminium curtain walls, white flat roof, natural circulation, your name projected by laser on all surrounding buildings, and the three large pot plants at reception?"

"Just the job yes—time I had a new office. Now, any idea how this might all total up?…"

Notes

Where does the money go?

1. As a result, in the UK, the Office of National Statistics last published a full set of input-output tables in 1995, opting instead to publish annual supply and use table (the unbalanced constituent parts of input-output tables) as part of the Blue Book (ONS, 2010a), and allowing academics to bid for funding to construct the full set of balanced tables. For example the UK-MRIO project (Wiedmann et al. 2007) produced a set of input-output tables for the UK 1992-2004 based on the supply and use tables published annually in the blue book (ONS 2011). The UK supply and use tables cover 123 sectors meaning that there are over 15,000 numbers to be collected. Most countries publish some form of input-output tables, however sector groupings differ from country to country and disclosure agreements can limit the amount of data that is made publicly available. The arduous process of data collection, verification and the balancing of tables (referred to in the literature as 'optimising') does not end there; to really understand the chain of purchases that are instigated by a product that is consumed in the UK (or conversely the ultimate source of demand for goods produced in the UK) we need to take into account trade. Queue another round of data difficulties: we need a concordance matrix to match up sectors that are grouped differently in different countries, and we need to make sure that everything adds up i.e. that, at the global level, imports are equal to exports when duly adjusted for tariffs, transport costs and suchlike. There are a handful of initiatives globally that have taken on this task, for example the GTAP database (GTAP, 2011), EXIOPOL (n.d.) and EORA (Kanemoto, 2011).

2. The data set we used was based on the most widely accepted collection of national input-output tables, known as the GTAP database (GTAP, 1997). To create a world input-output data, we added up national input-output tables, taking care to avoid double-counting activities related to trade.

The development of today's steel industry

3. The British national organisation for the steel construction industry produced a history of steel in construction to mark the Centenary of the metal (BCSA, 2006).

4. US Steel still exists and this information was taken from the history section of the company's website (US Steel, 2011)

5. The history of the steel industry produced by the BCSA (2006) states that Austin Chamberlain suggested a 5-10% tariff on imported steel in 1904 in order to guard against other countries (that were themselves beginning to erect trade barriers) dumping surplus output on the UK market. It was many years before this policy was implemented in the UK.

6. Aylen (1998) tracks trends in the international steel market.

7. Ibid 6.

8. Each year, the World Steel Association produce "World Steel in Figures" (World Steel Association, 2010) which includes annual production by region and by method.

9. Tim Bouquet & Byron Ousey (2008) describe the exciting journey that led to the formation of ArcelorMittal.

10. Ranieri & Gibellieri (1998) provide a commentary on the steel industry in the new millennium.

11. In 2006 the UK Parliament commissioned a report on globalisation in the steel industry (Parliamentary business, 2006).

12. The annual statistical publication by the World Steel Association (2010) provides production data for the top 49 steel companies.

13. Data collected by mining industry analyst Barry Sergeant (2010).

The development of today's aluminium industry

14. Zheng Luo & Antonio Soria (2007) produced a comprehensive appraisal of the aluminium industry for the European Commission.

15. Data supplied by industry analysts CRU (2011).

Global trade in steel and aluminium

16. Datamonitor provides regular industry reports for most sectors including Global automobile manufacturers (Datamonitor, 2007).

17. Every year the Financial Times identifies the top 500 companies by market capitalisation. A sector breakdown of these companies is also available (Financial Times, 2010).

18. Datamonitor reports for the containers and packaging industry (2008).

with one
eye open

PART II

7. Energy efficiency

To reduce the energy required to make steel and aluminium, the obvious first focus is the current processes which use most energy. However, because energy has always been a significant cost to the operators of the intensive processes, they have already sought out and applied almost every available option. What are the limits to future energy efficiency, and what remaining options are there to approach these limits?

8. Opportunities for capturing heat

Part of the energy required to convert ores to metals is required to drive chemical reactions, but most of the rest is heat used to melt or soften the metal and to allow diffusion. Virtually all of this heat is lost to air. It sounds as if we should try to capture this heat, either for re-use within the same process, or by cascading it through other industrial processes which require heat at a lower temperature. What's the opportunity to achieve this?

9. Novel process routes

If we could invent a new way to extract liquid metal from ore, could we find new emissions savings, or could we drive the reactions by electricity and find a source of clean electricity that would reduce our total emissions?

10. Carbon sequestration

If there are no alternative routes to making the metals, and if we continue to expand production, could we reduce total emissions not by saving energy, but by separating CO_2 from other gases emitted in production, capturing it and burying it underground?

11. Future energy use and emissions

If we bring together our assessment of all the options we've identified to reduce energy requirements and emissions from the existing production routes for steel and aluminium, and if demand grows as we anticipate, will it be impossible to make a 50% absolute cut in emissions by 2050?

7 Energy efficiency
in existing processes

To reduce the energy required to make steel and aluminium, the obvious first focus is the current processes which use most energy. However, because energy has always been a significant cost to the operators of the intensive processes, they have already sought out and applied almost every available option. What are the limits to future energy efficiency, and what remaining options are there to approach these limits?

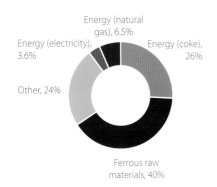

Figure 7.1—**Costs in steel production**

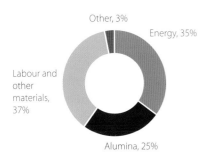

Figure 7.2—**Costs in aluminium production**

In the TV series *The Apprentice* a group of highly motivated candidates compete to be chosen for a well paid job through a series of episodes designed to test what we're told are their 'business skills.' In fact, virtually all episodes test the same skill: marketing a new product or service into an already well populated commodity sector, whether perfume, magazines, fish or chocolates. This is of course one important business skill. But our friends who teach entrepreneurship tell us that while most new businesses that fail in their first year, do so for lack of sales and hence the skills being tested in *The Apprentice*, the most likely cause of failure in the second year is a failure to control costs in delivering the products. Costs don't make good TV, but they are at the root of all business decisions in the materials processing industries because, regardless of marketing, the products are essentially indistinguishable. We have agreed international standards for steel and aluminium (and also cement, paper and plastic) which specify the composition, processing and properties of all the standard products, so buyers can switch suppliers easily. If all suppliers are equal, the price is in effect fixed at the lowest price any supplier can sustain. And if, as a supplier, you can't control the price, then your profits depend on controlling your costs. So next time we get the chance to run the BBC, we'll be moving on from *The Apprentice* because we've now learnt that focusing ruthlessly on your own advancement is the skill that gets the prize, and instead we'll be screening *The Cost Manager*—it already sounds like a hit!

The two pie charts show a typical breakdown of costs in primary steel and aluminium production. Energy purchases account for a third of the costs of both basic steel and aluminium production. As a result, these energy intensive industries have, for more than a hundred years, had a strong incentive to pursue energy efficiency. These costs will continue to motivate managers of average or poorly performing sites to raise their standards to those of current best available technology.

Gospel, blues

If it costs you, what you must use, you gon-na use it e-ffi-cient-ly,

In the Atomic Club in chapter 5 we saw that we need energy to drive reactions to raise the temperature of metals to allow diffusion and to make deformation easier. In this chapter we'll start by defining the least energy we would ever need to make our two metals. Then we'll evaluate the efficiency of existing processes to make metal from ore and from scrap.

How little energy could we use to make metal goods?

Iron and aluminium are both chemical elements appearing in the periodic table as Fe and Al respectively, but are rarely found in nature as pure elements. Only if you happen to stumble upon a meteorite. This is because iron and aluminium have a natural affinity for oxygen. When they are mined as ores, they are in the form of oxides with the pure elements tightly bound to oxygen atoms.

Haematite

Iron ore occurs naturally in several forms. The two most common forms are magnetite and haematite, both of which are oxides, with different ratios of iron to oxygen atoms. Ore deposits are commercially interesting if the ores make up at least a quarter of the extracted rock, the rest is typically quartz (silica) which must be removed. To do this, the rocks are crushed, and the ore is separated from the remainder, by use of magnets for magnetite, and by flotation in water for haematite. Iron is then extracted from these oxides by a chemical reaction in which the iron oxide is mixed with a stream of hot carbon monoxide, which itself is made by blasting a stream of hot air through coke. (Coke is made from coal by baking at around 1000°C in a low oxygen atmosphere, to remove water, coal-gas and coal tar without combustion.) At around 2000°C, the oxygen atoms in the iron oxide have a stronger attraction to the carbon atoms in the gas than to the iron atoms in the mined ore, so bond to the carbon to form carbon dioxide (CO_2) and leave behind a nearly pure pool of liquid iron, as shown in Figure 7.3. This 'pig iron' also called 'blast furnace iron,' retains about 5% carbon, and is a stiff but brittle metal. In an odd quirk of language, steel is actually a purer form of iron than 'cast iron'. Bessemer's invention, mentioned earlier, was to blow pure air

Bauxite

through the liquid pig iron to remove the remaining carbon by igniting it, to form carbon monoxide or carbon dioxide. In 1948, the Swiss engineer Robert Durrer discovered that this process was much more efficient if oxygen rather than air was used, and this is the basis of most current steel making.

Aluminium is most commonly found in the earth's crust as an oxide within bauxite, which contains about one third aluminium oxide (also known as alumina). Aluminium atoms have a stronger attraction to oxygen than iron or carbon, so aluminium cannot be separated as easily from its oxides by the same process as iron. Instead, the mined ore is first purified in the Bayer process, before being separated by electrolysis in the Hall-Héroult process. Karl Bayer, working in St Petersburg in Russia in 1887, discovered that if Bauxite is washed in caustic soda (sodium hydroxide, NaOH), the alumina within it dissolves, and after being filtered, dried and heated to 1050°C, is released as a white powder. The remainder of the Bauxite in the caustic soda is the 'red mud' which we identified in the first chapter as an environmental concern because it is strongly alkaline, and because we make roughly twice as much red mud as alumina. Alumina has a melting point of around 2000°C, but dissolves at 1000°C in liquid cryolite from which pure aluminium can be extracted by electrolysis. (Cryolite—meaning 'chill stone'—sounds like an invention in a James Bond film, but is a naturally occurring mineral compound of sodium, aluminium and fluorine, first found in Ivittuut, West Greenland in 1799. Despite being at one end of the only road in Greenland connecting two towns, and despite having Greenland's highest recorded temperature (30°C), the town was abandoned when the cryolite deposit was exhausted in 1987. A synthetic version of

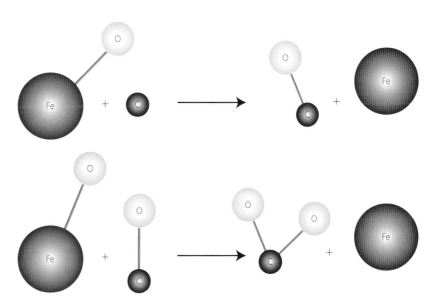

Figure 7.3—**Schematic of the iron reduction process**

cryolite is now used for aluminium production, and presumably Greenland's Road Atlas business has also collapsed.

The electrolysis process involves passing a large current through the solution of alumina in liquid cryolite, from a carbon-based positive terminal (the anode) through to the graphite negative terminal (cathode) as shown in Figure 7.4. As a result of the electric current, the aluminium and oxygen are separated: the aluminium forms a bath of liquid metal at the base of the cell, and the oxygen bonds with carbon from the anode, which is consequently consumed and converted into CO_2.

We've given a little detail about these chemical reactions to demonstrate that both require high temperatures, and both release CO_2 as part of the process. In looking for efficiencies in these two processes, a good starting point is to understand the limits to energy requirements for the reactions, and we can do that by turning to the work of Josiah Willard Gibbs, an engineer at Yale University, in the second half of the 19th Century. There is an unbeatable limit to the amount of energy required to heat water to 100°C before making your coffee, and it doesn't matter how much money you offer to inventors, they will never beat this limit. Gibbs showed us that there is a similar limit for extracting metals from ores.

Gibbs examined chemical reactions, such as those that transform metal oxides to pure metal, and showed that they involve an exchange of energy with the external world. Energy may be released during a reaction, as occurs during combustion of fuels or in oxidation, for example when iron rusts: the energy stored in gases and solids after the reaction (the atoms of the fuel or iron bonded to oxygen atoms) is lower than that of the separate fuel or iron and oxygen. Alternatively, energy may be required (absorbed) by a reaction, as happens when pure metals and oxygen are separated (deoxidation, described above), because the energy stored in the separated metals and oxygen is greater than when they were combined. Because oxidation releases energy, it can occur without any external energy input, and this is why metals are found as oxides in nature. Gibbs showed that the energy required to drive the chemical reaction of deoxidation is the absolute minimum energy we could ever use for producing a metal from its oxide. As a result of Gibbs' work, we know that the absolute minimum energy to make steel from ore is 6.7 GJ/tonne and for aluminium is 29.5 GJ/tonne of liquid metal produced[1].

The best technology in use today is able to extract pure aluminium and iron from their oxides using just over double the absolute theoretical minima calculated by Gibbs[2]. In contrast, a typical car operates much less efficiently, at around 10

Ivittuut

Sustainable Materials with both eyes open

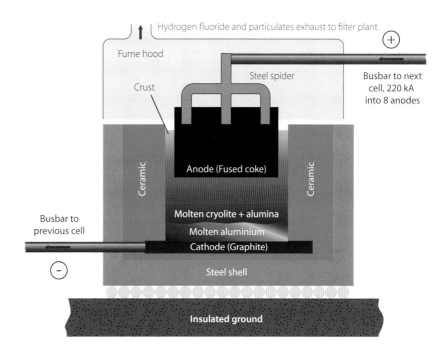

Hydrogen fluoride and particulates exhaust to filter plant

$+$

Fume hood

Steel spider

Busbar to next
cell, 220 kA
into 8 anodes

Crust

Ceramic

Anode (Fused coke)

Ceramic

Molten cryolite + alumina

Busbar to
previous cell

Molten aluminium

Cathode (Graphite)

$-$

Steel shell

Insulated ground

Figure 7.4—**A Hall-Héroult cell**

times the theoretical limit. Achieving the absolute minima predicted by Gibbs would require an impossibly ideal process: mining of ideal pure oxides without any impurities, perfect insulation, and perfect heat re-capture over an infinite area and infinite time. The fact that the ratio of current best technologies to the theoretical limit is so low signifies a remarkable maturity of the two technologies and this is of great importance as we consider the future of both industries.

The difference between average and best practice energy use

Gibbs has given us an invaluable definition of the absolute limit to energy efficiency in making metal from ore, and best practice is around double that limit. In Chapter 9 we'll take a look at attempts to develop novel processes that take best practice even closer to the limit. However, before reviewing these efforts, we can ask a simpler question: what's required to raise the performance of today's average processes to the standards of best practice?

This question has motivated substantial efforts led by our colleague Professor Ernst Worrell in Utrecht, who has over many years published thorough and comprehensive surveys of energy efficiency options for our two metals. Some general strategies that apply to most energy efficiency initiatives include improved process control and better scheduling of operations. Many of the specific options for efficiency in producing metals are about heat, either using less of it or capturing waste heat and re-using it, and this is the topic of the next chapter. In the rest of this section, we'll explore five opportunities revealed by Prof. Worrell's surveys: coke substitution in steel making; more efficient electrolysis for aluminium production; better use of by-products; energy efficient furnaces; efficient motor driven systems. We'll end by assessing the total savings we could achieve with all our options for energy efficiency.

Coke substitution in steel making

Producing coke for steel blast furnaces is both energy intensive and expensive. However, coke can partially be replaced by injecting pulverised coal, natural gas or oil directly into the blast furnace as a fuel. Pulverised coal is cheaper than coke because it can be made of lower quality coal and grinding coal takes little energy. In some countries, oil and natural gas may be a cheaper fuel than coke, and natural gas releases less CO_2 per unit of heat. However, as well as providing heat and acting as a chemical reductant (removing oxygen from iron ore) coke also has a structural role in the blast furnace. Unlike coal, coke remains hard at the high temperatures in the blast furnace, creating an open structure through which the hot gases can flow easily, giving a more efficient reaction. This structural function cannot be replaced by other fuels, so some coke is always required. Trials suggest that up to half of the coke currently used in a blast furnace could be replaced by pulverised coal[3]. Coke substitution, particularly by pulverised coal injection, is already widely applied, but could be increased in the future.

More efficient electrolysis for aluminium production

The key inefficiencies in average primary aluminium production relate to maintaining a constant alumina concentration in the electrolysis cell, removing accumulated gases that increase the electrical resistance of the cell and maintaining operating conditions at their optimal level. Point feeders are increasingly used to add alumina in smaller, more regular amounts around the centre of the cell to help maintain a more constant alumina concentration. Cutting transverse slots into the anodes, facilitates easier removal of the CO_2 generated during the electrolysis reaction. Operating an electrolysis cell can be made more efficient through better computer control of a range of operating parameters, including the temperature, current and electrolyte concentration within the cell.

Better use of by-products

Processes that convert ore or scrap to liquid metal create other by-products, such as gases that could be combusted for energy or used to drive a turbine, and solid slags with both chemical and thermal energy. In steel production, around 80% of the energy released from processes is contained in exhaust gases, and most of this is chemical energy in gases that can be combusted. The hot gases released from coke-making are rich in hydrogen and carbon monoxide, providing as excellent fuel which can be used to run the coke ovens and replace natural gas in other parts of an integrated steel plant. The energy content of the gases from the blast furnace and basic oxygen furnace are dilute compared to traditional fuels, so are typically mixed with natural gas before combustion, and may be used on-site to generate electricity or as a fuel for furnaces in downstream processes such as hot rolling. Blast furnace gas can reach pressures of around two and a half atmospheres and if driven through a top recovery turbine, can generate electricity at an efficiency of around 20%. A different opportunity for efficiency which is already used widely in some countries is to trade solid wastes with other sectors. In particular, blast furnace slag may be granulated and used as a substitute for clinker in cement with no compromise in properties. Cement may have slag contents up to around 85%, giving energy savings up to 2 GJ/t compared to the UK average[4]. A much wider example of this type of trade in by-products, often called industrial symbiosis, is the Kalundborg site in Denmark, which is described further in the box-story.

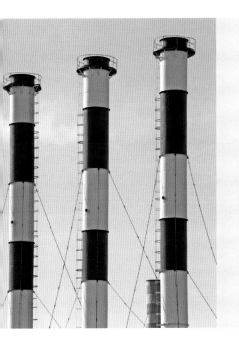

Industrial symbiosis in Kalundborg, Denmark

'Industrial symbiosis' refers to the practice of trading waste between businesses. The hope of such trading is to find mutual benefits to businesses, through cost savings, and to the environment, if the total consumption of resources and generation of waste is reduced.

The most famous example of industrial symbiosis is the Danish industrial park in Kalundborg, where energy, water and by-products are traded between Asnaes power station, Statoil refinery, Novo Nordisk Pharmaceuticals, the municipality of Kalundborg, Lake Tisso and others. For example, cooling water from the refinery is piped to the power plant, where it is treated and used in the plant boiler. After generating steam and electricity, the hot water, may be used for district heating in the town.

These partnerships began in 1959 and continue to develop with little intervention from government or other bodies. Analysis of the trading, particularly of water, showed that the main economic benefit does not come from the revenue generated by selling waste, but from other internal savings such as avoiding expensive treatment of waste water[16].

Energy efficient furnaces

Figure 7.5 shows a continuous process heating up some material. The material is fed in at room temperature, heated within the furnace and, having experienced whatever reaction was required, leaves at a high temperature. In the furnace, fuel is combusted with oxygen, and the material is heated through radiation or by convection of the gases in the furnace. The fuel and oxygen must be heated up to the temperature of the flame as part of the combustion process, and this requires energy, so the available heat is less than the chemical energy in the fuel. Typically, only 30–50% of this chemical energy provides useful heat for the process, and 20–30% preheats air. Most of the remainder is lost in exhaust gases, with other losses including heating the furnace itself, conduction through walls to the environment, hot gases escaping, and through cooling water used to ensure that critical equipment does not over-heat. The options for designing efficient furnaces are well known: burning the correct air-fuel ratio or using pure oxygen rather than air; recovering heat from exhausts; increasing capacity, and operating furnaces continuously to reduce start up energy and losses through walls; using higher performance insulation; reducing air leakage through improved charging and better seals; improving control systems and sensing to reduce heat demand. Using these strategies we can already make very efficient furnaces, achieving heating efficiencies (heat delivered to the material being processed divided by chemical energy in the fuel) close to 70%. However, many existing furnaces in the materials processing industries are old and operate well below this optimum level[5].

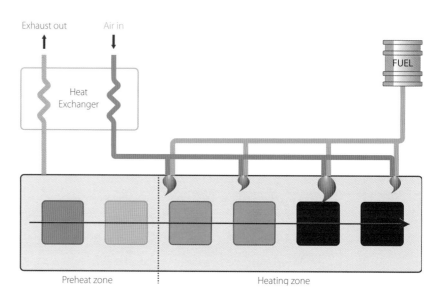

Figure 7.5—**Continuous heating furnace with heat recovery**

Sustainable Materials with both eyes open

For some furnaces, heat loss is actually a requirement to avoid damage to the equipment. In aluminium smelting, heat is deliberately lost to maintain a thermal insulating and protective solid layer of cryolite at the cell walls (liquid cryolite is highly corrosive, particularly for steel). Other low volume batch furnaces are only run intermittently, requiring additional energy to warm up the furnace after each stoppage. The box story below discusses how to use less energy in these cases.

The IEA's analysis of energy efficiency finds that the majority of remaining improvements in the steel industry are in blast furnace improvements and about half of the remaining improvements in the aluminium industry are in smelting improvements, such as better furnace insulation. Efficient furnaces are already a high priority.

Efficient motor driven systems

In industry as a whole, about 60% of electricity is used in motor driven systems[6]. The steel and aluminium industries are both exceptions to this average, due to the intense electrical requirements of electric arc furnaces in secondary steel production and smelting in primary aluminium production. However, we estimate that 19% of all primary energy in making steel products (combining energy required by the steel industry with that for downstream manufacturing) is used in electric motor driven systems and the equivalent figure for aluminium products is about 5%[7].

Minimising heat loss from intermittent furnaces

In small batch furnaces, with frequent cycles of heating and cooling, significant energy is used in each cycle to heat the furnace shell to the operating temperature[17]. The heat input (Q_T) needed to warm up the furnace can be found by multiplying the average temperature of the furnace walls, by the mass (m) and specific heat capacity (c_p) of the wall material (usually steel), using the formula:

$$Q_T = mC_p \left(\frac{T_{inside} + T_{outside}}{2} \right) \qquad\qquad Q_w \approx \frac{k}{w}$$

It takes more energy to heat a thick heavy wall than a thin wall. But this must be balanced against the thermal heat loss through the walls (Q_w), which depends mostly on the wall thickness (w) and thermal conductivity (k) of the insulation material: a thick, well-insulated wall loses less heat. When a furnace is operated continuously, as is the case for most larger furnaces, the heat required to heat up the furnace walls can be ignored.

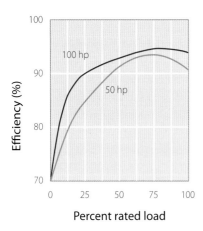

Figure 7.6—**Variation of motor efficiency with varying load**

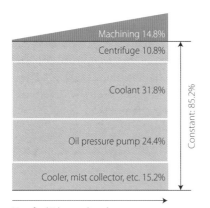

Figure 7.7—**Energy requirements for a machine at Toyota**[18]

Electric motors, at their best, convert electrical energy to mechanical work with nearly perfect efficiency. Conventionally each motor is designed for a particular speed and load, so 'at their best' means that the motor is used at this rating. Figure 7.6 demonstrates firstly that larger motors are usually more efficient than smaller ones, and secondly that motors become inefficient when they are used far below their capacity. The second point arises remarkably often, both because actual demands vary, and because designers specify bigger motors than required, to ensure they don't burn out. However, this inefficiency which is now well known, has led to intense government efforts to promote the use of 'variable speed drives' which improve overall efficiency over a much wider range of loads.

Variable speed drives are well covered in other places[8], but instead we want to think about two other aspects of efficiency related to electric motor driven systems: can we reduce the total amount of work they're asked to do? can we ensure they're only turned on when we need them? The IEA reports that avoiding over-specifying motors, by selecting them according to their actual torque and speed, could save around 20 to 25% of current electricity use. To find out if we can also reduce their specification, we conducted a detailed survey of motor driven systems, used in pumps, fans, forming and machining, handling equipment, compressors and refrigeration. We found that in applications related to pumping, an increase of a quarter in pipe diameter and reduction in pipe-bends would reduce loads by two thirds, and that in materials forming and removing systems, loads could typically be reduced by a half[9].

Figure 7.7 shows an analysis of a machine tool used by Toyota, with the total electrical energy input on the y-axis, and the fraction of the capacity of the machine being used on the x-axis. The graph is very surprising: even when the machine is doing no useful work, it is using 85% of its maximum power. That seems crazy, but occurs because the work of machining, cutting away pieces of metal, is very small compared to the effort of running the machine's cooling, lubrication and material handling systems, yet all of these remain turned on even when the machine is doing no productive work. We've seen similar results for other machine tools[10], which seem to reflect two decisions: sometimes machine designers simply don't think about turning off these 'auxiliary' features of their machines when they're not working, because energy efficiency wasn't part of the design brief given to them; other times, machines have some inertia which requires a start-up or stabilisation period, and if the arrival of work cannot be anticipated, it apparently makes sense to leave all the auxiliary systems running to avoid delay overcoming this inertia. Clearly this could also be addressed by different approaches to design.

Sustainable Materials with both eyes open

We suspect that the really big motors used in the early stages of metals processing, for instance to power the hot rolling mills, are already operated with high efficiency. However, further downstream, in manufacturing and construction, it's likely that there's more opportunity for future efficiency. Through a combination of correct specification, reduced loads in use, and better motor management when not in use, we estimate that we could save 50% of all energy used in electric motors throughout the production chains for steel and aluminium goods. This translates to about 9% of the total energy used for steel products and 2.5% of that for aluminium goods.

Overview of energy efficiency options

Reviewing the five reasons for performance variations in making metal that we've discussed here, the IEA estimate that upgrading all sites to best available technology would save 13% of current emissions for steel, and 12% for aluminium[11]. On top of this we have estimated an additional saving due to improvements in electric motor driven systems of 9% total energy for steel products and 2.5% of that for aluminium goods.

To conclude the section with a small caveat, the efficiency options we've examined here would all lead to energy saving, but one feature of metal production may lead to increased energy intensities. For both steel and aluminium production, significant effort is required to grind and separate the basic oxides from their naturally occurring forms in rocks. As more readily-available ores are mined, we may in future have to exploit less perfect sources with more impurities, leading to an increase in energy requirements. Already, in the aluminium industry, the electrical power needed to produce one tonne of primary aluminium has increased over the last ten years, due to a reduction in the quality of the bauxite available[12].

Recycling as efficiently as possible

We opened this chapter by defining three sub-sections, and in the first of them we described the chemical reactions required to extract liquid steel and aluminium from ores. We need to return to the reactions at the start of this section, because they raise an important question about recycling: when we're melting used metal and mix up a range of alloys with different compositions, can we remove any elements we don't want, or can we only deal with unwanted elements by dilution? It is difficult to remove metallic elements from liquid aluminium so dilution is common. Therefore, the mixed-up melt must be 'downgraded' to the highest grade alloy that can be made with whatever composition we've stirred up. Aluminium casting alloys have a much higher silicon content than wrought alloys, so unseparated aluminium is usually recycled into casting alloys. We saw earlier that aluminium recycling for drinks cans can be achieved within a 'closed loop' but even then the melt is 'sweetened' with at least 5% pure virgin aluminium, to ensure the composition is within required limits. Zinc and tin are common contaminants of steel scrap (zinc is used for galvanising and tin for tin-plating of packaging) but in both cases we have processes that can remove these surface coatings prior to steel melting.

Because it's so difficult to remove unwanted other metals from the melt, and the quality of products made by recycling depends strongly on the separation, it's better to separate different alloys during collection. Both our metal flow Sankey diagrams earlier showed that most recycling of both metals is of scrap generated during production, rather than for post-consumer scrap. This is partly because of the volumes available, but it is also easier to use, because production scrap is generally better sorted. However, in chapter 4 we predicted that future supplies of post-consumer scrap will increase, so separation will become more important if we want to maximise the benefit of recycling. Designers today should plan how their products are to be recycled at the end of their life to avoid degrading quality. Our overall capacity for secondary production must increase significantly, and in turn this gives us a great opportunity both to invest in the most up to date equipment, and to bring the recycling processes closer to where new metal is required. Potentially we may also introduce more sophisticated separation of the waste stream in future, with alloy compositions separated appropriately. Technology already exists to achieve this, but its cost and speed are not commercially attractive.

Recycling involves melting, and then adjusting the composition of the liquid metal. Generally, different types of furnaces are used for the two metals. Most steel is recycled using an electric arc furnace. In this process (which sounds like a Chinese firework display in a submarine), a strong electric current is passed across the scrap, initially causing a lightening storm of sparks, until sufficient metal has melted. The process is attractive because it removes surface contaminants and has proved to be less energy-intensive than other designs. In contrast the challenge in recycling aluminium is that it oxidises rapidly when heated: the relatively pure aluminium atoms will bond with oxygen during melting, unless the oxygen is excluded. We can minimize this oxidation by excluding oxygen from the molten surface, by operating the process in an inert atmosphere. Alternatively, when melting small pieces with a high surface area to volume ratio (such as swarf from aluminium machining) the scrap feed is sunk under the surface of an existing pool of liquid aluminium, to prevent additional contact with oxygen[13]. Aluminium recycling furnaces are typically gas powered, and come in three types. Reverberatory furnaces are used for melting a narrow range of feedstock, for example, scrap with a known composition, by passing a hot stream of combustion gases over the aluminium. Rotary furnaces, which as the name suggests rotate during operation, can be used to melt a wider range of scrap feedstocks and therefore require a greater quantity of flux to mop up impurities. A third type of furnace, the induction furnace, which uses electricity rather than gas, is used for a small proportion of aluminium recycling, and typically only for very clean scrap.

As we saw in chapter 4, it looks as if we will be able to recycle a maximum of 90% of the steel and aluminium that reaches the end of its life. Robert Ayres suggests that achieving this will rely on the development of new separation technologies to remove copper from recycled steel[14]. Improvements in furnace technology may reduce the energy used in recycling metal, and another focus will be technology to separate different types of metal scrap from the waste stream. As steel is magnetic, even small amounts of steel scrap can be separated easily. Aluminium which is not magnetic is currently separated by use of eddy-currents, but this method is imperfect. The key challenges for future aluminium recycling are to increase recovery of small amounts of aluminium, for example, the aluminium foil used in packaging, and separate wrought from cast alloys[15].

Outlook

Existing metal production processes, both from ore and from scrap, are already extremely efficient, because the strong commercial motivation to reduce purchase costs has driven extensive research and development. It will be difficult to invent significantly more efficient chemical reactions, but there are some opportunities to improve furnace design and operation, and potentially the use of electricity to power motor drive systems could be halved. Recycling will become more effective as we separate our waste streams by alloy type.

In the next chapter we'll ask whether we can save energy through better heat management along the production chain. If you're a gas molecule who's been combusted, we can try to use your heat again, but we can't recycle you as gas because, as they might say at the end of an episode of *The Apprentice*, "you're fired!"

Notes

1. Standard chemical exergy (exergy is described fully in chapter 8) values for elements have been recently updated by Rivero and Garfias (2006).

2. Worrell et al. (2008) describe the best practice energy intensity values for selected industrial sectors: 14.7 GJ/t to make cast steel from iron ore (2.2 times the minima); 70.6 GJ/t to make cast aluminium from bauxite (2.4 times the minima). These intensities are direct energy values (i.e. the metered fuel and electricity at the production site), which is a practical minimum equivalent to the case where all electricity is made with renewables or hydro-power. If instead primary energy values are used, assuming an electricity generation and distribution efficiency of 33% raises the cast steel value marginally to 15.9 GJ/t (2.4 times the minima), but has a more dramatic effect on the electricity intensive making of cast aluminium, raising the value to 174 GJ/t (5.9 times the minima). However, hydro-electric plants contribute 50% of the electricity for aluminium smelting (IEA 2009), and using the IEA methodology (IEA 2010c) of counting hydropower as the gross electricity production, gives a more realistic primary energy intensity of 124 GJ/t (4.2 times the minima).

3. Pulverised coal trials are described in IEA (2008a).

4. Hammond et al. (2011) have surveyed the UK materials industries to determine the average and best practice embodied energy and carbon emissions for a range of building materials with results periodically updated in their 'Inventory of Carbon and Energy'.

5. Based on the efficiency savings identified as part of the US Department of Energy's Industrial Technologies Program and reported in US DOE (2007), which has worked with industry to identify and implement best practices for process heating furnaces.

Efficient motor driven systems

6. From IEA (2009) page 191, electric motor drives are used extensively in industry and it is estimated that they account for 30% of all electricity use.

7. USDOE (2004) reports a breakdown for fuel/electricity use in the steel industry – roughly 60% fuel and 40% primary energy in the form of electricity. Subtracting electric arc furnace consumption, and taking 60% of the remainder as being used in motors (IEA (2009)), approximately 19% of energy use in the supply chain for steel products is in electric motors. Using a similar method with a breakdown of 80% primary electricity in aluminium production from Worrell et al. (2008) and subtracting smelting, we find 6% of energy use in the supply chain for aluminium products is in electric motors.

8. International standards exist for defining the efficiency class of three-phase motors for example IEC 60034-30:2008 described in CEMEP (2011).

9. Energy savings through more accurate motor specification are detailed in IEA (2009). The calculation of further energy savings from motor load reduction are described in Cullen et al. (2011).

10. For example, Avram & Xirouchakis (2011) find the highest energy is consumed when a milling machine is idle and Devoldere et al.

(2007) find 65% of the energy consumption of a press brake is used when it is not producing parts.

11. These numbers come from the IEA's (2009) report on Energy Technology Transitions for Industry. The percentages are calculated compared to 2008 direct and indirect emissions for steel (2.9Gt CO2) and 2007 emissions for aluminium (360Mt CO2). The direct and indirect emissions values do not include emissions for product fabrication, as we couldn't find any information on energy efficiency improvements in fabrication operations. If the fabrication emissions had been included, the percentage emissions reductions would be even smaller.

12. The lowest electricity intensity for primary aluminium production was 15,100 kWh/tonne in 2002, but since then, the electricity intensity has been higher. IAI (2011b) report the electricity intensity in 2008 as 15,400 kWh/t.

13. Boin and Bertram (2005) give metal yields for aluminium scrap melting ranging from 70% for foil to 95% for building scrap.

14. Ayres (2006) claims that recycling rates for steel, aluminium, and copper will approach 90% once a process for removing trace contaminants is developed.

15. In the USA, the DOE is supporting research into advanced sorting and recycling technologies for aluminium, particularly in anticipation of an increase in the amount of wrought aluminium used in vehicles. Two technologies being investigated are: laser-induced breakdown spectroscopy to separate wrought and cast scrap, which uses lasers to vaporise a small amount of aluminium so that the chemical composition can be measured; selective etching plus colour sorting to separate different wrought alloy grades, where different categories of wrought aluminium turn a different shade (bright, gray or dark), when etched with a chemical (Secat, 2005).

Box Stories, Figures and Tables

16. Energy use breakdown based on data collected by Toyota Motor Corporation and published by Gutowski et al. (2005).

17. This theoretical analysis of furnaces is reported in more detail in Ashby (2009).

18. Further details of Kalundborg are given by Jacobsen (2006).

8 Opportunities for capturing heat

and ways to use it

Part of the energy required to convert ores to metals is required to drive chemical reactions, but most of the rest is heat used to melt or soften the metal and to allow diffusion. Virtually all of this heat is lost to air. It sounds as if we should try to capture this heat, either for re-use within the same process, or by cascading it through other industrial processes which require heat at a lower temperature. What's the opportunity to achieve this?

Lego® Bricks

In this chapter we're going to play with Lego blocks—but it's a special type of Lego we've invented: each block represents a process in the long chain of processes required to convert ores into final steel and aluminium goods. Metal in some form flows through each block, being upgraded as it passes. There are also other inputs to each block, and other by-products are exhausted. We could include a long list of these other inputs and exhausts—money, energy, lubricants, labour, chemicals and so on—but the only other inputs and exhausts we'll consider here are heat energy. Armed with the right box of blocks, we can now build a model of the whole connected set of processes that interest us. In the last chapter, we asked whether we could make any individual block more efficient. In the next one we're going to explore whether we may in the future invent any new blocks. In this chapter our concern is about how they're connected. If we connected our blocks together in a different way, could we save significant energy? The processes in use today have been developed independently, so would it make a big difference if we were allowed to design them all in one go? For example, we visited a steel factory in the North of England and watched red hot metal at around 800°C being rolled, but then left to cool in air, even though we knew it would be reheated later on. In Lancashire we saw aluminium cans being melted and poured into ingots which cooled in air, so they could be shipped to Dusseldorf where they are reheated for re-rolling. In Wales we saw scrap steel recycled in an electric arc furnace and poured into long thin 'blooms', then transported two miles, and re-heated prior to rolling. In each case it looks as if heat energy could be saved if we (had an unlimited budget and) could reconfigure our processes. So let's play with Lego.

Temperature histories for case study products

If every component made of steel or aluminium is different, then every product must be made using a different set of processes, which makes it a little difficult to generalise in our search for opportunities to move Lego blocks around. The only way we can begin the search is to look for representative case studies that will illustrate the key points. We've done that, and Figure 8.3 on the next page introduces our nine case study parts, split between steel and aluminium, and with a range of different geometries and process routes.

To understand the requirements for heat energy in making these parts, we've talked to all the companies involved in making them—along the journey from ore to finished part—to obtain their temperature histories, and we've shown these in the Figures 8.1 and 8.2. This data is as comprehensive as we can manage—although different manufacturers might use slightly different temperature cycles

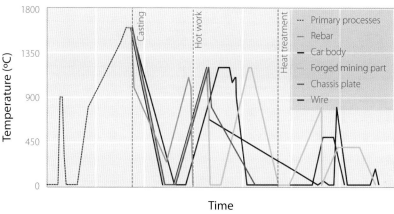

Figure 8.1—**Time/temperature histories for steel products**

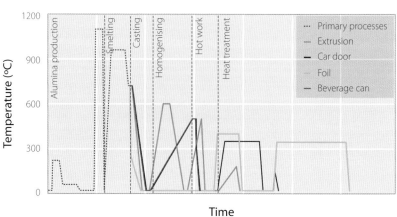

Figure 8.2—**Time/temperature histories for aluminium products**

Sustainable Materials with both eyes open

(a cycle here is a single peak on the graph—heating and cooling) for the same product. You can see that we've been a little cavalier with the time axis—because our primary concern is about the peak temperature in each cycle, rather than its duration. On each graph the lines are all identical up to the point of casting—because they all require the same primary processes, apart from the need to add different alloying elements to create the right composition for each part, and this doesn't influence the temperature. The lines diverge from casting onwards.

Forged mining part ●

Forging steel allows complex, high strength parts to be produced. A billet is softened by heating and compressed between shaped dies to achieve the desired geometry. A heat treatment consisting of quenching and tempering gives a strong and tough product.

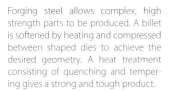

Car body ● ●

In both steel and aluminium, car doors have exacting requirements for both surface quality and formability. The surface must be free of defects in casting and quality is improved through subsequent hot and cold rolling stages

Rebar ●

Steel rebar is cast as square billets which are hot rolled to the desired bar diameter. Strength and ductility required are imparted by quenching and self-tempering, where the outer surface is cooled rapidly to form a brittle high strength microstructure, and tempered by the still-hot core to restore ductility.

Beverage can ●

Aluminium beverage can bodies require a formable sheet for drawing to the can shape, high strength to reduce sheet thickness and material costs, and a high surface quality for aesthetics. Hot and cold rolling processes give uniform formability, while cold rolling also work hardens the material to increase strength.

Wire ●

Steel wire has very high strength and ductility along its length. Cast billets are hot rolled to make wire rod, with the properties achieved by controlled cooling followed by work hardening as the rod is drawn to make wire.

Foil ●

Aluminium sheet is continuously cast and cold rolled through multiple passes. Annealing heat treatments are necessary to restore ductility so that large reductions in thickness can be achieved.

Heavy machinery chassis plate ●

Plate steel is cast as thick slabs and hot rolled to achieve the desired strength. The plates are cut, bent and/or welded during fabrication to produce the finished chassis part.

Extruded window frame ●

Complicated profiles are produced by extruding aluminium billets through a shaped die. An age hardening heat treatment increases strength.

● Steel parts   ● Aluminium parts

Figure 8.3—**Case design products**

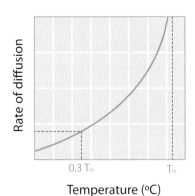

y-axis: Rate of diffusion
x-axis: Temperature (ºC)
(markers: 0.3 Tₘ, Tₘ)

Figure 8.4—**Effect of temperature on rate of diffusion**

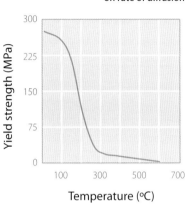

y-axis: Yield strength (MPa) — 0, 75, 150, 225, 300
x-axis: Temperature (ºC) — 100, 300, 500, 700

Figure 8.5—**Effect of temperature on yield strength of an aluminium alloy (AA6061-T6)**

We'll explore the processes used to make these parts in a moment, but let's first check that the peak temperatures in the two cycles make sense. At the Atomic Club in chapter 5, we saw that we need energy for three reasons when making metals: to drive chemical reactions, to allow diffusion, and to soften or melt the metal so that forming to shape is easier. In the last chapter we saw that the chemical reactions required to release metals from their ores occur more rapidly above their melting temperatures which for steel and aluminium alloys are around 1500°C and 660°C respectively. Diffusion, in which atoms move within the lattice of the solid metal, occurs at a rate related to temperature, and may occur even at room temperature. However the rate increases dramatically as the temperature approaches the melting point as the graph to the side shows. Softening, the reduction in the strength of the metal with temperature, evolves in the manner shown in the second graph to the side. In this case, a useful reduction in strength, say to 10% of the cold value, occurs at around 1200°C for steel and 550°C for aluminium. Our two temperature history graphs for our case study products show that casting and the primary production processes occur above the melting temperature, and subsequent processes all occur at a temperature that allows significant diffusion, with higher temperatures when deformation is required—so the graphs tie up with our understanding of why heat is required.

Now that we understand their temperature requirements, we can build our Lego models of the process chains for the case study products, and on the next page we've shown just two of them—for a car door (in steel) and a window frame (in aluminium). These diagrams allow us to estimate the heat energy inputs to the blocks. By looking at the histories and checking with the companies who do the processing, we can also show the heat energy discarded.

On adding up the energy flows into the two chains, we can see that making the car door requires 700 MJ, while making the window frame requires 4880 MJ. Most of this energy is 'lost', in the form of heat energy discarded in exhausts, radiated through walls, and as hot metal cools in air. We know that energy is neither created nor destroyed, so the 'lost' energy cannot really be lost. Bearing this in mind, how much of this discarded energy could we capture and re-use, to save on the inputs?

Sustainable Materials with both eyes open

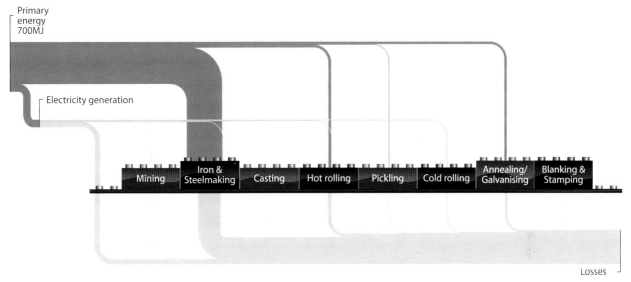

Figure 8.6—**Energy used in steel car door production**

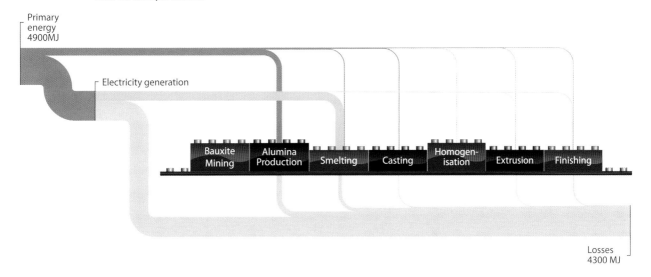

Figure 8.7—**Energy used in aluminium window frame production**

Exergy flows for the whole of steel and aluminium component production

100 litres at +5°C

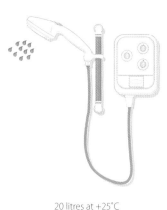

20 litres at +25°C

Figure 8.8—**Both the bath and the shower require the same energy, but we'd rather have the hot shower!**

It looks as if we've just made a typing error in the title. "Exergy"? Surely we meant "energy"? No, we did mean it, but "exergy", a word invented by the splendidly named Zoran Rant of Slovenia—is a largely unfamiliar word, but a very important one for us now. To find out why, we'll borrow an anecdote from our colleague Dr Rob Miller, who teaches thermodynamics in our department:

Let's imagine you're in the pub, and a dodgy character in an old coat sidles up to you and says "I've got a few megajoules of heat energy in my van round the back—are you interested?" Naturally you are—we're all concerned about the price of heating our homes, and keen for a good deal when some spare energy drops off the back of a lorry, know wot I mean? But your first reaction to the offer should not be "how much?" That way lies ruin. The right first question is "what's its temperature?" You should be ready to pay more for the same number of megajoules, if they're at a higher temperature.

The heat energy in a smaller mass of material at high temperatures is more valuable than the same energy in a larger mass of material at lower temperature. (Figure 8.8 illustrates this with a bath-time example of exergy).This is because the higher temperature energy can be used for heating or to generate other useful forms of energy, such as movement. In contrast the lower temperature energy cannot usefully be transformed or exchanged.

Heat is our main concern in this chapter, but the other forms of energy of interest when transforming metal ores into products are:

• chemical energy that may be released during combustion of fuels;

• electrical energy in electrical currents used to drive aluminium smelting as well as the motors and pumps used in most industrial equipment;

• mechanical energy contained in moving objects such as the rolls in rolling mills.

Could we 'capture' heat from the exhaust gases of furnaces, or from the hot metals we produce, and use it—either at a lower temperature, or by converting it to one of these three forms?

Let's imagine we wanted to use the few megajoules of heat on offer in the pub to drive a train: the question of whether we can convert heat energy into mechanical energy depends on the temperature of the heat. We cannot avoid this, and we've known about it since Nicolas Léonard Sadi Carnot, after his release from the French army on Napoleon's final defeat in 1815 (paving the way for the eventual accession of his nephew Napoleon III who's getting ready to open our next chapter), wrote his 1824 book *Reflections on the motive power of fire*. Carnot showed that the maximum work you can obtain from heat depends on the ratio $(T_1 - T_2)/T_1$ where T_1 is the (absolute) temperature of the heat supplied, and T_2 is the temperature of the operating environment. We can't do much about T_2, so the maximum work depends on the temperature of our supply of heat, and therefore hotter is better.

So, although it cannot be created or destroyed, not all energy is equal: electrical energy can be used for heating or moving, chemical energy may be used to generate heat or electrical energy, and hotter heat energy is more useful than colder heat energy. Zoran Rant's term "exergy" allows us to sort this out. Exergy is defined to be the maximum useful energy we can extract from some source of energy[1]. In effect, therefore, we should be using exergy in every discussion of efficiency we ever have—we don't want energy efficient homes, we want them to be 'exergy efficient' because if we can use fuel that burns at a lower temperature to heat our living rooms, we can save the most precious high temperature fuels for where they're really needed. For this reason, our first Sankey diagram in chapter 2 showing the global transformation of energy sources into useful services was drawn using units of exergy—the maximum work that could be obtained from each energy source feeding our system.

And we can connect our interest in exergy in this chapter to the work of Gibbs, whom we met in the previous chapter. Gibbs explored the fundamental limits to energy requirements for chemical transformations from one compound to another, now known as the Gibbs free energy. More recently, Jan Szargut a Polish engineer, has related Gibbs free energy to a list of compounds present in the environment to determine the standard chemical exergy of compounds. Chemical and physical (heat) exergies are happily related and consistent: the chemical exergy is a measure of the work required to form compounds from their natural state by separating and reforming atomic bonds; the physical exergy is a measure of how much work some heat at a given temperature can do while cooling to ambient temperatures.

Unlike energy, exergy is not conserved. Take for example water falling over a waterfall, potential energy is converted firstly to kinetic energy and later to thermal energy. Energy is conserved throughout. Yet at the bottom of the falls we no longer have the option of installing a water wheel to extract useful energy—the energy has been degraded to a lower quality and we have "lost" some exergy. Exercising exhausts excellent exergy to external extremes? Exactly!

So exergy is the right measure of our heat flows in making steel and aluminium components, and we can now return to our Lego models of the two process chains from earlier. Instead of showing mass and energy flows as before, the two revised Lego models in Figures 8.9 and 8.10 show exergy flows: the chemical exergy of the metal, the physical exergy inputs and outputs to each Lego block, and the lost exergy from each process. High temperature upstream processes, such as iron-making in a blast furnace or aluminium smelting, have recoverable exergy outputs in the form of combustible gases and hot flows of metal and exhausts. These outputs potentially could provide a useful service. For example hot exhausts can be used to preheat air coming into the process. In contrast, low temperature downstream processes have little or no recoverable exergy.

In order to introduce the idea of exergy flow we've so far concentrated on two of our case study products. However, in Part I of the book, we assembled enough

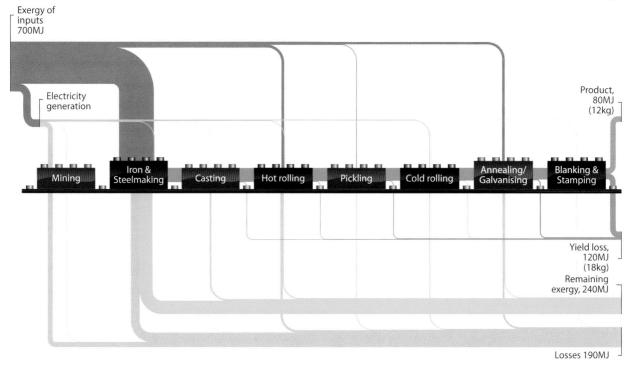

Figure 8.9—**Exergy flow in steel car door production**

Sustainable Materials with both eyes open

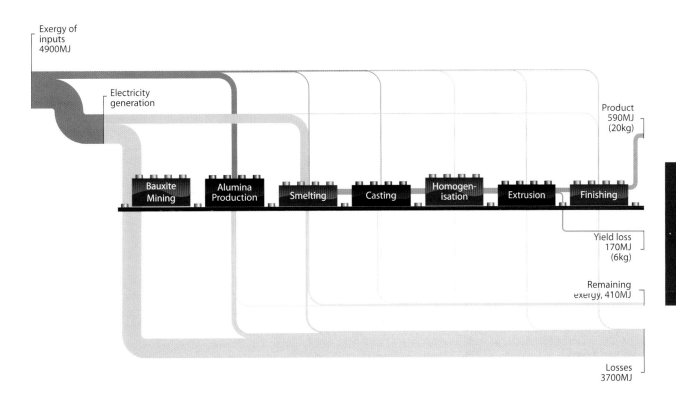

Exergy of
inputs
4900MJ

Electricity
generation

Bauxite
Mining

Alumina
Production

Smelting

Casting

Homogen-
isation

Extrusion

Finishing

Product
590MJ
(20kg)

Yield loss
170MJ
(6kg)

Remaining
exergy, 410MJ

Losses
3700MJ

Figure 8.10—**Exergy flow in aluminium window frame production**

information to make an estimate of the exergy flows of the whole global process of making steel and aluminium components, and these are shown in Figures 8.11 and 8.12. The chemical exergy flow looks very similar to our earlier metal flow Sankey diagrams, because once the liquid metal has been extracted from ore, its chemical exergy hardly changes as the geometry changes. No further chemical reactions are involved. In addition to this flow of chemical exergy, we can also see the exergy flows associated with fuel and electricity use throughout the process. Had we shown energy flows rather than exergy flows, while we could see energy being discarded from processes we wouldn't be able to 'value' it—because we could do little with it if it was at low temperature. Instead, these two diagrams show exergy flows so the exergy discarded is, or at least could be, recovered to do useful work. We can see that around 10% of the output exergy in steel and aluminium is recoverable. This is an upper estimate based on the temperatures of the flows just as they leave the processes. Some of this output exergy is already recovered, as we'll see later in this chapter. The remainder of the exergy input is lost: diluted to useless low grade heat, dissipated through furnace walls and destroyed by the chemical reactions themselves.

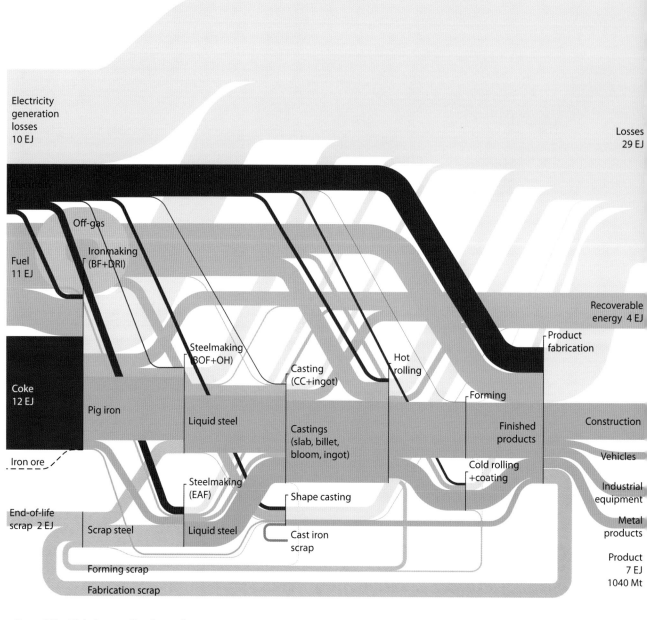

Electricity
generation
losses
10 EJ

Losses
29 EJ

Electricity

Off-gas

Fuel
11 EJ

Ironmaking
(BF+DRI)

Recoverable
energy 4 EJ

Product
fabrication

Steelmaking
(BOF+OH)

Casting
(CC+ingot)

Hot
rolling

Coke
12 EJ

Forming

Pig iron

Liquid steel

Castings
(slab, billet,
bloom, ingot)

Finished
products

Construction

Iron ore

Cold rolling
+coating

Vehicles

Steelmaking
(EAF)

Shape casting

Industrial
equipment

End-of-life
scrap 2 EJ

Scrap steel

Liquid steel

Cast iron
scrap

Metal
products

Forming scrap

Product
7 EJ
1040 Mt

Fabrication scrap

Figure 8.11—**Global exergy flow for steel**

The key message of these two diagrams of exergy flows is that energy used in the downstream part of the process, supplied as electricity, does work and is converted to low temperature heat with which we can do very little. However, the energy lost in the earlier part of the supply chain as heat at higher temperatures has significant remaining exergy value—and we'd like to exploit it.

Sustainable Materials with both eyes open

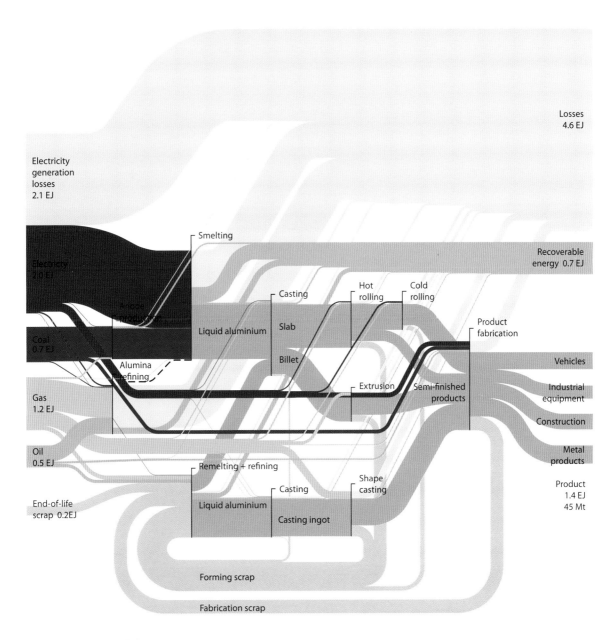

Figure 8.12—**Global exergy flow for aluminium**

Labels within figure: Losses 4.6 EJ; Electricity generation losses 2.1 EJ; Electricity 2.0 EJ; Coal 0.7 EJ; Gas 1.2 EJ; Oil 0.5 EJ; End-of-life scrap 0.2 EJ; Smelting; Anode production; Alumina refining; Casting; Hot rolling; Cold rolling; Liquid aluminium; Slab; Billet; Extrusion; Product fabrication; Semi-finished products; Recoverable energy 0.7 EJ; Vehicles; Industrial equipment; Construction; Metal products; Product 1.4 EJ 45 Mt; Remelting + refining; Casting; Shape casting; Liquid aluminium; Casting ingot; Forming scrap; Fabrication scrap

So our use of exergy has revealed two opportunities: if we can cut out thermal cycles in the processing of our components, we can reduce the need for exergy input; where we're discarding heat at higher temperatures, we are also discarding useful exergy. The next two sections explore whether we can reduce the number of thermal cycles, or we can recapture those lost exergy streams?

Cutting out thermal cycles

Ideally we would make all steel and aluminium products with just one well controlled thermal cycle: we'd heat up ores to extract liquid metal, adjust the composition of the liquid, cast it, deform it to shape and provide time for required diffusion processes, so that by the time the metal returned to ambient temperature it was perfectly ready for use. The only immutable barrier to this ideal is that some metallurgical treatments depend on a second thermal cycle. For example, the processes of age hardening of aluminium alloys and tempering steel require high temperatures for diffusion but must occur after quenching (rapid cooling) to a lower temperature. Similarly, heat treatments such as annealing must be carried out after cold deformation to restore ductility to the metal and allow forming. Even in this case, the thermal cycle need not be as deep as in the graphs we showed for our case study products—if diffusion largely stops below one third of the melting temperature, we don't need to cool as far as ambient temperatures.

Even in cases where we need a second thermal cycle, we're still using more thermal cycles than absolutely necessary, and there are three good reasons for this: we may not have all the required equipment in the right place; it may be difficult to co-ordinate the flow of metal through all the appropriate equipment at the right time to catch the right temperature; some processes must be operated at ambient temperatures. We'll investigate these through a few examples of process innovation.

In early steelmaking practice, the Bessemer process, or subsequently Robert Durrer's basic oxygen process, occurred in a separate thermal cycle from the blast furnace. This was clearly costly, so all modern steelmaking processes are coupled: the pig iron from the blast furnace is transferred as a liquid to the basic oxygen furnace to avoid the extra thermal cycle. However, aluminium smelting in the Hall-Héroult process uses a lot of electricity, so production sites have traditionally been located near to sources of cheap electricity. These locations may be far distant from the next process, so the aluminium is cast as 100% pure aluminium ingots at the smelter, transported to the site where casting will occur, and then re-melted. Around 25% of the world's aluminium is re-melted in this way, for no metallurgical benefit—just because the equipment is in different locations. At a smaller scale, as we've already seen, aluminium recycling always involves 'sweetening' with pure ingots, and similarly pig iron is charged as a solid into electric arc furnaces. In both cases there is no benefit in starting from solid rather than liquid metal, and energy would be saved by avoiding remelting if the recycling equipment could be co-located and co-ordinated with the primary liquid metal processes.

The next opportunity to cut out a thermal cycle occurs between casting and hot rolling. We've seen in our Sankey diagrams of metal flow that most metal is rolled, both to control its geometry and to break up the grain structure created by casting. In the past in both steel and aluminium production, the liquid metal was cast as an ingot and cooled, and then re-heated prior to hot rolling. The steel industry has begun to move away from this practice. Instead of casting in ingots, steel is cast in longer thinner strips, using "continuous casters". This has the double advantage of allowing faster cooling rates for the liquid metal, and reducing the total amount of deformation required in subsequent rolling. The output of these continuous casters is cut into plates, and without cooling is immediately given some re-heating ready for rolling; this is known as hot charging, and obviously saves the energy required to cool and reheat the cast material. A recent innovation in Italy, described in our box story, one step beyond this hot-charging, connects

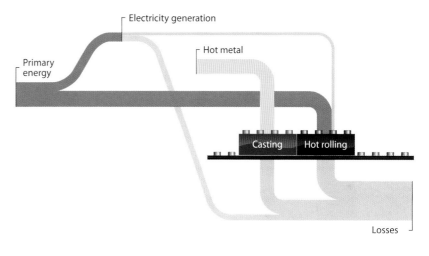

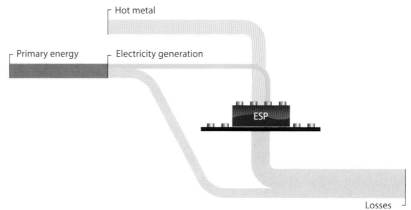

Figure 8.13—**Comparison of Arvedi Endless Strip Production with separate casting and hot rolling steps**

the continuous caster directly to the hot rolling line for production of steel strip. This process has therefore cut out the thermal cycle between casting and hot rolling, as shown in the Lego-block model of Figure 8.13, and as a result reduced total requirements for energy input.

In the aluminium industry, around 30% of the world's sheet and foil products (15% of all aluminium products) are made without hot rolling, by twin-roll casting. The box story on the next page explains the process and outlines the benefits. However, the process is most applicable to nearly pure alloys such as foil, because the lower alloy content gives a smaller freezing range and also because downstream processing is not as critical for pure alloys. Directly cast strip is more susceptible to surface defects such as porosity and 'surface bleeds', where the liquid metal breaks through the thin solidified surface. These defects occur due to the difficulty of maintaining consistent solidification with rapid cooling and unlike conventional casting of thick slabs, after twin-roll casting there is little opportunity for removing the surface layer or rolling. In the future, twin roll casting may extend to low alloy content, heat treatable aluminium products (perhaps inner panels for car bodies) and microalloyed steel products, removing the thermal cycle involved in hot rolling and saving 2-3 GJ/t.

Arvedi Endless Strip Production[7]

Thin slab casting technologies link the caster and rolling mill via a soaking furnace, where the temperature of the slab is homogenised and the production of the melt shop and rolling mill can be separated for easier scheduling. The heat retained from casting reduces the energy input in reheating for hot rolling. However, the largest energy savings are claimed by the Arvedi 'Endless Strip Production' (ESP) process operating in Cremona in Italy, where the cast slab is fed directly into the integrated rolling mill to produce an endless strip.

This process has a fast casting speed to achieve high productivity through the single line, liquid core reduction and direct high reduction at caster exit to improve internal quality, and inline induction heating for precise control of temperature.

A wide range of products may be cast and rolled through ESP, with energy savings of 1.25GJ/t compared to reheating strip from cold. Additional benefits include reduced formation of scale on the metal surface due to the metal spending shorter time at high temperatures, more uniform coils as the entire strip undergoes an identical temperature and deformation history, and lower thicknesses than can be economically achieved by conventional processes.

Most aluminium (the remaining 85% of global production) is not twin-roll cast, but cast into large ingots, typically around 2m wide, 0.5m thick and 8m long. Because the ingots are so large, they solidify gradually from surface to centre, so the composition of the resulting metal changes through the thickness. The fast cooling rate creates a different microstructure and alloy concentration at the surfaces, so every face of the cast ingot must be removed or scalped. To allow scalping, the ingot must be cooled to ambient temperature because we don't yet have cutters that operate at hotter temperatures. This is expensive because the next process, hot rolling, operates at high temperature, so we have added an extra thermal cycle.

Twin roll casting: liquid metal to strip in one process

Twin roll casting is the most widespread method of continuously casting thin strips in both aluminium and steel. Liquid metal is fed between two cooled counter-rotating rolls, with solidification occurring on contact with the roll surfaces. Two shells form and grow towards the roll pinch, where they are fused into sheet by a combination of heat and pressure. Typical thicknesses are 2–4mm in steel and 4–8mm in aluminium. The process was originally proposed by Henry Bessemer and first commercialised by Joseph Hunter in the 1950's for casting aluminium strips. Today, aluminium twin roll casters are used to produce more than 30% of all aluminium sheet and foil products. The process works best with a short freezing range

(and therefore low alloy content), so is mainly used to make non-heat treatable alloys.

Steel strip casting has taken longer to develop due to the higher required process temperatures, but several plants worldwide have demonstrated the process for low carbon and microalloyed steels[5]. Twin roll casting has demonstrated large energy savings relative to conventional routes, but there are still practical difficulties in achieving a high quality and consistent surface finish and in improving the lifetime of key components, particularly the casting rolls and liquid metal containment.

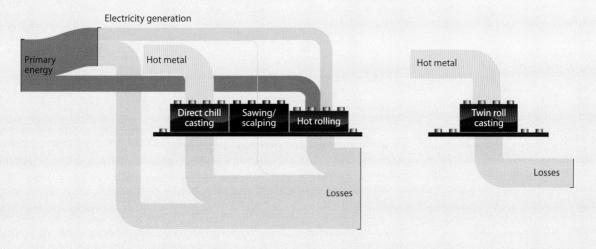

After casting and hot deformation, the remaining thermal cycles in our case study products are required for heat treatments. Various innovations have aimed to reduce the need for these cycles, particularly by integrating a heat treatment into the period of cooling occurring after hot deformation. For the steel chassis plate and the forged mining part among our cast studies, the steel is typically quenched (rapidly cooled to freeze it into a strong but brittle crystal form called martensite) and then reheated for tempering (where diffusion allows some rearrangement of the atoms in the martensite to increase its ductility and toughness). In a clever innovation, in producing reinforcement bars, quenching and tempering take place in line with the rolling mill: the surface of the hot rolled bar is quenched by a water spray, to create martensite at the surface of the bar. Sufficient heat remains in the core of the bar that its temperature averages out to allow tempering. This quench and self-tempering process could save about 1-1.5 GJ/t and is theoretically possible in all cases, although it may be difficult to achieve in some forgings where thermal stresses can cause distortion and cracking.

We've seen that it is possible to cut out most thermal cycles as we move towards the ideal of only having a single thermal cycle, but many practical limits remain. There's also a clear commercial limit: it is easiest to create a single thermal cycle process for one particular product—one geometry of one alloy made in high volume. But the reality of customer needs denies this ambition. When production chains must produce a wide variety of different products, it is more difficult to co-ordinate them efficiently. However 'shorter' production chains are possible, and with the energy savings that may be made we should do all we can to implement them.

Recovering and exchanging heat

Having looked at cutting out thermal cycles, what about using the heat discarded from the various processes: can we exchange heat between one process and another? If we don't exchange it, can we do anything else with the heat?

Heat exchangers are familiar in daily life. The radiator in our car (at the front, where it experiences maximum air flow) exchanges heat between the hot water circulating round the car engine and the outside air. In turn the hot engine exchanges heat with the cooler water leaving the radiator in order to cool the engine. The fins at the back of our refrigerator exchange heat from the inside of the fridge with the air in the kitchen. And the radiator that warms our living room exchanges heat from the hot boiler with the cooler air in the room.

The amount of energy transferred by a heat exchanger depends on its area (the larger the better), the materials between which heat is transferred (liquid to liquid or gas to gas transfer is generally better, and solid to gas or gas to solid worse), and the temperature difference across them (the smaller the better). That last feature causes us a problem if we try to capture and reuse heat in steel and aluminium making: we can transfer most energy when there's a small temperature difference, but if we want to transfer the heat energy quickly (and therefore economically) then we need a large temperature difference. So we must find a compromise between quick and efficient heat recovery.

How effectively can we transfer heat between a hot gas or solid and a cool solid? Figures 8.14 and 8.15 show the 'recoverable exergy' from our earlier Sankey diagrams of global exergy flow and our options for recovering heat energy to provide a useful service.

The hot output flows are in the form of exhaust gases, cooling liquids, waste by-products (typically granulated solids) and the metal itself which is solid. In steel processing, the exergy in off-gases dominates, containing approximately 80% of the recoverable exergy of the outputs. In aluminium processes, the heat lost through pot walls while smelting is most significant despite being at a relatively low temperature of around 250°C. The most common way to recover heat is to use it to preheat inputs to furnaces (either air, fuel, or the material to be charged to the furnace and heated) or to generate electricity. These may be combined with cascading heat recovery (where heat recovered is used at high temperature first and then subsequently in lower temperature processes) for further savings.

The heat in exhaust gases is transferred to air or fuel by recuperators or regenerators. Regenerators are more suitable for higher temperature and dirtier applications as they are less susceptible to corrosion and dirt. Incoming (solid) material may also be preheated through direct contact with exhaust gases, for example through aluminium stack melters, or with the Consteel® process described in the box story on the next page. Exploiting these energy savings requires investment in a container or conveyor for preheating, and the preheat temperature must be controlled to avoid creation of harmful volatile organic compounds from dirty scrap. Preheating can increase furnace productivity and may reduce metal losses by trapping dust particles from exhaust gases and reintroducing them to the melt.

We've looked so far for opportunities to capture heat and re-use it within the same industry, but potentially we could exchange heat between different industries. This book is primarily concerned with five key materials, and like

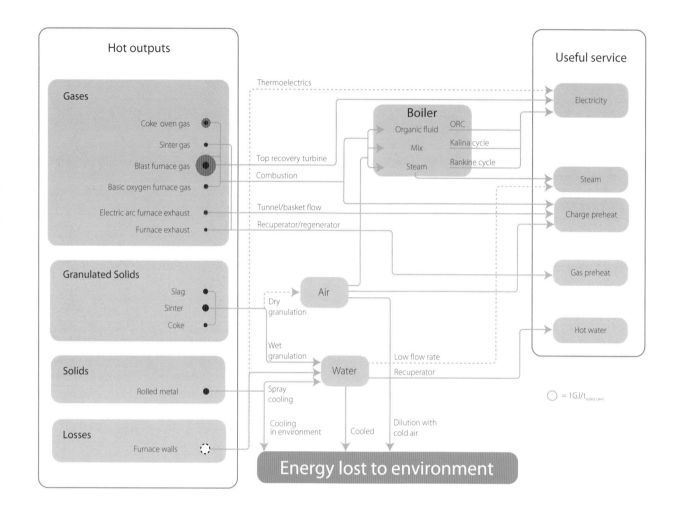

Figure 8.14—**Exergy available in outputs from steel production and possible paths for waste heat recovery**

steel and aluminium, cement requires very high temperatures (around 1450°C for clinker production), but the paper industry requires heat at around 150-200°C to evaporate water from wet pulp. Plastics manufacture also operates at lower temperatures (most thermoplastics melt under 200°C). In Oxelösund and Luleå in Sweden waste industrial heat is used to warm neighbouring houses[2], and we've encountered a pilot project looking at the use of waste exhaust gases to grow algae symbiotically with steel production, where the algae also sequester a small fraction of CO_2[3]. So, if we were given a free hand (and a huge budget) could we build an integrated materials processing facility sharing heat among several industries, as the industries in Kalundborg, described in the last chapter, share by-products? Integrated thermal design is common in the chemicals industries, where most heat transfer is from liquid to liquid, the most efficient mode for heat exchange. A

Sustainable Materials with both eyes open

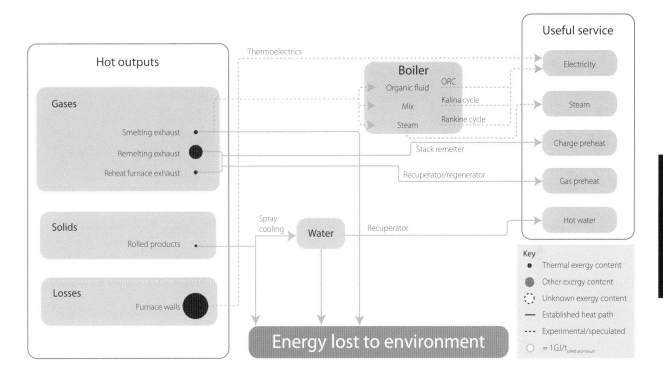

technique called 'Pinch analysis' is often used to optimise such designs. The box story contains some details of pinch analysis, and we anticipate that analysis of a wider set of materials processing industries could reveal new opportunities for heat exchange.

Finally, could we develop a heat recovery technology to exploit the heat in solid hot metal? This could be possible with radiant heat transfer to boil a fluid, by preheating air using convective heat transfer or by conducting heat away from the solid surface, for example in heat pipes. Unfortunately, although our chart shows significant exergy value in the processed metals, in practice recovering it is difficult. Effective heat transfer requires high contact pressures, which might damage product surfaces. Allowing the metal to cool more slowly to permit heat exchange would allow the growth of unwanted surface oxide layers and lead to larger than required grain sizes.

In this section we've seen that while there is significant exergy available in the exhaust gases, by-products, and processed materials of both the steel and aluminium industries, it is difficult to exploit, mainly because it is in gases or solids and we would like to transfer it to incoming solids. As a result existing practice is mainly focused on heat exchange between hot and cold gases or on the use of exhaust gas for pre-heating scrap.

Using waste heat to generate electricity

As well as heat exchange, it's also possible to generate electricity with waste heat or novel thermo-electric cells, and as electricity generation itself discards waste heat, could we usefully combine it with our other processes?

In modern power stations, the turbines are driven with steam at 500°C and a pressure of around 30 atmospheres. Blast furnace gas cannot create these temperatures or pressures, but recent research has shown that it can drive turbines via steam from liquids such as benzene or ammonia instead of water. A related development has shown that blast furnace slag can be cooled with air, rather than water, and the resulting hot air stream can also be used to heat a working fluid.

Thermoelectric conversion offers a different approach to generating electricity directly from heat with a solid state semiconductor converting heat flow into electrical power. To date, commercial thermoelectric devices have low efficiencies, around 5%, and are very expensive. However, these efficiencies may increase, and this approach may be able to use waste heat that cannot be exploited by any other

Energy recovery from EAF exhaust gases by Consteel®[8]

The Consteel® electric arc furnace (EAF) directs hot exhaust gas over an incoming conveyor of scrap in an insulated tunnel. This warms the incoming scrap to around 300-400°C through a combination of heat transfer and combustion of remaining carbon monoxide in the exhaust[6]. The preheated scrap falls from the conveyor into a molten bath of steel within the EAF, where it is heated further until it melts. This approach reduces the electricity needed to heat the scrap, and savings of 0.74 GJ/t have been reported.

As well as energy savings, preheating can increase furnace productivity by reducing the time needed for melting with a given electrical current. Metal losses in the exhaust are reduced by trapping dust particles and reintroducing them to the melt, and as the furnace maintains a molten bath (a 'hot heel'), noise is reduced as there are no sparks generated as normally occurs with a bed of solid scrap.

Sustainable Materials with both eyes open

route. For example, thermoelectric generation might be used to exploit the heat that must be conducted through pot walls in aluminium smelting to maintain a solid, unmelted layer to prevent corrosion of the refractory lining.

Power stations for electricity generation discard heat, and this could be used in production processes, in an approach, generally referred to as "Combined Heat and Power" generation or CHP. Electricity generation generally produces only low temperature heat (up to 200°C) which is not very useful in the high temperature steel and aluminium industries. However, in aluminium production, this heat can be used to generate steam for the initial stages of the Bayer Process for purifying alumina, and this application saves 15% of current primary fuel consumption[4]. Integrated steel plants have their own power stations for combusting the off gases of primary production, and steam may also be produced for use on-site.

Outlook

Steel and aluminium production requires many thermal cycles and the exhaust and hot outputs of these processes contain valuable exergy. It is possible to reduce the number of thermal cycles in many cases, but this may require new investment,

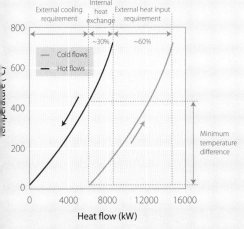

Pinch analysis of the steel and aluminium industries

In the chemicals industry, pinch analysis is commonly used to derive a target for site-wide energy consumption. This target is based on the thermodynamic maximum amount of heat that can be recovered. Hot material flows (those at high temperature with heat available for recovery) and cold flows (requiring heating) are surveyed and combined to generate a graph of heat availability and demand at different temperatures. For a given minimum temperature difference that depends on the nature of the flows (solid, liquid, gas) and the cost/area of heat exchange, a 'pinch point' is defined and these composite flows will have a region of overlap that signifies the theoretical maximum amount of heat recovery that can take place. Outside of the overlap, the heating and cooling requirements must be supplied by external sources; heating in furnaces and cooling in air in the case of steel and aluminium.

To achieve the targeted maximum heat recovery, heat transfer across the 'pinch point' temperature should be avoided. We have found that further energy savings could be achieved beyond implementing current technologies, but that a more complicated heat exchanger network would be needed to achieve these savings.

and could be inhibited by the need to maintain process flexibility. Heat exchange, while theoretically very attractive, is difficult to implement because of the flows in which heat is available and required.

Having begun this chapter with Lego, and in passing met Napoleon III who at the time his uncle was deposed, was aged four, so presumably would have been playing with it if only it had been invented 130 years earlier, let's now find out how he developed as an adult...

Notes

Exergy flows for the whole of steel and aluminium component production

1. In more detail, exergy is always defined relative to some reference state – such as ambient temperature and pressure at sea level. Exergy is then the maximum work that can be extracted from some source of energy while bringing the source to the same state (temperature, speed, voltage, pressure) as the surrounding environment. In metal casting, for example, the exergy of the liquid metal might be defined as the maximum work that can be done by the heat in the liquid metal as it cools to room temperature.

Recovering and exchanging heat

2. SSAB, a steel producer in Sweden, supply 70% of the population of Oxelösund and Luleå with heating using exhaust gases from their processes (SSAB, n.d).

3. Tata Steel and Sheffield University recently conducted a research project at Scunthorpe steelworks, described by Zandi et al. (2011), where power plant exhaust gases rich in CO_2 were bubbled through an algal bioreactor. The algae grow and sequester CO_2 through photosynthesis.

4. The predication of a 15% saving in primary energy by co-generation is based on research completed for the European Union by Luo and Soria (2007).

Box stories

5. The Castrip® process operated by Nucor Steel in Crawfordsville, IN., has successfully cast and sold steel sheet by the twin-roll casting method. The current range of grades and their properties are documented by Sosinsky et al. (2008).

6. Memoli and Ferri (2008) describe the Consteel® technology and how both heat transfer from the exhaust and combustion of remaining carbon monoxide in a preheat tunnel contribute to energy savings.

Box stories

7. Image credit: Siemens press picture

8. Image reference: Tenova Consteel EAF plant

9 Novel process routes

and clean energy

If we could invent a new way to extract liquid metal from ore, could we find new emissions savings, or could we drive the reactions by electricity and find a source of clean electricity that would reduce our total emissions?

When eating as the guest of Napoleon III in the 1850's, basic dignitaries, Royal princes of the poorer countries, and ordinary nobles, had to make do with the day to day gold plates and think themselves fortunate. But when he wanted to put on a show, to mark the arrival of the King of Siam for instance, there was no choice—gold was simply too common. For a big splash, the Emperor would bring out his very best the aluminium plates[1].

Napoleon III with his run-of-the-mill gold jewellery

Aluminium was first extracted from ore in 1825 by Hans Christian Oersted. On hearing about the metal, Napoleon III invested in its development so Henri Sainte-Claire Deville was able to begin commercial production in France. He used an inefficient chemical reduction process with huge costs: in the 1850's the metal was as expensive as platinum. Thirty years later, in Ohio in 1886, a 22 year old chemistry student Charles Hall, by passing electricity through a bath of molten cryolite into which he had poured aluminium oxide (alumina) powder, produced a few globules of aluminium metal. Entirely independently, Paul Héroult achieved the same result two months later. So the process, known ever after as the Hall-Héroult process, was commercialised, led to great reductions in cost and hence increases in application, and is the core of aluminium production today.

Steel making has a similar history, though we've been unable to find stories of Royal patronage. Iron has been in use for thousands of years, but its properties are impaired by naturally occurring impurities such as carbon, silicon and manganese. In 1855, the engineer and inventor Henry Bessemer patented an industrial-scale process to remove these impurities, by blowing air through the iron while liquid. Oxygen in the air reacts with the impurities to form either gases, which escape from the metal, or solid oxides, which collect as slag. As a bonus, adding air doesn't cool the liquid metal as might be expected, but instead the oxidation reactions produce heat, which improves the rate of reaction, and in turn this releases more heat, and so on. The resulting steel, which is purer than the original cast iron, has greatly improved properties, so Bessemer's invention opened the opportunity for a great expansion in applications of steel. Bessemer's process remained in use for over a hundred years until Robert Durrer in Switzerland showed in 1948 that replacing the air with a stream of pure oxygen was more effective. Today's steel is made with Durrer's 'basic oxygen' process.

We've started with these two stories of step changes in the processes of making aluminium and steel because we want to make an informed guess about whether it's likely that further step changes will occur in the future. Is there another student in Ohio waiting to be stimulated by a great lecture to invent a new process? According to our friends in the department of Economics this question is easy: the answer is always yes, and the real question is "what incentive do you need to provide to stimulate the next improvement?" This sounds reasonable, and at present is certainly true for the fuel consumption of cars, but in processing materials there are fundamental physical limits that we just can't beat. Whatever the incentive, a standard 3 kilowatt kettle will never be able to heat a litre of water from 10°C to boiling point in under two minutes, and similarly there are absolute limits to the energy required to make steel, aluminium and our other key materials.

We saw in Chapter 7 that pursuing all options for energy efficiency and reducing the CO_2 intensity of existing processes is allowing us to inch our way towards the minimum energy required to produce liquid steel and aluminium, but could we make bigger gains by developing novel technologies?

Novel processes for steel making

The world's steel makers are currently exploring three alternative ways to make iron—direct reduced iron, smelt reduction and electrolysis, and three options for using less coke—through substitution of other fuels, the use of hydrogen and through top gas recycling.

The earliest approach to making iron, from around 1,000 B.C., was to heat the ore without coke, over a fire of coal or natural gas. Hydrogen and carbon monoxide released on igniting the fuel allowed reduction (the removal of oxygen atoms from the iron oxides) and created 'sponge iron.' This precursor metal has a high concentration of carbon and other impurities, so the steel-makers of 3,000 years ago hammered, folded and hammered the sponge iron, while hot, to oxidise (and remove) carbon, and distribute other impurities uniformly through the metal. One option for novel production of steel is therefore to go 'back to the future', starting by reducing ore directly to sponge iron. This is now called direct reduced iron (DRI), illustrated in figure 9.1, and because the reduction occurs at a lower temperature (typically 800–1,000°C) than in a blast furnace and does not require production of coke, it uses significantly less energy than the blast furnace. However, direct reduced iron has too great a concentration of carbon and impurities. It could be refined in a basic oxygen furnace, but this would be energy intensive as production of DRI is solid not liquid. Instead, DRI is fed (hot) into the conventional electric arc furnace used in secondary steel making. The total primary energy used by the DRI route is greater than that in conventional steel making because of the electric arc furnace, but total emissions are lower because coke is not used. However, most DRI sites use natural gas to heat and drive the reaction, and this gives off-gases with a high concentration of CO_2 which could be captured and stored. If the electric arc furnace was powered by 'clean' electricity, this would further reduce emissions to a low level.

Smelt reduction is a two stage process, with the first being similar to direct reduction leading to sponge iron. However, rather than continuing on to refine the sponge iron in an electric arc furnace, in smelt reduction, it is fed into a closely connected pool of molten iron, and through further heating, is melted, as seen in Figure 9.2. The reduction reaction (removal of carbon and impurities) from the

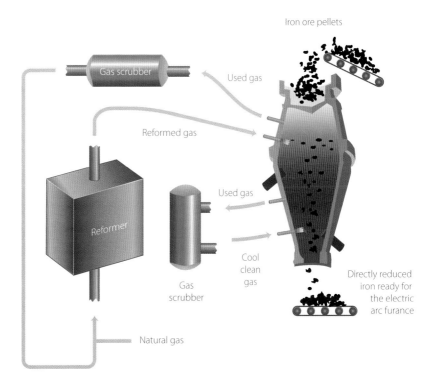

Iron ore pellets

Gas scrubber

Used gas

Reformed gas

Reformer

Used gas

Gas scrubber

Cool clean gas

Directly reduced iron ready for the electric arc furance

Natural gas

Figure 9.1—**Direct reduced iron production**[15]

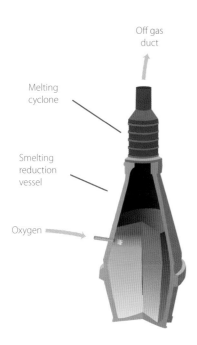

Off gas
duct

Melting
cyclone

Smelting
reduction
vessel

Oxygen

Figure 9.2—**Smelt reduction process**[15]

sponge iron occurs more rapidly in the liquid form, and is driven by direct injection of finely ground coal and oxygen into the liquid melt. The fine coal quickly turns into gas and combined with the oxygen, this drives the chemical reactions of reduction, and provides the required heat. Like DRI, the main efficiency of smelt reduction is the elimination of the coking process, but more energy is required as the process uses more coal and requires pure oxygen, which itself is an energy intensive product. Because oxygen rather than air is used in smelt reduction, and all other gases are fully combusted in the reduction vessel, the off-gases have a high concentration of CO_2 so could be stored.

The third novel process route aims to produce iron from its ores by electrolysis. Two electrolysis technologies, shown in Figure 9.3, are being explored: electrowinning, in which a strong electrical current is passed into an appropriate liquid via a positive terminal made up of unrefined oxide, so that pure iron is electro-plated onto the negative terminal where the current flows out; iron ore pyroelectrolysis where current is passed from an inert positive terminal through molten iron ore, at 1600°C so that liquid iron will form at the negative terminal while pure oxygen is released. Electrolysis eliminates the need for coking and ore preparation, but is electrically intensive, so would only offer emission savings if powered by low carbon electricity, and as yet has been proven only at a very small scale.

Some of the coke used in conventional blast furnaces can be substituted by charcoal, biomass, or waste plastics, shown in Figure 9.4. As we saw in chapter 7, the coke provides support for the ore, generates heat, and releases carbon, to trigger the reduction reaction. Each of these substitute materials can achieve part of this function. Waste plastic, which is in effect oil, combusts to generate

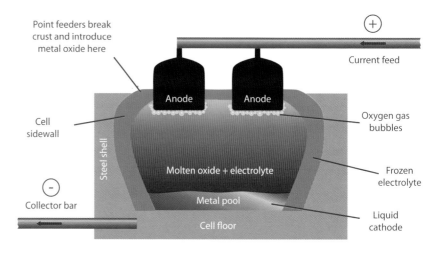

Point feeders break
crust and introduce
metal oxide here

Current feed

Cell
sidewall

Oxygen gas
bubbles

Steel shell

Molten oxide + electrolyte

Frozen
electrolyte

Collector bar

Metal pool

Cell floor

Liquid
cathode

Figure 9.3—**Schematic of iron ore pyroelectrolysis**

Sustainable Materials with both eyes open

heat, and we'll see later that even though any individual plastic can be recycled if well separated from other materials, waste plastics are often mixed together so incineration is potentially a good solution. Both biomass and charcoal are good substitutes, but an expansion in use is limited by the rate at which we can harvest biomass. If we replaced all coke in all 30 Mt of our steel consumption in the UK, we'd need to use nearly half the surface of the UK for charcoal production[2]. So even though biomass substitution for coke is technically feasible, it isn't in any meaningful way a 'sustainable' solution.

An alternative approach to coke substitution is to use hydrogen rather than carbon to drive the reduction reaction. This would eliminate process emissions, as the iron ore would react with the hydrogen to form iron and steam. However, the overall emissions impact of this option depends on how the hydrogen is produced and how the blast furnace is heated to its operating temperature. At present large-scale adoption of hydrogen substitution looks extremely unlikely, even by 2050[3].

Figure 9.4—**Possible fuel substitutes**

A final option to reduce requirements for coke is to apply top gas recycling. The off gases from the blast furnaces contain a mixture of gases, including carbon monoxide (CO) and others. In top gas recycling, the CO is separated from the gas stream and recycled back into the blast furnace, where it can reduce the iron ore, to form CO_2. In this case, the CO is acting as the reductant, rather than new coke. In a conventional blast furnace, preheated air is used to provide oxygen for combustion, so that a large volume of nitrogen is also present in the off gas, and this inhibits separation of the CO. If pure oxygen, rather than air is used, there is no nitrogen in the off gas and the separation of CO will be easier. Top gas

Figure 9.5—**Reduction of iron ore with hydrogen**

recycling reduces CO_2 emissions from the blast furnace by 5 to 10%[4] but if oxygen rather than air is used, the blast furnace could be coupled with CCS. In this section we've looked beyond the best-available technologies of chapter 7. Existing blast furnaces could be modified to use less coke or to use top-gas recycling, and this would reduce emissions by up to 10%. Or, we might in future replace the blast furnace to extract metal from ore by direct reduction, smelt reduction, electrolysis or hydrogen reduction. Of these, direct reduction is widely used already in countries with natural gas supplies, and demonstrations of smelt reduction are planned (see the box story about the HIsarana pilot plant at IJmuiden in The Netherlands). We learnt from Josiah Gibbs that existing steel production is already impressively energy-efficient, so unsurprisingly none of these new processes would save much energy. Instead, they could be configured to release off-gases with high concentrations of CO_2, which could potentially be captured and stored.

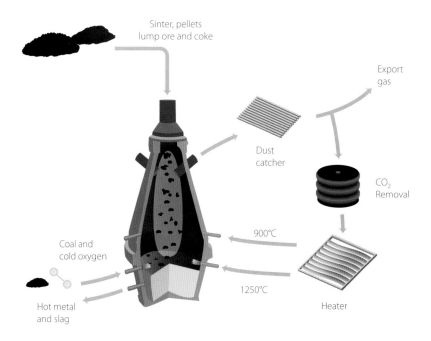

Figure 9.6—**Top gas recycling**[15]

Sustainable Materials with both eyes open

Novel processes for making aluminium

In order to reduce electricity consumption, developers in the aluminium industry aim to decrease the separation between anode and cathode in the Hall-Héroult cell. This could be achieved with inert anodes in conjunction with wetted drained cathodes and the anode-tilt system. Multipolar cells could increase productivity and two alternative chemical routes, carbothermic and Kaolinite reduction reactions, may lead to more efficient aluminium production.

The aluminium industry has been trying to develop inert anodes for at least 40 years. Many material options have been examined, particularly titanium diboride, an electrically conducting ceramic. In contrast with the carbon anodes in current use, inert anodes would not be consumed during electrolysis, eliminating both CO_2 and PFC (perfluorinated compound) emissions from carbon anode production and use. Furthermore, because an inert anode would not change shape in use, the separation between the anode and the cathode in the cells could be reduced giving improved energy efficiency. This would require care to avoid short-circuits between the anode (positive terminal) and the liquid metal in contact with the cathode (negative terminal). Two technologies aiming to reduce the chances of such short circuits are wetted drained cathodes[5], and the anode-tilt system[6].

Inert anodes could also lead to use of the multipolar cells, shown in Figure 9.7, with many anodes and cathodes in parallel in the same cell. This could increase productivity and electrical efficiency and could allow lower temperature operation of the cell.

HIsarna IJmuiden

HIsarna, a pilot plant for steel production by smelt reduction has been constructed at IJmuiden in The Netherlands. Comissioning has begun and production of up to 60,000 tonnes per year may start by 2020[7]. Unlike the conventional blast furnace the HIsarna process has two reduction stages: pre-reduction takes place in a cyclone converter furnace and then the final reduction takes place in a bath of molten oxide. Elimination of coke making and sintering steps should reduce the emissions of the HIsarna process, and in future it could be combined with CCS technology.

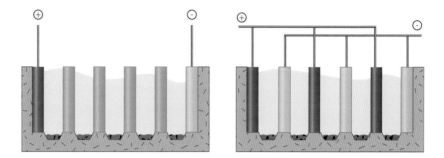

Figure 9.7—**Multipolar electrolysis cell**

Carbothermic reduction is a two-step process in which alumina and carbon react at around 1900°C to form an alumina-aluminium-carbide mixture, which is passed into a second reactor at about 2000°C, where the aluminium carbide is reduced by alumina to form aluminium. This process, shown in Figure 9.8, will produce more direct CO_2 than the existing route, but requires less electricity so gives an overall reduction in emissions. At present, development is inhibited by the high temperatures required. Alternatively, in Kaolinite reduction, alumina is first converted into aluminium chloride before reduction to aluminium in an electrolysis cell. Kaolinite reduction promises only a small reduction in CO_2 emissions, but can use lower quality ore than the Hall-Héroult process.

Electricity is a major cost in making aluminium, motivating intense research on the novel processes in this section for at least 40 years, yet they are still not ready for operation. It is unclear whether the industry can overcome the problems, so although 15-25% savings in emissions are forecast, we cannot yet plan for their implementation.

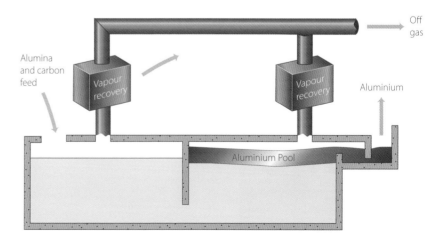

Figure 9.8—**Carbothermic reduction**

Sustainable Materials with both eyes open

Powering processes with 'clean' electricity

Both steel and aluminium making consume a lot of electricity. Our emissions would be reduced greatly if we could use 'clean' electricity, generated without emissions. To find out about that, we can turn directly to David MacKay's "Sustainable Energy without the hot air"[8]. Here's our very short summary:

Sheffield in the late 1800s, polluted by steelmaking

- There are many ways to generate energy 'renewably', for example from sunlight, wind, waves, tides, hydropower, plants or algae. All of them produce relatively little energy for a large commitment of land. The key numbers are summarised in Table 9.1 shown against our estimates of the total power use of a country divided by its surface area. To meet the UK's total energy requirements by renewable generation only, our most effective current options are either that we cover a quarter of all our land with solar cells, or that we cover more than half of our land with wind turbines. This won't happen.

- Nuclear power can deliver nearly carbon free electricity and is widely used. The main arguments against expanding nuclear power are that (i) we think it might not be safe, (ii) we will in due course run out of nuclear fuel and (iii) no electricity company can afford to insure a nuclear power plant, so in effect all nuclear electricity is subsidised by government, and the subsidy would be better used elsewhere. David MacKay provides clear evidence that (i) and (ii) are not right so while (iii) is true, it should only be used with a specific second part—where else should that money be spent? It seems that nuclear is probably a very good option for creating nearly carbon free electricity, and we should be very pleased we have the option.

Renewable electricity source	Power per unit area (W/m²)[9]	Country	Energy consumption per unit area (W/m²)[10]
Rain-water	0.2	Australia	<0.1
Plants	0.5	Brazil	<0.1
Wind	2	Canada	0.1
Offshore wind	3	China / USA	0.3
Tidal pools	3	France	0.6
Tidal streams	6	UK / Germany	1.3
Solar PV panels	5–20	Japan	1.9
Concentrating solar power (deserts)	15	World	0.1

Table 9.1—**Land requirements for renewable electricity generation**

- We discussed the first part of Carbon Capture and Storage (CCS) above for steel making—how do you generate a pure stream of CO_2 from steel making? With exactly the same motivation, developers of electricity generation stations are aiming to create pure streams of CO_2 when burning coal or gas. We'll discuss this further in the next chapter.

So, nuclear power is a mature technology that can be expanded relatively rapidly, Carbon Capture and Storage might be deployed in future but as yet doesn't operate at scale anywhere, and renewable sources are disappointingly intensive in land requirements. Is a nuclear powered materials industry the answer to all our problems? Possibly, but other sectors are banking on nuclear as well. Our map of global energy flow in chapter 2 showed us that nuclear sources currently provide around 6% of global energy or, as it's all used for electricity generation, about 15% of global electricity. If all existing industry were to be powered by nuclear electricity now, that would require a 5 times increase in current capacity. We expect that demand for industrial output will double by 2050, so that increases our nuclear expansion to 10 times. But in addition, guess what the car industry is planning as its low carbon model for the future? Electric vehicles, which of course are only low carbon if the electricity comes from renewables, nuclear or CCS sources, so let's assume that all future vehicles are powered by nuclear electricity, and that their number doubles. And to crown that, our house builders are going to promote ground or air sourced heat pumps as the low carbon solution. In other words, not just all future electricity, but all future energy must come from nuclear power. So if demand doubles, we need to expand global nuclear installation by 32 times in the next 40 years. The world currently has around 422[11] reactors operating, so we need to anticipate about 13,400 reactors by 2050. That requires a building rate of about 320 new reactors per year (in addition to the conversion of all steel plant to new electrical technologies.) This is around 10 times the world's maximum historical construction rate[12], so is technically feasible but difficult to believe.

So we're carrying on with this book because, although we can envisage a future materials industry powered solely by nuclear electricity, it seems to us unlikely that that will occur as there are so many other sectors competing for the same 'carbon free' electricity. So, let's keep looking for other answers, and when we assemble our forecasts of the future of materials processing in chapters 11 and 19, we'll return to our estimated need for nuclear power.

Outlook: will these novel processes be adopted?

We've focused on technological possibilities in this chapter so far—to check what sort of brake we need to apply to the idea that incentives lead to innovations. So, now back to the incentives. Will the steel and aluminium industries adopt new processes, CCS or be electrified, and if electrified, will there be enough nuclear power? Can we expect the market to choose the best solution? History tells us that we can't; there are many examples of successful inferior technologies (the QWERTY keyboard on which we're typing this book being the most well known of them)[13]. Such technologies succeed because they get an early foothold in the market. As their market share increases they benefit from economies of scale, achieve cost reductions with experience, benefit from greater publicity and the development of auxiliary technology. These advantages (referred to by economists as increasing returns to scale) amplify the way chance events affect outcomes. In effect what this means is that no single technology can be considered to be best, it can be best only in a particular context but that context is itself affected by the technology chosen. This logic undermines the axioms of neo-classical economics and has motivated economists to turn to evolutionary theory to understand transition[14]. The role of government in this context is, in the words of Brian Arthur the father of complexity economics, "not a heavy hand, not an invisible hand, but a nudging hand". The trouble is that evolution takes time and we don't have much time however big the nudge.

We've found several developments of novel processes in this chapter, but none offering a 'step-change' and none that are close to mass exploitation. A running theme in the chapter has been the separation of CO_2, both from the processes of metal-making and from electricity generation. Separating and storing CO_2 is currently a popular option in discussions on responses to climate change. So having looked at separation in this chapter, we need to put on our black suits, turn the page, and set off to the funeral.

Notes

1. We've done our best to find an original reference for this story, which we've found told in many different forms—always with Napoleon III, but with different visitors, and many different options for the table ware—plates, cutlery, serving dishes that were aluminium and not gold. Our earliest reference is an article in the February 1936 edition of "Popular Science" by Edwin Teale—who credits Napoleon with aluminium forks only, but with giving the King of Siam an aluminium watch fob as a gift. We've used plates, as the most commonly reported bit of tableware—and as our colleagues in the History department tell us that facts are far less important than the way you tell them, let it be plates from now on!

Novel processes for steelmaking

2. On average we can harvest 1 kg of dry biomass per year for every square metre of land (Vitousek et al., 1986) and we need 10 kg of biomass to make 1 kg of charcoal (Tribal Energy and Environmental Information Clearinghouse, 2011). We've estimated that the UK's 'steel footprint' is around 30 Mt and producing this requires 10 Mt of coke. To make this coke we therefore need 100 Mt of biomass, which is the average product of 100,000 km². This is about 40% of the UK, so it's not going to happen. Charcoal does not have the strength to support ore in the blast furnace, so can substitute no more than half our current use of coke. However 'biocoal', a new processed charcoal may have sufficient strength to allow complete substitution (IEA, 2009).

3. According to a recent review of the technical abatement potential in the UK steel sector "Hydrogen-based steelmaking is believed to be technically sound but there remains no sufficiently sized low/carbon free source. Nor does the industry think this likely even with a 2050 time horizon" (Adderley, 2011).

4. These estimates come from an overview of low CO_2 emission technologies for iron and steelmaking by Xu and Cang (2010).

Novel processes for making aluminium

5. Wetting here refers to the interaction between a liquid and a solid surface. For example, a droplet of liquid on a non-wettable surface will remain as a perfect sphere, whilst a droplet of liquid on a wettable surface will spread out to form a thin layer, as shown in Figure 9.9. In wetted drained cathodes, new materials are used to make the surface of the cathode more wettable so that the liquid aluminium formed during electrolysis spreads more uniformly and so the anode-cathode distance can be reduced.

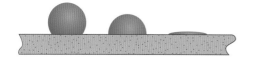

Figure 9.9—**Wettability**

6. Movement of the fluids and equipment within an electrolysis cell causes a wave to ripple through the liquid aluminium as it forms at the bottom of the cell. The distance between anode and cathode must therefore be sufficient that the wave of aluminium does not cause a short circuit. The anode-tilt system aims to avoid this problem, by tilting the anode in phase with the wave in the liquid aluminium, as shown in Figure 9.10.

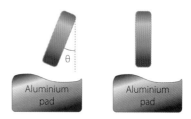

Figure 9.10—**Anode tilt system**

Powering processes with 'clean' electricity

7. The current status of the HIsarna pilot plant is described in a Tata news release (Tata, 2011b)

8. David MacKay's (2009) book, like ours, is published by UIT press, and also available on-line for free at www.withouthotair.com.

9. This table comes from David MacKay's analysis on renewables (Table 25.1) (MacKay, 2009).

10. The power per unit area is equal to each country's energy use in 2008 from the U.S. Energy Information Administration (2011) divided by the land area as reported in Table 3 of the United Nations Statistics Division's Demographic Yearbook (2008). The electricity consumption of the countries in the table accounts for 70% of global electricity consumption.

11. The European Nuclear Society reports that as of 19th January 2011, there were 422 nuclear reactors in operation and 65 under construction.

12. David MacKay estimates that the world's maximum historical construction rate of nuclear reactors was in 1984, when 30GW of nuclear power was completed, or 30 1GW reactors. (MacKay, 2009) page 171.

Outlook: with these novel processes be adopted

13. Other examples of successful inferior technologies quoted in Arthur (1989) include the alternating current, the narrow gauge of British railways and the programming language FORTRAN.

14. See Arthur (1999) for an explanation of complexity economics.

15. Parts of these graphics have been adapted from World Steel Association images

10 Carbon sequestration

If there are no alternative routes to making the metals, and if we continue to expand production, could we reduce total emissions not by saving energy, but by separating CO_2 from other gases emitted in production, capturing it and burying it underground?

We had an argument about writing this chapter: "We have to have more pictures"; "I don't like the colours"; "This is too political"; "That joke about the Belgian, the strawberry and the treacle is totally inappropriate"... and so on. But we've had a lot of arguments now, and all that stuff from the relationship councillors about airing our different opinions and respecting each other just seems like too much effort—so we're going to bury our resentments, and carry on with gritted teeth.

Welcome to the world of carbon sequestration (also known as storage): we've got an environmental problem? Don't worry—let's bury it. Nuclear waste? Hole in the ground. Red mud? Open lakes out of sight. Toxic chemicals? Down the drain. We have a long history of literally burying our problems, so if we're worried about carbon emissions, why not just trap the CO_2 and push it underground?

Which rather sounds as if we're avoiding facing up to the real problem, and by hiding CO_2 underground it looks as if we're creating a short delay and leaving an even worse problem behind for our children. But to some extent, we have no choice but to consider burying at least part of the problem. Behind all discussion on carbon sequestration is the big black hand of coal. Globally we're currently using more and more coal for electricity generation, and 75% of the world's coal reserves are held by just five countries: the United States, Russia, China, India and Australia[1]. To date, Russia, China and India have steadily increased their use of coal to drive their economic development, and there is not yet sufficient political will in the USA or Australia to inhibit further coal development. Coal gives more CO_2 emissions for each unit of energy produced than any other form of electricity generation[2]. (The UK's emissions reductions in the 1990's which allowed Prime Minister Tony Blair to be first to sign the Kyoto Protocol occurred mainly because of a switch from coal to gas fired electricity generation.) If we're inevitably going to increase coal combustion, the only way we can reduce associated emissions is if we capture the CO_2 and bury it.

What does that have to do with materials production? Well, if we can't avoid emitting CO_2 when producing materials, and we've seen that that's the case for primary production of both steel and aluminium, maybe we can join the bandwagon of the 'clean coal' movement, and having separated the CO_2 using one of the novel processes in the previous chapter, we could also compress, transport and store it.

Carbon Capture and Storage (CCS) technologies are at a very early stage of development, and certainly we would be taking a grave risk if we bank all our hopes for emissions reductions on this unproven approach. Therefore in this chapter we aim to review current thinking on the second part of CCS: what are the main options for storage? what are the risks? what are the costs? If we can make a balanced assessment of those questions, we'll be in a better position to evaluate our options for reducing emissions from future materials production.

Where can CO_2 be stored?

The world's natural carbon cycle involves continuous exchange of carbon between four major 'pools': the atmosphere, oceans, plants and soils. These flows are large, much larger than the additional emissions arising from fossil fuel combustion, but essentially balanced. For example, each year plants absorb around 120 billion tonnes of carbon from the atmosphere through photosynthesis, release about 60 billion tonnes through respiration, and store about 60 billion tonnes as biomass in soils. In turn, soils release about 60 billion tonnes of carbon to the atmosphere through respiration. In parallel, the oceans exchange about 90 billion tonnes of carbon with the atmosphere each year. These two cycles are essentially balanced so, as George Bush said, "what's the problem? Emissions from fossil fuels are tiny compared to nature's emissions." Well, that's right, but emissions from fossil fuel combustion are not balanced by an equivalent withdrawal from the atmosphere. So, when we talk here about storage, we're specifically thinking about storing additional carbon beyond what's always happened within the Earth's natural cycles. Incidentally, in case George is reading, we should also flag another common confusion: this paragraph has described tonnes of carbon, where the rest of the book considers carbon dioxide, or CO_2. Which is heavier —a tonne of carbon or a tonne of CO_2? Of course they're the same weight (well done George), but a tonne of CO_2 contains only 270 kg of carbon, because an oxygen atom is a third heavier than a carbon atom. So to convert carbon emissions into CO_2 emissions, we need to multiply by 11/3, or about 3.7.

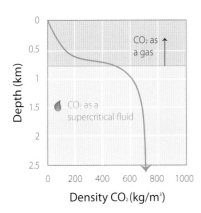

Figure 10.1—**Behaviour of CO$_2$ at increasing depth and pressure**

What else can we do to store emissions from industrial processes? Some options depend on photosynthesis to extract carbon from the atmosphere, but we'll ignore these general approaches as our focus is specifically on burying emissions captured at materials processing factories. Other options involve burying the gas below the earth's surface, and the graph illustrates the benefit of this: as you descend below the earth's surface, either in the ocean, or under the 'water table', the surrounding pressure increases. This compresses the CO$_2$ gas and eventually its becomes a liquid with a volume 370 times less than the gas at atmospheric pressure.

There are three main storage options: we can pump CO$_2$ under ground into current or past oil and gas reservoirs, into coal seams or into other porous rocks; we can dissolve CO$_2$ in the ocean or store it as a 'lake' at great depths; we can convert CO$_2$ gas into a solid through mineral carbonation, consume it in industrial processes or use it to grow algae for bio-fuel.

Oil and gas have been stored under the earth's surface for millennia, so presumably we can replace them with stored CO$_2$. This could either happen during extraction (it may be easier to extract the oil if we 'push it out' with an injection of CO$_2$ called 'enhanced oil recovery'), or it could occur after a field has been exhausted. In effect we could run the extraction process backwards, and push CO$_2$ back in. Both approaches have been tried in practice, see the box story on the following page for more details. Oil and gas fields are potentially attractive storage sites because their geology is already well studied, they are below sealing layers of impermeable rock, and some of the required infrastructure (wells, pipelines) is in place. However, a lot more development would be required to switch from oil extraction to carbon storage[3].

The coal industry is particularly interested in injecting CO$_2$ into deep coal seams, especially those that can't be mined profitably. As the CO$_2$ is absorbed into the coal, methane (natural gas) is emitted. If we then collected this gas we could burn it to offset some of the cost of CO$_2$ injection, although doing so would release CO$_2$ and hence reduce the net amount stored[4]. Obviously if the seam were subsequently mined, and the coal burnt, the exercise would be pointless.

CO$_2$ could equally be pumped into any porous rock covered by an impermeable layer, as illustrated in Figure 10.2. Abandoned mines, salt caverns, basalt layers and shale formations have all been tested but found unsuitable for large scale storage. The most promising locations appear to be salty lakes (saline aquifers) deep within porous rock formations where the CO$_2$ would be physically trapped by the rock and would over time dissolve into the water. Several estimates suggest that we have sufficient capacity world wide to store the CO_2 emitted during several centuries of human activity[4]. However in contrast with fossil fuel geologies, the relevant rock layers are less well mapped and understood, and we do not know how the carbon dioxide would react with the surrounding minerals and microbes.

Sea water absorbs CO_2, and the deep layers of oceans are the earth's largest natural pool (or 'sink') of carbon storage. We could pump CO_2 deep into the oceans (a thousand metres or more below the surface), and release it to bubble up through the ocean and be absorbed into the water. The gas could be released using existing oil transport systems, for example from fixed pipelines with diffuser valves or from pipes trailing behind huge tankers. We do not know how this form of storage would affect marine life over a few hundred years, the oceans would release the stored carbon and eventually reach an equilibrium with the atmosphere. Trials of this type of storage have been attempted off Norway and Hawaii but were halted due to local opposition.

CO_2 storage test sites

There are three sites worldwide where storage of CO_2 has been tested at scale (i.e. more than 1 million tonnes per year for at least five years). Each project is expected to store 20 Mt CO_2 in total:

- At the Sleipner West field in the Norwegian North Sea, CO_2 separated from gas has been injected into a saline formation (lying above the gas layer) since 1996.

- At the Weyburn oil field in Canada, CO_2 is injected to increase oil production and then stored. The CO_2 comes from the gasification of coal across the border in North Dakota and is transported via a 320km pipeline. Similar schemes are operating at a smaller scale in Texas.

- At the In Salah gas field in Algeria, CO_2 separated from the gas is re-injected back into the field, albeit into a saline formation adjacent to the gas reservoir.

These examples suggest that for fixed-location sources like steel and aluminium plants, storage is feasible. However we would require 2,800 such facilities to store our current carbon emissions from steel and aluminium (2.8Gt per year divided by a facility capacity of 1 Mt/year). Even if compressed to 800 kg/m³ —the highest density at which CO_2 is injected —this would require 3.5 billion m³ of storage, equal to three quarters of the volume of crude oil we currently extract each year. And this is only the emissions for steel and aluminium, which are only 10% of the total emissions from energy and processes…

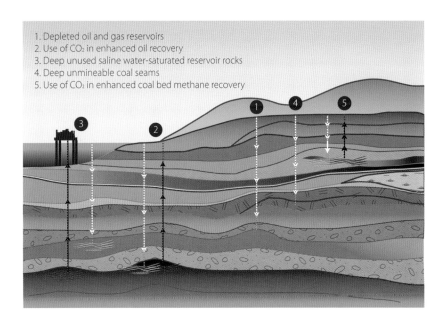

1. Depleted oil and gas reservoirs
2. Use of CO_2 in enhanced oil recovery
3. Deep unused saline water-saturated reservoir rocks
4. Deep unmineable coal seams
5. Use of CO_2 in enhanced coal bed methane recovery

Figure 10.2—**Ground storage options for CCS**[11]

At higher pressures, liquid CO_2 has a greater density than sea water, so below about 3,000 metres will form a liquid lake that sinks. CO_2 stored in this way would dissolve into the water slowly so might remain in storage for 10,000 years as the oceans are more stable at these depths. This approach hasn't yet been tested, and if deep sea currents stir up the CO_2 lake, the storage time could be cut to as few as 30 years[3].

Many of the earth's surface rocks are silicates (compounds of silicon and oxygen atoms) containing metal oxides, which over a very long time react with carbon dioxide to form limestone or other carbonates (compounds which include a carbon atom bonded to three oxygen atoms). This process can be accelerated dramatically at raised temperature or pressure, so could be used as a means to store CO_2 as a solid material. The attraction of mineral carbonation is that the resulting solid is indefinitely stable, so the CO_2 will not be re-released. However it is energy intensive, to the point that it might consume virtually all the energy generated by a power station, and the weight of silicate required is 2–4 times greater than the weight of CO_2 stored. In order to sequester all 28 Gt of our current yearly emissions we would have to mine 84 Gt of silicates per year, equivalent to about seven times our current extraction of fossil fuels[5]. The process also uses intense intermediate chemicals such as hydrochloric acids so it isn't yet a clear environmental winner. A demonstrator project has been initiated in New South Wales to combine carbon dioxide with the serpentinite rock abundant in the area. This would store the CO_2 as magnesium carbonate which could be used as a building material. However, significant technology improvements are required before mineral carbonation becomes a viable option.

Some industrial processes use CO_2, for example as a solvent or refrigerant. It would be sensible if, rather than investing energy in manufacturing CO_2 for these purposes, we used captured CO_2 instead. Unfortunately the total volumes of CO_2 required by industry are small, no more than 200 Mt per year, and the CO_2 is often released again within a year, so this approach would have little benefit[4].

Finally, we could bubble a stream of CO_2 through a pool to stimulate growth of algae, which can be harvested and converted to biofuels. This approach is at an early stage, currently has a low yield, and as well as needing sunlight, and water, also uses a large area of land. We would need a 50 km² pool to store the carbon output from a (small) 100 MW power station[6] so the approach may well be prohibitively expensive.

Current global emissions from energy use and processes are around 28 Gt CO_2/year or just under 8 GtC/year. Table 10.1 shows that the options above could potentially have sufficient capacity to store this amount of CO_2 for many years but how risky is this, and what will it cost?

Storage option	Lower estimate of worldwide capacity (GtCO₂)	Upper estimate of worldwide capacity (GtCO₂)	Storage integrity ('permanence')	Environmental Risk
Oil & Gas Reservoirs	675	900	High	Low
Coal Seams	3–25	200	Medium	Medium
Saline aquifers	1,000	Possibly 10,000	Medium	Medium
Oceans	1,000	Every 2,000 increases acidity by 0.1pH	Medium	High
Mineralisation	Theoretically very high but high energy cost and raw material requirement		Highest	High
Industrial Processes	0.1	0.2	Low	Low
Algae	Limited by land requirements		Low	Medium

Table 10.1—**Estimated global capacity for different storage options**

Sustainable Materials with both eyes open

Lake Tanganyika

What are the risks of storing CO_2?

If you sit on a balloon, eventually it bursts. If we blew up a balloon at atmospheric pressure with the world's annual 30 thousand million tonnes of CO_2, it would contain about 16,700 cubic kilometres: enough to cover Belgium to a depth of half a metre, or roughly the same volume as Lake Tanganyika, the world's second largest freshwater lake. If we compress it 370 times, as discussed earlier, we're down to a volume of just 45 cubic kilometres per year: around eleven times our current oil production. What happens to that if we sit on it for ever?

The obvious danger of storing this high pressure balloon underground is that it might leak out. It could do that at the place where the CO_2 was pumped into storage, or it could escape through the rock—slowly by permeating the porous rock, or rapidly if it encountered a geological fault[3]. The effect of such a leak would be twofold: firstly, the emissions would return to the atmosphere and contribute to global warming; secondly because carbon dioxide gas is slightly denser than air, when released as a concentrated cloud it initially stays close to the surface of the earth, until dispersed by the wind. Our lungs can only reject CO_2 at a certain rate, so if the concentration of CO_2 in the atmosphere becomes too high, we are eventually unable to take in enough oxygen, and die. Tragically, on 21st August in 1986, a 1.6 million tonne (or 1.2 cubic kilometre) bubble of CO_2 was spontaneously released from Lake Nyos in Cameroon—a lake which naturally has high concentrations of CO_2. Before this bubble could disperse, around 1,700 people lost their lives. Clearly no one will invest in carbon storage unless they have high confidence that this disaster will not repeat, so extensive modelling and experiments have explored the expected safety of storage. Models predict that it is very likely that more than 99% of CO_2 stored would remain in storage for 100 years[3]. However, this figure depends on assumptions —and safety will remain a concern until we have more practical experience.

Sad Finnish Folksong

You can't hide clouds in the ground for e-ver, You can't hide words in your heart

If we need to transport CO_2 from where we made it to where we want to store it, will it leak out of the pipes? We already have some experience in this area, transporting CO_2 in pipelines in the USA for use in enhanced oil recovery. So far the pipelines have proved to be as safe as those used for natural gas, but sulphur

Process	Approximate Energy Use (GJ/tCO2)
Post-combustion separation (chemical absorption)	2.7–3.3
Pre-combustion separation (physical or chemical absorption)	2.3–5.0
Oxyfuel	3.2–5.1
Compression	0.4
Mineralisation	1.1

Table 10.2—**Energy estimates to operate different carbon capture and storage processes**

Site and Capture technology	Cost US$/t captured (2002$)
Steel Blast Furnace	
Pre-combustion (DRI)	10–25
Post-combustion	18–30
Power Stations (for Steel and Aluminium Electric Furnaces)	
Pre-combustion	11–35
Post-combustion	23–35
Oxy-combustion	16–50

Table 10.3—**Cost estimates for different carbon capture technologies**

and other impurities in the flow increase the rate at which the pipes corrode so they must regularly be inspected.

Finally, if CO_2 is stored in oceans, it may change the acidity of the water and in turn change the living habitat of certain species. We don't yet understand how increases in either carbon content or water acidity will affect marine life, but high levels of either will cause death, as in mammals. Experiments in which various species were exposed to CO_2 produced mixed results ranging from avoidance to attraction to death. Potentially, because deep sea fish respire more slowly and have fewer young than their near surface relatives, they might be less affected by increases in carbon or acidity, but this also remains unknown[3]. It is hardly surprising that the marine protection treaty organisation OSPAR[7] announced a decision in 2007 to prohibit the storage of carbon dioxide on the sea-bed[4].

What are the energy and money costs of storing CO_2?

Because CO_2 storage is still only in development, we cannot predict its costs with great certainty. But we know that it entails equipment and infrastructure similar to existing gas extraction, storage and distribution systems, and if you've ever been in charge of the balloons at a 5-year old's birthday party, you'll be aware that it's also going to take a good deal of energy.

Dealing with energy first, the table to the side shows estimates of energy inputs required per tonne of CO_2 stored by several of the routes discussed earlier. Table 10.2 shows that most methods of capture have similar energy requirements[8]. After capture, energy is required to compress the gas from about 10 to over 200 times atmospheric pressure, but this combined with the energy required for transport, is small compared to the energy of capture[3]. The only storage route requiring significant energy input is mineralisation as discussed above.

The costs of operating this system include the capital and operating costs of separation and capture, the additional energy costs to drive the process and the capital and operating costs for storage. Again, these can only be estimated, but Table 10.3 presents a range of current estimates from the IPCC[3].

As well as costs, we also need to consider the scale of the change required to introduce sufficient storage to influence our net global emissions. We mentioned earlier that our annual volumes of CO_2, once compressed at high pressure to liquid, would be about 11 times greater than our current oil production. So if

Sustainable Materials with both eyes open

Storage Option	Cost Estimate (US$/t stored) (2002 dollars)
Oil & Gas Reservoirs	0.5 - 13
Coal Seams	0.5 - 8
Saline aquifers	0.2 - 30
Oceans:	5 - 30
Mineralisation	50–100
Industrial Processes	-
Algae	Land cost

Table 10.4—**Storage cost estimates**

The 'Batillus' built in 1976 for a subsidiary of Shell Oil, was one of the largest boats ever with a net tonnage of 275,268 tons, being 414m long and 63m across at her widest point. Fully laden, she could carry almost five million barrels of oil, or about 7% global production for one day. If we were to transport our annual CO_2 emissions by ship we would need over 56,000 tankers of this size, which, if laid end-to-end would stretch from pole to pole.

we want to address our emissions target (50% absolute cut in emissions by 2050, while demand doubles) we have 39 years remaining to set up an industry that must operate at 10 times the scale of the current oil industry. This took one hundred years in development and had powerful economic drivers. Challenging…

Outlook

We started the chapter in an argument, and against the advice of our counsellor decided to bury it under the carpet, to avoid dealing with the issues. In exploring carbon storage we've seen that our relationship analogy conveys some truth: storage aims to allow us to continue emitting CO_2 at whatever rate we wish, rather than reducing our emissions. However, that's only part of the story. On the one hand, storage looks like the only viable approach to deal with emissions from coal combustion, and unless a very strong driving force changes their behaviour, it's likely that the countries with the largest coal reserves are going to burn them. On the other hand, carbon storage is in its infancy: only three sites operate at scale, and most of what we have discussed about technology, risks and costs is based on prospective research. A pilot electricity generating plant in Schwarze, Germany demonstrates that carbon can be captured effectively, but as yet it is released and not stored—see the box overleaf. We have seen that there are many possible storage options, but to implement them at sufficient scale to make a big difference requires implementation at an unprecedented rate.

Commercially and politically, storing carbon has a particular attraction: if we could make it happen, we could address our concern about emissions without requiring any change in the behaviour of consumers or voters. It appears to offer unlimited capability to take the problem away, and while we are discussing but not really implementing it, the question of "who pays" can happily be reduced to "I'm not going to pay, you'll have to." By not answering the question of who pays, everyone can recommend CCS as a key part of our future: incredibly, for a technology that barely exists, the International Energy Agency projects that 19% of our emissions will be sequestered in the year 2050[9], and this is a cornerstone of all their projections for emissions abatement.

For both the steel and aluminium industries, storing carbon, whether from primary processes or from electricity generation, is equally attractive as a 'catch all' solution that would solve the problem, if only someone else pays for it. In Europe, where we have set aggressive targets for emissions reduction but not offered any border protection to our industries, it is inevitable that the steel industry in particular must pursue storage: they have no chance to achieve emissions reductions targets and stay in business without it. This position would change with border controls that ensured that steel makers anywhere supplying customers in Europe were subject to the same targets as producers in Europe.

But back once more to our opening argument: we actually have great evidence from relationship counsellors that the way to solve problems is not to hide them, but to address them. All over the world, for the past 30 years, we've been teaching our manufacturing students that the great secret behind Toyota's commercial success is their production system which aims to make problems visible, to find their root causes, and then to solve them so well that the problems can't ever recur. If the problem is that we're emitting too much CO_2, isn't it better to emit less than to bury it? Oh no it isn't. Oh yes it is...

Schwarze Pumpe CCS demonstrator[12]

In 2008, at Schwarze Pumpe in Germany, a pilot plant was commissioned to demonstrate oxyfuel combustion of coal generating 30 MW of steam (sold to a neighbouring paper mill) and a relatively pure stream of CO_2 for carbon capture and storage. The demonstrator has achieved a carbon capture rate of 90 % but although liquefied CO_2 is stored onsite in tanks and can be transported by trucks, it is currently released into the atmosphere. Failure to resolve long term liability for storage has prevented its implementation[10].

Notes

1. Data from the annual BP publication (BP, 2011).

2. Data from the International Energy Agency shows that while 27% of the total primary energy supply comes from burning coal, 43% of emissions due to generating this energy are from coal, more than any other source. 'CO$_2$ emissions from fuel combustion — highlights', IEA (2008b).

Where can CO$_2$ be stored?

3. The Intergovernmental Panel on Climate Change produced a special report addressing CCS, IPCC (2005). It goes through capture, transport and storage options in great detail, giving data on processes, logistics, risks and costs.

4. The International Energy Agency has produced reports investigating the feasibility and scale of CO$_2$ storage. The information in these paragraphs is from 'CO$_2$ Capture and Storage: A Key Carbon Abatement Option', IEA (2008b).

5. Vaclav Smil's book 'Energy Myths and Realities' (Smil, 2010) neatly summarises the current state of many carbon storage technologies and computes figures to put the issues in perspective.

6. Outline calculations have been done by the IPCC (2005).

What are the risks of storing CO$_2$?

7. The OSPAR Convention (OSPAR, 1998) is the current treaty regulating environmental protection in the North-East Atlantic. It builds on previous accords limiting marine pollution. The OSPAR Commission, made up of government representatives) carries out work under the convention.

What are the energy and money costs of storing CO$_2$?

8. These values are primarily drawn from examples of gas and coal-fired power plants with CCS. The exact energy consumption will depend on the configuration of the power plant, exact technology used for capture, and carbon dioxide concentration in the gas stream to be separated. The typical range for CO$_2$ concentration in these examples is 3–14%; ULCOS blast furnaces are aiming for CO$_2$ concentrations around 40vol% in the gas entering the separator and therefore should be able to achieve lower energy use for carbon capture according to Danloy et al. (2008). For comparison current blast furnaces have a concentration of 22vol% as detailed in the blast furnace mass and energy balance found on http://www.steeluniversity.org.

Outlook

9. IEA (2010b) includes projected energy use, carbon emissions and 'technology roadmaps' that outline what improvements and savings could be made to reduce them.

Box stories

10. Details of the project are provided on the company's website (Vattenfall, 2011) and a more detailed analysis of initial results has been carried out by Strömberg et al. (2009).

Images

11. Adapted from CO2CRC (http://www.co2crc.com.au)

12. Image author: I, SPBer. Used under Creative Commons Attribution 2.5 Generic Licence (http://creativecommons.org/licenses/by/2.5/deed.en)

11 Future energy use and emissions

with one eye open

If we bring together our assessment of all the options we've identified to reduce energy requirements and emissions from the existing production routes for steel and aluminium, and if demand grows as we anticipate, will it be impossible to make a 50% absolute cut in emissions by 2050?

Isaiah in the Piazza di Spagna in Rome

We ought to start a chapter about forecasting with a word from a prophet:

"What will you do on the day of reckoning, when disaster comes from afar? To whom will you run for help? Where will you leave your riches?" (Isaiah 10:3)

This is a chapter of reckoning: in the last four chapters we've explored every option we can identify 'with one eye open' by which we mean with all possible efficiencies but ensuring that any demand for metal is met. However the target of an absolute 50% reduction in CO_2 emissions by 2050 is snapping at our heels. The European steel and aluminium industries certainly feel that tighter regulations on emissions being applied in the EU, but not elsewhere, have chewed up their heels so it's increasingly hard for them to stand up. In our survey of energy efficiency options, have we identified enough options for further improvement that there's a chance of it all adding up, or is disaster coming from afar?

Our job in this chapter is to do the adding up carefully. We've been clear from the outset that we face uncertainty in every number we use, so our adding up must reflect our uncertainty. But we've also seen some things which are not uncertain: no one, by any means and whatever the incentive, will ever be able to extract metal from ores with less than the standard chemical exergy; while global demand is growing, we can keep increasing our recycling volumes, but we absolutely cannot achieve a circular or closed-loop economy.

We'll develop our forecasts in two stages. Firstly we'll predict the features of our metals economy in 2050. Then we'll use them to forecast how much CO_2 we'll emit.

What will the metals economy look like in 2050?

We will be able to predict emissions in 2050 if we know how much metal is made, by which processes, how much energy those processes use per unit of output, and how much they emit directly or as a result of energy use. We've examined all of those issues in the earlier chapters of this Part of the book, so in this section we'll draw together our evidence and choose values for the parameters we need to make our forecasts.

We developed forecasts of future demand for both metals in chapter 4, and we'll use these as average values within a range of ±10% for steel and ±20% for aluminium based on the projections of the IEA. We'll use the models of stocks and product life-spans from chapter 4 to calculate future scrap availability, and assuming that post-consumer scrap collection rates improve to 90%, we can then predict the fraction of metal demand that will be met by lower emitting secondary production.

In chapter 7 we found that we could make only small savings in the energy required to drive the chemical reactions to extract metal from ore, some savings in furnace management, and further savings in downstream processes, where energy is mainly used in electric motors. However, in predicting the gains available from these process improvements we don't know the distribution of current operating efficiencies across the world: how near are we on average to current best practice? Our exploration of opportunities for heat capture and exchange in chapter 8 leads to a similar uncertainty. We've resolved this by assuming that the IEA's predictions of gains from energy efficiency exclude electric motors but include everything else so we can achieve a 14% emissions saving for steel production and a 12% saving in aluminium by energy efficiency. We won't use a range for these values because they arise from proven technologies, and have a clear economic incentive, so it seems likely that over 40 years they will be adopted universally.

In chapter 9 we found that most current efforts at innovation in steel making are related to carbon capture and storage, principally because the existing routes are so extremely efficient compared with Gibbs' absolute limit. The one exception was to use electrolysis to produce steel, but this is far from commercialisation. We also saw that the candidate process innovations for aluminium production have been known for a long time, and the problems that inhibit their development persist. In tables 11.1 and 11.2 we have summarised what we learnt from chapters 7-9 about the emissions abatement potential of efficiency and process innovations for the two metals.

Option	CO_2 abatement potential
Energy efficiency—best available technology	14% for all processes
Direct reduced iron	20% compared to the blast furnace
Smelt reduction	20% compared to the blast furnace
Electrolysis with nuclear power	80% compared to the blast furnace assuming low carbon electricity
Top gas recycling and fuel substitution	10% compared to the blast furnace
Electric motors in fabrication	50% reduction in energy

Table 11.1—**Summary of the emissions abatement from energy efficiency and novel technologies for steel**

Sustainable Materials with both eyes open

Option	CO_2 abatement potential
Energy efficiency—best available technology	12% for all current processes
Inert anodes with wetted drained cathodes	30% for smelting but double for anodes
Carbothermic reduction	Smelting increases by 12% and no anodes required
Electric motors in fabrication	50% reduction in energy

Table 11.2—**Summary of the emissions abatement from energy efficiency and novel technologies for aluminium**

Will future steel and aluminium production be powered by 'clean' electricity? It is unlikely that renewable sources will power future materials processing, although an expansion in nuclear power could occur. But the other options for clean electricity, and all the other options for process innovations, require carbon capture and storage (CCS). And for our future rate of implementation of CCS, based on what we found in chapter 10, we can choose any number we like: at the optimistic end of the scale, we can say CCS is tremendous, we're going to apply it to all our industrial processes, and all our electricity generation, and in fact we're going to treble our electricity output because in future we'll have electric cars and heat our homes with electric heat pumps. Joy for all, we're going to bury bury bury the problem. At the pessimistic end, well, CCS has been tried in three sites around the world but not yet attached to an industrial process or power station, it's going to reduce the power output of each process by a quarter[3], it's going to cost a lot, it carries risks and the public may not accept it, even if anyone does generate electricity with CCS every other sector will want it too so there won't be any left for industry, and it seems to us the only rational way to explore future emissions linked to materials processing is to choose zero. If we depend on CCS to solve the problem for us, we need take no other action, and the risk of that approach is too great. So let's support intelligent development and evaluation of CCS, to build up our understanding of what it will cost, how it will operate and how difficult it is to implement. But let's not dream of it taking the problem away. We'll just park it—and have as a caveat to all our predictions "unless CCS is implemented on a massive scale". However, we will assume some decarbonisation of the global electricity system. This is also a risky assumption as demand for electricity is growing significantly with population, economic development and fuel switching. But given strong political commitment at present, and because we could achieve this by more nuclear generation, we'll assume that by 2050 between 10% and 30% of the world's electricity is carbon free.

We started this section by asking how much metal will be made in 2050, by which processes, with how much energy and emissions. Having reviewed our options, the parameters we'll use to make our forecasts are shown in tables 11.3 and 11.4. We're going to assume without uncertainty that all remaining energy efficiency options are fully adopted, and that recycling rates rise to 90% by 2050, but for all other choices, the table shows a range of values. To reflect the uncertainties of forecasting 40 years ahead, we've given an optimistic, medium and pessimistic value for every number: the optimistic values include lowest forecasts of demand, and the most aggressive possible implementation of emissions saving options, so would lead to the lowest future emissions figure we can imagine. The pessimistic

	Low	Medium	High
Demand projection (Mt)	2300	2500	2800
Electricity decarbonisation	30%	20%	10%
Iron reduced by:			
Blast furnace with top gas recycling and fuel substitution	50%	60%	75%
DRI	20%	20%	15%
Smelt reduction	20%	15%	10%
Electrolysis	10%	5%	0%

Table 11.3—**Features of our forecasts for future production of steel goods**

	Low	Medium	High
Demand projection (Mt)	110	130	150
Electricity decarbonisation	30%	20%	10%
Aluminium reduction by:			
Conventional Hall-Héroult implementation	0%	25%	50%
Inert anode implementation	85%	65%	45%
Carbothermic reduction implementation	15%	10%	5%

Table 11.4—**Features of our forecasts for future production of aluminium goods**

values lead to the highest possible emissions forecast, and of course the medium values are in between.

Forecast emissions in the steel and aluminium sectors

Now we can start adding up for our day of reckoning in 2050. Firstly we've scaled our forecast of global demand from chapter 4 according to the values in tables 11.3 and 11.4. Then we've run our model of stocks and recycling to predict the volumes of the two metals made by primary and secondary routes. We've applied our energy and emissions intensities from the tables, and converted electricity to emissions as appropriate. Unlike forecasts made by the steel and aluminium industries, we've included downstream manufacturing and construction processes in our calculations, because these sectors are the key drivers of demand. Finally, we multiplied each process emissions intensity by the relevant metal flow, and summed up the process totals to predict future emissions. We repeated this exercise for optimistic, average and pessimistic settings in the two tables, to arrive at a range of forecast emissions in 2050. For comparison we also predicted a 'business as usual' forecast of emissions, by assuming that demand would increase, but emissions intensities would not change.

Our results are shown in figures 11.1 and 11.2 and are devastating: we have done all we can to reflect every possible move that would lead to improved energy efficiency and emissions abatement in making goods in steel and aluminium, and we simply cannot reach the target 50% cut, if demand grows as we anticipate.

For steel, if we pursue the energy and process efficiency options identified in table 11.3 with extraordinary worldwide commitment, CO_2 emissions would remain at approximately current levels, despite nearly a doubling in steel demand. However, this would be an astounding achievement as the required changes involve a huge upheaval in the industry. A fifth of iron would be produced by gas-powered DRI and all blast furnaces would be retrofitted with top gas recycling and incorporate further fuel substitution. Significant investment would be needed in the commercial development of smelt reduction and electrolysis and we require the optimisation of all downstream electric motors. Our proposed widespread use of ironmaking technologies other than the blast furnace would dramatically reduce the need for coking and sintering plant while significant investment would be required to build capacity for new ironmaking technologies and recycling.

Sustainable Materials with both eyes open

Figure 11.1—**Emissions forecast for steel**

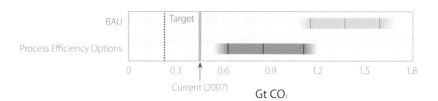

Figure 11.2—**Emissions forecast for aluminium**

The forecast for aluminium suggests that our likely performance will be even further from the targets, with CO_2 emissions nearly doubling as demand for aluminium grows. Even to get to this level of emissions requires a significant change in production technology. The long-anticipated inert anode system is critical to achieving these reductions and would replace the majority of conventional electrolysis. We will need to double our current capacity for primary production, and increase further our capacity for secondary production of aluminium from recycled material. To achieve the emissions levels in our forecast, the aluminium industry while increasing capacity, must develop and deploy a technology that has remained elusive for the last 25 years. This would be an unprecedented achievement.

The most uncertain variable in our forecasts are the rates at which we think different technologies will be adopted by industry. As we discussed in chapter 9, many novel technologies are in the early stages of development and need significant scientific breakthroughs to become commercially viable, so our forecasts may well be optimistic. We're also aware that the emissions abatement potential of these new technologies can only be estimated after full scale implementation, so the numbers we're using for novel process performance may be ambitious.

We can of course re-interpret the results by saying "OK, now we know how much we can gain from efficiency, that tells us how much CCS we need" but we don't think this is reasonable given the current state of the technology. However, if we don't pin our hopes on CCS, these charts show us that we cannot reach our target emissions numbers by efficiency measures. If the climate scientists are correct to be calling for a 50% cut in global emissions to avert serious global warming, the chart has two consequences: either we continue forwards knowing that we are creating irreversible harm to our children's lives; or we accept that as the effects of global warming become more severe, governments will take bolder action to limit emissions, and will eventually ration the output of the steel and aluminium industries. And as we said at the beginning of the book, we're using CO_2 emissions as a proxy for environmental harm more generally: if you're concerned about other problems that inhibit future sustainability, whether emissions to water and land, or resource depletion, or national security—we anticipate that similar analysis will lead to similar results. If you want to reduce harmful side effects while global demand increases, simply aiming to be more efficient within the materials industries is unlikely to make a big enough difference.

Wrought iron railings being collected for the war effort [2]

But the reason we wrote this book is that we don't have to look ahead with only one eye open. If we assume that we must meet any future demand for new metal, we now know that we can't reduce our impacts to sustainable levels solely by pursuing efficiency measures within the industry. We have to do something else, and we raised the 'threat' of rationing above simply because, in a crisis, that's exactly what happens. During the last world war, the UK's population were asked to give up any spare iron or steel in their possession to create materials for the military forces—so iron railings, for example, rapidly disappeared[1]. When forced, we can cope with rationing and our lives do not fall apart.

But we don't want to live between the two precarious extremes of industry efficiency and eventual rationing, and we don't have to if we open our other eye. If we assume production must grow with demand, we can't make enough difference, so why not consider meeting demand with less production? That's what we mean by having both eyes open, and specifically we want to explore the idea of 'material efficiency' to balance the 'energy efficiency' we've looked at so far, with our one eye. We purchase steel and aluminium components as part of goods which we use to deliver a service. Let's call this a 'material service' such as 'transporting us between Cambridge and London' or 'providing a comfortable workspace in town, near to my colleagues'. The objective of making materials is not to have the materials themselves, but to provide material services. So, with both eyes open, can we deliver material services, even allowing for growing demand, while requiring less material production? That's the theme for the rest of the book. In Part III we'll look with both eyes open at the services provided by steel and aluminium. We'll expand on this to look at cement, plastic and paper in Part IV, and then in Part V reflect on how to make enough difference.

Let's turn the page with Isaiah, *"then will the eyes of the blind be opened… and a highway will be there… no lion will be there.. and sorrow and sighing will flee away"*.

The clear conclusion to Part II, is that with one eye open, we can't make enough difference. We need to look instead with both eyes open.

Notes

Forecast emissions in the steel and aluminium sectors

1. John Cole, a child in London during the Second World War describes how in 1943, the wrought iron railings in the front gardens along his street were removed for use in the war effort after Lord Beaverbrook, Minister of Aircraft Production, started a campaign to collect scrap metal. (Cole, n.d).

2. This picture shows the railings from Whitehall Road Recreation Ground being removed in 1942 (Rugby Advertiser, 1942)

3. David MacKay states that cleaning up the gases from a coal-fired power station and storing the CO_2 underground "would reduce delivered electricity by about 25 %" (MacKay, 2009).

with both eyes open

PART III

12. Using less metal by design

We use so much metal that we've designed and optimised our production processes to make it with great efficiency. However a feature of that efficiency is that it is much cheaper to make a large volume of material of the same shape than to make each piece of metal a different shape—there are significant economies of scale related to tooling costs, and the speed of continuous as opposed to discrete processes. As a result, it's almost always cheaper to make components with simple geometries, than to use less metal.

13. Reducing yield losses

Separate from component design, our maps of metal flow showed that at least a quarter of all liquid steel and 40% of liquid aluminium never makes it into products, as it is cut off as scrap during manufacturing. What can we do to reduce these losses, and how much can we save?

14. Diverting manufacturing scrap

With high yield losses currently in production, and with additional scrappage from defects and over-ordering, could we avoid sending scrap for recycling by melting and instead use it elsewhere?

15. Re-using metal components

Having looked at diverting production scrap back into use without melting, can we apply a similar approach to components from products at the end of their first life? For larger components, particularly for steel beams used in construction which are generally not damaged at all in use, we may not need to recycle them by melting: instead, could we reuse them directly?

16. Longer life products

In developed economies, where our demand for metal has largely stabilised, we mainly purchase metal as replacement rather than due to growth. So, if we keep our products for longer, that would slow down the rate of replacement and hence reduce our need for new metal. Could we really use products for longer?

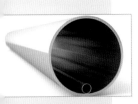

17. Reducing final demand for metal services

If we can't find enough options to meet our emissions targets through energy or material efficiency, we need to consider the possibility of demand reduction also. Does this automatically mean impoverishment—the reverse of development—or are there other options?

18. Options for change

19. Future energy use and emissions

Now that we've identified a new set of options 'with both eyes open' we can return to the catalogue of products we identified in Part I to find out to what extent each strategy can be applied to each product.

12 Using less metal by design

We use so much metal that we've designed and optimised our production processes to make it with great efficiency. However a feature of that efficiency is that it is much cheaper to make a large volume of material of the same shape than to make each piece of metal a different shape—there are significant economies of scale related to tooling costs, and the speed of continuous as opposed to discrete processes. As a result, it's almost always cheaper to make components with simple geometries, than to use less metal.

The Wright brothers' Flyer

Henry Ford's Model-T

1903 was a good year for engineering: Wilbur and Orville Wright took to the skies in the first powered flight at Kitty Hawk in North Carolina, while a few hundred miles away, Henry Ford set up the Ford Motor Company in Dearborn, Michigan, a suburb of Detroit. The Wright brothers' main contribution to flying was to invent three-axis control, but they also worked on wing geometries and cutting down the weight of their Flyer. And how did they cut down the weight? They removed every possible strut from the airframe, made the rest as thin as possible, used the right materials and built their own engine, with—thanks to the leadership of Napoleon III—a cast aluminium engine block. In order to fly, the Wright brothers had to learn how to design the lightest possible plane, and the aerospace industry has pursued lightweight design ever since. But meanwhile, in Dearborn, Henry Ford was gearing up to produce the Model T, which launched in 1908, and which transformed the world of motoring. For the first time, a car was cheap enough that the people who worked in Ford's factory could afford to buy one. In transforming the car from a luxury product to an affordable one, Henry Ford set in train the whole history of 20th century manufacturing, converting luxuries into commodities, and he did it by ruthlessly pursuing standardisation. Famously Ford's offering was "any colour so long as it's black." In effect Ford discovered and exploited the economies of scale in production: making a high volume of identical parts and goods is significantly cheaper than making a wide variety, because there is no delay moving on from one part to the next, and the people, tools and systems to make parts all improve with experience.

So, in our snapshot of 1903, on the one hand we have the Wright brothers doing anything possible to reduce the weight of their vehicle, and on the other, we have Henry Ford doing everything possible to standardise his. Standardised parts are generally heavier than optimised ones, and that sets up the story of this chapter:

can we use less metal by optimising the design of components? If we optimise the design, what will it cost us?

We'll start with optimising weight, and try to establish guidelines for designing parts with minimum weight. As most components are not perfectly optimised, we'll examine a set of case studies to see how metal saving plays out in practice, and try to understand why we don't minimise weight at present. We'll then revisit our design principles to develop some practical guidelines, and use these to estimate how much of the world's metal could be saved by better design. Finally, we'll look at the business case for saving metal: metal costs money, so why wouldn't you take every opportunity to use less of it?

Basic principles of lightweight design

Since the 1970's the subject of 'structural optimisation' has developed computer aided tools to design components of minimum mass. This is a wonderful subject[1], but mathematically intense, so always demands the best available computers. For any specific problem, it's unlikely that we could beat the computer by hand, but if we rely on the computer, we won't learn how we might try our hand at some other problem. As a result, apart from aerospace applications, optimisation is rare and usually limited to small parts that move rapidly. For example it's worth optimising the heads in an inkjet printer, because reducing inertia allows increased print speed. So in this section we'll try a different approach, and see if we can learn some general principles.

Figure 12.1 shows the simplest example we can imagine, a point load supported by an arm (a cantilever) some distance from a strong stiff wall must deflect less than some limit. This picture might represent a crane, a balcony on a building, or the arm of a robot. We must also ensure that the arm is strong enough but, usually design for stiffness is more demanding than design for strength.

The arm in Figure 12.1 is uniform, so it is most likely to break at the wall. For a stronger arm, we'd want to make it deeper nearer the wall, and by similar logic, less deep near the load. It turns out that if we want stiffness not strength, the same logic applies. Figure 12.2 shows a more optimised design: the depth of the arm varies so that the arm is as stiff as possible for the load at its tip. This design is 16% lighter than the first one: already good news for the Wright brothers, but bad news for Henry Ford as it's going to be more difficult to manufacture.

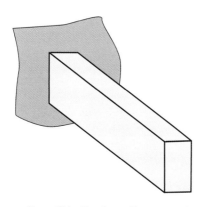

Figure 12.1—**Simple cantilever example**

Sustainable Materials with both eyes open

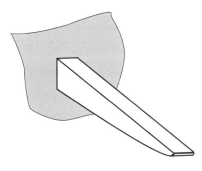

Figure 12.2—**Rectangular beam with depth optimisation**

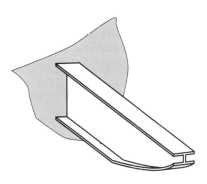

Figure 12.3—**Depth optimised I-beam**

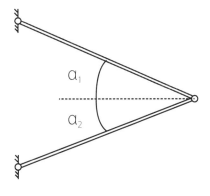

Figure 12.4—**Pin jointed truss**

Although the first beam would fail at the wall, the second one should fail all along its length at the maximum load. However, the whole beam does not fail at once. Failure will start at the upper and lower surfaces. You can easily show this if you have a packet of spaghetti to hand, and don't mind a bit of sweeping up: grasp the bundle of spaghetti firmly at each end, and steadily bend it into a curve of increasing severity. Which is the first strand of spaghetti to snap? It is always the one on the outside of the bundle, the strand at the centre is least likely to snap. Similarly with our beam, failure is most likely at the upper or lower surface, so this is the most useful place to have material, and we can make the middle of the beam thinner. Our third design in Figure 12.3 combines this arrangement of material with the design in Figure 12.2 and now the cross-section of the beam looks like a capital "I". This is the standard form in which structural steel is used in buildings but, because of Henry Ford's concerns, we usually use constant cross-section I-beams, not the variable type we've shown here. I-beams are usually made by rolling with specially shaped rollers, and it's a lot more convenient to make them with the same cross-section along their length. If we'd converted the first design into an equally stiff I-beam but with constant cross-section, we could have saved 54% of the mass, but with the variable depth I-beam in the third picture, we've now saved 85%.

Our variable depth I-beam is beginning to look like two spars working towards a point, and resembles a 'truss' which is familiar from the roof supports of large span buildings such as airports, and from railway bridges. So now let's move to the fourth picture, the simplest possible truss. We have two choices in this design: what's the angle between the two bars in the truss, and what cross-sectional area should they have? For the stiffest design, the best angle between the bars is a right angle, 90° (or equivalently in our picture, angle α_1 and α_2 should be 45°), if we assume that the structure is symmetric. Strictly, the lower strut is in some danger of buckling so might need some extra bracing. At this angle, the distance between the two supports at the wall will be twice the distance of the load from the wall, which may be a problem if we need to conserve space beneath it, but we'll worry about constraints later.

The truss design turns is extremely efficient. If we pick up the bundle of spaghetti again, and grip the two ends firmly, but now just pull, then each strand experiences the same load and is equally likely to fail. This means that we are using the material perfectly efficiently: we will always use less material if we can align loads with members to avoid bending. If the hinges in Figure 12.4 are frictionless, the loads in our truss align perfectly with the spars, so we can use members with constant cross-sections (good for Henry Ford) with just enough area to take the load, and no material wasted (terrific for the Wright brothers).

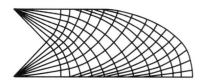

Figure 12.5—**A Michell truss**

We've nearly finished our simple case study, but will end with a remarkable ideal design developed by Anthony Michell—an Australian lubrication engineer, who invented the widely used 'Michell Bearing", set up the Michell Bearing company and as an aside explored the design of 'minimum frames'. In keeping with the theme of the chapter, Michell did this work in 1903 and showed that all minimum frames comprise bars which "form curves of orthogonal systems." So our final solution to the example problem is one of Michell's trusses illustrated in Figure 12.5. The design comprises two 'fans' of lines which always intersect at right angles—that's the meaning of "curves of orthogonal systems." For the Wright brothers, this design looks very interesting, but for Henry Ford rather less so, as the truss requires a complex set of ever shorter bars.

Our simple example has established two key principles for using less metal:

- Avoid bending by using trusses. Truss spars loaded along their length are always more efficient than members loaded in bending.

- If a member must experience bending, it should be designed (like an I-beam) to have the material as far away from its bending axis as possible. If the bending varies along the member, it should have a variable cross-section.

These two rules give us a great starting point for trying to design components with less metal, but before we go on to our case studies, we can add three further principles to guide our search for metal savings.

Firstly, once we've chosen our basic efficient design, we must choose the cross-sectional areas of each member, and as the loading increases, or the required deflection reduces, so the area must increase. Therefore, prior to starting our design, we should aim to reduce the required loads and increase the allowed deflections as much as possible. This seems rather obvious, but in practice, clients or letting agents will often over-specify requirements "to be on the safe side." That's comforting when we're in an aeroplane, but may be quite wasteful if our office is strong enough to have a swimming pool on each floor.

Secondly, our simple example required that we support just one load. What if we also had a second load that should be supported from the same base? Should we support it with a second independent structure, or should we support both loads

Sustainable Materials with both eyes open

with the same structure? In most cases we'll save material using one combined structure rather than two separate ones.

Thirdly, we haven't yet discussed the material we're going to use to make the arm, but of course if we use a stronger stiffer material, we'll generally use less material. Material selection is a big topic, because as we saw in chapter 3, there are so many properties we might consider. But fortunately, and as before, we can return to our colleague Professor Mike Ashby, who's book and associated software and databases show us how to choose the best material[2]. We'll illustrate his approach by going back to our simple truss design solution to the example problem. We said that the design must withstand the required load without failing (strength limit) and without exceeding some deflection (stiffness limit). If we set the load at the strength limit of the material, its deflection will decrease as the stiffness increases, or equivalently we can say that the deflection is proportional to the strength limit divided by the stiffness. Our chart in Figure 12.6 shows the properties of a few materials plotted on axes of strength against stiffness, with contours along which the ratio of strength to stiffness is constant.

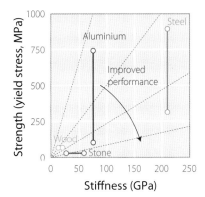

Figure 12.6—**Material selection chart or Ashby chart**

Materials on the same contour, such as steel and aluminium in this case, give similar performance and the arrow shows the direction in which we should move to choose the best material. According to the graph the best material is stone. We could perform a similar search considering other properties: density, for example if the weight of the truss is a significant component of its loading, or cost, or availability and so on.

We've now done enough with our simple example to derive five principles for designing products and components with less metal:

Five principles for using less metal

- Support multiple loads with fewer structures where possible
- Don't over-specify the loads
- Align loads with members to avoid bending if possible
- If bending is unavoidable, optimise the cross-section along the member
- Choose the best material

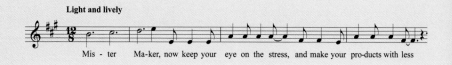
Light and lively

Mis - ter   Ma-ker, now keep your   eye on the stress, and make your pro-ducts with less

How can these principles be applied in reality? To find out, we'll look at what happens in practice today.

Case studies to explore using less metal in practice

To explore the reality of material saving through efficient design, we've examined five case studies—universal beams, deep-sea oil and gas pipeline, car bodies/crash structures, rebar, and food cans. Globally, annual production of these components uses around 400 Mt of steel and aluminium, nearly 40% of the total production of the two metals. We spent time with the companies making these components to learn about current practice, then we applied our principles from the previous section to propose a new lighter weight design. Then we went back to the companies to see what they made of our suggested change.

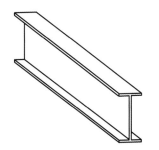

Figure 12.7—**A standard universal beam**

Standard universal beams as illustrated in Figure 12.7 are the key components of steel-framed buildings. They are designed for bending stiffness, and used as horizontal beams to support floors or roofs. They are manufactured in a standardized set of geometries, and listed in catalogues provided by steel producers. However, their geometry, which has a constant cross-section, is chosen for ease of manufacture, so is not perfectly efficient, as we saw with our simple example in the previous section.

In this case study, in order to estimate how much metal we could save through optimised design, we designed a series of beams to cope with a set of standard load cases and then evaluated our findings with experts in the construction industry. Our different beam designs are shown in Figure 12.8 and comprise: standard I-beams; composite floor beams where the concrete floor slab is part of the bending system allowing use of smaller steel sections; open-web joists which are truss structures suitable for lighter loads such as roofs; cellular beams where shaped cells are cut from the web of the beam to save weight; variable cross-section beams where the beam depth or width varies and is optimised for a given loading.

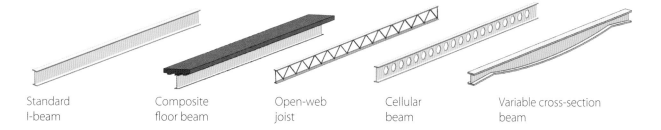

| Standard I-beam | Composite floor beam | Open-web joist | Cellular beam | Variable cross-section beam |

Figure 12.8—**Comparison of different beam designs**

Structural engineers design buildings according to codes of practice written by standards agencies to ensure building safety. In the UK, designs must satisfy European building codes (Eurocode 3 for steel design). So we optimised our beam designs[3] to satisfy these codes in two contexts: for floors and roofs. Our results are summarized in Figure 12.9, showing the weight of steel required for each design.

Composite floor beams are the most common solution for floors in the UK at present, so used these as a reference for the floor load cases. For the roof load cases the current standard design is a standard universal beam. Our results show that weight savings of at least 30% can be achieved by applying our design principles, and higher weight savings are possible in cases where composite floor beams are not currently in use. When we discussed these results with building designers, they said that the improved designs were technically feasible, but would cost more. Clearly this is true, but if Boeing can assemble millions of parts to make a 747, it can be done—and, remembering the brief sketch with which we began chapter 6, the additional cost will be relatively small compared to the total cost of the building.

So, with the Wright brothers, we might be able to reduce the amount of steel in steel framed buildings but what would Henry Ford think? We mentioned earlier that I-beams are currently made by hot rolling with special roll shapes, so when we started thinking about this issue, we also got to work in our lab, and have found a new way to roll optimised I-beams[5]. We hope that Henry would approve.

Although in this case study we've aimed to optimise the cross-section of beams subject to bending, let's not forget our other design principles: we should combine loads, and avoid over specification. The box story on the Velodrome at the 2012 London Olympics on the next page shows that combining loads (supporting the seats and the roof in the same structure) was a key strategy in delivering a materially efficient building.

Roof beam

o Cellular beam

o Cellular beam

o Variable web depth beam

o Variable flange width beam

o Open-web joist

Floor beam

o Cellular beam

o Variable web depth beam

o Variable flange width beam

0   20   40   60   80

Weight saving relative to benchmark (%)

Figure 12.9—**Weight comparison of alternative beam designs**

Our principles also tell us not to over-specify loads. Over-specification occurs in construction because of a process called 'rationalisation'. Typically, a keen young civil engineering graduate might design a building according to the standard codes, and choose the optimum beams. A wizzened old hand then reviews the design, and reduces the number of different beam sections required, because it simplifies life for the contractors who build the building. The cost of steel is low compared to the cost of labour in developed countries, so it's generally cheaper to save labour (by avoiding variety on the construction site) than to save material.

London 2012 Olympic Park

As CO_2 emissions related to the use of buildings are reduced through energy efficiency measures, more attention is focused on the embodied carbon emissions in construction. At the London 2012 Olympic Park more than 90% of embodied carbon is in just three construction materials: concrete, reinforcing steel and structural steel. Each material accounts for approximately 30% of the total. An effective means to reduce embodied carbon in construction projects is to set targets early in the design, preferably in the brief. We found two different stories at the Olympic park.

The architects for the Velodrome had a vision to build a minimum structure building 'shrink-wrapped' around the sport and spectators. As a result the geometry was governed by the track layout and required sightlines; this 'saddle' shape allowed use of a lightweight cable-net roof system where the steel is used in tension to span 130 metres between supports. Despite initial concerns about costs and risks, the contractor could save money and time by using this system and the client approved. The cable-net roof saved 27% of the steel that would have been required in an alternative steel arch option. An advanced dynamic analysis of the seating structure showed that combining the roof, stand and façade support systems, gave performance within accepted limits despite being lighter than code recommendations.

The contract for design the Aquatics Centre was awarded to a signature architect asked to design an iconic building for the London 2012 Games. The roof is a key element—'an undulating roof sweeps up from the ground as a wave'. The shape of the roof could be supported only by a conventional truss system. This was optimised during design but is still over five times as heavy as the roof of the Velodrome's, which has a similar span and area.

The story of these two stadia at the London Olympics demonstrates that specifying lightweight design early in a contract allows significant material savings: finding a favourable form at the start yields greater savings than highly refining a heavier option later on.

Our initial studies, with confidential data, have shown that this two-stage process of rationalisation leads to significant extra use of steel.

So in our exploration of beams in construction, we've see that there are significant opportunities for using less metal, but we don't currently pursue them because of the relative costs of materials and labour.

Deep-sea oil and gas pipeline connects off-shore drilling rigs to shore, and may be installed more than 2 km under the sea. At these depths, a pipe is subjected to a very high water pressure which would tend to crush it if empty, but when in use, oil or gas is pumped through the pipe at a pressure similar to the external pressure. The oil and gas inside the pipe supports the pipe wall, which experiences only a small pressure difference, and could therefore be quite thin. In this case, the pipe wall-thickness would be chosen to avoid dangers from corrosion.

Sections of a pipeline

However, it isn't just the use of the pipe that determines the amount of steel required. We also have to solve a different problem: how do you install a 250 km length of pipe two kilometres under the surface of the sea? 2000 metres of water creates a pressure of approximately 200 atmospheres. At that depth there's no sun light, the temperature's around -5°C and you might bump into a Humpback Anglerfish, so it's a difficult environment for lining up and welding steel pipes.

As a result, deep sea pipes are not installed in-situ, but instead are dropped down from the surface. Typically a pipe is made of 30–50 mm thick high grade steel plate. After hot rolling, the plate is cut into lengths, typically 9 m or 12 m, rolled and welded into pipe sections with lengths of around 10 m. Pipes of this type cannot be coiled without damage, so are laid from a ship that slowly steams out to the target oil or gas well by welding each new section onto the existing pipe. This pipe 'string' initially hangs between ship and shore, and as it becomes longer, slowly sinks down to the sea bed. The photo shows the Saipem 7000, one of the worlds' largest pipe-laying ships.

A humpback anglerfish
(Melanocetus johnsonii)

During regular use, the pipe has to withstand only a small pressure difference across its wall. But during laying, the most recent section of pipe to be welded onto the string must support the weight of about 2.5km of the string as it descends to where it reaches the sea bed, and the pipe also experiences significant bending just before it settles. To reduce the weight of the pipe it is laid empty, so the buoyancy of the air inside the pipe reduces its effective weight. Even so, the loading on the pipe during installation, due to self weight and to bending as it is draped onto the sea bed, greatly exceeds the loading it will experience during service.

The Saipem 7000 pipe laying vessel[6]

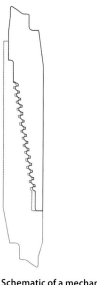

Schematic of a mechanical
pipeline connector

Applying our principles for designing with less metal to this case study, we considered whether we could reduce the loads, and whether we had any other material selection options. We could try to reduce the loads during laying by pressurising the pipeline internally during installation, and our calculations suggest that this could reduce the weight of the pipe by around 30%. However, we learnt from industrial partners that the need for corrosion protection may reduce these savings to 10% and generating an internal pressure of 200 atmospheres in the pipe during laying may lead to safety risks.

Alternatively, as the loads during installation, not service, determine metal requirements, is there a different installation system that would allow a reduction in metal use? In shallower water, some pipelines are constructed on the seabed using mechanical connectors like those shown to the left. Could this practice be extended to deeper waters? Alternatively, could we make the pipe from a different material, either to increase its strength to resist crushing pressures, or to improve its corrosion resistance? Potentially "yes", but both solutions need extensive development.

This case study has revealed an important barrier to saving metal by design: line pipe in use today is overweight, not because of over-specification of the design loads, as we saw with beams in construction, but because the pipe experiences much higher loads during installation than in service.

A modern car body

Car body structures originally comprised a stiff chassis on which the body was erected. However, although this is still the basis of truck and heavy vehicle design, most cars today are constructed without a chassis but based on a monocoque: a cage around the passenger area giving better safety than a chassis based design of the same weight. When we look at a car, we can't see this monocoque. Instead we see cosmetic body panels which are only lightly attached so they can be replaced easily if damaged. Their main function is to hold up the paint! The priority design requirements for the monocoque are that it should absorb energy in a crash and provide sufficient strength and stiffness for normal operation. However, the monocoque has many additional functions, such as providing mountings for the engine, drivetrain and wheels, comfort for passengers, and an aesthetically exciting shape that attracts customers, and it must be possible to manufacture the body at acceptable cost. As a result, the design of a car body structure is extraordinarily complex, involving a series of trade-offs between competing intentions. If we skewed this trade-off towards saving weight, how much could we save?

Sustainable Materials with both eyes open

The Lotus Seven lightweight vehicle

One very simple answer to this question comes from the great car designer Colin Chapman, founder of Lotus Cars in the UK. Chapman's design principles included the aim to "simplify and add lightness" and, famously, although we can't endorse this one, "any car which holds together for a whole race is too heavy".

At 500 kg, the Lotus Seven (now produced by Caterham) is one of the lightest cars on the road today. Its lightness is generally used to give very high acceleration, but in a recent competition for fuel efficiency a Lotus Seven was raced for economy, and with a change only to its tyres, and with a different driving style, achieved 160 miles per gallon. So Chapman's commitment to weight saving is inspiring in our quest for a more sustainable future both for reduced fuel consumption, and of course for reduced metal requirements.

We're hoping that our head of department will soon be buying us a Lotus Seven so we can learn more about lightweight design, but meanwhile we'll focus on one part of a more conventional body structure, the car door, and return to our principles for using less metal. The car door must be convenient for passengers, support a window, house various electronic features including loudspeakers, and resist impact in a crash. Applying our five principles in turn:

- **Support all loads with the same structure:** conventionally a car door is designed with the support structure separate from the 'door skin'. If these separate structures are combined, they can be made lighter.

- **Don't over-specify the loads:** the loads on impact are specified by national standards in crash tests, so depend on an average of other vehicles on the road. In future, separating heavy and light vehicles on roads would allow great improvements in safety for lighter weight vehicles.

- **Align loads with members to avoid bending if possible:** doors are supported round their perimeter, so are inevitably loaded in bending. The bending would be minimised if the door were as small as possible but customers prefer larger doors so this strategy has little short term potential.

- **If bending is unavoidable, optimise the cross-section and allow it to vary:** doors would be lighter if thicker in the middle, but this may conflict with passenger comfort or external aesthetics. The schematic to the side shows various alternatives to the conventional door design that would allow weight saving. These designs are currently inhibited by the need to withdraw the window entirely within the door.

Alternative car door designs

- **Choose the best material:** Using Professor Ashby's material selection tools, we can examine a wide range of alternative materials for the car door. Carbon fibre composites or magnesium sheets could offer weight savings for equivalent energy absorption. However making these materials requires more energy, leads to greater emissions, and composites cannot be recycled. So there is a trade-off between emissions in production and use, and we'll explore this in detail in chapter 16 when we look at life extension. Manufacturing with composites is also more complicated than with metals so costs would increase.

Our principles have revealed many options for saving weight in car body structures. To validate them, we've spent time with a team at Jaguar Land Rover, who are reviewing their door designs, and are now aiming at a 30% reduction in door weight over the next five years. The details of their approach are confidential, but their ambition confirms that a significant weight saving can yet be achieved in these familiar and already highly engineered components.

Steel reinforcing bars

Steel reinforcing bar, commonly known as "rebar" is used extensively to provide structural reinforcement for concrete in buildings and infrastructure. Concrete is a ceramic, so strong in compression but weak in tension, and steel rebars are therefore embedded within it to provide tensile strength. The design of rebar is often constrained by strength, rather than stiffness as we saw in the earlier case study on structural beams, so if stronger steel is used to make the rebar, less mass is required.

Running through our five design principles for using less metal, two apply particularly to the use of rebar: material selection and avoiding over-specification.

In China, where an astonishing 60% of the world's rebar production is used at present, most rebar is made of relatively low strength steel, around two thirds of the strength we generally use in Europe. If we could upgrade all Chinese rebar, from the current mix of strengths to the best in Europe, we would save about 23 Mt or 13% of global rebar production. Why isn't this happening? Improving the strength of Chinese rebar requires a change in composition (in particular an increase in vanadium used in alloying). Vanadium is expensive, but even so this upgrade would reduce costs by around 20%. However, local producers are reluctant to invest in the equipment required for pre-straining, heat treatment and improved control, so Chinese rebar still has low strength.

Are we using the right amount of rebar? We discussed over-specification of loads in construction earlier, but a different issue arises with rebar, where even if the building as a whole has been designed without over-specification, designers, detailers and contractors may make choices leading to excess rebar use. This is because it is easier and quicker to lay out rebar in simple geometries, at a single spacing and with as few different bar diameters as possible. Of course simple layout also reduces the risk of mistakes and makes inspection easier. What would Henry Ford and the Wright brothers make of this?

You can have any rebar you like, provided it's all the same diameter and of the same length.

If you say so, but then we'd use far more than we need, we'd need a lot of time to lay it out on site, so it will end up costing us a lot more.

I see your point. OK, I'll find a way to weld the rebar into regular grids and cages, to help with the spacing on site—but it's still got to be all the same diameter and length.

Thanks—those grids and cages really help, but now you've got your automatic grid welding system set up, any chance we could vary the spacing sometimes?

Alright—with the new computer system, that works pretty well, and I've found that I can also cut different lengths and position them along the mesh at points where the bending moment's greatest.

Terrific—that saves a lot of steel, and it's just as easy for us to install. Now—what about varying the diameter of the rebar as well?

Well—with the price of steel going up, I can just about justify buying the extra tooling now, so OK.

Fantastic—it's looking really good, and we've now saved a lot of steel. Now then, so far we've always had the bars lined up on a square grid—any chance of some diagonals?

Grrrr—NO!

… and that's about where we've got to with the use of rebar today. It is designed carefully, and apart from the simplest applications, it's welded into grids and meshes to ensure the right spacing and separation. Modern computer control systems such as used by Qube in the box story, can design meshes with varying lengths, spacing and diameters, but as yet we still only use meshes aligned with square grids: no diagonals.

However that's the best of what's currently possible, not necessarily what happens in practice. After discussions with industry experts, we estimate that by truly optimising sizes and placement, we could save a further 15% of global rebar production, assuming optimised rebar solutions could be used in 65% of building projects and 50% of infrastructure projects. If we moved to non-orthogonal layouts, yet further savings would be possible, but with increased project complexity and cost.

Food cans experiencing greater loads in the warehouse than at home

Around 100 billion **food cans** are produced each year. In contrast to drinks cans, which have become lighter by around 20% over the past 30 years, food cans have had only modest decreases in weight, and remain around 30% heavier than a drinks can of equivalent volume and aspect ratio. Lighter cans could be produced using existing manufacturing equipment, but this has not been done. Why not?

The performance specifications of food cans are dictated by downstream processing requirements, where the food manufacturer fills the can, caps it, and then sterilises the contents in a cooking process known as "retorting", before stacking the cans to great heights for storage. During the retorting process, the can experiences an implosive pressure of around one atmosphere (the equivalent of being 10 metres below the surface of the sea) due to pressure in the cooking oven, followed by an explosive pressure of nearly three atmospheres as the contents heat and expand. Later, when cans are stacked in a warehouse the can must withstand the weight of all the cans on top of it—potentially as many as 50. Both features of this loading, which occurs before the can is sold to final customers, differ from the treatment of other food packaging such as aluminium pouches, plastic pots and Tetra Pak™. These are sterilized in a balanced retorting process at pressures of around a half an atmosphere, boxed instead of stacked, and handled more carefully. If the same were true for food cans, the can body could be 30% lighter, and in some cases can ends could be replaced by foil closures.

Once safely in customers' homes, cans need be no stronger than drinks cans, so just as with the deep sea oil and gas pipes above, their weight is determined by loads that occur before final use. It is possible to reduce these additional loads:

Reinforcing steel optimisation

Reinforced concrete designs generally include a degree of 'rationalisation' in the selection and layout of reinforcing steel, i.e. bars of the same diameter and same spacing are used across large areas to simplify detailing, identification, laying and checking of the installed reinforcement. This can typically add between 15% and 30% more reinforcing steel than is strictly required to meet performance and code requirements. Qube Design minimise this over-specification by using an advanced finite element approach for designing and detailing reinforcement using the Bamtec prefabricated rolled reinforcement carpet system. Bamtec carpets typically comprise smaller diameter bars (including in addition to normal stock ranges: 14, 18 and 22 mm diameter) which are placed at a reduced spacing to achieve the same reinforcement area required by the design. Bamtec 'rolled carpets' are robotically manufactured with the reinforcement read from the detailed drawings. Complex sequences of bars are used to significantly reduce the degree of rationalisation in the slab, without any loss of stiffness, and with increased crack control. Each bar is spot welded to thin gauge steel straps during manufacture and rolled up, for quick roll out on site. The rolled carpets, together with prefabricated edge curtailment and cages are mainly manufactured offsite. The combination of Qube's approach to design, and the Bamtec carpet system is an attractive example of intelligent innovation leading to real material savings[7].

the balanced retorting process used for foil food pouches could be used for cans, additional support could be provided for light cans in the existing process, and additional (reusable) supports could be used to allow can stacking with reduced total loads. We currently don't do this, because it's cheaper to pay for the additional metal. But if, for example, we had a choice between saving metal or paying for the infrastructure and energy costs of carbon capture and storage, metal saving might be much cheaper.

Practical barriers to saving metal by design and means to overcome them

Armed with our five principles for using less metal by design, we've found significant opportunities to use less metal in each of our case studies, but we've also found that we don't currently take these opportunities because of various practical barriers. Some of these barriers relate to cost: it can be cheaper to use excess metal than to pay the costs of using less. However, our ambition in the book is to look ahead to identify all possible options to cut emissions to 50%

of current levels by 2050, assuming demand for metal services doubles, and we expect that some of them will not be profitable immediately, or they would have been implemented already.

Let's summarise the barriers we identified in the case studies, and look at how we might overcome them:

- **Requirements before final use dominate design:** The service provided by metal components is often multi-faceted. Components may appear to be over-specified for their final use if their design must also satisfy other criteria: the food can must withstand higher pressures during retorting than on the shelf, and the deep-sea pipe experiences higher stress during laying than when pumping gas or oil. However, in both cases we've seen ways to reduce these additional loads to avoid adding metal: the can could be supported during retorting and stacking; the pipe could be joined on the sea bed rather than dropped in a string. So, in response to requirements prior to use: **look for alternative means to reduce loads occurring before final use**.

- **Asymmetric risks of using less metal:** It is generally cheaper to incur extra material costs for an over-designed component than to carry the risk of component failure. As a result, designers are inherently conservative, and in the long chains of companies involved in making final metal products, this conservatism is applied repeatedly. For example, we saw that the beams eventually used in buildings can be significantly over-specified after repeated rationalisation. The solutions to this issue are contractual, and depend on more precision in agreeing risks. For example, current building regulations in the UK specify *minimum* required sections or rebar designs to carry given loads. As a result, everybody involved is motivated to exceed the minimum of their predecessor. However, if the building regulations were changed to specify a target section or rebar requirement instead of a minimum, there would be no motivation to exceed it. So, in response to asymmetric risks: **write standards that specify target not minimum design requirements**.

A novel flexible spinning process in our lab

- **Manufacturing minimum weight designs may cost more:** we saw that making variable section structural beams would save weight, but cost more to produce, and in our imagined dialogue between Henry Ford and the Wright brothers, we found that current use of rebar is a compromise between material cost and manufacturing effort. But we also found that there's space for innovation in manufacturing, creating flexibility in forming processes to produce more optimal designs with less metal[4,5]. We won't save metal if optimised parts are

cut out of big blocks, as occurs in aerospace manufacture: the value of weight saving is so high for aeroplanes that material costs are irrelevant, and typically aircraft manufacturers turn more than 90% of the high quality aluminium they purchase into chips (called swarf). So, in response to concern about manufacturing costs: **develop new flexible metal casting, forming and fabricating processes**.

Two other barriers to using less metal, that came up in discussions with the companies in the case studies, are that customers may perceive lighter weight products as lower quality (this is a concern for luxury car makers for example), and that optimised components may be less robust than those with excess capacity. Both issues could be addressed by good design.

The key to achieving the material savings in these case studies is to foster more detailed collaboration among all the companies involved in converting liquid metal into final components. If product designers, component suppliers, manufacturing bosses, equipment makers, and the producers of intermediate metal stock products—in fact all decision takers between liquid material and final use—were to collaborate in the definition of material service requirements, the assessment of risk, and the build up of manufacturing costs, and evidence is that they could overcome all the barriers that prevent us using less metal.

How much metal could we save and how does this influence emissions?

The table summarises our estimates of potential weight savings in our five case studies, showing an average of about 30%. If we assume this estimate also applied to the remaining 60% of steel and aluminium use not covered in our case studies, using less metal by design looks like a dramatic opportunity for saving material: so potentially, we could use 30% less metal than we do at present, with no change in the level of material service provided, simply by optimising product designs and controlling the loads they experience before and during use. In fact, if our estimated reduction is applied across all metal using products, it translates directly to a saving in emissions: optimising designs could lead to a 30% reduction in all emissions associated with steel and aluminium production. In Chapter 11, we found that with one eye open we could save 10–30% of current emissions by efficiency in existing production systems, but now in our first chapter with both

	Global demand (Mt)	Potential savings (Mt)	
Beams	49	8-21	20–50%
Line pipe	25	3-8	10–30%
Car body	48	10-20	20–40%
Rebar	170	51	30%
Food cans	8	2	30%

Table 12.1—**Estimated weight savings for case study products**

eyes open we've found an opportunity greater than this with just one strategy—although it's a strategy that won't be pursued by the metals industries themselves.

In fact the consequence of our 30% saving in metal production would actually be a greater saving in emissions than we've estimated so far, due to three co-benefits we identified in the case studies:

- In any application where a product moves, so particularly in transport, fuel consumption increases with vehicle weight, so lighter vehicles use less fuel as we saw in Figure 2.2. Fuel efficient cars are light weight cars. (Sadly, the recent history of car making is that we've reduced the weight of car body structures, mainly by using higher strength materials, but average car weight has increased, as we continue to want more luxury items in commodity cars. We all now expect air conditioning, electric window winders, great audio systems, and buttons to move our seats around, and no doubt within five years we wouldn't be seen dead in a super-mini that didn't have built in back-massaging in every seat…) If we could only stop compensating for weight saving by translating more of the features of luxury homes into our cars, we'd have lighter cars with lower fuel consumption.

- Lighter weight products may have improved performance: lighter cars accelerate, brake and turn better, lighter robots work faster, and lighter shipping containers can be lifted more rapidly.

- One lighter component may lead to another lighter component, compounding reductions in weight. This is true in office blocks where self-weight exceeds the weight of users, but also applies to oil rigs where the weight of the structure below the surface depends partly on the weight of the topsides, and to trains where lighter weight trains lead to reduced rail wear.

We can't estimate the impact of these co-benefits, but will return to the trade-off between fuel consumption and the use of metal in vehicles in chapter 16.

The business case for using less metal

A sustainable future may not be cheaper than an unsustainable one. But in some industries, for instance in making aluminium drinks cans, using less metal has been a core strategy for many years, driven by profit. So in this section, we'll

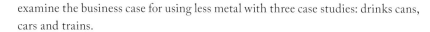

Cost savings per unit mass saving (£/kg)

■ Material costs   ■ Energy costs in use
■ Maintenance costs

Figure 12.10—**Cost saving distribution for example metal products**

examine the business case for using less metal with three case studies: drinks cans, cars and trains.

To start, we'll estimate the lifetime benefit of using less metal. For each kilogram of metal saved, we save one kilogram of material purchasing. For the drinks can that's the only benefit, but as we saw earlier, the car and train also benefit from reduced fuel consumption over their whole life (say 10 years for the car and a 7 year franchise life for the train). The lighter train gives a further benefit through reduced track wear. Figure 12.10 shows how these costs add up to a predicted benefit to the final consumer.

It looks as if the train owner should have the greatest motivation to save weight, and the car owner and can purchaser should have equal motivation. Is that true?

Aluminium drinks cans today are 35 % lighter than they were 30 years ago, driven by the fact that about two thirds of the cost of making a can is the cost of purchasing the aluminium. We use a massive number of these cans (in Europe alone we're using over 50 billion per year) so for the can making industry it's

FLEXX Eco-Bogie

Based on early bogie development work by British Rail Research in the early 1990's, Bombardier's FLEXX Eco-Bogie (previously known as the B5000 bogie) is an example of component lightweighting in the rail industry. The integrated design reduces bogie weight by 30 % (blue versus grey in plan view), saving approximately two tonnes per bogie. More importantly for track damage, the unsprung mass—that is the mass that is in direct contact with the rail with no suspension—is reduced by 25 %, approximately 1 tonne per bogie. The FLEXX Eco-Bogie was developed as part of Bombardier's ECO4 Energy, Efficiency, Economy, Ecology initiative and aims to deliver savings in energy costs, network access charges and maintenance costs. Bombardier estimate that the new bogie results in a 25 % lifecycle cost saving. In the UK, where expected track damage influences network track access charges, the lightweighted bogie is expected to save 17 % of these charges in the 200 km/hr 16 tonne axle load class compared to a conventional bogie. The lightweighted bogie design is suitable for commuter, regional and high-speed rail applications. Over 1000 units are in operation worldwide. Further units are being manufactured for the Norwegian Railways (NSB) and for the new Bombardier Turbostar.

worth investing in research and development that leads to any possible saving. Surprisingly though, the contracts for can making link the can price to the material price: any reduction in weight achieved by the can maker reduces material purchased, saves money for the can purchaser but gives no benefit to the maker. However, can makers also complete with plastic bottle producers, so are motivated to continue reducing weight to maintain their share of the overall market for drinks packaging.

Cars have grown heavier in the last 40 years, and a typical family car is now around half as heavy again as its 1970's equivalent. The main reasons for this gain in weight are improved comfort, more features, improved performance, larger size and increases in safety. And of course these changes arise because they're what customers want: fuel efficiency is typically about ninth in a list of customer preferences, far behind performance, comfort, style and safety. Customers will pay more for cars with diesel rather than petrol engines—giving better fuel consumption—but only if there is no compromise in other features. If customers won't push the development of lighter weight (and hence fuel efficient) cars by preference, they must then be promoted by legislation—which is precisely what's now happening in Europe, with target emissions for new cars set at $95\,gCO_2/km$ for 2020, compared to a current average of $145\,gCO_2/km$.

Trains in the UK, having had a constant weight during the 1980's, have become a quarter heavier in the years since to provide increased reliability (for example through having more powered vehicles in the same train), more air conditioning and passenger service systems, better safety and higher performance including tilting bogies. However, this increase in weight is surprising given the dual benefits of reduced power requirements for moving lighter trains, and reduced rail wear which in turn reduces track maintenance and replacement costs. We've found that the low priority given to weight savings for trains in the UK appears to be due to the way the rail industry was privatised: the track is owned by one company, the rolling stock by another, and the trains are operated by a third. So the rolling stock company wants versatile trains with high residual values (which are typically heavier), the track company would like lighter trains causing less wear, and the operating company wants to maximise profits during a relatively short franchise period which is not long enough for it to influence rolling stock development.

In summary, our three case studies have shown quite different motivations for or against reducing metal requirements in these three different industries, not at all linked to our predicted costs: it's not just the size of the benefits of saving weight that motivate change, but their size relative to other costs (only for the can maker was metal purchasing a large fraction of cost) the preference of customers for fuel efficiency against other features and the structure of the industry. So in contrast to our prediction that the train owner should have the highest motivation for weight saving, it's only in drinks cans that this has occurred: both trains and cars have become heavier.

Outlook

We've seen in this chapter that it is possible to define some simple principles for designing goods with less metal, and that if we apply the principles, it looks as if we could reduce global metal production by an amazing 30% without loss of final service. We've identified barriers to adopting this change, and shown they could be overcome, and have also seen that reducing weight has other benefits. However, we've seen that contracts, customers and industry structures may prevent the adoption of weight saving practices, and this suggests that we may need help from policy makers. Given that the massive implementation of carbon capture and storage would also require an input or two from policy makers this isn't too daunting, but we'll leave policy until we've completed our exploration of opportunities with both eyes open.

This chapter would have been much the less without 1903, the Wright brothers and Henry Ford, so let's not forget that in 1903 M.C. Escher, then aged five, moved with his family to Arnhem possibly clutching his first teddy bear invented in 1903 of course, and his box of Crayola crayons first made in 1903, with which he would learn to draw tessellations—which later become a crucial part of his artistic world, and which are central to our exploration of manufacturing yield losses in the next chapter.

Notes

Basic principles of lightweight design

1. Bendsøe and Sigmund (2003) give a thorough introduction to the field of topology optimization. For a more hands on introduction, you can try topology optimization for yourself at http://www.topopt.dtu.dk/.

2. Ashby and Jones (2005) provide a detailed analysis of material selection. Typically the designer will specify the key material parameters, such as strength or stiffness. By comparing these parameters among different materials and classes of material, the most suitable material can be chosen.

Case studies to explore using less metal in practice

3. The design cases we used were a 5 metre long beam taking a floor loading of 50kN/m or a 5 metre long roof beam taking a load of 7.5kN/m.

Practical barriers to saving metal by design and means to overcome them

4. Allwood and Utsunomiya (2006) give a detailed summary of flexible forming processes in Japan, many of which are now being more widely explored.

5. Carruth and Allwood (2011) describe our approach to rolling optimized I-beams.

Images

6. Image author: TeeGeeNo. Used under creative Commons Attribution ShareAlike 3.0 licence (http://creativecommons.org/licneses/by-sa/3.0/

7. Image thanks to Qube design

13 Reducing yield losses

Using less metal to make the same things

Separately from component design, our maps of metal flow showed that at least a quarter of all liquid steel and 40% of liquid aluminium never makes it into products, as it is cut off as scrap during manufacturing. What can we do to reduce these losses, and how much can we save?

A mosaic in the Nasrid Palace, Alhambra

Aged 68, M. C. Escher said, "filling two-dimensional planes has become a real mania to which I have become addicted and from which I sometimes find it hard to tear myself away." Escher was particularly interested in finding tessellating patterns, in which a small number of images can be replicated with some degree of regularity, in order to fill a plane completely, with no gaps. In turn he had been inspired by the incredible decorations of the 14th Century Moorish Alhambra palace in Granada, Spain. The Alhambra, now surrounded by a beautiful forest of English elm trees brought by the Duke of Wellington in 1812, three years before he defeated Napoleon I (and so, as we know, paving the way for Napoleon III to accede and promote aluminium), has walls, ceilings and floors decorated in mosaic tiles: Islamic art does not represent living beings so this exemplar of 'Paradise on Earth' takes the idea of repeating geometry to an extraordinary limit. Five hundred years before Yevgraf Stepanovich Fyodorov, Professor of Geology at the Moscow Agricultural Institute proved it in 1891, the 14th century artists of the Alhambra had identified that there were 17 possible forms of translational symmetry and exploited them all in their tilings.

Tessellation provides the starting point for this chapter, because as we've seen, the steel and aluminium industry produce intermediate stock products including plates and rolled up coils of sheet metal, which must be cut into shapes before being formed into components. If those shapes do not tessellate, some of the metal is scrapped, so we have to make more liquid metal than we really want. And in fact, tessellation isn't the only reason we do this: we also cut off significant fractions of our cast metal as part of normal manufacturing practice, generally because we only want to use perfect quality metal or because the shapes made with great efficiency by the steel and aluminium industry are not the shapes finally required by customers.

A car door panel

Our metal flow Sankey diagrams in chapter 4 showed us that the combination of poor tessellation, quality constraints and cutting out, causes us to scrap 26% of all liquid steel and 41% of all liquid aluminium. So this chapter is motivated to see if this is absolutely necessary. We'll start by checking our global numbers for yield loss with some product-based case studies, and then identify how yield losses influence the 'embodied energy and emissions' in components. We can then explore the causes of yield loss in current production systems, look for options to reduce them, evaluate the emissions benefit of reducing yield losses and finally examine the business case for better yield.

Case studies of yield loss

A steel I-beam

There are no national data sets about yield losses, so to find out more about how much metal we currently scrap, we conducted a series of case studies, in which we track backwards from a finished component, visiting all the companies along the journey of production, until we arrived back at liquid metal. We wanted our case studies to span both steel and aluminium, and to cover both sheet (thin) and bulk (thick) products, so the components we followed were a steel I-beam, a car door panel made either in steel or aluminium, the body of an aluminium drinks can (i.e. with no lid or opener) and the aluminium wing skin of an aeroplane. At each stage, we asked about yield losses, and also about energy and CO_2 emissions associated with each process, to build up a complete picture of the production process. Inevitably these data are commercially sensitive so, while our numbers reflect real commercial practice today, we can't identify our sources.

An aircraft wing

We had to be rather careful in defining yield loss. It's not just sensitive externally, where customers might be able to exploit yield information in negotiating prices, but in larger companies the figure is sometimes used for comparison between different production sites, so local managers wanted to give an optimistic view of their own yield figures. This is particularly true in early processes where production scrap can be re-melted: at one site, where liquid metal is made from recycled scrap, we found that around 20% of each batch of liquid metal was discarded, cooled to solid and then immediately recycled. In our eyes this is a major yield loss, because 20% of the energy used by that process was to melt metal cycling forever around a loop. However, the local manager told us that his reports on yield counted only the ratio of metal entering his factory to the weight of products leaving it, so what we saw as a 20% yield loss did not feature in his reports. Our numbers in this chapter are therefore process yield losses: for each process, the yield loss is the difference

A drinks can

between the sum of all metal entering the process and the weight of metal moving onto the next process downstream.

We've summarised our five studies of yield loss in the column charts below. In each case we've normalised the results, to start with one tonne of liquid metal, and the different sections of each column show the metal lost at different process stages. The I-beam is extremely efficient: around 90% of the liquid metal makes it into the finished component. For the sheet products, the car door panels and the drinks can, the losses stack up to around 50% of the cast metal, and for the wing skin panel, the losses are an amazing 90%. As we saw in the previous chapter, weight is so important to the aerospace industry, that they will do anything to reduce it: so if we measure the outputs of an aeroplane manufacturer by weight their main product is swarf, the scrap of machining processes, and aeroplanes are a mere by-product!

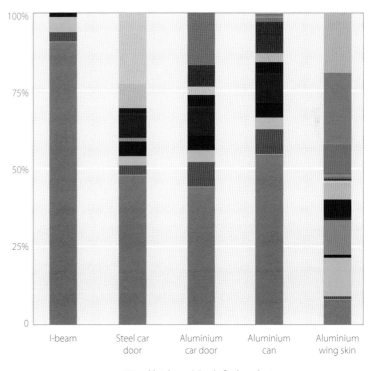

Figure 13.1—**Yield losses for the case study products**

Our case studies have confirmed the overall estimates of yield losses we saw in the Sankey diagrams of metal flow in chapter 4, and have drawn attention to the extreme losses in the aerospace industry. The overall yield ratios shown on the metal flow diagrams, are repeated in Table 13.1. Yield losses in forming components in aluminium are greater than those in steel, because cast aluminium ingots must be scalped, surface finish requirements for aluminium products are usually more demanding, and because more aluminium components are made by extrusion and direct casting which have higher yield losses than rolling. Yield losses in fabrication depend on the required change in geometry from stock to finished product, so depend on both product design and process route, but are remarkably similar for both metals.

The aim of the rest of this chapter is to explore how we can reduce these losses. However, before doing so, we can draw a further interesting insight from our case studies, by looking at the 'embodied' energy in each of the five components.

Process	Steel		Aluminium	
	Output (Mt)	Yield loss	Output (Mt)	Yield loss
Liquid metal	1400		76	
Forming	1280	9%	54	28%
Fabrication	1040	18%	45	18%
Overall		26%		41%

Table 13.1—**Global yield losses in steel and aluminium production**

The effect of yield loss on embodied energy and emissions in products

We discussed in chapter 2 the difficulty of attributing emissions to individual products or services. However, in the case studies of this chapter, having looked in detail at what physically happens at each process step, we can attempt an attribution. We have only collected data on processes, and haven't been told what else drives energy use at each site, so cannot correctly allocate all energy used in these factories to the products that they make: for example, managers who've talked to us informally about their energy use in downstream manufacturing businesses, have told us that around half of their energy purchases are to keep people warm or cool at work, and this energy is never allocated to products.

Using just our process data, we can show how the cumulative energy required to complete a component builds up, at the same time that yield losses reduce the

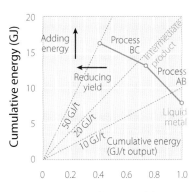

Figure 13.2—**Example graph of energy against yield**

fraction of the original cast metal remaining in the component. We'll define the cumulative energy divided by the remaining metal as the energy embodied in the component. When metal is cut off as scrap, we won't attribute any energy to the scrap, because what concerns us is the total energy inputs required to make the component, and this is what we mean by 'embodied.' (The energy 'embodied' in the component is quite different from the energy 'embedded' in the product. The embedded energy is what we could recover from the metal, and as we know from chapter 8, this is its exergy, which is largely defined by its composition and uninfluenced by all other processing).

To show how embodied energy builds up in our case study parts, we've invented a new graph. The x-axis of our graph shows the ratio of mass remaining in the component to the mass that was cast and is just like the column graphs of Figure 13.1. The y-axis of the graph shows the cumulative energy of all processes involved in making the component. We've also scaled this axis by the mass of metal cast (not by the mass remaining at each stage) so that both axes are scaled by the same fixed number. This allows us to plot contours of a constant ratio of the y-axis to the x-axis, equal to the cumulative energy divided by the mass remaining in the component, and these contours show the embodied energy in the component. The results of our cases studies are plotted on these new axes in Figures 13.3 and 13.4. In both cases making the liquid metal uses most energy, so we've truncated the y-axis.

The striking message of these graphs is that the liquid metal process dominates the cumulative energy, but yield losses dominate the embodied energy: in the most extreme case of the wing skin panel, the cast liquid metal required 100 GJ/tonne, but the embodied energy of the final panel is 1500 GJ/tonne because 92 % of the liquid metal has been scrapped. More typically, the embodied energy for the sheet products (can and car panels) has nearly trebled mainly because of yield losses greater than 50 %.

Liquid metal production is already highly optimised as we saw in chapter 7, so the graphs tell us that if we want to make a large reduction in embodied energy it will be more effective to try to reduce yield losses than to improve energy efficiency. To illustrate this message, in Figure 13.4 we've redrawn the graph for the aluminium door panel a further time, with axes of absolute cumulative energy against mass. On this graph efficiency improvements would reduce the y-axis height of the finished component. We've shown three lines on the graph: the aluminium car panel exactly as in the earlier graphs; the panel as if all downstream manufacturing processes were 20 % more energy efficient; and the panel as if all

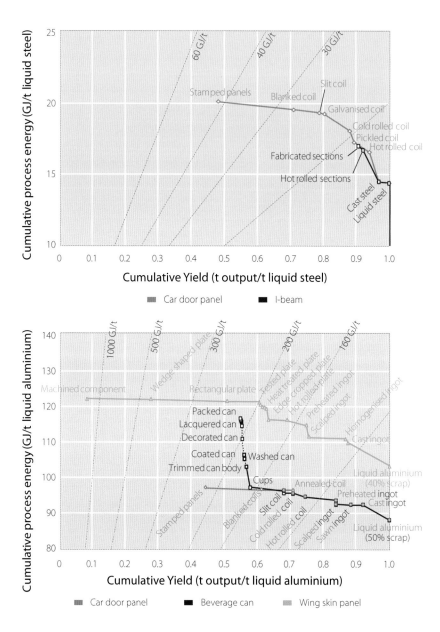

Figure 13.3— **Accumulated energy against cumulated yield for the metal products**

downstream processes had a 20% lower yield losses. The improvement in yield gives a much greater reduction in cumulative energy, because the panel required less liquid metal.

The energy embodied in the liquid metal depends on its recycled content. However, the graph for our aluminium case study parts, which includes two different starting

Sustainable Materials with both eyes open

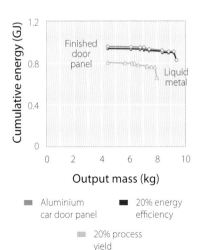

Cumulative energy (GJ)

Finished door panel

Liquid metal

Output mass (kg)

■ Aluminium car door panel
■ 20% energy efficiency
■ 20% process yield

Figure 13.4—**Absolute values of cumulative energy against mass for the aluminium car door panel**

points, demonstrates that the strong effect of yield losses in driving up is similar in both cases. Without question we want to make the liquid metal with as much efficiency as possible —that's what our "one eye open" strategies were all about. But these case studies have shown that yield losses greatly increase the amount of liquid metal required, and therefore greatly drive up the embodied energy of final components.

We can draw one last lesson from these graphs. When we visited the can-making company for our case study, they gave us estimates of the process energy required to coat the can with external paint and internal lacquer. Both processes require a baking cycle, to harden the coating after it has been applied, and the aluminium graph above shows that these baking cycles are energy intensive. In fact baking adds as much to the cumulative energy axis as all the manufacturing stages required to make the can from liquid metal. We have similar estimates for the car body panels —the paint baking operation is the most energy intensive process in manufacturing car bodies from coiled sheet. Remembering back to chapter 2, where we looked at both global and Chinese total energy use, we found that manufacturing components from stock products used about 5% of industrial energy (compared to 25% for steel and 3% for aluminium). If baking cycles (and other furnaces) are a major driver of energy use in manufacturing, the contribution of metal shaping and cutting to total energy requirements must be relatively small. Therefore the development of shaping and cutting processes to support a more sustainable future should prioritise the reduction of yield losses.

The causes of yield loss

Why on earth are we making so much scrap? More than a quarter of all liquid steel, and nearly half of all aluminium never makes it into a component, and instead is perpetually cycling round an internal loop with each cycle costing us energy and creating emissions. What's gone wrong?

We've seen from our case studies that the losses arise from a combination of quality problems at metal surfaces, from the fact that the intermediate products made by the steel and aluminium industry are the wrong shape, from the need to grip metal components while shaping them, and from defects and errors. We'll look at each of those in turn.

When liquids solidify, they do so from outer surfaces towards their interior, and for liquid metal with complex compositions, during this process, the composition

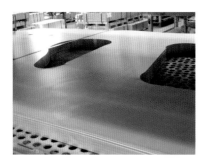

Blanking[6]

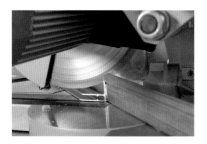

Cutting aluminium with a circular saw

Machining aluminium and making swarf

of the remaining liquid changes. As described in chapter 8, different cooling rates at the surface and centre of an aluminium ingot lead to a different, lower quality, microstructure and composition at the surface. As a result, 150 mm is currently sawn from the head and tail of each cast aluminium ingot and the outer 20 mm from the top and bottom surfaces is removed by 'scalping'. (Scalping, which is also applied to the hair of new army recruits, is a large scale machining process.) This problem does not occur for steel, although rapid growth of steel oxides (known as scale) causes some loss of steel when the brittle scale breaks away from the surface during rolling. After casting, most steel and aluminium is rolled at least once, and while rolling has tremendous throughput, it is most effective in the middle of each coil or plate—so the head and tail of any rolled material is always cut off, and the edges, which crack during rolling, are trimmed. Overall these problems at surfaces cause around 25 % of all yield losses in steel[1] and around 40 % of all yield losses in aluminium.

The second major cause of yield loss is that the stock products made by the steel and aluminium industry are the wrong shape. They are chosen as useful average shapes, so we can achieve economies of scale, but very few customers actually want the shape they purchase. The most extreme example of this in our case studies was for the aluminium wing skin where we saw the aluminium supplier producing a thick long rectangular plate of perfect proportions. But this perfect plate is machined into a wedge shape, because aircraft wings are thinner at the tip than the centre so much of the perfect plate is immediately scrapped. In reality, the aeroplane manufacturer never needed a uniform plate. However, this is merely an extreme. Can makers want circular disks of aluminium sheet to make cans, but instead receive 2 metre wide coils of sheet, from which they punch out circles and then send back 15 % of the coil for remelting. Car body panel makers also don't want continuous coils of sheet: they want cut-out shapes to form into panels, often with holes where the windows will be. They too return 10 % or more[2] of the coil after 'blanking' (cutting out the shape they really wanted). In fact all material removal processes applied to stock products cause yield loss, which occurs because the intermediate product was the wrong shape.

Sheet and plate materials are supplied flat, but usually are not flat in use, having been shaped in some way. The most common process for shaping sheets, 'deep drawing', illustrated in Figure 13.5, forms the flat sheet into shape, and can create incredible shape change, such as when forming a cup or box out of a single sheet without joining. If you form a sheet without firmly gripping its edges, you can only make a very shallow cup before the sheet tears. Equally, if you don't restrain the edges at all, as you begin to form the cup, the edges will wrinkle. So deep

Sustainable Materials with both eyes open

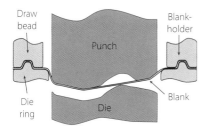

Figure 13.5—**Deep drawing**

drawing works using drawbeads to grip the edges of the sheet, which prevents wrinkling, but allows the sheet to draw inwards to prevent tearing. Deep drawing is a fantastic, efficient process but the material gripped by the drawbeads, about 25mm around every finished part, must be trimmed off. This leads to a yield loss of about 15% for a typical deep drawn part[3].

Finally, no manufacturing process is perfect, but customers only want perfect parts, so any error, defect or imperfection in manufacturing leads to yield loss. This is naturally an area where every manufacturing business is highly motivated to improve, but errors persist and around 5% of all yield losses are due to defects and errors.

Options to reduce yield losses

When we began discussing yield losses with the various companies we visited in preparing this chapter, their immediate reaction was "well of course we wouldn't generate scrap if we didn't have to, so of course we can't improve." Strictly that statement should be "we wouldn't generate scrap unless it was cheaper for us to do so" because, as always with high labour costs in Europe, decisions are based on the balance between material costs and labour. But as we continued to explore the cumulative effect of yield losses along long production chains, we found that few if any of the companies we visited understood the yield losses of their suppliers or customers. It seems that current yield losses are as much a function of habit as necessity.

Convertible car doors often don't have frames surrounding their windows

...unlike conventional cars

We've therefore looked at three stages of the life of each metal component, to ask if a different practice at one stage could influence yield losses elsewhere: can component designers influence yield losses in manufacturing? can the design of cast geometries reduce the need for downstream yield loss? could we invent new manufacturing processes that reduce our need for trimming, cutting and machining?

We can start back at the Alhambra palace: designers of metal components at present are largely unaware of the implications of their geometric choices on yield losses, but potentially could design with tessellating or nearly tessellating shapes, and so radically reduce yield losses. This could constrain product geometry, which might be unacceptable to customers, but the issue is so little in the minds of designers at present, that some significant gains will be possible. A simple example is in the two photographs of car doors to the side: the door with an integrated window would require more than double the amount of metal than the door in the convertible car in which the window projects upwards. We've also been lucky enough to attract help from one of the UK's emerging new kitchen stars, Roseanna, who in the box story demonstrates the material efficiency of her hexagonal jam tart cutter.

Roseanna's hexagonal jam tarts

1. Roll out two identical sheets of pastry

2. Check that both sheets measure around 275x320 mm

3. Carefully position your hexagonal cutter in one corner

4. Continue cutting hexagons till you have filled the sheet

5. Cut out the other sheet with a circular cutter

6. Lift the cut tarts into a lightly greased patty tin

7. Check which cutter gave lower yield losses.

8. Fill both sets of tarts, and bake at 200°C for 15 minutes

9. Leave to cool, serve, and see which tarts your friends prefer.

Trimming the edge off a roll of paper

CNC machine cutting and
perforating fabric

There are obvious limits to tessellation: at present we can't form drinks cans out of square, or hexagonal blanks, so in the short term we can't approach perfect yield in cutting sheets. But equally there is significant space in which to improve: paper makers, like sheet metal producers, produce long coils of constant width stock products, which are then cut to size according to customer preferences. Over years of development they have learnt to optimise the two-dimensional cutting of their stock to minimise waste. Arguably this is an easier problem than faced by metal sheet users, as most paper is used in rectangular shapes which naturally tessellate well. However, the clothing and textiles industry faces a challenge at least as difficult as that for the sheet metal makers and now use sophisticated computer algorithms to maximise the yield of clothing from rolls of fabric. In fact advanced clothing manufacturers now automate not only fabric layout but also cutting, with fast laser cutters to translate the optimised blanking pattern into action.

One of the lessons we've learnt from the mathematicians working on the 'two-dimensional cutting stock' problem, is that yields improve when the most possible shapes are tessellated. This is obvious: if you have a larger variety of shapes, you increase the chance that you can find small pieces to fit between the larger ones. At present, two features of metal product design mitigate against this: firstly, product designers tend to optimise material selection for each component, so the 200 sheet metal components in a typical car will be made of many different alloys, and many different thicknesses; secondly, the blanking presses used in cutting parts from coils of sheet metal are designed to cut one piece from the coil, then index forward the sheet, and cut the same piece again. This gives very little opportunity for tessellation. So if car designers used fewer alloys and thicknesses, they could improve yield ratios, and these would be realised if new approaches to blanking could allow more sophisticated tessellation. At present laser cutting of metal, while common in James Bond films, is relatively slow, so the approach of fabric cutting cannot yet be translated into metal sheets. However, there is great scope for innovation in blanking press design to cut more than one shape at a time.

He - xa - gon,　　　He - xa - gon,　the　best　darn　re' - lar　fit - tin'　paoh - ly - gon

A completely different strategy to reduce yield losses, is to start by forming the liquid metal to a shape nearer to that of the final component. We've found three approaches: continuous thin strip casting where the liquid metal is cast into the nip between two chilled rollers into a continuous strip; direct casting in a mould;

Figure 13.6—**Direct casting of a steel part in a sand mould**

A part made by additive manufacturing (selective laser melting)[5]

and additive manufacturing. The aim of these approaches is to make components with fewer processing steps and reduced yield losses. But unfortunately, none of them are as good as existing process routes. Thin strip casting saves the need for reheating prior to hot rolling, and for aluminium can also avoid yield losses in scalping, sawing and hot rolling. However, it is difficult to control, and the resulting sheets often have poor surface quality, unless they are rather pure alloys. Cooking foil, which is a nearly pure form of aluminium, is made by thin strip casting, rolling and coiling, but as yet this approach is not used for alloys with more complex compositions. The geometry of components made by direct casting must be simple enough to ensure complete filling of the mould, and as we saw in chapter 3, the properties of steel and aluminium depend on both composition and processing. Without deformation it isn't possible to increase the strength of direct cast components by breaking up large grains or work hardening. As a result the properties of direct cast components cannot match those achieved by conventional process routes involving deformation such as hot rolling.

Many additive manufacturing technologies are under development, and the whole area of "3D printing" has attracted great excitement in research over the past twenty years. It's a very easy topic to "sell", because the dream that we might in future somehow not just order our goods over the internet, but have them magically appear in our domestic 3D printer is a compelling media image: all we need is the magic powder that can be James Bonded at home! Some parts of this dream are quite real: the photo shows a part made additively, and the aerospace industry is pursuing the technology for making complex parts in titanium. In one common process, 'selective laser melting', a bed of powder is placed under a scanning laser which 'draws' the pattern of a layer of the product. The laser melts and bonds the powder then a new layer of powder is laid and the process repeats. Unfortunately, there are several drawbacks: the process works with powdered metals, which must be made from liquid metal in an energy intensive process using spraying and freezing; lasers are themselves energy intensive; production rates are low because each product is built up in layers; as with direct casting, the properties of the product are limited by the absence of deformation; and surface finishes are poor and must be improved by subsequent operations.

Our interest in additive processes was motivated by energy efficiency, related to yield losses. Figure 13.7 compares the energy embodied in a part made by a conventional process chain (with yield losses) against one made by the selective laser melting process (with no yield losses). The graph shows results for mild steel, stainless steel and titanium because aluminium parts cannot currently be made with the required density[4]. The graph shows that for steel parts, the additive

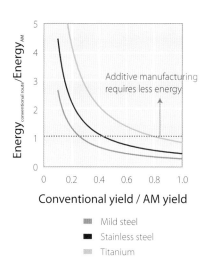

Figure 13.7—**Comparison of energy use in conventional and additive manufacturing processes showing a dependence on process yield**

(chart) Energy$_{\text{conventional route}}$/Energy$_{\text{AM}}$ versus Conventional yield / AM yield

Additive manufacturing requires less energy

Mild steel
Stainless steel
Titanium

process leads to lower embodied energy if the conventional process has yield losses worse than 75%. In contrast, the yield losses need be only 20% before selective laser melting saves energy for titanium components, because this method produces parts with acceptable properties, it is commercially attractive. For steel parts, there would be no energy saving, and it is not currently possible to overcome the other drawbacks listed above.

All three routes to nearer net shape production will continue to develop, but we do not have a clear winning technology to replace existing production routes for steel and aluminium components. The steel and aluminium industries will therefore continue to sell intermediate stock products requiring subsequent shaping.

If we are largely restricted to existing stock products, can we look downstream and find new manufacturing processes with lower yield losses? We discussed above the need for trimming after deep drawing: but is it possible to replace deep drawing with a different process that does not require trimming? The older and slower process of metal spinning can make parts with geometries similar to deep drawing but without trimming, so maybe in the future, novel derivatives of spinning processes will be able to take over from deep drawing. The whole class of machining processes, those which remove material by cutting chips from it (drilling is the simplest version), is used in manufacturing only because the geometry or quality of the parts made by upstream forming processes is insufficient. In the companies we've visited where machining removes a substantial fraction of purchased metal, we've identified opportunities to remove less metal by forming metal closer to final shape. For example, with modern control systems, the rolling mill used to make thick aluminium plates as part of wing-skin manufacture could be adapted to roll a variable thickness, eliminating the machining step.

It appears that we have many options for reducing yield losses. Although we need more development before net shape casting can replace existing processes, we have seen opportunities both for designers to reduce losses by tessellation, and for process innovations to reduce scrap. How would these savings influence emissions and does it make business sense?

Emissions savings from reducing yield losses

When we explored embodied energy earlier in the chapter, we found that the embodied energy in a product is significantly increased by yield losses. In most cases, yield loss is a greater driver of embodied energy than the energy of

	Steel	Aluminium
Energy savings	17%	6%
CO₂ savings	16%	7%

Table 13.2—**Global energy and emissions benefit of eliminating all yield losses in steel and aluminium**

downstream manufacturing. So reducing yield losses should have a significant effect on emissions overall.

It does, but the scrap metal which arises from yield losses is mostly recycled at present. The effect of reducing yield losses is therefore to reduce the supply of metal sent for recycling by exactly the same amount that we reduce our demand for liquid metal. In other words, yield losses create a permanent loop of recycling in the two metal flow Sankey diagrams of chapter 4, and reducing yield losses reduces the size of this loop. The strategy of designing goods with less metal that we examined in the last chapter leads to an overall reduction in demand for all liquid metal. But in contrast, the strategy of reducing yield losses simply reduces the mass of metal that is permanently cycling round the secondary production route as production scrap. The table shows how the elimination of all yield losses would reduce total energy requirements and associated emissions in the steel and aluminium industries.

The business case for better yield

The initial reaction of businesses to our exploration of yield loss was 'if we could save it we would.' However, our work in this chapter has revealed that collaborative design and process innovation would exploit further opportunities for reducing yield losses. Collaborative examination of yield losses along long metal production chains would not be expensive and we anticipate that some of the resulting opportunities will be cheap and may be immediately profitable. The business case for others will depend on the trade-off between economies of scale and increased variety in product specification. Generally a loss of economies of scale in production can be compensated by development of more flexible equipment and we've shown that this could occur.

The ideal target in this chapter has been to reduce yield losses to zero. This would eliminate production scrap, so would reduce recycling at the same rate that it would reduce demand for secondary production. However, it will take time to do this so before we reach the 'paradise on earth' of the Alhambra's mosaic artists, we'll look in the next chapter for opportunities to make use of the scrap before we send it off for recycling by melting.

Sustainable Materials with both eyes open

Notes

The causes of yield loss

1. Based on data collected by Worldsteel (2009). Yield improvement in the steel industry.

2. Depending on the part being made, blanking losses may be as large as 80%, though for most mass produced car parts, the losses will be considerably lower (Tata Steel Automotive, 2010).

3. The draw bead dimensions and exact yield loss due to edge trim after deep drawing depends on the geometry of the part and tooling, so the figures of a 25mm edge trim and 15% yield loss are quoted for a typical automotive drawn part.

Options to reduce yield losses

4. We've assumed that making the metal powder requires 40 GJ/tonne for steel and stainless steel and 45 GJ/tonne for titanium. Data from Cambridge Engineering Selector software, CES (2011).

Images

5. Image courtesy of Renishaw Inc.

6. We would like to thank Tata Steel for their picture of the blanking process.

14 Diverting manufacturing scrap
to other uses before recycling by melting

With high yield losses currently in production, and with additional scrappage from defects and over-ordering, could we avoid sending scrap for recycling by melting and instead use it elsewhere?

The European Magpie is a remarkable bird: thought to be the most intelligent of animals or birds, its neostriatum—a region of the brain associated with the executive functions required to cope with novel or unusual situations—has the same relative size as that of humans. The Magpie is of course black and white, so with the pungent poetry for which contemporary football is famous, the English teams of both Newcastle United and Notts County, who play in black and white, are nicknamed 'The Magpies'. And of most interest to us, the Magpie has a reputation as a thief and hoarder, particularly of shiny objects. In Rossini's opera La Gazza Ladra (The Thieving Magpie), the lovely Ninetta escapes by seconds a sentence of death imposed on her for stealing silver cutlery, only because the true culprit, the Magpie, is caught re-offending.

The European Magpie

A quick survey of our nation's garages and sheds would reveal that in fact we're all Magpies. We're attracted to shiny, or not so shiny, metal objects that have passed through our hands, and store them because 'they might come in useful'. We have an instinctive sense that old metal objects have value.

Could we be more intelligent in hoarding our shiny production scrap? If we chose to keep our scrap and not melt it, would we find a different use for it? We'll separate our answer to this question across two chapters: in the next chapter we'll look for opportunities to re-use components at the end of their first useful life, but in this one, we'll examine whether we can divert scrap arising along the production chain. We've seen in the Sankey diagrams of metal flow, and in the last chapter on yield losses, just how large this supply of scrap is—is it always best to melt it in a recycling loop, or could we divert some of the scrap back into use, with less energy?

We'll start by examining scrap as it is created: what have we got and in what volume? Then we'll look at opportunities to divert scrap of different types into use, and finally move on to looking at the barriers to increasing scrap diversion in future.

Where does metal scrap arise and in what form?

The magpie in British folklore is a bringer of bad luck, a harbinger of bad weather, and foreteller of death. So, is collecting metal scrap good news, or a prophecy commercial doom? In contrast to the post-consumer scrap favoured by magpies, manufacturers know precisely the composition and history of steel and aluminium scrap generated in production, so can avoid mixing up different alloys. Such scrap is also typically in good condition, without surface corrosion (although it may be covered in a lubricant), and has not been assembled into a product, so requires no disassembly. So we are likely to have better luck looking for opportunities to divert scrap from production than after use.

A typical 'skeleton', left over after blanking

According to our Sankey diagram of steel flows, 30% of steel scrap comes from the forming processes of the steel industry, from the beginning and ends of castings, and from trimming the heads, tails and edges of rolled material. The remainder arises in fabrication and manufacturing. Our work in the previous chapter suggests that yield losses for long products such as the I-beam are relatively small, so the largest fraction of steel scrap arises from cutting out non-tessellating shapes from blanking rolled strip and trimming after forming. The sheet and plate material left after blanking is called the 'blanking skeleton' and this is probably the most useful form of steel scrap. Half of all steel fabrication scrap comes from rolled strip and plate, and from the last chapter let's assume half of this is due to trimming after forming, so around 60 Mt of steel per year scrapped as blanking skeletons. What else could we usefully cut out from the blanking skeleton? One answer is shown in Figure 14.1: if we wanted to cut out smaller versions of the same shape (circles in this case with diameter around 15% of the original), this would reduce the blanking skeleton scrap by about half. Extrapolating this simple estimate, around 30 Mt of steel sheet and plate blanking skeletons might be diverted into use, if we could find customers for the smaller shapes.

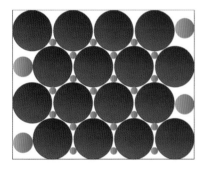

Figure 14.1—**A possible use (blue) of material left over after cutting circular blanks**

The Sankey diagram of aluminium flow tells quite a different story, with two thirds of aluminium scrap arising within the aluminium industry, particularly due to cutting heads and tails off ingots, ingot scalping, and machining parts from cast products. Just one third of aluminium scrap arises in downstream fabrication and manufacturing. The heads and tails of ingots are large blocks, but scalping and machining scrap is in the form of swarf, or aluminium chips. Our yield loss case studies in the previous chapter showed that around 10% of metal cast for the aluminium car door panel becomes swarf. However over 60% of the metal cast for the wing skin panel is turned into swarf, and for directly cast products, all scrap will be in the form of swarf. So, looking at the global Sankey diagram, we

Sustainable Materials with both eyes open

Aluminium machining swarf

Over-ordered material, in excellent condition, being transported for scrap

estimate that of the 76 Mt of liquid aluminium produced each year, between 10 and 20 Mt of it will be made into swarf.

One final important source of scrap arises due to over-ordering. This is common in construction, where projects will be delayed at high cost if there is a delay finding material. Over-ordered material is generally collected and recycled efficiently, but of course it could also be resold. A high profile example of this form of scrap diversion occurred during construction for the 2012 London Olympics: the roof trusses of the main stadium are made from over-ordered oil and gas pipeline. More details about this in our box story.

We don't know the volumes of over-ordered steel and aluminium components that are sent for recycling. However, through visits to metal scrap yards in the UK, we found that scrap merchants increasingly keep such good quality material separately while searching for customers who will re-use it directly.

Our survey of scrap creating, has identified two interesting high-volume streams of scrap: steel skeletons and aluminium swarf. Can we divert these streams back into use without melting?

Truss structure in the Olympic Stadium, Olympic Park London

The truss structure for the Olympic Stadium uses 2,500 tonnes of "non-prime" steel tube, over-ordered from an oil and gas pipeline project. The original stadium design had specified large diameter steel tubes, but the fabricator was concerned that the delays in purchasing new steel, and the difficulty of manufacturing these specialised sections, might delay construction. So the Olympic Delivery Authority (ODA) and Team Stadium chose to use this over-ordered stock to remove the risk of delays and to reduce the embodied emissions in the stadium.

The second-hand tubes were supplied without certification, so coupon tests, using small lengths of steel cut from each tube, were conducted to confirm their mechanical properties. Each 12-metre tube length was tested and then welded into 15-metre span lengths while the structural design of the truss was modified. The additional design time was modest, and despite having to over-specify some structural members, no additional weight was added to the structure. As a result of this action, 20% of the steel used in the stadium is diverted scrap. Although their motivation was to reduce project risk, and despite the additional design and testing effort, Team Stadium were delighted to find that reusing steel gave a small reduction in total project costs.

What opportunities are there to divert scrap into use?

According to Shakespeare's Macbeth, in his growing madness, "Augurs and understood relations have by magpies and choughs and rooks brought forth the secret'st man of blood." So if the magpie can lead to revelations about murder, can we reveal opportunities to extract value from our shiny scrap?

Blanking skeletons are a supply of perfect quality material from which smaller blanks could be cut. There is no technical difficulty in this apart from the problems with blanking-press design discussed in the previous chapter. The best solution for diverting scrap from blanking skeletons would be to use blanking presses to exploit every last square millimetre of each sheet. That however requires process development, while at present, on many blanking lines, the skeleton is chopped into small pieces for easier collection. An alternative, if the skeleton can be removed from the press intact, is to ship it to a separate business who will cut out the large pieces. Step forward Abbey Steel in Kettering, described in our box story, who for thirty years have purchased blanking skeletons and other trim (such as the window cut-outs in door panels) from car manufacturers in the UK. They then cut regular shapes from these skeletons, and supply them as blanks to firms making small parts. Abbey Steel exemplify the profitable diversion of blanking scrap, and tell us they could serve more customers if only they could persuade more car manufacturers to hand over their scrap.

Scrapped structural steel sections

The other major source of scrap that could be diverted is aluminium swarf. This sounds rather unpromising: our childrens' guinea pigs go to sleep at night on a bed of wooden chips, but surely not even a magpie would feather its nest with aluminium swarf? Surely no-one wants swarf except for melting. Yet several years ago we learnt of a series of trials carried out in Wrocław in Poland, by Professor Gronostajski and his son, Professor Gronostajski, examining the solid bonding of aluminium chips. Aluminium is a very reactive metal, and as we learned in chapter 3, under normal conditions 'naked' aluminium will rapidly and within milliseconds react (join) with oxygen atoms in the air to form a thin protective layer of aluminium oxide. However, if we were able to bring together two 'naked' surfaces of aluminium, with no oxygen present, the two surfaces would instead react with each other, and bond. So, pure aluminium will weld to itself at room temperature, and this gives us a chance to re-use aluminium swarf without melting.

This solid bonding is related to techniques developed in Japan over 1,000 years ago to make the Katana (刀), the traditional sword of the Samurai. Iron sand and charcoal would be heated in a traditional Japanese furnace, known as a tatara, to

A 'Katana' or Samurai Sword

produce the crude tamahagane steel for the sword. The master swordsmith would then carefully pick the right pieces of steel for making the sword. The colour of the steel determined his selection, as it is indicative of the carbon content: too little carbon and the blade will not be hard enough to give the required razor-sharp cutting edge; too much carbon and the blade will be too brittle for use. Small pieces of the selected steel were then heated to just below the melting point, and hammered into a welded block. This block would be repeatedly heated, folded and beaten, the interface between each layer welding under the compressive pressure of repeated blows. More than ten such folding operations produced hundreds of layers in the steel, spreading the carbon content and impurities more evenly and creating a fine grain size and an excellent sword. The katana sword was used by the samurai for centuries, and is an iconic symbol of weaponry and metal artistry.

So the Samurai warriors gained strength from swords that were folded and welded while solid but hot. The aerospace industry has explored a similar approach to create very high strength aluminium sheets by accumulative roll bonding[1]. One strip of aluminium is stacked on top of another, then joined by rolling. As the two strips pass under the rolls, the oxide layer cracks and naked aluminium is squeezed through the cracks to meet naked metal from the other sheet and so weld. This process can, in principle, be repeated many times to produce a very fine grain size, and hence strong material. The Professors Gronostajski set off on a different route to both the aerospace industry and the master sword smiths of ancient Japan, using extrusion. Extrusion (squeezing metal through a small die), elongates the original

Abbey Steel

When blanks for car body parts are cut from coiled steel strip, 10% or more of the material is wasted because parts do not tessellate perfectly. When they are subsequently pressed on average 50% is lost due to cut-outs (e.g. for car windows) and edge trimming. Abbey Steel, a family run business in Stevenage, has for 30 years bought, trimmed and re-sold around 10,000 tonnes per year of these cut-outs. They are used for noncritical parts by manufacturers of small components including filing cabinets, electrical connectors and shelving. Abbey Steel pays a premium over the scrap price to collect the cut outs, trims them into rectangles according to demand and sells them on at a discount relative to new stock. The business would grow more if press shops could segregate more cut-outs for resale.

material while compressing it and extruding clean aluminium swarf, creates a new, well-bonded solid with remarkably good properties: similar strength, but reduced ductility, compared with the original material. An attraction of this approach is that it saves over 90% of the energy directly associated with melting in conventional recycling. In addition, recycling chips by melting gives a yield of around 50% but by solid bonding has a yield nearer to 90%.

Solid bonding of swarf is still in development, and with our colleagues at the University of Dortmund, we're attempting to understand it better (more details in the box story). But with around 10–20 Mt of aluminium swarf to play with, this looks like it might be an attractive option for the future.

In this section we've seen that two major streams of scrap might be diverted from melting, as there are viable low energy routes to making use of the scrap without melting.

Dark and exotic

Your scraps could be my feast, your crumbs could make my bread.   Your waste is my de-light...

What are the barriers to scrap diversion and can they be overcome?

The magpie is a common national symbol in Korea, where it's seen as a bird of great good fortune, of sturdy spirit and a provider of prosperity and development. Both of our routes for diverting scrap are technically possible, but neither has yet led to widespread prosperity and development. Is it just the lack of a sturdy spirit that's holding back the adoption of scrap diversion?

Most downstream manufacturing and fabrication businesses do not see their scrap as part of their core business. Typically, scrap handling systems are designed to prevent disruption, and to dispatch scrap as rapidly as possible. Production lines have generally been designed without considering value in scrap so, as we saw, larger blanking skeletons are chopped into small pieces for ease of handling, and swarf in machining shops while separated by metal family is rarely separated by alloy. One aeroplane manufacturer told us that they sell their swarf with all alloys mixed and for a price of around 1% of what they paid for it, yet swarf is 90% of their output. If the solid bonding process is developed further, this manufacturer

Early solid bonding trials to create a box section

might in future have an extrusion press adjacent to its machining line, to convert swarf into bars of known single alloy composition. These could either be used directly, or recycled by melting but with much higher yields and value than at present.

Upstream, we have seen careful handling of different alloys, but only in 'melt shops' where aluminium casting occurs. Here, the heads, tails and scalping swarf from ingots of different alloys are carefully segregated, so they can be fed back into future melts without disrupting composition.

So lack of awareness, the design of current waste handling systems, and alloy mixing in waste streams all inhibit the opportunity to divert scrap from recycling by melting. In addition it may be necessary to clean scrap prior to diversion, to remove rust, coatings or lubricants, and because scrap is only traded at present prior to recycling by melting, finding customers for blanking skeletons may take time and require stock-holding.

Scrap diversion, and indeed all recycling, would be simplified if we could reduce the variety of alloy compositions in use. Competition between metal suppliers tends to have the opposite effect, and each year the number of alloys on the market

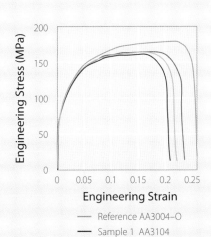

Solid bonding trials

In ongoing trials, we're working with our partners at the University of Dortmund to develop and evaluate solid bonding, aiming to promote the technique as a commercial alternative to recycling by melting of aluminium swarf.

We have tested the process using AA3104 (drinks can body material), AA6060 (automotive bright trim), and AA6061 and AA7070 (aerospace machining swarf), and all tests have produced specimens of high quality. The graph presents tensile test data for samples made from extruded AA3104 chips. The solid bonded material shows similar performance to the reference material, with reductions of around 10% in ultimate tensile strength and 15% in ductility. We anticipate that with further development we will be able to reduce these differences and in parallel we're assessing process reliability.

In many applications (such as aluminium window frames or decorative trim) the full strength and ductility of the original aluminium is not required, so potentially solid bonded material could be used instead. We're currently working with a leading car maker to produce automotive bright trim for a new car from aerospace swarf.

increases. Each new alloy is optimised for a particular application, and as we saw in the last chapter, careful material selection can facilitate lighter designs. However, this variety inhibits re-use and recycling, so designers now, and policy makers in future, may choose a reduced range of alloys.

Outlook

We've estimated that up to 30 Mt of steel blanking skeletons and 10–20 Mt of aluminium swarf could be diverted to other use rather than being recycled by melting. This is technically possible, but inhibited by various features of current practice. If we could achieve this diversion, how would it affect global emissions figures for the two sectors?

Diverting scrap would create a new loop on our metal flow Sankey diagrams—from scrap back into fabrication. This would reduce the flow of metal entering secondary production, while simultaneously reducing demand for metal made by this route. The two options for scrap diversion in this chapter require little further processing energy, so compared with existing recycling processes, they might save 11 GJ/tonne for steel, 13 GJ/tonne for aluminium, or equivalently about 0.7 tonnes CO_2/tonne for both metals.

Diverting scrap is potentially a significant emissions abatement strategy but as we saw in chapter 13, because it diverts metal from secondary production not primary, it has less effect on total emissions than reducing total demand for metal through design, as discussed in chapter 12.

In Norway, the magpie has a wonderfully diverse role in legend: cunning, a thief, associated with the devil and guardian of the household. For any negative connotations we now have the Samurai's sword to silence the magpie for good, but instead let's leave him in a positive role: a playful, loud Norwegian magpie is a bringer of good weather, so we'll keep playing with solid bonding and shouting loudly about the opportunity to improve the weather by diverting swarf and blanking skeletons into other uses.

Notes

1. In the 1990s severe plastic deformation of metals was investigated as a method of producing ultra-fine grains less than 1 μm in diameter, producing associated high strength. However, most of the processes investigated were only suitable for small samples due to the high pressures involved. Saito et al. (1999), however, developed a repeatable rolling deformation for the intense straining of bulk materials. This process is known as accumulative roll bonding.

15 Re-using metal components
without melting them

Having looked at diverting production scrap back in to use without melting, can we apply a similar approach to components from products at the end of their first life? For larger components, particularly for steel beams used in construction which are generally not damaged at all in use, we may not need to recycle them by melting: instead, could we reuse them directly?

Cambridge white bricks

Boring red brick

Shipping containers designed for long-term reuse

Property prices in Cambridge are high, and planning restrictions tight, so the town has a community of builders specialising in house extensions. Loft conversions, kitchen extensions and garage alterations abound as we all try to maximise our living spaces on our small plots of land. The great expansion of housing in Cambridge, which between 1800 and 1950, as the town's population grew from ten to ninety thousand, was constructed principally using the Cambridge White brick[1]. However, as we expand our houses today, we have a problem, because the Cambridge White is no longer made, and although we can buy prosaic red wire-cut bricks cheaply from the local Builders' Merchant, we'd rather keep the style of our houses consistent. So there is an active market in reused Cambridge White bricks, and they currently cost around £0.85 per brick, compared to £0.50. Any demolition work is done with care to preserve the value of the bricks, which are mainly undamaged from their first 100 years use and can be deconstructed easily, because 19th century lime mortar is weaker than today's Portland cement.

The story of the Cambridge White has raised all the key issues for us in this chapter: there is demand for old Cambridge Whites, so there's an incentive for builders to deconstruct rather than demolish old buildings, and most bricks are undamaged so ready for reuse after simple cleaning. How does this translate for steel and aluminium?

In the last chapter we looked at diversion of scrap and components that had not yet been used, and in the next one we'll look at extending the life of whole products, which is also a form of reuse. There are also some goods, such as shipping containers and steel sheet piling (see our box story overleaf), which are designed for long-term reuse. In contrast to these approaches, in this chapter, we're looking at the opportunity to reuse components, after they have been used in a product 'in anger.' Our motivation for this is obvious: for both steel and aluminium, recycling

Inventive reuse of steel

"Carhenge" in Nebraska[9]

by melting saves energy compared to making metal from ore, but is still energy intensive; reuse without melting potentially offers a very low-energy supply of components, if the only energy required is for dismantling and re-assembly (in the case of the old Cambridge Whites). Are there opportunities for re-using steel and aluminium, and if so, how extensive are they, and how can we develop them further?

It takes little thought to realise that steel and aluminium are already being reused in various ways. To start with a couple of extremes, the pictures to the side are a reminder of the creative reuse of metal goods in one of the world's poorer countries, and the extravagant "artistic" reuse of metal in the richest one. But neither picture illustrates a future business model, so let's turn to some more commercial examples:

- Car dismantlers and salvage companies break up damaged or old vehicles to re-sell components as low price spare parts. This approach has gained momentum with the use of the internet to reach a larger market, and is particularly strong for heritage vehicles.

- Rail track is regularly reused—firstly by swapping over the left and right rails on a track, as the train wheels wear away only the inner edge of the rail, and later by 'cascading': when rails are no longer suitable for main-line use, they are ultrasonically tested for cracks, cut and welded to length and reused on secondary lines with lower traffic. The box story describes a new strategy for re-using rail even more.

Sheet steel piling

Steel piling is used on construction sites as a temporary structure to hold back soil or water while foundations or retaining walls are erected. Once the permanent structure is strong enough the sheet piles are removed, cleaned, trimmed of any buckled portions and then reused on another site. This process can be repeated 5-6 times per year, after which the main UK manufacturer of steel piling will buy the sheet at a pre-determined rate if in good condition.

Carrwood Park

Recovered ship plate ready for re-rolling

- The British Construction Steelwork Association's new headquarters building at Carrwood Park is one of several examples we've found, where new steel-framed buildings have been constructed from used steel. In fact we think that the opportunity for steel reuse in buildings is so important that the second half of this chapter will focus entirely on construction.

- Famously, around half of the world's retired ships are beached on the shore at Alang in North West India and then manually dismantled. Major components are re-sold, but the steel plate from which the ships are constructed is cut with oxy-acetylene torches into plates that can be lifted off the beach manually, and eventually these are heated, and re-rolled for reuse. The destination of this steel is not very well documented, but we understand that much of it becomes reinforcing bar for construction across India, and in 2008, ship-breaking was contributing up to one eighth of all Indian steel demand[2].

- By law, all oil drilling equipment installed into the North Sea must, at end of life, be removed. In 2007 BP's North West Hutton rig was decommissioned, and dismantled by Able UK in Teesside. Able UK chose to reuse the 'topsides' of the rig (the accommodation block) as their own office, and also broke the steel jacket (the legs) into sections that could be re-rolled. Over a quarter of the 20,000 tonne rig was profitably reused.

Re-use of steel and aluminium components is already viable, and exactly as we found with Cambridge White bricks, each of our examples has included (a) dismantling to separate an end-of-life product into components, (b) cleaning and processing of the old component to prepare it for reuse, and then (c) delivery into a willing market. We can look in turn at these three features, to understand the potential to reduce demand for liquid metal production by reusing components.

A novel track design for increased reuse

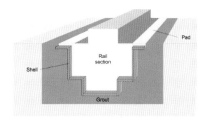

A common mechanism of failure in rail-track is wear of the railhead. Replacement is often due to the deterioration of only the surface material. Re-usable designs are looking to extend the life of the remaining material. One idea is to redesign the shape of the rail with a double or quadruple headed rail, supported in a continuous bed of concrete instead of sleepers, but mounted so that it can be withdrawn and rotated when worn, to provide a new contact surface. We've looked at the total embodied emissions of this design—accounting for increased concrete and reduced steel use—and if the rotation doubled the life of the rail, the total embodied emissions of the track per year of service would be greatly reduced.

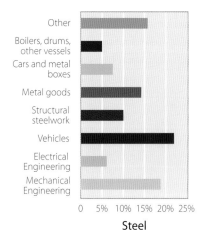

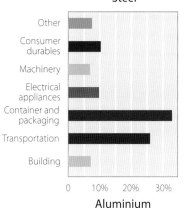

Figure 15.1—**Estimates of scrap availability**

Dismantling end-of-life goods to create a supply of components for reuse

What components could be reused? We could give a great answer to this question if we could station a few students at the nation's metal scrap yards, and ask them to keep a detailed log of everything that came in over a year or so. Remarkably, several students around the world have done exactly this and we salute their commitment! But fortunately we can make a useful estimate in a different way. We looked earlier in the book at the flow of metal into products, and made estimates of the life-span of different product types. So, armed with a history of production in each main sector, we can predict the types of products currently being scrapped and sent for recycling which might instead be reused. Figure 15.1 shows our estimates[3]. The distribution has changed from the product catalogues in chapter 3, because some goods last longer than others.

To reuse components we need to extract them without damage and at low cost. We can extract them either by cutting them out, or by disassembling a product into its parts, so it seems rather obvious that products should now be designed with mechanical joints (such as nuts and bolts) so they can be taken apart later. However, there are several other requirements too, mainly driven by the fact that disassembly is much more expensive than assembly. A key to this is because, unlike assembly where tasks can be standardised to gain economies of scale[4], in disassembly each task is different, so costs more. The UK's wonderful facility for shredding one million fridges per year (we'll come back to it in chapter 16) does have sufficient repeating tasks (if only it didn't…) to standardise the removal of key components prior to shredding. However, building deconstruction must occur on-site, so is always a 'one-off', and vehicle disassemblers must process whatever cars arrive—generally each car is different from the one before. Without standardisation, disassembly is expensive unless products are designed with disassembly in mind. For example, it should be easy to identify parts, and it should be possible to remove any one part without having to remove several others first. Table 15.1 provides a summary of what we've learnt about design that supports cost-effective component extraction for reuse[5].

If we ignore cost, almost all assembled products can be disassembled, and the principles in the table give a basis for designing products now so that in future their components can be more easily reused. However, if we want to start re-using components now, we must cope with what's in current designs.

Sustainable Materials with both eyes open

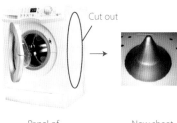

Cut out

Panel of
washing machine

New sheet
metal part

Figure 15.2—**Reforming metal
from reclaimed products**

Preparing components for reuse

Having separated a component from its parent product, what should we do to maximise its value? Car dismantlers might do very little, for instance to a working engine part, and simply re-sell the component for use elsewhere. Or they might need to re-spray a body panel, and it's technically possible to clean and re-coat used steel food cans. Every metalworking shop keeps a stock of off-cuts or parts from old jobs, which can be cut into smaller pieces for new uses. We described re-rolling old ship plates earlier, and Professor Erman Tekkaya and colleagues at the University of Dortmund have demonstrated that you can form a used car body part into a new part[6]. In fact most sheet goods retain sufficient ductility that they could be re-formed. Small parts from a previous use or even swarf can be joined into larger parts, as we saw in chapter 13, or as happens in car body repair. So between re-sale and re-melt there's a wide range of options for reuse, which we've summarised in Table 15.2.

In a crisis we would immediately adopt all of these strategies, to conserve the value in existing materials. In our economy at present, manufacturing is so efficient that any reuse requiring additional labour is unlikely to compete with the use of new material, and therefore most of these options are dormant.

However, we've listed the options in order of increasing likely cost, and as we look ahead for options to reduce total demand for liquid metal, we can use this table as a guide. Superficial change—removing a coating, or reapplying one, can be cost effective already—particularly for larger, custom made parts, which are currently sprayed by hand, and 'subtractive reuse' is generally much cheaper than deformative reuse: metal can be cut with generic tools, but can only be formed with special costly tools.

Looking for opportunities for future reuse, we want to find components that can easily be separated from their parent product, and can be reused directly or require only superficial change or simple trimming. To look for candidates, we can now return to the bar charts of scrap availability. Any component that can be reused without change, will be reused already if the cost is attractive, so reuse will increase if the relative difference in price between new and used components expands, or if the cost of labour decreases relative to the cost of the new component. Vehicles and equipment feature prominently in the scrap charts of Figure 15.1 but for different reasons both are difficult targets. Body panels in vehicles are potentially a large source of used sheet steel but by the time cars are scrapped, their design has usually been superseded, so the market for component re-sale without change

No change: the product is resold e.g. second-hand sales of books and clothing, modular construction/deconstruction

Superficial: only the surface of the product is changed, e.g. refurbished cardboard boxes (label/print/tape removal), thermal cleaning, non-abrasive blasting

Subtractive: Material is removed from the original product e.g. dye-cutting of used cardboard, rust removal, cutting new shapes from used steel plate

Deformative: the component is reshaped, e.g. reforming steel columns, re-folding cardboard boxes, re-rolling of steel plate

Additive: components are joined together e.g. solid bonding of aluminium swarf, welding processes (selective recasting, laser cladding, wire-arc spraying), gluing plastics and paper

Destructive: conventional recycling

Table 15.2—**Different options for component reuse organised by increasing cost from top to bottom**

is small. If in future, cars were designed with a common architecture, panel reuse could be valuable, but at present there is little opportunity beyond the existing spare parts market. Re-use of components from equipment is also difficult: equipment is assembled with a wide variety of specialised components, so the market for any particular part is small. With increased standardisation this could change. Packaging is the largest source of post-use aluminium scrap, particularly foil containers and drinks cans. However, regulation on food packaging, the fragility of the packages once emptied, and the logistical difficulty of collecting used packaging strongly inhibits reuse.

So where should we look for the chance to expand reuse? We need an application that uses big pieces of metal that will be useful even if trimmed, that aren't damaged in use or afterwards, and that are sufficiently standardised that they will continue to be useful after first use. And no doubt by now you're thinking that this sounds exactly like the world of steel-framed buildings. We agree, and weren't the first to think of it: step forward David Rose from Suffolk in East Anglia whose family-run business Portal Power takes down, restores, and reuses single story portal-framed buildings. Take a look at the box story on Portal Power to find out more.

Re-use of structural steel looks to us to be a great opportunity that is likely to grow rapidly in the near future and we'll discuss it more shortly. However, before narrowing our focus to this specific application, we need to explore the third aspect of reuse thrown up by our opening story about Cambridge White bricks: where's the market?

Identifying markets

The bricks of Cambridge are reused with a chain of three players: the owners of the old building who decide to sell the bricks; the builders who take down the old building, clean the bricks and often act as stockists; the owners of the new building who specify reused bricks as a requirement. So a market for reused metal will evolve if the three equivalent players all want it to happen:

- The end-of-life chain for scrap metal is mature and efficient: nearly all scrap metal arising in the UK is collected for recycling (by melting). The decision to supply metal for reuse rather than recycling therefore depends on whether a higher price is offered for reuse to pay for the inconvenience of disassembly and careful handling.

- A sufficient network of stockholders exists already, world-wide, to meet the needs of existing manufacturers and constructors for metal. These stockholders already have the required contacts in the market, so are the natural suppliers of reused metal, and will do so if customers are prepared to pay a price for old metal that sufficiently compensates any additional costs related to sourcing, remediating and stocking. The box story shows that for James Dunkerley Steels in Oldham, there is indeed sufficient compensation.

- Clients, designers, contractors or manufacturers would specify reused material over new, either if there was a price incentive or if they found a brand advantage in doing so. However, they will only consider reused metal if the quality of the material, which might need certification, is appropriate to their needs.

Apparently we have defined a clear economic principle about reuse: everyone will do it if the price is right. Clearly that's true, but potentially reuse could also be driven by a changed business model related to modularisation and we'll be exploring that opportunity in chapter 16. There are many opportunities to create modular designs around standard grids, and this approach would greatly increase the value of components at end-of-first-life, by increasing the number of potential second applications. The largest opportunity we can identify for developing reuse appears to be in steel framed buildings, and we'll now explore that specifically.

Portal Power

Portal Power is a business specialising in the design and erection of portal frame buildings. Over 40% of their 2,000-3,000 tonnes annual throughput is in pre-used portal frame buildings. Portal Power oversees the whole process from deconstruction, through any modification, to final erection in a new location. Deconstruction generally takes 3-6 times longer than demolition, and is not always possible. For example, if column bases have been embedded in concrete, it is too costly to extract them without damage. Changing insulation standards for cladding have also prevented reuse of some cladding sheet in commercial buildings.

After deconstruction, Portal Power stores the steel while waiting for a buyer. When a customer is found, Portal Power can modify the building, adding value to their business. Portal Power provides structural drawings to the new owner, and is investigating shot-blasting and repainting the reclaimed steel to add further value. Portal Power does not currently test the steel, and the majority of the reused buildings they sell are for agricultural use.

Re-use of steel sections in construction

All over the world, large buildings are based on structural frames made either with reinforced concrete or structural steel. In the old days we used to use large blocks of stone, and all we could manage were buildings like the Cathedral of Notre Dame in Paris, Machu Picchu in Peru, Angkor Wat in Cambodia, King's College Chapel in Cambridge and the Taj Mahal in Agra, but our sense of design has moved far beyond that now and instead we make towers and hangars. 8,000 years of development, and global architecture has become a single perfectly harmonised style, so that wherever you are, if you're in a city you're surrounded by towers, and if you're in a shop, a factory, warehouse or airport, you're in a hangar. Towers and hangars, the greatest achievements of design, and we build them all with only two possible material options—reinforced concrete or structural steel.

In France and Italy they still mainly use reinforced concrete, but in the UK, we have steadily shifted towards steel frames: plenty of concrete still to make the floors, and often the central core, but the basic structure is steel. The graph shows an estimated history of construction steel use in the UK, and the second line, the same line, smoothed and shifted forwards by 40 years, is an indicator of the upcoming availability of structural steel in buildings reaching their end of life. We have a growing supply of used structural steel.

James Dunkerley Steels (JDS)

JDS are a steel stockist in Oldham. Up to 20% of their stock is used steel and they sell around 3,000 tonnes of used steel sections per year. They are known nationally as a buyer of used steel and have a long-standing, established business. JDS employ a full-time buyer who visits demolition sites and quotes a price for the steel. The business pays a premium over the scrap price to cover the additional time and effort of deconstruction. To encourage careful dismantling, the steel is inspected on the ground before payment. The steel is then transported from the demolition site to the stockyard in Oldham.

JDS do not test or certify reclaimed steel, but instead 'downgrade' its specification to that of basic mild steel. The turnover of stock is generally 3–4 months, however for steel of standard sizes this may be reduced to just one week. The main customers for reclaimed steel are civil engineering firms, who use the steel for temporary structures and road plate. JDS also sell to local builders and developers, and have a fabrication shop to provide added value to their customers.

Steel framed buildings are bolted together from sections, which form the beams (horizontals) and columns (verticals) of the building frame. Steel sections are not degraded in use, unless the building is damaged by fire, so the supply of steel in the graph could be used to make new buildings. Furthermore, steel sections are standardised, so geometries made 40 years ago are still regularly specified today. And although some sections are limited by strength, which has improved with 40 years of technology improvement in steel making, most are limited by stiffness, which is unchanged. There are no fundamental technical barriers to designing steel buildings now, with 40-year old steel.

A small number of steel-framed buildings have now been built with sections reused from previous buildings, and our colleague Professor Mark Gorgolewski from Ryerson University in Canada has documented several of them. We've worked with him to make an estimate of the emissions benefit of steel reuse, and the box-story overleaf tells the story of those buildings. Overall, we've found that steel reuse requires very little energy, so if we can make a one-for-one substitution, re-using a tonne of steel section gives an emissions benefit equal to making a tonne of an equivalent new section[7]. We have to be careful though—and as the box story on the following page shows, the emissions benefit of reuse in the different buildings is not the same in each case, mainly due to over-specification. This occurs because reuse is not common practice, so in several cases larger cross-sections were used than would be chosen in a new design, and the total mass of steel used was therefore higher. The processes of deconstruction and reclamation required very little energy, and we found no evidence that reuse influenced the energy required to heat or cool a building in use.

Figure 15.3 shows a simple process flow for building a new building with reused steel. Once the old steel reaches the fabricator (the people who cut the steel to length, and weld end-plates and other fixtures to it ready for assembly) there is no difference between this process and that for a new building, so the key stages of reuse are: sourcing the old steel; deconstruction; reclamation; certification; design. We'll now take a look at each of those stages in turn.

When a property developer buys a site, they first decide whether to refurbish the existing buildings on the site, or replace them. If the decision is to replace, they design a new building, seek planning permission, identify contractors, and wait till they have a client to occupy the new building. During this process the old building stands empty, but when all four elements are satisfied and the programme of work starts, the first contractor onto the site is the demolition agent who is told to clear the site as rapidly as possible. Any delay to demolition causes a delay in the whole

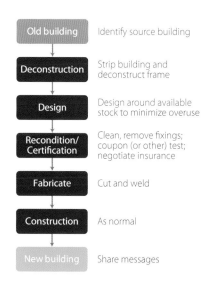

Figure 15.3—**Schematic for designing a building from reused components**

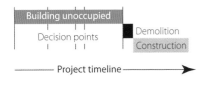

Figure 15.4—**Time-line for building demolition**

programme, and therefore an expensive delay before the tenant starts to pay rent. The quickest way to clear a site is to knock the building down, and current health and safety laws in the UK aim to avoid having people near the building until all the materials are at ground level. Once the building is reduced to rubble, a simple sorting occurs—and in particular old steel is separated and sold as a commodity for recycling. Because they will be melted, it doesn't matter if the steel sections are damaged during demolition. So, if we want to reuse the steel sections from this site, we have to deconstruct the building rather than demolish it.

The time-line in Figure 15.4 re-emphasises the amount of time that the building stands empty before demolition begins—this occurs because nothing happens until all contracts are in place. However, if the developers used separate valuations for a site with an old building and a clear site, they could begin deconstruction earlier without delaying occupancy of the new building. Because deconstruction takes longer than demolition, it costs more, so even if they have time, demolition

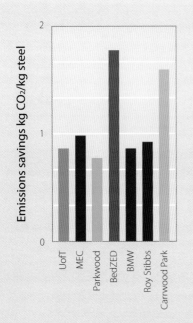

Figure 15.5—**Emissions savings from building reuse**

Re-use of buildings

University of Toronto, Toronto: 16 tonnes of structural steel were recovered from the deconstruction of the nearby Royal Ontario Museum and used in one wing of the student centre.

Mountain Equipment Co-op, Ottawa: About 90% of the original structural steel in the old grocery store was reused in the construction of the Mountain Equipment Co-op store on the same site.

Parkwood Residences, Oshawa: During the adaption of an old office complex into a new residential development, about 90% of the original steel frame was reused.

BedZED, London: 98 tonnes of structural steel were reclaimed from local demolition sites and used for a housing and commercial development.

BMW Sales and Service Centre, Toronto: During the adaptation of an old factory into a BMW Sales and Service Centre, about 80% of the original steel frame was reused.

Roy Stibbs Elementary School, Coquitlam: Following a fire, the Roy Stibbs Elementary School was rebuilt incorporating 466 steel joists recovered from a deconstructed school to speed up construction.

Carrwood Park, Yorkshire: An office-park development reused 60 tonnes of structural steel from existing structures on site and from a private stockpile.

Sustainable Materials with both eyes open

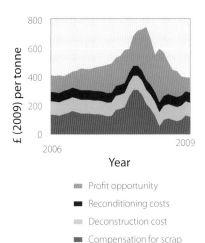

Figure 15.6—**Profit opportunity from steel reuse**

- ▦ Profit opportunity
- ■ Reconditioning costs
- ▨ Deconstruction cost
- ▦ Compensation for scrap

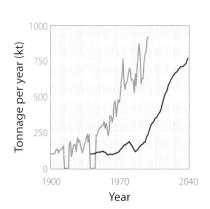

- ▦ Annual consumption of structural sections
- ■ Predicted annual availability of reclaimed sections

Figure 15.7—**Forecast availability of scrap structural sections in the UK**

agents will only do it if they're paid more. Is that likely? Figure 15.6 shows the history of the price for new steel sections in the UK (top line) and for scrap steel sections sent to recycling (bottom line) between 2006 and 2009. The gap between these is the potential profit opportunity motivating deconstruction rather than demolition. From talking to demolition contractors, we've estimated that the cost of deconstruction is an additional £100 per tonne of steel, compared with demolition, and we've added £70 per tonne for cleaning up the used sections ready for resale. The blue area therefore shows the profit opportunity if reused steel can be sold as a substitute for new steel. The graph suggests that there is enough money available to cover certification costs (to be discussed below) and to offer some incentive to purchasers to choose reused steel over new steel. Despite this opportunity, which is sufficient to motivate James Dunkerley Steels as described in the earlier box, the UK's market for reused sections hasn't yet flowered. We think it very likely that it will: Figure 15.7 suggests that supply will increase rapidly.

Many other business models are possible in sourcing reused steel sections. Table 15.3 shows four ways that clients have already found steel for reuse, three of which do not involve a stockholder. In fact there is a further option which we're now trying to develop into a demonstrator: large retail chains who own their own buildings currently expect the buildings to last for around 20 years, after which the needs of local shoppers or the actions of competitors will create a commercial incentive to redevelop the store. Currently each store is built to order, and demolished destructively at the end of its life. Instead, the retail chains could retain ownership of the building components, and reconfigure them either on the same site or elsewhere to maintain the value of the materials and allow faster construction.

Steel framed buildings are bolted together—fabricators weld plates with holes onto each steel beam or column with sufficient precision that the building is delivered as a kit of parts and rapidly bolted together on site. If we need to demolish buildings rapidly and without people on site, as at present, un-bolting is currently not possible, and instead the weapon shown in the photo is used to smash the facades off the building, and cut the steel sections into pieces. Operating one of these things must be a testosterone fuelled thrill, albeit a depressing one, but they are, of course, extremely effective: we've recently watched one of these monsters eat up a four story office block on the road to our local train station in just two days. If we want to use the steel again, we need a different strategy, and with a change to health and safety laws, we could allow people back onto the site, applying the same safety rules as when constructing new buildings, and either un-bolting or cutting the joints. Alternatively we could look for new approaches to joining steel

A delicate tool for smashing the façades off buildings

that facilitate remote deconstruction: see the box story to the right for a survey of current innovations in the area while the other specifically looks at the problem of separating reinforced concrete floors from the steel frame of a structure.

Steel sections extracted undamaged from old buildings require some reclamation, after which they are visually identical to new sections. However, there is one important difference: new sections are supplied with a certificate that guarantees their properties, and allows for the transfer of responsibility for building failure from the contractor back to the steel supplier. How can this transfer be achieved for reused steel?

New steel is certified based on an audit of the steel mill where it was made. The quality of the whole process from liquid steel to final product is regularly tested with statistical sampling, and each section is certified to have properties at a specified level. The steel companies are highly motivated to get this process right, as they would be legally liable if a building failed because the steel was below specification. We need an equivalent quality guarantee for reused steel

Table 15.3—**Factors affecting the decision to specify reuse in construction**

Existing reuse models	Information and certification	Design	Timing and project management
		Reuse of steel in construction	
In-situ reuse: an obsolete building is bought and either adapted, or deconstructed so that components can be reused.	Reduced need for testing: possible access to engineering drawings, current loads known.	Adaptive design based on known materials purchased up front. Possibility to reuse entire building systems.	Single client manages deconstruction, design and construction. Timing naturally aligned.
Relocation: a steel structure is dismantled and re-erected elsewhere, e.g. Portal Power.	Reduced need for testing: same configuration, same loads.	Adaptive design based on steel structure purchased up front.	Buyer is tied to seller's project schedule, possibility of delay.
Direct exchange: steel sections or modules are sold for reuse without an intermediary.	Testing and certification required unless beams are downgraded or buyers trust sellers.	Material pre-ordered or design drawn up with a flexible specification in order to increase likelihood of finding suitable stock.	Buyer is tied to seller's project schedule, possibility of delay.
Stockholder: sections, steel frames or modules are bought, remediated and stocked until a demand presents itself.	Testing and certification required unless beams are downgraded. May only accept standard products.	Material pre-ordered or design drawn up with a flexible specification in order to increase likelihood of finding suitable stock.	Delays can be avoided as stock is supplemented with new material if necessary in order to guarantee supply (this affects reuse content).
		Reuse of manufacturing scrap	
Stockholder: offal from the pressing process is bought, cut to regular sizes and sold for reuse.	Material properties known. No additional testing. Sold for non-critical parts.	Unaffected as irregular offal is cut into standard sizes.	Delays can be avoided as stock is supplemented with new material if necessary in order to guarantee supply (this affects reuse content).

sections. In future, it may be possible to do this simply by providing information, although guaranteeing that paper records are kept safe and can be found would be complicated. Alternatively, a permanent marking on each section could specify its performance. For either of these approaches to work, the insurance industry must learn to trust that the properties of the section are unchanged during first use. At present, they don't accept this, so the required assurance must be provided by testing each reused section. This involves cutting a test sample from each beam, and stretching it in a testing machine to measure its strength. This process requires labour, so is expensive and is an important barrier to reuse. However, as the box story shows, there are other cheaper ways to provide an equivalent test, and part of our ongoing work will be to develop an affordable standard for testing reused steel which is acceptable to the insurance industry.

So, armed with undamaged, clean, certified reused steel sections, designers can now proceed with the new building—but not quite. New steel sections are made

Reversible joints

Joints that lock mechanically and with fewer bolts may allow quicker and safer deconstruction. The chart below presents a range of common and novel structural connections. The joints are grouped into two families: simple connections which resist shear forces (as commonly used in low-rise buildings) and moment connections which also resist bending (as used in portal frame construction). Novel joints such as Quicon, ATLSS, and ConXtech simplify demounting of the beams. Quicon offers simple removal, and ATLSS and ConXtech provide stability with male/female interlocking secured with bolts. Specifying these more novel joints may allow greater reuse in the future.

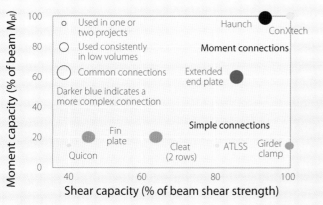

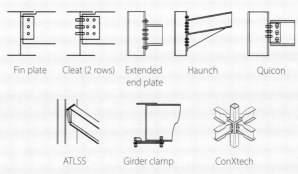

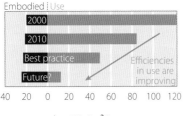

Embodied : Use

2000
2010
Best practice
Future?

40 20 0 20 40 60 80 100 120

kg CO_2/m²/year

Figure 15.8—**The balance between energy in use and embodied energy in buildings is changing**

continuously, so designers using new material can specify any length, and the range of cross-sections available today is greater than in the past. Design with reused sections may require some modification to the overall design to make best use of available materials. For some clients this could be an advantage: promoting the use of reused steel as a symbolic statement was an important part of the motivation of the case studies examined by Mark Gorgolewski. However, in general, it seems likely that a mix of reused and new steel will give the right combination of design freedom and reduced embodied energy or emissions.

Overall we've seen that re-using steel in construction looks to be a big opportunity in our quest for future material efficiency: reused steel can be used as a direct substitute for new steel, re-certification could be developed, and the supply of steel sections for reuse will grow. We anticipate that the motivation to pursue reuse in construction will grow also. Figure 15.8 gives an estimate of the balance between annual energy use in a retail building, and the embodied energy in the building divided by its anticipated life-span. Improvements in insulation, sealing, and heating and ventilation are driving a rapid improvement in annual energy use, while a tendency towards shorter life-span buildings is driving up the annualised embodied energy. Building operators are already aware of this trend, so looking ahead for opportunities to reduce embodied energy and material reuse offers the biggest impact. At present, the certification standards used to demonstrate energy efficiency in buildings (BREEAM in the UK, see the box story at the end of the chapter, and LEED in the US) are insensitive to embodied energy in the building—but both standards are under review, and proper reflection of embodied energy in these standards will increase the motivation for reuse.

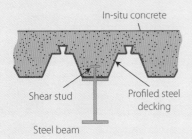

In-situ concrete

Shear stud

Profiled steel decking

Steel beam

Composite floor removal

Multi-storey non-residential buildings account for approximately 45% of the steel used in UK buildings. The most popular floor design in these buildings since the early 1990's has been the composite steel and concrete deck, combining the tensile strength of the relatively expensive steel at the bottom and the compressive strength of relatively cheap concrete at the top. However it is difficult to deconstruct such floor systems because of the difficulty of ensuring the safety of the deconstructing team and because of the cost of slow unbolting in contrast with fast cutting or shearing of joints. Novel joints might allow quicker separation of the floor modules from their supports, and of the concrete from its coupled steel work, for instance by cutting out segments. A major demolition contractor told us that cutting out would currently take at least 3 or 4 times longer than conventional demolition.

Sustainable Materials with both eyes open

Outlook

This chapter started with reused Cambridge White bricks, and has ended with a focus on the reuse of steel sections in construction, because it looks like such a big opportunity. To promote it we need some lead users, perhaps retailers seeking brand advantage, or the government through its procurement policies, to stimulate demand. The supply of reused steel will follow demand, and could be increased with changes to demolition practice, either driven by changes to regulation, or new approaches to reduce the costs of deconstruction in comparison with demolition. We're currently working hard to stimulate some demonstrators of reuse in the UK.

A Meccano inerter

We've left to the end what's probably the most obvious and well-known example of metal reuse: the famous Meccano kit. Invented by Frank Hornby in 1901 the first Meccano kit used reversible joints (nuts and bolts) with regular spacing between bolt holes, to ensure that components can mate. Since then the number of parts has increased a little, but the number of designs is limitless. Does reuse limit design creativity?

One of the most exciting inventions we've seen in the past 10 years is the inerter invented and patented by Professor Malcolm Smith. The inerter is a new member of the family of basic mechanical components, which includes springs, masses and dampers and allows new designs for car suspensions[8]. It's a great invention, and the photo shows Professor Smith's first model inerter, made of course, in Meccano. Design constraints in reuse? Not that we can find!

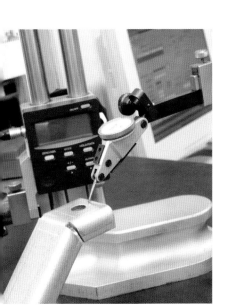

Rapid cheap testing of used steel

The Vickers hardness test was invented in 1924 to estimate the hardness and yield stress of a material. A cone indenter is pressed into the surface of the material, with the Vickers hardness defined as the applied force divided by the area of the indented shape. Empirical studies have estimated the yield stress as a third of this hardness value. Portable hardness testing can be much cheaper and quicker than the coupon tests currently used to recertify reclaimed steel. However, the error between hardness testing results and actual yield stress is often greater than 20%, an unacceptable level of error for insurance companies. Professor Tekkaya at the University of Dortmund has shown that we can reduce this error by considering the changing behaviour of the material as it deforms around the indenter. For a given batch of reclaimed beams, a combination of portable hardness testing, and a small number of coupon tests could allow a satisfactory degree of confidence in the properties of the material.

BREEAM and embodied energy

Voluntary eco-standards such as BREEAM give accreditation for the sustainability features of buildings. Buildings are scored across a number of sustainability criteria. The resulting credits are then combined to produce a single overall score on a scale of Pass, Good, Very Good, Excellent and Outstanding.

The materials category of BREEAM includes an assessment of the embodied life cycle impact of buildings but this is not based on publicly available data, and no minimum targets are set. And while embodied carbon in the structure typically constitutes over 20% of a building's lifetime impact, it is surprising that only approximately 5% of total credits are allocated to reducing its footprint; instead the emphasis is very much on use phase savings. By contrast the Australian Green Star rating system was revised in February 2010 to drive best practice in steel production and fabrication and to encourage dematerialisation of steel structures. Performance criteria for Green Star include minimum strength for rebar and structural sections and offsite optimised fabrication of rebar.

Notes

1. Two of our colleagues in the department of Earth Sciences provide a marvellous introduction to the building materials in Cambridge with their "walking tour around the historic city centre" online (Woodcock and Norman, n.d.)

2. Larger ship plate sections are hot-rolled to a thinner gauge to get rid of imperfections. Smaller sections are cut into ribbons, heated and fed into dies to roll into rebar. The re-rolled plate is sold for use in low-grade construction. There is no certification, and quality is assured only by the re-rolling mill's reputation. Re-rolled plate commands approximately 60% of the certified product price. Professor Asolekar of the Indian Institute of Technology in Bombay, has documented the environmental implications of this practice in two papers: Asolekar et al. (2006) and Tilwanker et al. (2008).

Dismantling end-of-life goods to create a supply of components for reuse

3. Empirical scrap data at the level required for this analysis is difficult to obtain, as waste regulations do not require data collection at a product level. Dynamic material flow analysis (MFA) using data on historic production and product lifetime distributions are used to model the outflow of goods from use by Davis et al (2007) to determine steel scrap flows in the UK, and these results are in good agreement with global discard of steel values produced by Hatayama et al. (2010). A breakdown of aluminium old scrap from Europe, the USA, China and Japan has been produced by Hatayama et al. (2009), again using a dynamic MFA model; these four regions account for about 80% of global aluminium consumption.

4. Although the most authoritative book on the Toyota Production System is that by Taichi Ohno (1988), who invented it, there's a very nice article by Dr Steve Spear of MIT (Spear and Bowen, 1999) that gives a definitive introduction for most of us who are unfamiliar with Japanese culture, so miss the nuances of Ohno's book.

5. Design for reuse principles are abstracted from recommendations and case studies by Addis and Schouten (2004) and Morgan and Stevenson (2005) on design for deconstruction, Kay and Essex (2009) on reuse in construction, and WRAP (2010) on a design team guide for civil engineering.

Preparing components for reuse

6. The remanufacturing of sheet metal scrap is investigated by Tekkaya et al (2008). Hydroforming, where high-pressure hydraulic fluid is used to press sheet metal against a die, is used to flatten contoured sheet metal parts, such as car bonnets. Incremental forming is used on already flat sheet metal parts, such as washing machine panels. Similar ideas on incremental forming of non-uniform sheet panels are investigated by Takano et al (2008).

Reuse of steel sections in construction

7. This is a little subtle—in the UK we actually don't make steel sections from recycled material, although they do in the US, but given that the steel in an old section would be recycled, on average, re-using it will reduce the amount of metal being recycled by one tonne, at the same time as reducing demand for liquid metal by one tonne, so the emissions saving from reuse is equivalent to the emissions of secondary production.

Outlook

8. The inerter looks like an ordinary shock absorber, where one end can be attached to the car body and the other to the wheel set. As the car moves over uneven ground, a rack and pinion or similar coupling causes the rotation of a flywheel inside the device. When combined with a spring and damper, the result is that the inerter reduces the vibration of the car body, allowing the car to have better road holding. Our colleagues in the control-engineering group have documented the advantages of this type of suspension in Smith et al (2004).

Images

9. Author: Plumbago at en.wikipedia (http://en.wikipedia.org) used under Creative Commons Attribution 2.5 Generic Licence (http://creativecommons.org/license/by/2.5/deed.en)

16 Longer life products

with delayed replacement

In developed economies, where our demand for metal has largely stabilised, we mainly purchase metal as replacement rather than due to growth. So, if we keep our products for longer, that would slow down the rate of replacement and hence reduce our need for new metal. Could we really use products for longer?

Caversham Road Bridge[13]

Ironbridge

Concorde

In three days during the 2011 New Year celebrations, the Caversham Road Bridge carrying nine train tracks over a road near to Reading Station in the UK was replaced, and the steel in it sent for recycling. There was no public outcry about the loss of the previous bridge, but if we proposed to replace Abraham Darby III's 1781 bridge at Ironbridge Gorge, we would incur not just public outcry, but the full legal might of the United Nations who have declared it a World Heritage Site. Every year in the UK we send 2 million cars to scrap[1], eventually to be recycled by melting, but we don't scrap old E-type Jaguars, because they epitomise a glamorous era of motoring whose aura we treasure. In total, 20 supersonic Concorde aeroplanes were built between 1966 and 1979. They no longer fly, but we'll never melt them all. NASA's four remaining space shuttles have retired to Museums in Florida, Los Angeles, Virginia and New York and we'll never discard them. The oldest surviving Watt Steam engine, the Old Bess built in 1777, is on display in the Science Museum in London, and we'll keep looking after it.

We connect with our past through stories and songs, through pictures and manuscripts, but also through physical objects. This connection is part of all cultures, and at some point objects become part of our heritage: we cease to consider whether they should be replaced by a newer or better model; we preserve them because they are part of what we are. This is as true of us individually as collectively, and in the same way that national charities and government organisations work to preserve important publicly owned buildings and goods, so privately we maintain family heirlooms and treasures.

So we know that if we choose to do so, we can maintain goods for much longer than normal, and in this chapter we'll explore whether keeping steel and aluminium products and components in use for longer would be viable or a good thing. The motivation is that, as we saw in chapter 4, in developed countries most of our demand for steel and aluminium is to replace goods rather than to expand our

Cars that failed to achieve heritage status

total stock. If we replace them less often, we will reduce our demand for new liquid metal, and so reduce the environmental impacts of production.

We learnt an important story motivating our work on this chapter in a previous project, where we looked at the future sustainability of clothing and textiles supply to the UK[2]. Between 2000 and 2005, in the UK, we increased the number of garments we purchase each year by one third. This incredible growth in demand was not, of course, triggered by a change in weather, but by the move towards 'fast fashion.' Prior to 2000, the fashion industry had a summer and winter season, and brought out new ranges twice a year to match. 'Fast fashion' now allows the introduction of new clothing ranges every six weeks, or even faster. This is a remarkable achievement, but most people reading this book can remember living in 2000, without worrying about being short of clothes. We buy more clothes because we can, and as a consequence, we throw them away at a greater rate. During our project on clothing and textiles, we met many inspiring people, and chief among them is Kate Fletcher[3]. Kate recognised that we discard garments so easily because they are commodities: they have no personal meaning. However, if your mother embroidered a shirt while you were ill, or if your child knits a hat, it isn't a commodity and you can't replace it.

What we learnt from Kate applies across a wide range of personal purchases, but we saw in our catalogue of steel and aluminium goods, that most metal is purchased by businesses not individuals. So in this chapter, starting from Kate's inspiration, we need to work our way carefully through the environmental, technical and business realities of steel and aluminium longevity.

We can anticipate the structure of this chapter by thinking about longer life cars. Firstly, if cars are becoming more fuel efficient, is it a good thing to keep them for longer, or should we actually replace them sooner, to gain improved fuel consumption? Do we replace the car because it is broken, because there's a new one we prefer, because it no longer meets our needs, or because it's no longer legal? Do we want to replace everything about our car, or just a few components? Finally, as car owners, or as car makers, how does longer car ownership affect us?

Power anthem

I don't need a new___ dress, I don't need a-no-ther car,

The angel of the north[14]

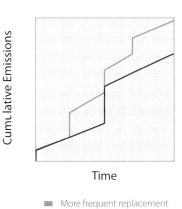

■■ More frequent replacement

■ Less frequent replacement

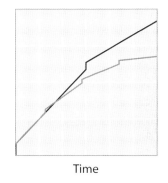

■■ More frequent replacement

■ Less frequent replacement

Figure 16.1—**Cumulative emissions profiles: products with low embodied energy and high rates of efficiency improvement should be replaced more frequently**

Is it more sustainable to keep goods for longer?

Keeping goods for longer reduces the rate of replacement demand, and for products that don't need maintenance and require little energy in use, this will save energy compared to replacing them. With absolute confidence we can state that the best strategy for minimising emissions associated with the Angel of the North, and indeed any other metal sculpture, is not to replace it. We can say the same about any products that use energy, but which have not become more efficient, since last purchased. However, if developments in technology, legislation or consumer preferences have led to more efficient products, we must evaluate the trade-off between increasing emissions by producing new metal for the replacement, against reducing emissions in use.

Figure 16.1 explores this issue. In the first graph, a product with high embodied energy, low energy in use, and little improvement in use should be replaced less frequently. In the second graph, energy in use is greater than that in production, and efficiency is improving, so the product should be replaced more often. We'd like to generalise the message of these two graphs and will do so with a simple calculation.

Let's assume we know the embodied energy required to make some product, and the annual energy consumed in use for this year's model. We'll also assume that each year, because of innovations, both embodied and annual use-energy are reduced at steady but independent rates—say 1% less embodied energy and 2% less energy in use per year, every year, for that year's model. Now let's assume the owner chooses to replace the product at a regular interval. For example, for the improvement rates we've given, if the user replaces the product every 5 years, then in 5 years time they will buy a model having 5% less embodied energy and 10% less annual-use energy than this year's model. For any product, if we know this year's embodied energy and annual-use energy, and the likely rates of future improvement in both, we can now calculate the replacement interval that minimises the total required energy.

We've done this for a range of these values in Figure 16.2. The graph shows us firstly that as the ratio of embodied to annual-use energy increases we should replace products less frequently (as we anticipated with the Angel of the North). But we can also see how that decision changes as either embodied or annual-use energy improve. Improvements in annual-use energy have a small effect, which is stronger at the right of the graph; improvements in embodied energy have a large effect all across the graph. This seems surprising but remember that the basic shape of the graph *already* tells us to replace products with large annual-use energy more frequently. If the annual-use energy improves, the effect of changing our replacement period is small because we will incur most of the annual-use energy anyway. However, if we reduce our replacement interval at all, the total number of times we buy the product goes up, and we incur the full embodied energy each time, so are highly sensitive to how it improves[4].

We've also shown on Figure 16.2 various familiar products—an office block, a car, an aeroplane, a train—for which we know current values of embodied and annual use energy[5]. For each product, we've shown typical replacement intervals in current practice (circles) and the replacement interval we estimate to be best— according to current rates of improvement (stars). The results show that in each case, albeit only marginally for the plane, we're replacing faster than we should do according to this criterion, so in turn, delaying the end of life for all of these products would save energy. This motivates us to explore the other reasons why we replace products, and will do so in the next section.

Figure 16.2 provides important general guidance about the value of delaying product replacement, and we could now use it as a start to exploring life extension for any particular product. In the rest of this chapter we'll assume that we're dealing with products for which life extension is beneficial, and focus on the realities of making it happen. However, before leaving the environmental case, let's anticipate one of our strategies coming up, and explore what happens if, rather than replacing the whole product, we're able to perform an upgrade to gain the benefits of improved energy requirements in use, without incurring the full

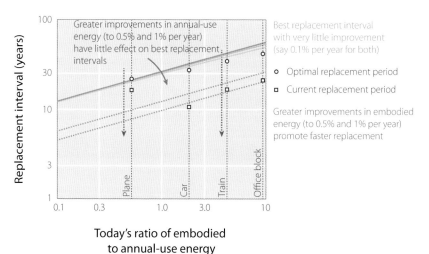

Figure 16.2—**Predicted product replacement intervals to minimise use and embodied energy**

Today's ratio of embodied to annual-use energy

Sustainable Materials with both eyes open

embodied energy cost or replacing the entire product. The box story examines the options for life extension and upgrades applied to a specific vehicle, confirming the potential benefit of upgrades.

Can we anticipate how this linkage between use and embodied energy and emissions will play out in future? Figure 16.3 shows estimates of current ratios between embodied and use emissions for buildings, passenger and freight vehicles over current life spans, showing that in all cases, total energy requirements are dominated by use. This is well known, and links right back to the pie charts on global energy use in chapter 2. The use of vehicles and buildings are two of the three major categories of global energy consumption, but unlike industrial production, they are currently inefficient and we have plenty of options to improve their efficiency. As a result, annual-use emissions will in future be smaller relative to embodied emissions from making buildings and cars, so by our analysis this will increase the value of life extension in future.

The conclusion of this section is that life extension is not always a good idea, if a product has high use energy requirements compared to embodied production

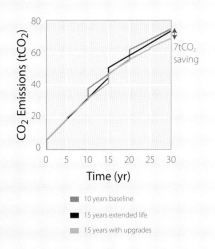

10 years baseline
15 years extended life
15 years with upgrades

Upgrade as a strategy for vehicle life extension?

In the graph to the left, the blue line represents a typical mid-size car (125 g CO_2/km tailpipe emissions) with a design life of 200,000 km over 10 years. At years 0, 10 and 20, the car is replaced creating 6.3 t CO_2 of embodied carbon emissions per car. The annual-use emissions are assumed to improve by 3.5 % every year (in line with the car-maker's targets and EU regulation) giving 128 g CO_2/km for the first period, and 90 g CO_2/km and 64 g CO_2/km for the following two periods. Total emissions of the 30 year period come to 75 tCO_2. Life-extension (the purple line) to 15 years requires only two new cars. This saves just 1.5 t CO_2 (2 %) of emissions, much less than the 6.3 t CO_2 embodied emissions saved, because the strategy delays upgrading to the latest engine technology. Upgrading (the green line) the car every 5 years with a new engine (at a cost of 15 % of embodied emissions in a new car, 0.9 t CO_2) takes advantage of improved engine technology to reduce annual-use emissions with a minimal penalty in embodied emissions. This strategy saves 7 t CO_2 (9 %) of emissions, which is more than a new car, and this could be an attractive business model for car manufacturers. In this case the total saving is relatively small compared to the cumulative emissions over the period, but greater savings will be achieved for products with higher relative embodied energy.

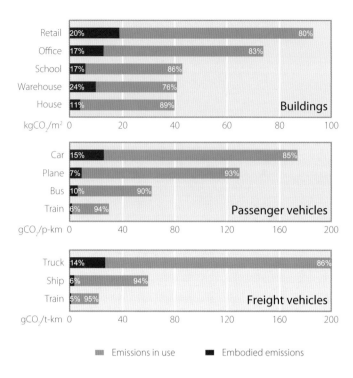

requirements, or if rapid technology change is occurring. However, for most existing products, life extension would lead to net savings. Therefore we'll now focus on life extension and the key question arising from our evidence in Figure 16.2 is 'what's making us replace things too soon?'

Why do we replace existing goods?

Some of us want new cars, with the latest styling and features, while others prefer to buy second-hand cars to have sufficient features at lower cost. Perhaps surprisingly new tractors, fridges and trucks are now all marketed with fashion and style prominent in the advertising messages while functionality is assumed. But if you're a salesman for steel rail track, your primary message will be about its life in service: we don't buy track because of its colour.

We've looked at dozens of case studies exploring why owners in different contexts replace products, and found that we can helpfully illuminate their different motivations by asking just two questions:

- is the product replaced because of its performance or because of its value?

- is the product being assessed relative to when it was purchased or relative to what's now available?

We've illustrated these options as the rows and columns of Table 16.1 to define four types of 'failure'[6].

	... relative to when it was purchased	... relative to what's now available
The product's performance has declined ...	Degraded e.g. rail track	Inferior e.g. washing machines
The product's value has declined ...	Unsuitable e.g. sports car	Unwanted e.g. single hulled oil tankers

Table 16.1—**Types of failure**

Looking in turn at each type of failure in Table 16.1:

- **Degraded** failure occurs when the product has deteriorated so can no longer perform its original function. For clothing and textiles, this obviously relates to clothes being worn out, but for metal goods, it relates primarily to surface wear (damage when two metal surfaces slide over each other) but may also occur due to fire damage, fatigue cracks (growing after repetitive cycles of loading and unloading) or over-loading or impact.

- **Inferior** failure occurs when the original product is still functioning as designed, but a newer product is more attractive. Flared purple trousers of the 1970's have largely met this failure mode, and it is also common in computing and telecommunications due to the rate of innovation. For steel and aluminium goods, this mode often drives replacement decision for cars and machinery.

- **Unsuitable** failure occurs when the users' needs have changed so that the original product is no longer as valuable to the existing owner. In clothing and textiles this failure mode occurs when (for some reason) the clothing no longer fits the owner, and perhaps relatedly, a two-seater car is of little value to a couple with a new baby. Changing customer behaviour could drive unsuitable failures in many contexts, public transport for example, or electrical distribution, or when a building no longer meets a tenant's needs. Unsuitable failure relates to the value of the product to its current owner, but other owners may value it differently.

- **Unwanted** failure occurs when a product still functions well, but is valued neither by its current owner, nor any other. It may occur due to changes in fashion, or due to legislation: for example, legislation which now favours double hulls in an effort to reduce the risk of oil spills has caused early replacement of single hulled oil tankers, which continue to operate according to their original design, but are now unwanted.

Armed with our vocabulary of failure modes, we can now return to our product catalogue from chapter 3, to explore why each product type is replaced. To create Figure 16.4, we've pulled together all the information that we could find on the reasons for failure product by product, and then verified our estimates with experts in each industry. We found that we rarely demolish buildings because their performance has failed, and instead, their value to owners or tenants has declined so they are unsuitable or unwanted. Second hand markets for vehicles and industrial equipment are strong, so although their original owners may replace them because they are unsuitable or inferior, eventually their final owners will discard them when degraded. Aluminium packaging is degraded in use, and so is replaced. At their original design load, electric cables could last for a hundred years, but due to growth in population and power hungry technology, older cables must often transmit power beyond this design load and so become 'unsuitable': they overheat, sag, and can cause power cuts.

	Steel	Aluminium
Degraded	32%	61%
Inferior	14%	3%
Unsuitable Unwanted	54%	36%

Table 16.2—**Failure mode shares for each metal**

Table 16.2 summarises our estimates of the fraction of steel and aluminium discarded for the three modes of failure shown in Figure 16.4. Our table of four different failure modes has helped us to identify and separate the reasons why steel and aluminium goods are replaced and soon we'll use it to search for opportunities to extend product life. But before doing so we'll ask a more forensic question: we know that steel and aluminium are always used to make components, so when goods containing the two metals are replaced, has the whole assembly of components failed, or does failure really apply to just a few components?

Sustainable Materials with both eyes open

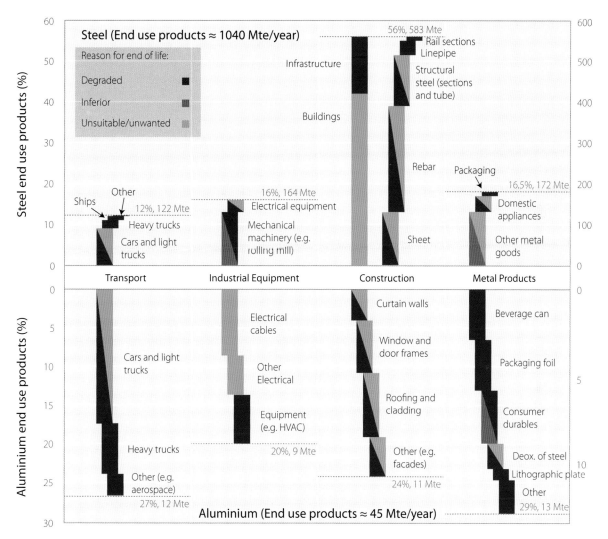

Figure 16.4—**Reasons for end-of-life**

Which specific components drive our replacement decisions?

High un-productivity in
UK fridge shredding

Among the many visits we made while preparing this book, we went to a metal scrap yard with a dedicated fridge shredding line. We have about 22 million households in the UK, with a fridge in each, and we throw them away when they're 10–12 years old, so we discard about 2 million fridges per year. We must dispose of them with care to avoid releasing the refrigerants (previously CFCs and now HFCs) into the atmosphere, so we've created dedicated un-production lines to shred them efficiently. And how wonderfully efficient we are! Our best fridge shredding line in the UK can shred one million fridges per year, as we apply in reverse all the skills we've learnt from Toyota about efficient car manufacturing. In the UK we make about 1.5 million (mainly Japanese) cars per year so we must be pretty efficient at manufacturing? Peanuts! Every year we destroy at least 33% more fridges that we make cars, and while our car output is declining, our fridge destruction rates are rising. Great news: UK un-productivity goes up!

What's wrong with all those fridges. Are they unwanted? No, we all want fridges. Are they unsuitable? No, we have two basic shapes of fridge, under the counter or cabinet size, and there hasn't been much change. Inferior? A few people with low self esteem purchase identical pink fridges to demonstrate their creative individuality, but essentially fridges aren't a fashion item. So they must be degraded? Not the outer case, not the door, not the interior fittings, not the heat exchanger, not the insulation… almost all of the mass of the fridge is in excellent working order when it's discarded. We mainly discard fridges either because the rubber door seals have changed shape, or because the compressor (the electric motor and pump that drives refrigerant around) doesn't work. And has the compressor fully degraded? Has the case of the compressor broken? The metal in the rotor and stator? The copper windings? Apparently the most common cause of failure in a compressor is that the bearings wear out, and in turn this occurs because the lubricant has escaped.

So the real reason why we're discarding and shredding so many fridges is that we are short of a few millilitres of lubricant in a couple of small bearings in the fridge compressor. Replacing the compressor is labour intensive, and generally the motors were designed as sealed units, so the bearings can't be replaced. But as we look for opportunities to reduce metal demand with a different business model based on life extension, it seems that we have found an opportunity here: it looks as if we could sell a fridge with a life-time guarantee, if we identified the likely causes of failure and designed into the original product a simple means to repair them.

The fridge is an assembly of components, and in our motivating discussion we've recognised that the components have different failure modes. So now we'll try to generalise what we saw in the fridge by proposing an 'onion-skin' model of products. At the core of many products is a structural framework, often provided by steel or aluminium, with a long expected life-span. Attached to this framework are layers of other components, and we'll organise them so that as we move from inner core to outer layer of the onion, the expected life-spans of the components decrease. If products are designed so that components in the outer skin of the onion, those with the shortest life-span can be replaced easily then we may be able to extend the life of the product and exploit more of the life-span of the inner components. To make more of this idea, we will simultaneously create an onion skin model showing cost shares. If more of the metal and more of the costs are at the core of the onion, we will find more motivation to extend the life of the product, by repairing or upgrading failed components in the outer layers.

We've applied our onion skin model of metal and cost shares to four different case study products in Figures 16.5–16.8, including two using both steel and aluminium. As usual, we've done this through detailed discussion with companies working in each area. The plate rolling mill is a great example of how the onion skin model explains motivation for life extension: about half the steel in a plate mill is in its structural frame and foundations, and this is a substantial part of the cost of a mill. So rolling mill frames tend to have long life spans, while other components are repaired or upgraded on failure. In contrast, although a large fraction of its steel is used in the structural core, the cost of steel in an office block is relatively small. So offices, which mainly fail in the 'unsuitable' mode, are often replaced rather than upgraded. Similarly for the car, the body and drive-train account for most metal use, but this is a smaller fraction of vehicle material costs, so there is little commercial motivation for life extension. However, no such inhibition is clear for the fridge where it seems that it is the cost of repair, rather than the value in the components, which motivates replacement over life extension.

Of our four case studies, life extension is normal for the plate mill, and one reason for this is that the value shares in the onion skin model are more closely aligned with the metal shares[7]. In contrast, the large fraction of metal at the core of the onion skin models of offices and cars is usually still functioning perfectly when they are discarded, but has a lower fraction of total value. Can we do anything about this?

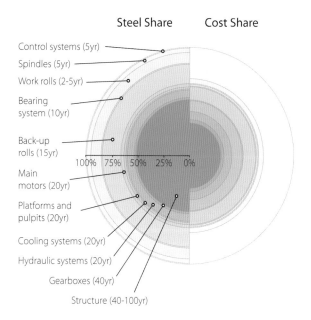

Figure 16.5—**Onion skin model for rolling mill**

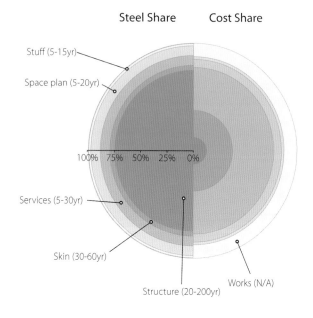

Figure 16.6—**Onion skin model for office building**

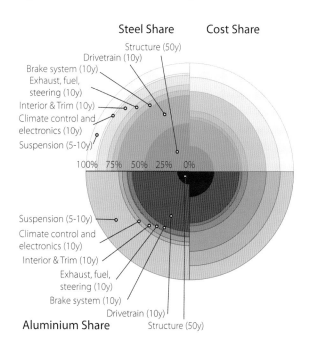

Figure 16.7—**Onion skin model for car**

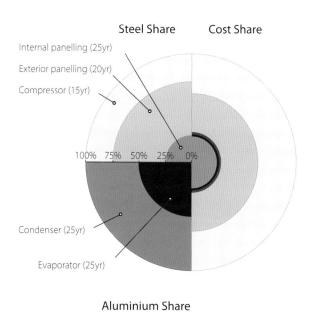

Figure 16.8—**Onion skin model for fridge**

Sustainable Materials with both eyes open

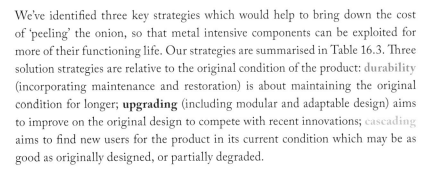
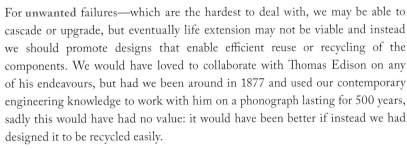

	... relative to when it was purchased?	... relative to what's now available?
Has the product's performance declined ...	Durability when degraded	Upgrade when inferior
Has the product's value delcined ...	Cascade when unsuitable	Design for recycling when unwanted

Table 16.3—**Strategies for 'peeling the onion'**

We've identified three key strategies which would help to bring down the cost of 'peeling' the onion, so that metal intensive components can be exploited for more of their functioning life. Our strategies are summarised in Table 16.3. Three solution strategies are relative to the original condition of the product: **durability** (incorporating maintenance and restoration) is about maintaining the original condition for longer; **upgrading** (including modular and adaptable design) aims to improve on the original design to compete with recent innovations; **cascading** aims to find new users for the product in its current condition which may be as good as originally designed, or partially degraded.

For **unwanted** failures—which are the hardest to deal with, we may be able to cascade or upgrade, but eventually life extension may not be viable and instead we should promote designs that enable efficient reuse or recycling of the components. We would have loved to collaborate with Thomas Edison on any of his endeavours, but had we been around in 1877 and used our contemporary engineering knowledge to work with him on a phonograph lasting for 500 years, sadly this would have had no value: it would have been better if instead we had designed it to be recycled easily.

Edison's phonograph[15]

Making components more durable

If components are degraded, we have three opportunities for intervention: design changes may delay the onset of failure; restoration may be possible to return components to their original specification; condition monitoring as part of maintenance in use may allow better prediction of when component replacement or restoration is required. All three of these practices are already in use, and could be applied more widely.

A wooden wagon wheel with a steel tyre for increased durability

Component degradation mainly occurs due to wear between sliding surfaces, crack growth due to cyclic loading, or corrosion. Blacksmiths and Wheelwrights understood the key principle of wear resistance, with strong iron horseshoes and tyres proving more wear resistant than horses feet or wooden wheels. The 'Archard equation'[8] predicts that wear will increase with load and sliding distance, and decrease with metal strength so modern rail track is made with high strength rail, and as our box story shows, this greatly extends the service life. Taking a lesson from the blacksmiths and wheelwrights, the Swedish innovation ReRail also mentioned in the box story is exploring the use of hardened but replaceable steel rail caps, to extend rail life further.

The well-painted Forth Road bridge

Corrosion may lead to failure of steel components, and a simple defence is to coat the steel: the alleged continuous re-painting of the Forth Bridge in Scotland is a well known example of this. A different problem with corrosion may occur in road bridges, if cracks in the concrete allow water to seep in so the steel reinforcing bars rust, and lose their bond to the concrete. This is a significant problem in the UK: several road bridges built in the 1960's had the wrong concrete mix, and reinforcement bars were placed too near to the surface, so water could reach the steel, cause rust and force early replacement. To avoid this problem we need better quality control in construction, or we could use stainless steel reinforcement bars which do not corrode, but cost four times as much. We've discussed wear and corrosion to show that we have good technical solutions to most cause of failure by degradation: if we correctly anticipate the loads a product must withstand, and the environment in which it will operate, we can generally find a durable design.

If degradation occurs, replacement may not be necessary if the component can be restored to its original condition. This is already familiar in tyre "retreading" where the worn rubber outer skin of the tyre is replaced, while the life of the highly specified steel wire in the tyre wall is extended. In this case, rubber is restored, but tram rails also wear away according to Archard's equation, and eventually will damage tram wheels, or impair safety. The cost of replacing tram rails is high, but if new metal is added to the rail in-situ in thin layers (by submerged arc welding) the temperature of the metal is carefully controlled and the right alloy is chosen, the rail can be restored with high strength. In fact, if the deposited steel has a high carbon content, the restored rail can have higher wear resistance than the original. More conventional restorations, for instance restoring coatings or other surface properties, are well established.

In safety critical applications such as flying, components may be replaced earlier than necessary, due to the terrible risks of component failure. This has led to a

Durability and wear in rail track

Replacing and maintaining rail track is expensive, not just because of the cost of materials (which only account for about 7% of the cost of track renewal) and the logistics of transporting materials and equipment to and from the work site, but also because of the economic penalty of lost track time when the line is closed. Therefore, increasing the life of rail track and decreasing the frequency of maintenance are important economic and environmental strategies for the rail industry. Four strategies to prolong rail life are being considered by the industry:

- Using stronger rail with a higher wear resistance reduces the frequency of maintenance and extends rail life. The graph below contrasts the emissions from material production and lifetime maintenance for two types of premium rail (heat treated and non-heat treated) with conventional rail and shows that significant emissions savings can be achieved even in a single life cycle.

- Thickening the rail head (see schematic) extends rail life by increasing the amount of sacrificial material that can be worn away. Assuming the wear rate is identical for both conventional and thicker head rail, extending the rail life in this way would save metal by delaying the manufacture of a completely new rail.

- Capping rail combines the previous two options—a stronger metal is used but only for the wear surface. The Swedish ReRail system uses a wear-resistant boron steel push-fit cap. With this system only 15% of the rail is replaced, offering a total carbon saving of 92%.

- In environments where corrosion may reduce rail life, high purity zinc coated rail can be used. In one such environment, the rail life at a busy crossing was extended from 3–6 months to more than 16 months using this method.

High performace heat treated rail

High performace non-heat treated rail

Conventional rail

Emissions (kg CO₂/m rail)

0   20   40   60   80   100   120

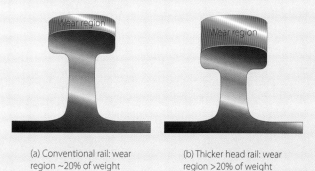

(a) Conventional rail: wear region ~20% of weight

(b) Thicker head rail: wear region >20% of weight

Turbine blades in jet engines are monitored to detect cracks

world of technology development known as "condition monitoring" which aims to give health checks to metal components. In the same way that medical doctors use technology for early detection of health problems, metal condition monitoring technologies aim to identify potential causes of failure early and as they become more precise, will allow extended component life spans with reduced risk. Typical techniques include ultrasound scanning and use of x-ray to detect small cracks. for example in the wings and turbine blades of aeroplanes. Alternatively, a series of sensors that measure movements, strains and other influencing factors can be used to support diagnosis of concrete cracking in monitoring infrastructure.

We have a wide range of options to design against degraded failures: although there will usually be a trade-off with cost, we can expect to design virtually all components to survive expected loads for indefinite time. If components fail, we have a growing range of techniques for restoring them to their original condition and we are developing diagnostic tools, to test the future health of components in service.

Upgrading products to extend the useful life of their embedded materials

When products fail because they are inferior, they can still perform their original design functions, but other products are now more attractive. We no longer make Penny Farthing bicycles for this reason. If an innovation has led to a complete change in a product design, there is little hope that we can extend the life of its predecessor. However, such radical innovations are rare. Most design progress is 'incremental' with smaller changes to an overall design used to attract new customers without the full costs of redesign, and it is more likely that upgrade can keep pace with such incremental changes.

Our onion skin model gives us clear guidance on upgrade opportunities: if the inferior components are in the outer layers of the onion, but the inner layers have significant value, upgrading will be attractive. Design to facilitate future upgrade therefore depends on anticipating which components are likely to require upgrade, and ensuring that the components can be exchanged.

To demonstrate how the structural core of products can outlast the original designers intentions we'll look at two case studies. The original office block built in the 1950's at 55 Baker Street is concrete-framed but by the early 21st Century it had become unsuitable, so was upgraded: the outer layers of the building,

Sustainable Materials with both eyes open

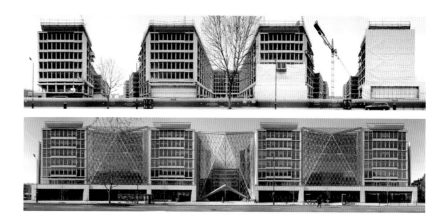

including the windows, cladding, internal trim, and heating and water services, were stripped out; stairs and lifts were reorganised centrally; floors were expanded to connect two adjacent wings; columns were removed; a new slender heating and cooling system was installed to increase ceiling heights. Around 70% of the original building structure was reused and the upgrade took a year less than would have been required for demolition and rebuild. In a different case study, Jonathan Aylen at the University of Manchester Business School, examined the life stories of seven strip rolling mills built in the 1950s, three of which still operate today. Since the 1950s steels have become stronger and the range of strip geometries expanded, but the volume of steel rolled each year has increased by 80%. Four changes supported this upgrade: the mills are used more intensively through better co-ordination in the factory; condition monitoring and regular maintenance have reduced interruptions to production; the quality of material arriving at the mill has improved fast roll changing; and better control systems have cut unproductive time.

In both case studies, upgrades allowed life extension and prevented failure by the unsuitable mode. However, in some cases products can't be upgraded. For example, air conditioning which was originally a luxury, is now an assumed feature of new cars. Air conditioning units are bulky, so it would be difficult to upgrade a car originally built without it, because there isn't space. Should we over-design products so we have more options to upgrade them later? To answer, we need to know which failure modes will cause end of life, what other innovations will occur, and what consumers will want in future? It's unlikely we'll ever have the answer, so we must be pragmatic, and the onion skin model helps us: we should arrange the product design so that components with shorter expected life-spans are easy to separate; if we can anticipate future performance requirements

Modular design of photocopiers allows reconfiguration

we should design the core of the product to achieve them; if not, better not to over-design, and instead plan for reconfiguration.

Modularity facilitates reconfiguration, and is useful in addressing all four failure modes. A modular design comprises modules connected according to some well-defined architecture so that each module can be replaced independently, and the number of modules in the product changed. Dell became the dominant supplier of personal computers in the 1990s by defining a set of rules for connecting modules: an 'architecture'. Customers choose their own modules so module suppliers can innovate independently[9]. Xerox supply photocopiers in a modular way, because owners want the latest model but the core of the copier changes slowly. Up to 80% of a new Xerox copier may actually be modules that have already been used but which are still perfectly serviceable[10]. With a related business model, Foremans in the UK refurbish building modules so that around 80% of the steel in old modules is reused after failure of the parent building.

Upgrading products that have failed because they are inferior or unsuitable is therefore also technically feasible, and already applied in some current businesses, but not a universal solution because the core of the initial design may prevent required upgrades. However, modular designs with an architecture that allows sub-products to be combined, are an attractive way to create adaptable designs that can be upgraded in response to all four failure modes.

Cascading products between users with different requirements

Owners requiring lower specification may be able to take over products that are degraded for their current owner, or may be able to adapt what was originally a higher specification product. In chapter 15 we explored the opportunities to cascade rail: by moving spent rail to lower duty branch lines and by rotating rail sections to reduce metal loss due to wear. We can also 'cascade' buildings. Typically this will involve refitting the interior and services while retaining most of the structure, but unlike the upgrade to 55 Baker Street, cascading may also involve a change in use. We interviewed a selection of structural engineers about this form of cascading and found that the key features of a structure that determine its value in different applications are the locations of entrances, stairwells and lift-shafts, the spacing of columns, the permissible loading on each floor and the height between floors. Having reviewed typical ranges for these features for different building types, we have drawn Figure 16.9 to indicate the relative difficulty of

Sustainable Materials with both eyes open

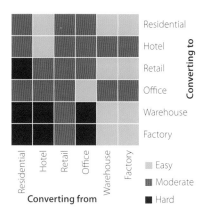

Residential
Hotel
Retail
Office
Warehouse
Factory

Converting to

Residential
Hotel
Retail
Office
Warehouse
Factory

Converting from

■ Easy
■ Moderate
■ Hard

Figure 16.9—**Building adaptation matrix**

converting buildings between uses. For example, the wide, high spaces typical of factories and warehouses allows easy adaptation to other uses. However residential buildings, which typically have smaller, more enclosed designs, cannot easily be adapted to other uses requiring greater volumes of uninterrupted space. The leading diagonal is not always green because homes and shops are often highly customised.

Cascading products between applications or user groups with different performance requirements is applicable where fashion and rapid innovation are not important drivers of demand. Cascading is already applied, and could usefully be extended, in applications where the core of the onion skin contains most of the embodied energy.

The business case for life-extension

If product life extension is technically possible, why doesn't it happen more and what could be done to promote it? In this section we'll explore how business decisions on purchasing act for or against life extension. In preparation we've conducted a series of structured interviews with producers and users of industrial machinery and equipment to find out about their purchasing and selling decisions.

Life extension in the eyes of the purchaser

If you have the opportunity to upgrade your existing equipment or to replace it with a newer model, how are you going to present the options to your boss? It's likely that you'll comment on at least five aspects of the decision: (1) how the new machine will affect other costs such as maintenance; (2) how you've taken into account future benefits; (3) whether the existing machine has already been 'written off' or not in the accounts; (4) how you think your needs will change in future, and whether the new machine is likely to meet them; (5) how much you'll get for the new machine if your needs change and you decide to sell it.

- **Which costs are taken into account as part of the purchasing decision?** More durable and reliable products are usually sold for a higher price in the hope of lower maintenance costs and delayed disposal and replacement costs. Although whole-life-costing is taught in theory, in practice many decisions are taken without fully adding up costs over time. At an extreme, when cash for investments is short, decisions are made to minimise initial purchase costs. Failure to take into account the full benefits of longer life products also occurs if managers allow only a short time for the cost of purchase to be paid back by the benefits of ownership. Payback periods can be as low as two years.

- **How are future benefits valued?** Figure 16.10 demonstrates how investors would examine the question "what share of future replacement costs would we take into account in our decisions today?" based on discount rates between 10 and 20% which were typical of the companies we talked to: at a discount rate of 10% only a third of the cost of replacement in 10 years is taken into account in decisions made today. Therefore, for longer-lived goods such as buildings, replacement costs don't even feature in decisions today so there will be no financial benefit in purchasing a longer lasting product.

- **Has the existing product already been 'written off'?** In company accounts the value of a purchase, say a piece of equipment, depreciates over time at some chosen rate. This depreciation is shown as a cost in the profit and loss accounts, and profitable long-lived equipment can be 'written-off' in the accounts, so it has a reported value of zero. Accountants think of this as an advantage because the cost of the equipment has been fully taken into account, managers may then be less motivated to maintain the value of what they own.

- **Will the product meet your needs in future?** The amount we're prepared to pay for more adaptable products depends on how sure we are that they'll be useful to us in future. If we want to promote longer-lasting equipment we must be confident that it is sufficiently flexible for our future needs.

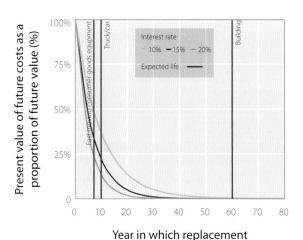

Figure 16.10—**The effect of discounting on future costs**

Sustainable Materials *with both eyes open*

- **For how much will you be able to re-sell the product in future?** Concerns about low second-hand prices can limit what we might pay for longer lasting products. For example, 15% of the value of a new car is lost on purchase with another 10% lost by the end of the first year and a further 10% lost in each succeeding year. As purchasers of second-hand goods, we don't trust the owners to assure us of the condition of the product, because they have a vested interest in exaggerating quality. If that quality is not easily tested, resale prices tend to be low and in turn, this deters purchasers from buying longer lasting goods.

With our five questions we've seen that there are many reasons why purchasers might be biased against more expensive longer lasting goods. Longer lasting and more reliable goods are more valued in industries for whom interruptions are more expensive, for example train or track breakdowns cause great disruption, and electricity generators are fined if they fail to deliver as promised. So to boost business for suppliers of longer-lasting products, perhaps instead it would be better to sell upgrades? We've seen that upgrades are already sold for some products such as rolling mills. We've seen in our case studies that the benefits of upgrades include reduced replacement costs, faster replacement and continuity in operation. In particular, for products with slow rates of innovation, upgrades may be particularly attractive.

The business case for upgrade of vehicles

The graph shows cumulative profit margins for three replacement and upgrade strategies for cars. We assume that an upgrade costs 20% of a new vehicle and increases fuel efficiency in line with the energy efficiency technology available in the year of upgrade (using the same fuel efficiency assumptions as the box story at the beginning of this chapter). Regular upgrade halves annual maintenance costs and yields a 20% profit for the producer (this is in line with profit margins after-sales automotive services). The upgrade strategy is found to be as profitable as the 10 yearly replacement cycle and offers more regular cash flows. If profits are not as high as those in after-sales automotive services then the producer will lose out unless they can increase prices.

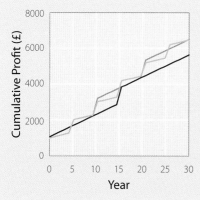

Cumulative Profit (£) vs Year

- No upgrade, replace every 10 years
- No upgrade, replace every 15 years
- 5 yearly upgrade, replace every 15 years

Having looked at the business case for purchasers, and seen that it might be easier to choose upgrades when products fail than to pay extra for longer lasting products at the outset, are sellers able to exploit this opportunity?

Life extension in the eyes of the seller

Now put yourself in the shoes of a producer. Would you choose to sell a more or less durable product? What if you could make money as your product cycles through different owners[11]?

- **Deliberate shortening of product life?** If you are serving a 'saturated' market, where most purchases are for replacement, you are more likely to want to shorten product life to generate more sales. But this means that you have to recoup any product research and design spending over a shorter period, which is easier in an industry with fast-changing technology development. How can you persuade your customers to keep buying a short-lived product? They're more likely to agree to this if the market is concentrated so you don't have too many competitors. So planned obsolescence, the deliberate shortening of product life, is more likely in saturated, concentrated markets with fast-changing technologies. In contrast, amongst our interviewees in the industrial equipment sector, which does not have these characteristics, we found that planned obsolescence would not succeed due to global competition, and the importance of building a reputation for quality.

- **Strategic, profitable product life extension?** Alternatively as a producer you can sell your product with a contract, such as a lease, a long-term maintenance contract or an upgrade contract, that gives you access to potentially lucrative downstream markets[12]. Such contracts also expose you to the costs of product failure and so increase your incentive to produce durable, adaptable and modular designs. The potential benefits of such contracts are far reaching, including more regular cash flows, better customer retention, greater differentiation from competitors, and, in some cases, higher profits. However this is a very different business model from the usual one in which producers focus solely on initial sales. It also moves away from the core capabilities of a traditional producers. Only if you change strategy to a service model can you profitably pursue product life extension, with these types of contract.

Outlook

We started this chapter celebrating the heritage objects that tell our national and personal stories, which we happily pay to maintain indefinitely, and throughout the chapter we've seen that we have plenty of options to maintain most of our steel and aluminium intensive goods for much longer. We can make them more durable, can upgrade them if their relative performance falls off, or we can cascade them between owners with different requirements. We've also seen that the environmental case for keeping goods for life depends on the ratio of embodied energy to annual energy in use, and on the likely rates of improvement in each. In looking at the business model for longer life goods, we've seen that it would be easier for purchasers to choose upgrades than to pay extra for longer-lasting initial purchases, and we've seen that producers will only promote longer-lasting offerings if they can replace sales related to replacement demand with income from servicing, maintaining, and upgrading existing stocks. As purchasers, we could choose now to treat everything we own as heritage objects to be maintained indefinitely, and in most cases this would be a more sustainable practice. That gives us the opportunity to dictate terms to producers—to encourage the development of new longer lasting goods, supported by different contracts. If we can purchase a standard new fridge for around £200, expecting it to last 10 years but guaranteed for only 3, we're unlikely to agree to pay £2,000 for a fridge with a 100 year guarantee, but we might agree to pay £40 per year indefinitely for a fridge that would always be maintained and upgraded to the latest standards. And if that's the case, we can offer the supplier double their income over a much longer period, compared with a single purchase with no commitment—and that might get them excited.

Notes

1. Approximately 1 million Certificates of Destruction and Notices of Destruction were issued under the UK End-of-Life Vehicles Regulations (2003) in 2006 but over 2 million cars were taken off the road in that year (Car Reg, n.d).

2. 'Well Dressed?' by Allwood et al. (2006) describes a government funded project that explored practical changes in the textiles and clothing industry that would improve the sector's performance on a range of sustainability metrics.

3. Kate Fletcher is a fashion designer who has developed the concept of slow fashion. Her book (Fletcher, 2008) explores the life-cycle impacts of fashion and textiles and presents practical alternatives, design concepts and social innovation. More information about Kate's work can be found on the website www.katefletcher.com.

4. Assume that in year t the embodied energy to make the product is $E(t) = \alpha^t E_0$ where α is the annual fractional improvement each year, which must be less than one, but only just. A 1% improvement each year would mean $\alpha = 0.99$. Similarly the use phase energy per year for a product made in year t is $U(t) = \beta^t U_0$. Provided α and β are strictly less than 1, we can then sum to infinity the total energy Z required if we replace the product every T years, giving:

$$Z = \frac{E_0}{1 - \alpha^T} + \frac{TU_0}{1 - \beta^T}$$

The optimum life span T is the value at which the derivative of this with respect to T is zero, which is when:

$$\left(\frac{E_0}{U_0}\right) \frac{\alpha^T \ln\alpha}{\left(1 - \alpha^T\right)^2} + \frac{1 - \beta^T + T\beta^T \ln\beta}{\left(1 - \beta^T\right)^2} = 0$$

For given values of (E_0/U_0), α and β, we can solve this and so plot T against (E_0/U_0).

5. We make the following assumptions: the office has embodied emissions of 3,200 kWh per m^2 and annual use 340 kWh it has a life of 40 years based on Ramesh (2010); the car has embodied emissions of 5.6 tCO$_2$ based on VW LCA reports (VW, 2006, 2010), annual use phase emissions of 2.6 tCO$_2$ and an expected life of 14 years; the train has embodied emissions of 17 tCO$_2$, annual use phase emissions of 3.7 tCO$_2$, and an expected life of 30 years (Chester & Hovath, 2009); the plane has embodied emissions of 52 tCO$_2$, annual use phase emissions of 100 tCO$_2$, and an expected life of 25 years; we assume use phase improvement rate of 2% and an embodied improvement rate of 0.1% for all products bar the plane for which the use phase improvement rate is assumed to be 0.1% and the embodied improvement rate 0.1%.

6. The matrix is based on the observation by Solomon 1994 that "replacement decisions arise from a deterioration in the actual value of the product or an upgrade in the desired state" and on the distinction between relative and absolute obsolescence made by Cooper 2004.

7. Aylen (2011) briefly discusses the possibility that mill stretch has been facilitated by initial over-design, e.g. the mill in Linz had a low initial rolling capacity but was contained in an excessively large building allowing the rolling line to increase within the building by just under 40%. In their paper on plate mill upgrade Bhooplapur et al. (2008) point to a second reason why mill upgrade has been possible. Micro-alloying is the favoured process for making modern high strength plate grades and in this process the greater strength of the steel is exhibited only in the late stages of rolling and cooling, limiting pressure on the mill stand and so allowing high strength steels to be rolled on mill stands that where built before these grades were envisaged.

8. The Archard equation states that the volume of worn material produced under sliding contact is proportional to the load on the surfaces times the sliding distance divided by the hardness of the softer of the two surfaces. John Archard, who after six years in the RAF subsequently moved on to working on the erosion of heavily loaded contacts and their lubrication, defined the most widely used prediction of metal wear under sliding contact.

9. Magretta (1998) interviews Michael Dell who stresses the importance of Dells "virtual integration" strategy in the company's success. This strategy is based on a customer focus, supplier partnerships, mass customisation and just in time delivery.

10. Kerr & Ryan (2001) explore the environmental benefits of the Xerox remanufacturing model and find that remanufacturing reduces resource consumption by a factor of 3.

11. We know that durable goods, such as cars, trucks, machinery and equipment often have multiple users over their lifetimes: yellow goods typically go through 3-6 ownership cycles before they are finally scrapped and Land Rover estimate that up to two-thirds of all Land Rover Defenders ever built are still on the road.

12. Moving downstream in this manner can be lucrative. Research by Dennis and Kambil (2003) has shown that, in the automotive sector, after sale service margins, including customer support, training, warranties, maintenance, repair, upgrades, product disposal and sale of complementary goods, are three to four times greater than new product sales margins.

Images

13. Image credit: Network Rail (sourced by Ramboll).

14. Author: David Wilson Clarke. Used under the Creative Commons Attribution 2.5 Generic License (http://creativecommons.org/licenses/by/2.5/deed.en)

15. Author: Norman Bruderhofer (http://www.cylinder.de) Used under the Creative Commons Attribute-Share Alike 3.0 Unported License (http://creativecommons.org/licenses/by-sa/3.0/deed.en)

16. Image credit: Zander Olsen, Make

17 Reducing final demand
for metal services

If we can't find enough options to meet our emissions targets through energy or material efficiency, we need to consider the possibility of demand reduction also. Does this automatically mean impoverishment—the reverse of development—or are there other options?

A Valkyrie on a horse in park

We're approaching a heroic theme in this chapter, so who better to help us on our journey than Richard Wagner, who's defining opera cycle "The Ring of the Nibelung" was first performed as a whole at Bayreuth in 1876, 21 years after Bessemer patented his steel making process, and 10 years before Charles Hall and Paul Héroult discovered a commercially viable route to produce aluminium. It's tempting to start with the Nibelung themselves, dwarves toiling at their forges in their underground cave of Nibelheim, under the merciless supervision of their insatiably greedy boss Alberich, and we could make something of the low yield losses of their process for forming the Rhinegold into helmets and rings. But instead, we'll turn to George Bernard Shaw's commentary "The Perfect Wagnerite" in which he draws an analogy between the ending of the reign of the Gods in the Ring Cycle (in the final opera, the great palace of the Gods, "Valhalla," which was completed just before the first opera begins, burns and subsides back into the Rhine) and the collapse of Capitalism. Alberich who, at the beginning of the cycle renounces love in order to steal the Rhinegold, symbolises capitalist leaders who, in the pursuit of profit, have forgotten their higher human values. The long narrative of the cycle of four operas tracks the deceitful tricks of those who pursue wealth and power at all costs, and finally they receive their comeuppance when Valhalla—the capitalist system—burns, and the Rhinemaidens can return to their opening innocence, with the gold in its rightful place, underwater.

Heady stuff—but this is a daring chapter. We set out in this book to examine all possible options to halve carbon emissions from producing materials, within 40 years while demand for material services doubles—and having looked at all possible efficiencies in existing processes, and then looked at all possible material efficiencies, we have one apparently apocalyptic option remaining: simply living with less. We'll explore three variants of living with less: using goods more intensely, so that our total demand for material services can be met with fewer goods; finding alternative means to provide the same services, but using less material; and reducing our overall demand for the services.

In public, no business leader and no politician or policy maker can propose an ambition of reduced profit or induced recession. But in private, after a glass of wine and a nice meal, virtually everyone we've talked to in those positions has said to us "of course, we all know we're simply consuming too much." And in developed economies we do all know that—because nearly all of us can remember consuming less a few years ago. If we read the gravestones in our local churchyard, we have yet to find one which says "Here lies John Smith, whom we remember because he owned a large pile of material". And if, from within our developed economy, we make a quick mental survey of our friends and colleagues, very few of us will be able to report that those who own most material live happier lives than those who's relationships, families, senses and imaginations are most vibrant. So, with a little inspirational help from Wagner, let us sally forth as heroes into the dark forests of demand reduction.

Providing more services with less material by more intense use

"The Ride of the Valkyrs" by John Charles Dollman

The third act of the second opera of The Ring cycle, begins with the famous "Ride of the Valkyries" during which eight Valkyrie, wild maidens whose regular line of business is the delivery of dead heroes to Valhalla, fly on winged horses to a meeting on the Valkyrie rock. The meeting will begin when eight of them have arrived, and their journey takes approximately eight minutes. The flying horses have little else to do in the whole cycle, so out of approximately 15 hours, are used for around 1% of the time. This is similar to our use of cars in the UK: typically we each spend 225 hours per year in a car, we have 28 million licensed cars in the UK with an average of 4 seats in each, and there are 60 million of us, so on average each licensed car seat is used for under 2% of the year. Do we really need eight flying horses? If the horses are strong, and the Valkyrie slender, could we mount two Valkyrie on each, and cut our requirements for flying horses to four? Alternatively, could we sequence the arrival of the Valkyrie on the Rock, starting earlier for example at the beginning of Act II during which neither flying horses nor Valkyrie are involved, and so deliver all eight of them with just one flying horse? Do we need fifty times more car seats in the UK than are, on average, in use at any time? What a fantastic material saving opportunity that suggests.

Sustainable Materials with both eyes open

We can use products more intensively either by using more of their capacity when they're in use, or by increasing the fraction of time we use them. We've illustrated this on the graph which shows in blue a 'use profile' for a notional product, the fraction of its capacity used over time. The grey box shows the full capacity of the product over its full life so the ratio of blue to grey area is a measure of how intensely we are using it: the visible grey area shows under-utilisation. What can we do to make better use of this spare capacity? Broadly we have two options: we can make more use of the product, or we can design products with less capacity, and these options are all illustrated on the graph.

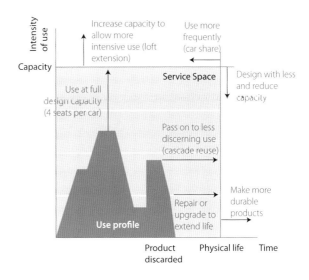

Figure 17.1—**Schematic of intensity of use**

Making more use of products is possible through using the product more frequently (to extend the blue use-profile sideways up to the physical life), and using more of its capacity, (to stretch the blue use profile upwards). The logic of public transport systems is that providing a larger capacity shared service allows more intense use of a greater fraction of capacity than if each user owns their own separate vehicle.

Designing products with reduced physical life and capacity sounds wrong after our previous chapter on life extension. However, if we are building products that will inevitably reach 'unwanted' failures, due to technical or style obsolescence for example, then as well as designing them to be recycled, we should try to match their physical life to their useful life, to avoid excess material use.

Using products more intensely will lead to material savings if increased use does not proportionately shorten their expected life. We've illustrated this in the box story on using vehicles more intensely which shows that making more use of capacity (more seats occupied) greatly increases the total service output (passenger miles) delivered by the car. However driving twice as far per year, with the same passenger load, simply shortens the life of the car without changing the total service output. We can explain this from what we learnt about the Archard equation in the last chapter: wear of the sliding surfaces in the car is proportional to both load and distance; doubling the number of miles driven per year, thus halves the time until the critical distance is reached; however doubling the passenger load has only a small effect on the total load, because the car is much heavier than its passengers.

Can we identify which products would show most benefit from more intense use? To examine this, we've created Figure 17.2 which plots our catalogue of steel and aluminium products on axes of intensity against lifespan. The contours on the plot show the equivalent time for which the products have been used at full capacity, and the radius of the data points is proportional to the fraction of total metal use. The chart shows that industrial equipment provides the highest equivalent years of service for both metals: such equipment is typically used intensively and

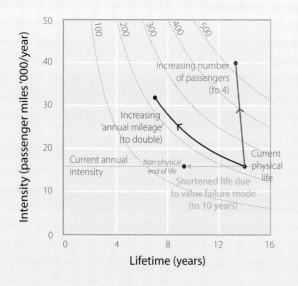

Using vehicles more intensively

We can see that increasing average passenger loading from 1.6 to 4 (the orange line) makes little difference to the physical life of the car (because the car weighs more than the passengers) but more than doubles service output. Doubling the annual mileage (the pink line) halves the physical life of the car but does not change the service output. This reduces the chance that a car is discarded before the end of its physical life e.g. because it is outdated. Finally reducing the average life of a vehicle from 14 years to 10 years with no change in utilization (e.g. due to an accident or as promoted, for example, by the expired UK scrappage scheme) decreases total service output by 30% (the green line).

Similarly, increased loading on trucks, trains, ships and washing machines causes a disproportionately small loss in product life, though the ratio will vary widely by product type. Offices are currently used less than a quarter of the time and could be used more frequently with no effect on building life.

Sustainable Materials with both eyes open

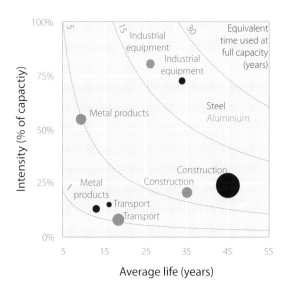

Figure 17.2—**Intensity and product life**

discarded due to severe degradation or changes in requirements. For example, electric transmission cables are in near-constant use over a 30 year lifespan, and are only discarded when they become unsuitable, typically because higher power must be transmitted.

However metal products, such as cars and domestic washing machines provide the lowest equivalent service level. Could this be improved by shared ownership? Could we use launderettes instead of owning our own washing machine, or car pools instead of our own car?

Shared ownership is related to renting, and in effect the recent growth in city bicycle share systems is a convenient form of short term renting. However, it is as yet quite difficult to set up such systems effectively. A study of a car pool system in Austria found that simply looking at the costs of each driven journey showed that around 70% of all households would save money by using a car pool[1]. However, the reality of car use is that the car serves many functions other than the journey, for instance as a convenient place to wait to meet someone, for storage, or as an indicator of prestige and so on, and with these factored in, only 9% of households would benefit from the car pool.

Shared ownership offers the potential for significant saving in material requirements but the real difficulty of sharing is that we associate ownership with development: part of the service provided by material goods is their instant availability and convenience. Shared ownership denies this, so requires some increased personal discipline and as yet we have identified few instances where people find this attractive.

Finding alternative ways to deliver services, using less materials

Discussing productions of The Ring always opens up opportunities for subversive humour, so we'll avoid the temptation to discuss having the Valkyrie arrive on skateboards, to save on the flying horse budget. Instead, let's explore a truly awful heresy. It's extremely expensive to put on a production of The Ring: apart from 24 lead soloists, seven other Valkyries, a chorus of Niebelungs and Gibichungs and an orchestra of a hundred, we also need, say, a hundred other backstage, front of house, production and marketing staff. If each of these people are involved in two weeks of rehearsals, and four full performances of The Ring (16 nights spread over three weeks) and are paid an average UK wage of £430 per week, the cost of the production is £540,000 before we rent a venue or pay for the advertisements, or offer incentives to our star singers. So double the total, and divide by 1000 seats and four rounds of the cycle, and your average ticket price is around £270 per person to see the entire Ring.

Bikes belonging to the cycle share scheme in London

So now the heresy: given the rise of computer technology, sound sampling, video games, and animation, maybe we don't need any people or the venue! Instead, armed with the latest Kinect sensor on our Xbox, we could conduct the whole Ring Cycle ourselves, while our friends come round to act out the leading roles, and direct the performance. We only need one copy of the score to scan into a good sound system, and we can create the whole piece—music, staging, lights and more, in our own front room, and not one artist required!

An awful heresy indeed, and although it's close to what's currently possible, it will be years (and we hope never) before simulated performances can really replace live ones. But more broadly, can metal services be delivered without the metal?

The most striking opportunity to avoid using metal is to use video-conferencing to avoid business travel. We can't imagine finding a non-material substitute for construction, equipment or most metal goods, but many of us would actively like to avoid business travel: why has video-conferencing not developed? Although there is no global data on the substitution between video-conferencing and air travel, national, survey-based studies show that the substitution rate is low, with video-conferencing competing for just 1–3% of the business travel market[2]. Video-conferencing has had some success in certain industries (e.g. banking, insurance, IT, oil and the chemical industry), especially to substitute for travel to internal meetings (which account for just 10% of business travel) but has failed to compete with business air travel more widely. The main reason for this appears to be that, despite more sophisticated video-conferencing packages, they cannot compete with face-to-face meetings for developing relationships so are not a viable substitute for negotiations and marketing demonstrations[3].

Substituting virtual for physical services has been much discussed, particularly with developments in the internet. The reality has been different, paper use is still growing, despite opportunities to use less paper by substituting electronic information storage as we'll see in chapter 22. Within the world of steel and aluminium, we have found very few opportunities to avoid metal use by providing a service in a different way.

Reducing our total demand for material services

On to the fourth opera in The Ring cycle, "The Twilight of the Gods", and after everyone who has owned the Ring has died, Valhalla falls, the unhealthy era of the Gods ends, a new era of human love is promised, and the Rhine is once more at peace. Or, within the analogy with which we opened, the ruthless pursuit of wealth and power has destroyed itself, and a collective view of well-being been re-launched.

Is it right? If we step away from wealth to other measures of well-being, would we save metal, and would we be better off? To ensure that we can reach our target of a 50% emissions cut while demand doubles, we need a fallback option: to reduce demand. This will never be a part of corporate strategy, and is unlikely to be prominent in public policy, at least partly because economic growth as we understand it at present is fuelled by borrowed money (debt) and the only way to pay back the debt is to grow. Yet, over the past century, recession has been a reliable predictor of emissions abatement[4]. Figure 17.3 shows how changes in the UK's GDP correlate closely with changes in our annual emissions of CO_2. Recession, or at least avoiding future growth, would constrain our demand for energy and materials, and therefore lead to reduced emissions. For fun, in his retirement speech from the University of Surrey, Professor Roland Clift suggested that a low-carbon lifestyle would involve spending our spare money on stone

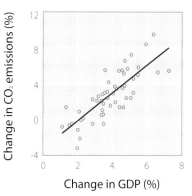

Figure 17.3—**The relationship between emissions and GDP**

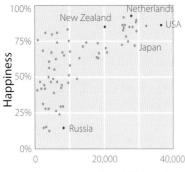

100%

Happiness

75%

50%

25%

0%

New Zealand   Netherlands

USA

Japan

Russia

0   20,000   40,000

Income per head ($/year)

Figure 17.4—**The relationship between GDP and happiness**

sculptures: which have low embodied energy but higher labour costs. But can we imagine whole nations ever wanting to pursue recession?

Surprisingly, the answer is yes, and a rapidly growing area of behavioural economics is examining what sounds like the un-definable topic of "happiness". We can create a defensible index of happiness for a country, because whatever measures we use seem to be well correlated. We might measure mental health statistics, self-assessment, divorce rates, drug abuse and many other measures of social wellbeing and they largely support each other, so various economists have created aggregated measures of national happiness. Once you have this index, the obvious first question is "are richer countries happier" and this is explored in Figure 17.4. The graph gives a clear message, which we've seen recreated using several different happiness measures: up to a national income around $15,000 per person, countries become significantly happier as basic needs for health, nutrition, shelter and security are met. Beyond that threshold, further increases in happiness rise slowly, if at all.

We've come a long way away from our core subject and need to refer you to other sources if this topic catches your interest (as it does ours)[5]. But the story of this section is that if to meet our emissions reduction target, we chose to reduce our demand for materials, we might well not be any less happy than we are now. It's very difficult to see governments or businesses pursuing that as a target, but it provides a rational basis for a social movement, when we compile our forecasts, and we need to retain it as our 'option of last resort' to guarantee that we can meet our overall emissions reduction target.

Outlook

In a war, natural emergency or other crisis, populations rapidly adjust to different patterns of behaviour, including reduced expectations about reasonable levels of demand. However this is largely induced by shortage of supply, so is accepted because there isn't a choice. In this chapter we've found two options to reduce demand for metal which could be acceptable before a crisis: through increased intensity of use and through service substitution. And we've found one option which depends on a major social change: through choosing well-being over wealth.

There is a time-delay between the actions that cause environmental harm and the harm appearing. Do we have any evidence that populations voluntarily choose demand reduction to cause less harm, before a crisis arises? Positively we can look at the wonderful range of both religious and secular charities through which the wealthy limit their own spending in order to contribute to development. Negatively, we can reflect in astonishment at the population of Easter Island (A.D. 900–1700) who caused their own demise by chopping down all the trees on their island[6]. What could possibly cause a population to undermine itself in this way? Maybe they were burning the trees to keep themselves warm? Or building shelters to keep themselves dry? No, their fatal vice was none other than building stone statues! It seems that the population of Easter Island were early pioneers of Roland Clift's carbon abatement strategy. So intense was their competition over stone statues (evident from the increase in statue size and their more elaborate designs) that it caused the demise of their civilisation. Two things are clear from this story: that mankind's competitive nature is inherent, and that we must continue to search for a low emitting, sustainable outlet for this behaviour.

And having raised our option of last resort, demand reduction, we're now ready to return to our adding up process, to find out whether we have enough options to reach our target, before we have to throw the Ring back in the Rhine.

Notes

Providing more services with less material by more intense use

1. This study was conducted by Prettenthaler and Steininger (1999).

Finding alternative ways to deliver services, using less materials

2. Denstadli (2004) finds that the substitution rate for Norway is 2-3%, obviating 150,000-200,000 trips 1998-2005; Roy & Filiatrault (1998) find a substitution rate of 1.8% for Canada.

3. Based on a survey of the Taiwanese technology industry Lu & Peeta (2009) show that video-conferencing is often adequate for information exchange, management meetings and training, but not for the face-to-face meetings required for negotiations and marketing demonstrations.

Reducing our total demand for material services

4. Bowen et al. (2009) explore the relationship between carbon dioxide emissions and GDP with a view to predicting the likely emissions impact of the 2008 financial crisis. They find that there are two effects on energy demand in recession: (1) demand for output falls and as a result demand for energy to produce that output declines, (2) if energy prices fall, firms may substitute energy for other inputs to production. They forecast that UK emissions will be up to 9% lower in 2012 than they would have been without the recession.

5. Layard (2005) gives an introduction to the field of happiness economics.

Outlook

6. The story of Easter Island is documented in Jared Diamond's book (Diamond, 2005) Collapse. The trees were used to make wooden platforms and rope for dragging the stones to location and leveraging them into position. The intense use of trees for these purposes coupled with a plague of rats that ate seeds, severely diminished tree stocks. The inhabitants of Easter Island prioritised statue building over building sea canoes, limiting their diet to small land mammals and birds and undermining the sustainability of these animal populations. The loss of animals that acted as pollinators and seed dispersers ultimately caused the end of the forest as well as the island's food stock.

18 Options for change
for the major steel and aluminium using products

Now that we've identified a new set of options 'with both eyes open' we can return to the catalogue of products we identified in Part I to find out to what extent each strategy can be applied to each product.

With one eye open, in chapter 11, we found that we didn't have enough options to achieve our target 50% cut in emissions while demand grows to 2050. However, since chapter 11, we've re-examined the world of steel and aluminium with both eyes open, and found that we have a new and wider set of options, through material efficiency and demand reduction. So in the next chapter we'll return to adding up, to find out whether we can combine all the options we applied in chapter 11 with those in our new armoury to reach our target. But in preparation for that, we first need to look at how each of our new options apply to the major product groups we identified in our catalogues in chapter 3.

We'll continue to use our forecast of future demand from chapter 4, and in the absence of any other detail, will assume that the forecast of demand growth applies not just in total, but also to each product in turn: we can't predict 40 years ahead whether growth in car ownership will occur at a different rate from growth in the use of drinks cans. However, having seen that materials are used to provide a service and not as objects in their own right, we can re-interpret our demand forecast as a prediction of demand for material services. Therefore the option to use products more intensely, may allow us to reduce material inputs while growing service outputs. And if we treat our forecast as a prediction of service demand, this allows us to apply our option of last resort, from the last section of chapter 17: as an absolute reduction in demand for material services.

As we look at how our new options apply to different products, we also need to be aware of other forces for change. Anticipating changes in consumer fashion and specific technologies is beyond us, but returning to the pie charts of chapter 2, we saw that after the industry sector, the next two big sectors of the global emissions pie chart were the use of buildings and the use of vehicles. While we are aiming at a 50% cut in emissions in industry while demand grows, we must expect that the designers of future buildings and vehicles also will be aiming at similar reductions.

We're going to set up a 'mixing desk' for our options for change, with sliders to indicate the degree to which we'll pursue each option. We'll have one slider for each of chapters 12–17 of this book, and in this chapter we'll estimate for each product the two extremes of the slider. The lower value on each slider will show where we are today, and the upper value will show the limit of what we think could be achieved. For example, cars in the UK currently have an average life of 14 years, but could in future have a life of 30 years. So our life extension slider for cars will range between 14 years (the present) and 30 years (the maximum we can envisage in future). Similarly the fleet average mass of cars in the UK is 1.3 tonnes at present, but we know that Colin Chapman's Lotus Seven weighs 500 kg, and Volkswagen's current L1 concept car, which achieves 189 mpg in a diesel hybrid configuration, weighs 380 kg. So we could allow our slider for using less metal by design in cars to range from 1,300 kg now to 300 kg as the minimum we can imagine. Each slider will describe a representative product, such as an 'average car' so we retain a physical sense of what our forecasts require—but if your car has a different weight or expected life at present, you can scale the slider appropriately. If we find we have to apply all six sliders at their limits and still can't reach our target, we'll have two further 'catch-all' sliders: one for carbon capture and storage (CCS) and one for a global reduction in demand for services.

How should we deal with material substitution between the two metals, or between either of them and some other material? The question 'is steel better than aluminium is better than steel?' is not for us interesting, because it is too small a

A mixing desk for emissions forecasting!

Sustainable Materials with both eyes open

Lightweight cars: Lotus Seven (top) and Tata Nano (bottom)[8]

question because we know demand for both metals is set to grow strongly. For the past 30 years, the aluminium industry has been promoting the use of aluminium in cars, and most engine blocks are now aluminium, but with a few exceptions, most car bodies are still made in steel. There will be further change in material composition in cars in future, but we don't know how it will develop. The much bigger driver of change in cars is that they must become significantly lighter in order to achieve better fuel economy, and this can be achieved with either metal: the two-seater 500 kg Lotus Seven is mainly made in aluminium; the four-seater 600 kg Tata Nano is mainly made in steel. So in our predictions about future product compositions, we'll stick with our global forecast from chapter 5—that steel demand will grow by 170% and aluminium by 250%—and assume that the relative proportions of the two materials in any particular product will always grow in this ratio.

We've looked at substitution of other materials in chapter 3, and found that there really aren't many options. We could potentially use more magnesium alloys in cars, with the advantage of a good ratio of strength to weight, and with low yield losses when the metal is injection moulded to final shape. However, casting magnesium currently requires intense use of the gas SF_6 (sulphur hexafluoride) in order to exclude all oxygen from the liquid metal (which would otherwise combust); SF_6 is the worst of all greenhouse gases with a global warming potential over 20,000 times worse than carbon dioxide. Studies of the substitution of magnesium into cars suggest that the emissions benefit of weight saving, and hence fuel economy, is currently eclipsed by the effect of this gas. We've seen that both Airbus and Boeing have made a significant shift from aluminium to composite materials in the past 10 years, and as we know, if you make aeroplanes you'll do anything to save weight. But producing composites is more energy and carbon intensive than manufacturing aluminium[1], and composites cannot in any meaningful way be recycled[2]. So although we are confident some material substitution will occur, there are no clear 'better' materials, and we could with some confidence join in the steel and aluminium industry's claims that they are (jointly!) key materials for our future. So we won't include any effects of material substitution in our exploration of future product options.

In the remainder of this chapter we'll look at the products from our catalogues in chapter 3, to anticipate how we could apply our options for the future, with both eyes open.

Construction

Steel in construction

In the UK, government legislation on energy consumption in commercial buildings requires that by 2019, every new building will be 'net zero carbon', i.e. designed with very efficient heating and cooling with energy supplied from carbon-free sources[3]. Governments in other countries are also aiming to reduce energy use in building, for instance Germany and Scandinavia promote ultra-low-energy 'passive houses', and in China low-carbon 'eco cities' are planned. However, the use of energy in a commercial building is largely unrelated to the structural frame that supports it. The key features of a building that determine its energy requirements in use include the ratio of window separation to ceiling height, the presence or not of atria or chimneys to boost natural ventilation, the location and design of windows to control radiant heating by the sun, and the exchange of heat between the interior and exterior via leaks, insulated surfaces, windows, and ventilation. Requirements for steel (and cement) are therefore not strongly influenced by evolving regulations on energy use in buildings.

Three main forms of steel are used in construction: structural sections, reinforcing bars and sheet steel used for cladding and 'purlins', the light, horizontal elements in 'shed' type buildings such as supermarkets and warehouses.

In our survey of options, we've seen that there is a significant opportunity to reduce requirements for structural steel in buildings through avoiding over-specification, avoiding excess rationalisation, and through applying 'using less by design' with new manufacturing techniques. Compounding these opportunities we've estimated that structural steel requirements could at best be reduced to around two fifths of current levels. We have seen that structural steel could be re-used extensively, and with a more standardised set of components we estimate up to 80% of structural sections in buildings could in future be re-used. However it is unlikely that much if any material from infrastructure projects could be re-used, as it is usually replaced only after problems with corrosion or fatigue damage.

In parallel we should be able to reduce our demand for reinforcing bar per unit of service through better optimisation of layout, and through a shift to higher strength steels. The second option is particularly important in China at present. As yet reinforcing steel has never been reused: if it is used below the ground it is in effect lost, as the cost of extracting old piles is so great that contractors on 'brownfield' sites prefer to build around old sub-surface structures than to replace

Reinforcing steel in a demolished building

or re-use them; if it is used above the surface, then at the end of the life of the building, as part of demolition, reinforcing steel may be separated from concrete (by shaking or hammering) and recycled, but it is never re-used. However, if in future we assemble buildings from modular reinforced concrete elements, parts such as standard floor-slabs in multi-storey buildings could be re-used, so we'll allow for 20% reuse of reinforcement in this application. It is difficult to envisage any change to our strategy of abandoning sub-surface reinforcement bars at end of life, so we will continue to exclude this metal from future recycling streams.

The third form of steel used in construction derives from rolled sheet—and is used for purlins and cladding. Purlins are often damaged during deconstruction, so although they can be re-used, we have allowed only a maximum of 50% re-use. Cladding, often made from stainless steel, is subject to changing standards for thermal insulation, so reuse is currently restricted to agricultural sheds. However, the opportunity to reuse cladding is likely to increase as the new insulation standards become widespread, so we've also allowed for up to 50% future re-use.

Structural steel and reinforcing bars are cut to length accurately during fabrication, leaving only small off-cuts. Also, the sheets used for cladding tessellate and can be cut to regular, often rectangular, shapes. Therefore, in these applications there is little opportunity to reduce yield losses in construction or to divert scrap to other applications. All three types of steel would see the same benefit if the life of the building or infrastructure were extended, or used more intensely. At present, when buildings are demolished, this is because of changed user preferences rather than degradation, so we can safely assume that all building lives could be doubled. The owners of infrastructure are already highly motivated towards life extension, but we found evidence suggesting that the UK's motorway bridges from the 1960's are failing earlier than intended, so some life extension will be possible through better control of the construction process. Most buildings could be used more intensely. If an office block has no other purpose, and if everyone using it works for 40 hours per week, it is unused for over 75% of the time. So we assume that the intensity of building use could double. Potentially, infrastructure could be used more, but in several cases we found that it is already used beyond initial specifications, for instance when national laws on maximum truck weights change. Therefore there is limited scope for using infrastructure more intensely[4].

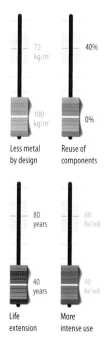

Steel in construction
(based on a 7-storey office block)

To set up our sliders, we've averaged the discussion in this section according to global average proportions of structural steel, rebar and sheet. So although we estimated that we could use two thirds less structural steel than at present by design, the overall limit to reduction in steel in construction is only one third—

because it is more difficult to save reinforcing bar and sheet. The numbers on the sliders are based on a typical office building, a 7-storey building with $100\,kg/m^2$ of steel and $10,000\,m^2$ of floor area. We assume proportionally similar savings for other building types.

Aluminium in buildings

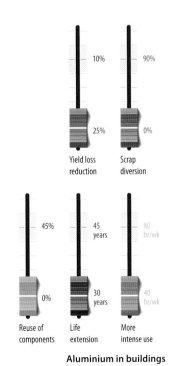

Yield loss reduction — 10% → 25%

Scrap diversion — 90% → 0%

Reuse of components — 45% → 0%

Life extension — 45 years → 30 years

More intense use — 80 hr/wk → 40 hr/wk

Aluminium in buildings

About half of the aluminium used in buildings is made by extrusion and of necessity must have a constant cross-section, so there are few opportunities for saving metal with efficient design: extrusion already allows excellent flexibility for designers wishing to optimise material use. There is some scope for yield improvements in extrusion[5] and solid bonding may allow efficient diversion of scrap from both production (the head and tail of each extrusion) and from cutting to length in fabrication. Re-use of aluminium window frames and other building components is not yet practised, and is inhibited by the difficulty of extracting used components without damage, by water staining of older frames, and by the fact that windows are generally removed when a higher specification is required. Reuse of aluminium building components is possible so we assume it will develop to some extent. The same issues apply to aluminium cladding as for steel, so we'll assume that up to 50% of it could be reused in future. More intense use of buildings would give the same benefit for aluminium components as for steel in buildings.

Rail track and line pipe in infrastructure

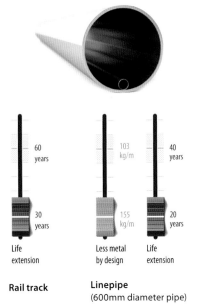

Life extension — 60 years → 30 years

Less metal by design — 103 kg/m → 155 kg/m

Life extension — 40 years → 20 years

Rail track

Linepipe
(600mm diameter pipe)

We've chosen rail track and line pipe as representative of non-structural applications of steel in infrastructure. We've seen several opportunities for extending the life of rail track, by cascading, by design with new higher strength steels, and by restorative processes. ReRail, capping worn rail with new high strength steel, is as yet unproven, but would allow significant life extension for the bulk of steel in the rest of the rail. As track wear is proportional to train weight, future design of lighter rolling stock would also support life extension. With intense development we estimate that we might double the life of future rail track. We identified two credible options to use less metal by design for deep sea line pipe: if we could find a different laying process, pipes could be assembled on the sea bed, saving around one third of current metal requirements. This might be achieved through remote welding, or by mechanical joining as used for pipes in shallow seas[6]; improved condition monitoring, for example by robotic 'pigs' that clean and monitor the inside of the pipe, would help ensure pipe safety over its life, and allow a reduction in over-design. Inevitable corrosion and fatigue restrict opportunities for reusing pipe at the end if its life.

Sustainable Materials *with both eyes open*

Vehicles

Cars and trucks

The average car in the UK weighs 1.3 tonnes, is used for 4% of the year, and when in use has an average of 1.6 occupants. So most of the time, most cars have significant excess capacity, and the car is significantly heavier than its cargo. Cars require much more fuel when accelerating than when driving at constant speed, and fuel consumption rises significantly beyond about 65 miles per hour. So a car designed to minimise environmental impacts would be light, be full of people, and travel more smoothly with a lower top speed. (All of this applies regardless of the power source used to drive the car, which is why we've argued that developing plug-in electric cars now is the wrong priority: vehicle weight should be addressed before switching to electric power.) As a result, we are confident in predicting that future cars will be lighter than today. How can this occur? Cars could be smaller. We know we could live without many of the gizmos (electric windows, seat angle adjusters) that attract us to shiny new cars, which as they are operated by heavy electric motors, add significant weight. Future control systems may help to reduce the danger of crashing, or we might accept lower speed limits, or lanes segregated by vehicle mass to ensure the safety of lighter cars.

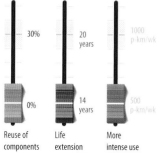

300 kg	20%	85%
1300 kg	40%	0%
Less metal by design	Yield loss reduction	Scrap diversion
30%	20 years	1000 p-km/wk
0%	14 years	500 p-km/wk
Reuse of components	Life extension	More intense use

Cars

The same benefits of different driving behaviour apply for trucks, but the vehicle mass is less important because trucks are designed to carry loads heavier than themselves. 'Road trains' with multiple trailers pulled by one vehicle offer fuel savings if fully loaded, and reduce requirements for metal per tonne of cargo carried. However, there are fewer opportunities to save vehicle weight for trucks than for cars. Car manufacture has high yield losses, and there are many technical options for developing more efficient production chains to reduce them. We learnt from Abbey Steel that car blanking skeletons can be cut into blanks for other users, so scrap diversion could be applied more aggressively in future. We already re-use car and truck components through salvage yards and second-hand dealers, and some component remanufacture occurs. However, as the design of engines and gearboxes changes rapidly, component reuse will remain limited. In future, as we saw demonstrated by Professor Tekkaya in Chapter 15, we may be able to re-shape sheet metal parts, but this still needs extensive development. Although the lifetime of cars could be doubled to 30 years, only the body structure, panels and closures are likely to last that long. The drive train, suspension and other moving parts of the car are likely to require earlier replacement or upgrade. We have averaged these opportunities according to component masses to predict a reduced upper limit of 20-years on our "Life extension" slider.

Ships and trains

In recent years ships have been scrapped at a high rate due to a decision by the International Maritime Organisation to force a shift from single to double hulled tankers. Currently 60% of shipping containers returning from the UK to China are empty, but that reflects the direction of world trade in goods, so we have few opportunities to increase the intensity with which we use our ships. At end of life, ship plate salvaged from ship-breaking in Gujarat is currently re-rolled, and with the Indian sub-continent dominating the global ship breaking industry it may be difficult to expand this activity further[7].

39 tonnes

47 tonnes

Less metal by design

Train

Meanwhile trains, which are a key part of any future lower energy transport system, have in the UK, become significantly heavier in the past 20 years: the average train (a combination of intercity, diesel and multiple electric systems) has grown from 39 to 47 tonnes. This has been driven by use of larger crash structures and by demands for the improved reliability provided by multiple powered vehicles. In contrast, high-speed trains in Japan have become lighter. The Shinkansen rail system has reduced train mass by 40% since the 1960s. As anticipated for future cars, improved safety control has reduced the chance of crashes, allowing weight savings in the crash structure. So we can safely promote the design of lighter weight trains to save metal in production and to extend the life of rail track. At a minimum, we can predict train weights will return to those of 20 years past.

Aeroplanes

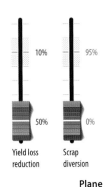

10%   95%

50%   0%

Yield loss   Scrap
reduction   diversion

Plane

Aeroplane manufacturers primarily manufacture swarf, so there is great potential to improve their famously poor 'buy-to-fly' ratio. The ideas we've discussed include rolling plates with a wedge profile, better forging processes to achieve nearer to net shape stock products, and diverting swarf back into use via solid bonding. Aeroplanes require a relatively small fraction of total aluminium use, albeit a high profile one, so despite their inefficient use of material, they are not our highest priority. However, given the very high and growing contribution of air travel to energy and emissions in transport, the difficulty of making significant step changes in future fuel consumption, and the problem of land area requirements for growing biofuel to replace kerosene, an important strategy in reducing future emissions must be for us all to fly less. We've aggregated all reductions in demand for final services into one slider in the next chapter but would like to prioritise demand reduction in flying, as it is such a significant and growing fraction of transport emissions in developed economies.

Sustainable Materials with both eyes open

50%

0%

Reuse of
components

**Transmission
cables**

60%

0%

Reuse of
components

Transformers

20%

0%

Reuse of
components

**Bus bars
and conduits**

Industrial equipment

Electrical equipment

Steel is used both to provide the structural infrastructure for electrical grids, and as an active electrical component in distribution and use. Galvanised steel towers (pylons) create electrical corridors that criss-cross nations as they distribute electricity from centralised power stations. The failure of one of these pylons would cause power-cuts and widespread disruption, so pylons are typically well maintained and only replaced when corrosion has undermined the integrity of the tower. Therefore there is limited opportunity to extend the life of the towers, and because their components are small and corroded in use, reuse at end of life is also unlikely. Electrical steels, with high silicon content, are used in large transformers throughout the electrical network, for example to step down the voltage from power stations to household voltage. The intensity at which the transformers are used determines their expected life, so there is little scope for intensity improvements in an already well-managed grid. However, at end of life, the steel tank surrounding the transformer could be reused, along with up to 60% of the transformer itself. The cost of transportation and disassembly currently inhibits this option.

Both steel and aluminium are used in electrical cables. The aluminium conducts the electricity while the steel provides the strength to span the long distances between pylons. The main cause of end of life for overhead transmission cables is that over time they are required to transmit more power than initially intended. This excess power causes the cable to heat up causing annealing and thus a permanent reduction in tensile strength. This, in combination with the tension in the cable, causes structural sag, prompting replacement before (we hope) or after contact with an obstacle such as a tree. This issue will become more complex if we move towards a more electrical future, and there is considerable debate at present about the development of a "smart grid" that would allow connection of widely distributed, intermittent low power supplies (typically renewable sources) of electricity to be switched in and out of different grid segments. Such a grid would be materially intensive, and also vulnerable to changes in future specification. It should therefore be designed in a modular manner to facilitate upgrades. Proactive overhead cable replacement in the future may allow reuse of cables on lower power routes, so we have assumed potential for up to 50% reuse.

When underground cables fail, they are usually repaired rather than replaced, unless additional capacity is required or the insulation has failed. Underground cables are not reused at present because they cannot be certificated, and the insulation could be degraded. This is unlikely to change in the future.

Aluminium strips (known as bus bars) are also used to connect elements in switchboards, and aluminium conduits protect wires and cables. Such conduits are small and dispersed, so reuse might be expensive, but there is no technical obstacle so we have assumed up to 20% could be reused.

Mechanical equipment

In our analysis of mechanical equipment, we focused largely on rolling mills, and found them to be an exemplar of our onion-skin model of design: most of the rolling mills ever made are still in regular operation, as the core metal providing the structural frame has survived undamaged and can still cope with expected loading. The outer layers of the onion skin, including rolls, bearings, drives and actuators, have been upgraded at appropriate intervals. We therefore have few suggestions about extending the life of current mechanical equipment. Given the complex geometries of many of their component parts, it may be possible to improve the yield in equipment manufacture, and we also identified an opportunity to develop replaceable wear surfaces, such as sleeved work rolls, to allow restoration of degraded components. We found that metal products in general could typically be made a third lighter by optimal design and manufacture so have assumed the same here. Fabrication of products from plate (a large proportion of steel in mechanical equipment) typically has a low yield, which could be improved by greater tessellation.

Mechanical equipment could be used more intensely, through better scheduling and co-ordination, both within and between factories. Increased flexibility in future equipment design may allow more continuous use of equipment while coping with the wide variety of products demanded by final consumers. Standardisation of reusable and modular products would reduce the variety demanded of mechanical production equipment which could further support more intense use.

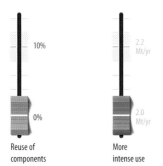

Less metal by design	Yield loss reduction	Scrap diversion
3,100 tonnes	10%	80%
4,700 tonnes	25%	0%

Reuse of components	More intense use
10%	2.2 Mt/yr
0%	2.0 Mt/yr

Mechanical equipment
(based on a 4,700 tonne plate rolling mill, with a production capacity of 2 million tonnes year)

Metal products

Packaging

Returnable or reusable packaging is easy to design, and normal in Germany, but would require a change in user behaviour, and possibly legislation, to be adopted in the UK. Steel food cans and aluminium drinks cans could be re-used, if the cans were stronger to avoid damage in use, and could be cleaned and recoated in a way that met food safety standards. Steel aerosol cans could equally be refilled and re-used.

Foil, used for the cooking and preparation of food generally, is a poor use of aluminium as the waste stream of this valuable material is highly dispersed. Foil is discarded in small pieces and mixed in other waste, so is hard to separate and therefore mainly lost to landfill or incineration after first use. With collection rates around 50–60%, nearly half the material in drinks cans is also lost after first use. So, it would be sensible to replace aluminium food and drink packaging with a material with lower embodied energy, and ideally with packaging that could be reused many times. It's unlikely that foil can be made much lighter, and drink can weights are also approaching a limit, but we saw earlier that there may be opportunities to reduce yield losses in can making. Food cans, as discussed in Chapter 12, could be a third lighter if they were cooked in a different way.

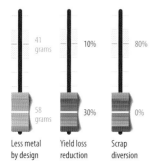

Less metal by design — 41 grams / 58 grams
Yield loss reduction — 10% / 30%
Scrap diversion — 80% / 0%

Food can

Goods and appliances

Use of our two metals in appliances is dominated by fridges and washing machines which, as we discussed before, are discarded after lives of around 10 years, due to the failure of small low cost components that are expensive to replace. Design for substantial life extension is therefore a big opportunity for these applications, so that rather than having a new fridge every decade, we buy one for life but with a service model for repairs and upgrades. Electric motors and fridge compressors can be remanufactured or reused, and the sheet metal panels in white goods could be reformed into alternative shapes. We'll also assume that yield losses from fabricating these appliances could be reduced, and that they could also be much lighter.

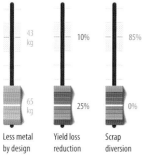

Less metal by design — 43 kg / 65 kg
Yield loss reduction — 10% / 25%
Scrap diversion — 85% / 0%

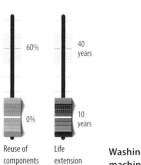

Reuse of components — 60% / 0%
Life extension — 40 years / 10 years

Washing machine

Notes

1. According to Granta Design (2010), the manufacture of primary aluminium requires approximately 200MJ/kg, whereas a typical composite, such as carbon fibre reinforced plastic, requires 270MJ/kg. In reality, manufacture of aluminium is a mix of primary and recycled, further reducing the energy requirement for aluminium. In contrast, there is no viable method for recycling composites.

2. Recycling of composite fibres has been investigated by Seok-Ho (2011). However, over 1.5 litres of nitric acid are required per 100 grams of composite, and therefore the environmental implications are awful. The recovered carbon fibres only have a slight reduction in tensile strength. As the process extracts only the fibres, not the energy-intensive resin, there is only a limited benefit in this approach to recycling composites.

Vehicles

3. The UK Government has undertaken consultations to formulate this strategy, following on from its requirements that homes be carbon neutral by 2016. Though the exact rules and details have yet to be finalised, further information is available at DCLG (2007).

4. Roads and bridges are designed for a certain maximum weight of vehicle, which is limited by law. These limits have been increased three times in the past twenty years in the UK, so we have had to re-examine existing bridges to see if they can take a higher loading than originally intended, or if they must be strengthened. Statistics collected by McKinnon (2005) to examine the use of trucks, estimate that they carry their maximum load 36 % of the time.

5. Yield losses in making commodity extrusion products, such as window frames are about 20–25 %. This is due to scrap generated at the start of each extrusion, and from the butt welds that form between billets as they are extruded one after another. With better modelling and control of this weld, we may be able to reduce these yield losses in future.

6. Merlin mechanical connections have been used to join oil pipe by remotely operated vehicles in the North Sea. They use a clamp and pressure seal connection. Using mechanical connections avoids the need for welding, so pipes can have a plastic lining, which increases corrosion resistance so prolongs their life. These connections are reusable and reversible.

Vehicles

7. India, Pakistan and Bangladesh dominate the ship breaking industry, with roughly half the world's ships dismantled in India alone. Tilwankar et al (2008) state that over the life-span of the ship, approximately 10 % of the steel is lost by corrosion. 95 % of the remainder is in the form of re-rollable sheet, allowing approximately 85 % of the ship's original steel mass to be reused. The predominant revenue stream of the ship breakers is from re-rolling the steel and so they are naturally motivated to maximize re-use.

Images

8. Author: High Contrast. Used under Creative Commons Attribution 3.0 Germany License (http://creativecommons.org/licenses/by/3.0/de/deed.en

19 Future energy use and emissions

with both eyes open

We can now recreate our analysis from chapter 11, but enhanced with the sliders on the mixing desk from the previous chapter, to bring in the options of material efficiency and demand reduction.

In effect the whole book so far has led up to this chapter. We've travelled, visited, talked, invented, imagined, cooked, fought, detected, explored, deduced, sung and calculated ourselves to this point to find out if we can create a sustainable steel and aluminium future, defined by our emissions target and with assumed demand growth. With one eye open, we looked for options that reduce emissions by process and energy efficiencies within existing businesses, but are hidden from to final consumers. And we found that we simply didn't have enough options to get close to the target, unless hiding behind the infinitely comforting blanket of carbon capture and storage.

With both eyes open we have a wider set of options, and at our most daring we've seen that, in the limit, we could live well with fewer material services. But this book isn't a radical call for the new richness of poverty: it's about exploring a set of options that have been forgotten, because the incumbent materials industry can't easily pursue them without some external impetus.

So in this chapter, we'll briefly discuss how to make use of the sliders we invented in the last chapter. Our main work is then to play with the sliders, to see whether we can reach the emissions target with our expanded set of options, or whether we need to bring in our slider of last resort, an absolute reduction in demand for material services. Then we can look at which sliders are most effective, and move onto anticipating what our forecasts tell us about future capacity requirements in different industries.

Anticipating energy and emissions with both eyes open

We can start our adding up by remembering where we were with one eye open: everything that was possible with one eye open remains possible, so we will continue to apply all the efficiency options from Part II. We'll stick with our previous forecast of demand, although we'll now interpret it as demand for services and not a demand for metal. As a consequence, the actual flows of metal in 2050 could be lower than before if, for instance, we make a shift towards lighter weight product design or more intense product use.

In the last chapter, for each product type we invented six sliders on a mixing desk to characterise the new options we've found with both eyes open. To forecast future metal stocks and flows, we will sub-divide the flows of both metals into the product categories, and modify the flows according to the sliders. We can move each slider between the limits we set in chapter 18, and to simplify our mixing desk, rather than having six sliders for every product, we'll assume that all sliders of the same type (e.g. all "scrap diversion" sliders) move together.

We also need two further sliders to affect the whole system: one for absolute demand reduction, which we'll apply equally across all products, and one for carbon capture and storage (CCS) which we'll apply to all emissions. We hope we won't need to use either of these sliders, but they are our options of last resort if full application of everything else isn't enough.

As before we will predict emissions in 2050 with a range of values, rather than a single number, to reflect our uncertainty about both demand, and about the scale and impact of our strategies. Our ambition is to reveal likelihoods, not to make precise predictions.

Forecasts of the future with both eyes open

Our first question in looking to the future with both eyes open is "can we meet the target without needing demand reduction or carbon sequestration?" We'll address this by assuming we move all the sliders (but not CCS or demand reduction) forwards together. The results are displayed in Figures 19.1 and 19.2.

For steel, we can see that even without pushing all of the sliders forward to their maximum positions, we can reach a 50% reduction in emissions compared to current levels. For aluminium, for which we're predicting greater demand growth, the story is different. Even if we implement all of our previous strategies from chapter 11, and if we then add material efficiency at the maximum rate we found credible in the previous chapter, our forecast emissions are still approximately 25% above the target. Actually the span of our forecasts, allowing for uncertainty, just reaches the target, but the mean forecast value is 25% too high. As a result,

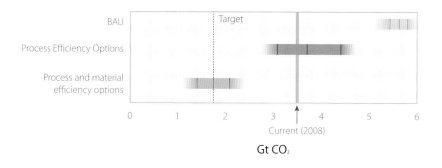

Figure 19.1—**Steel emissions forecasts and sliders**

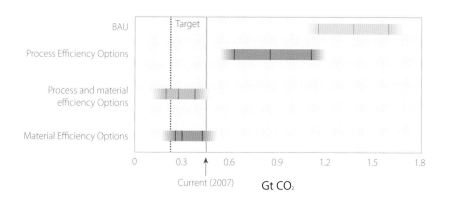

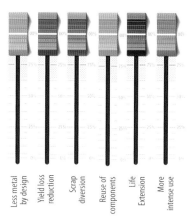

Figure 19.2—**Aluminium emissions forecasts and sliders**

in order to meet the target, we will need to use our sliders for CCS and demand reduction: we could meet the target for aluminium either by using CCS to remove a further 20% of emissions in producing electricity, or by reducing demand for aluminium services by 14%.

These two results are good news: it's been worth reading the book! We can reach the target for steel and nearly reach it for aluminium, without having to foment a revolution in behaviour or believe in the questionable dream of CCS.

Now we have an answer to our overall question, "can we get there?", we can now move on to a more nuanced one and ask what sort of journey we'd like to take to reach the target? To address this, we'll consider alternative ways to move the sliders. In particular we'll look for at two contrasting approaches:

- **Process and technology led change:** what happens if we have a preference for changes that can be implemented within industry? We'll examine this by moving forwards the sliders for using less by design, yield loss reduction, scrap diversion and component re-use, twice as far as those for life extension and more intense use. This approach demands more effort from within the industry, but less change of behaviour by consumers.

- **Behaviour led change:** in contrast, what happens if material efficiency becomes a social norm, and is driven by behaviour change? Here we'll shift the sliders more related to behaviour (life extension and more intense use) at twice the rate of the others, to examine what would happen if consumers took the initiative.

In Figure 19.3, we've contrasted these two approaches and can see that for steel, we can achieve the target with either strategy. If we have a preference for behaviour change, we can achieve the target with the sliders at lower values than when we prefer process and technology change. For the aluminium sector, the results in Figure 19.4 show that we still need to rely on CCS and demand reduction to meet the targets. The effect of the alternative preferences above is to move some sliders to only half their limit, while the others remain at full implementation. This increases our need for CCS or demand reduction. As with steel, a preference for process and technology change is less effective than a preference for behaviour change, so results in higher settings for these two sliders.

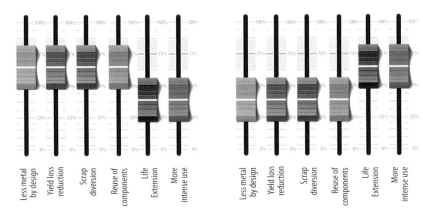

Figure 19.3—**Alternative steel strategies**

Technology moving at twice the rate of behaviour

Behaviour moving at twice the rate of technology

Sustainable Materials with both eyes open

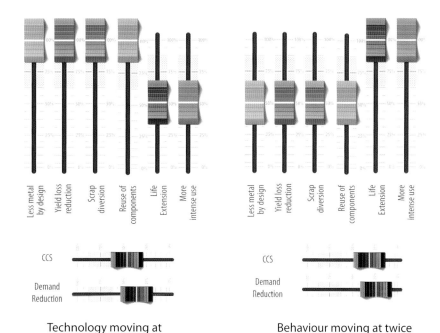

Figure 19.4—**Alternative aluminium strategies**

Technology moving at
twice the rate of behaviour

Behaviour moving at twice
the rate of technology

We've established that the target we set for ourselves can be met—but we've seen that behaviour options appear to be more powerful than those related to technology. In the next section we'll explore this further.

The relative sensitivity of our different options for change

In chapter 2 we established that options for reducing energy use are not all additive, because if you reduce demand for some output, you also reduce the potential for savings from delivering that output more efficiently. So, we must be cautious in exploring the effect of moving each of slider separately. However, we now want to try this, because we've been careful in setting up limits for each slider, so can give physical meaning to small movements of each slider relative to the present. Exploring the sensitivity of overall emissions to each slider will help us to establish priorities for short term action.

Figures 19.5 and 19.6 show the emissions saving from moving each of our sliders forwards by 1%, while leaving the other six at present levels. We've included the slider for demand reduction in order to give some comparison of scale.

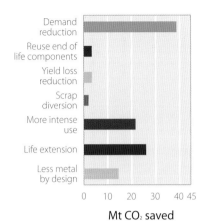

Figure 19.5—**Sensitivity analysis for the steel options**

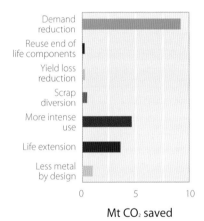

Figure 19.6—**Sensitivity analysis for the aluminium options**

These results are not additive: if we applied two of the strategies together, we would not necessarily see a total emissions reduction equal to the sum of the two applied separately. However they show us the relative impacts of starting to implement each strategy. Scrap diversion, yield loss reduction and component re-use have the least effect. Even though these are the easier strategies to implement, because they are 'internal' to the industry, they apply only to a subset of the secondary stream of metal which will be recycled, so has a lower emissions intensity than primary production. In contrast, life extension, more intense use, and design with less metal all lead to a reduction in total material demand, so are more effective. This result is highly significant as we plan for a sustainable materials future. To date, virtually every effort related to the goal of sustainable materials has focused attention on the sites where material is produced. The forecasts of chapter 11 and those here, show that this simply won't have a substantial effect—because these sites are already operating remarkably well. Instead, the three strategies that we've found give a big effect. All cause a reduction in demand for production of new materials. By designing with less material we continue to produce the same number of goods, but use less material when doing so. The other two strategies aim to provide the same service with fewer new goods, by maintaining existing goods for longer and using them more intensely. A sustainable materials future therefore has reduced materials production, and for materials producing businesses with no other revenue stream, this is bad news. However, it is not bad news for the economy as a whole, as we've seen that lost revenue in materials production can be replaced by increased activity in maintaining, repairing, and upgrading existing stocks. So a sustainable materials future requires a change in the balance of our activity, but does not require a recession.

We'll conclude our exploration of options for change by developing two more forecasts for steel. In both cases we'll move forwards all six sliders at the same rate, but in the first we'll include capture and storage of 25% of all emissions and in the second we'll include reduction of demand for final services by 25%. Contrasting these results in Figure 19.7 with the earlier ones, we can see that this level of CCS or demand reduction, requires that the other sliders move forwards about 40% less.

Capacity requirements and roadmaps

We don't know which of our options will be implemented at which rate, so having worked to establish credible limits for each strategy in each product area, we'll stick to our first forecast with no demand reduction and no sequestration, but all

Sustainable Materials with both eyes open

Figure 19.7—**Steel slider options with CCS or demand reduction**

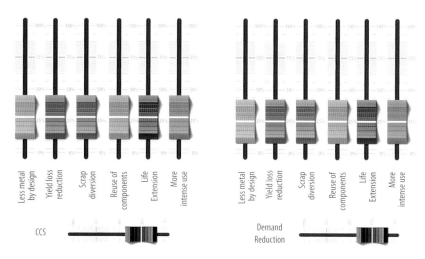

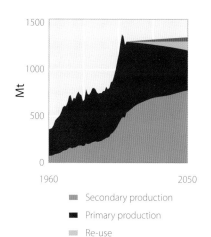

Secondary production

Primary production

Re-use

Scrap diversion

Figure 19.8—**Capacity required for steel processes to 2050**

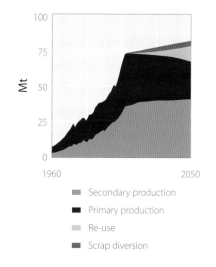

Secondary production

Primary production

Re-use

Scrap diversion

Figure 19.9—**Capacity required for aluminium processes to 2050**

sliders moving together. If we apply this approach to our model of metal flow, we can now extract two further useful insights.

Firstly, for both metals, we can anticipate the total global capacity required for each major stage of production, between now and 2050. The graphs in Figure 19.8 and 22.1 show that: we already have enough global capacity for steel and aluminium primary production; we must increase our capacity for recycling steadily between now and 2050; we must grow our capacity for processing diverted scrap and reusing components. These graphs give an unequivocal message to politicians considering emissions reduction targets: if we wish to achieve a 50% cut in emissions, we must not build any new primary production facilities. Instead, globally, we need to reduce primary production by around one third over the next 40 years. This is a direct consequence of primary production driving most emissions in materials processing. Reduced emissions requires reduced primary production, and the options for change we have identified throughout Part III are about living well with less new material. We've found plenty of those options, but we cannot avoid the simple fact of these graphs: to cut emissions globally we have to cut global primary production.

Secondly, we can develop start to predict the changes required to allow changes in metal service delivery to take place. Over the next four decades, changes in capital investment (related to plant capacity) will be required, alongside technology innovation (for example new manufacturing process development) and new approaches to design (for instance to enable component reuse) are required in order to meet the targets. Changes in the systems (such as safe lightweight cars), legislation and behaviour required to help us meet the targets will be our focus in Part V of the book.

Outlook

The great news of this chapter is that a sustainable material future looks much more feasible with both eyes open than it did with just one. We have now identified enough options for big change to have a choice about how to reach our emissions target. In Part IV we'll explore whether similar approaches would allow similar relative reductions for other materials.

other
materials

PART IV

20. Cement

Cement is the second of our five key materials emitting almost as much CO_2 as steel—in fact steel and cement drive nearly half of all industrial emissions. Cement is the ubiquitous building material of the world, with most demand in the most rapidly developing countries. What fraction of these emissions can we save by energy and process efficiencies, and what else could we do?

21. Plastic

Plastic waste is in the public eye, but we already know from the labels on packaging that plastic recycling is complicated. Is plastics production as efficient as the production of other materials, and what can we do to use less, recycle more, or use plastics for longer?

22. Paper

Paper is a natural product—closely related to trees—so its energy and emissions impact can be surprising: energy is mainly needed to convert trees to a lignin-free wet pulp, and then after papermaking to remove excess water by evaporation. Are there other efficiency options, or can we reduce demand for paper?

20 Cement

Cement is the second of our five key materials emitting almost as much CO_2 as steel—in fact steel and cement drive nearly half of all industrial emissions. Cement is the ubiquitous building material of the world, with most demand in the most rapidly developing countries. What fraction of these emissions can we save by energy and process efficiencies, and what else could we do?

We haven't managed a really good conspiracy theory yet, so now's the time: they may have been trying to deceive us about how the Great Pyramid of Giza in Egypt was made … Of course we all know that in fact it was made around 2560 BC by slaves carving blocks out of rock, rolling them on wooden poles under the watchful eye of Elizabeth Taylor, and heaving them up with hemp ropes while singing the chorus of the Hebrew slaves from Verdi's Nabucco … but maybe that's just a cover-up—because actually it could have been much easier than that. For at least some of the blocks, all they needed were moulds and buckets because they're not rocks at all—they're just blocks of concrete poured into moulds to look like rock.

The Great Pyramid of Giza: carved or poured?

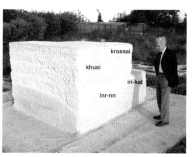

Dr. Davidovits standing before four blocks of 'pyramid' limestone concrete, totalling 12 metric tonnes[25]

This very interesting theory was proposed in the 1980's by Dr Joseph Davidovits, a materials scientist working in France, and has not been widely accepted by Egyptologists, but the debate is still very much alive. In 2006, an academic paper by Professor Michel Barsoum at Drexel University in Philadelphia, and two colleagues, provided detailed analysis of samples of material from the pyramid[1]. The pyramid samples contained a high density of very small grains of material with high silicon constituents, none of which were found in the limestone found in the area. Professor Barsoum and colleagues deduced that this would occur if the pyramid material had at some point been a solution (in water) and the small grains had formed as part of the chemical reactions during solidification of what must have been an early cement. Professor Barsoum and co. are very careful not to overstate their results, and other authors have subsequently argued against them. But, if they're right then, as they conclude, they have found that the Egyptians had discovered how to make a very sophisticated lime based cement that has survived for nearly 5,000 years.

3,000 years later, and we know for sure that the Romans were using cement: the dome of the Pantheon in Rome, originally designed for Marcus Agrippa in about

The Pantheon Dome

Roman ruins in front of Mount Vesuvius

The Great Wall of China

AD 31, but rebuilt by Hadrian around AD 126, was made with about four and a half thousand tonnes of Roman concrete. The strength of this concrete has been tested to be not less than half that of modern concrete made with Portland cement. We know about the production of Roman concrete through the writings of Marcus Vitruvius Pollio, whose "De Architectura" from about 25AD, gives details of lime mortars and the ratios in which they should be mixed with small stones to form concrete for different applications. The word 'concrete' itself comes from the Latin 'concretus', meaning 'compounded'.

The basis of both the postulated early Egyptian cement and the definite Roman material is limestone (largely $CaCO_3$): when it is heated to 1000°C in a kiln, carbon dioxide is released to leave behind 'lime' (CaO). This is then mixed with water and sand in certain proportions to make mortars which harden when exposed to the atmosphere as carbon dioxide is reabsorbed. Mortars made in this way are called 'non-hydraulic' as they must be exposed to air to set, i.e. they cannot set underwater.

Around 100 BC the Romans discovered that they could make a much stronger mortar if they used sand from the slopes of Mount Vesuvius, and what's more, it would set underwater. This was because this 'sand' was in fact fine volcanic ash, which contained silica and alumina that combine chemically with the lime to give a 'hydraulic' mortar which, when mixed with water, sets in a chemical reaction called 'curing'. Though the Romans did not understand the exact chemistry of the new material, they used it for over half a millennium, even trying (unsuccessfully) to reinforce it using bronze bars. Most of their knowledge was lost with the fall of the empire, and we reverted to using predominantly non-hydraulic lime cement for the next thousand years. Most of Europe's royal palaces, Cambridge's colleges, the fabulous 12th Century rush of French cathedrals and the Great Wall of China are held together with lime cement (though apparently the ancient Chinese added in sticky-rice to improve strength)[2], and it was not until the mid-18th Century that serious efforts were made to improve upon the traditional formula. In particular, the search for better cement was motivated by the limited strength and slow setting time of non-hydraulic cement, and the fact that it couldn't set underwater.

John Smeaton, who was commissioned to build the third Eddystone lighthouse, conducted a survey of available options to find a strong cement that would harden sufficiently between tides that it would not be washed away. He concluded that limestone containing clay (which has the important silicas and aluminas in it) gave the desired results and achieved a cement comparable to what the Romans had used, so that the foundations of 'Smeaton's Tower', completed in 1759, remain

Sustainable Materials with both eyes open

A masonry footbridge

Smeaton's tower

to this day (the tower itself was dismantled and moved in 1876). Smeaton did not develop his findings further, so no progress was made for 30 years until Rev. James Parker noticed that certain stones found in clay, once burnt, could be ground up to make a 'natural cement' that was strong and hydraulic, but set quickly (within 15 minutes). This setting time was too rapid to allow accurate block placement, and the natural cement had such low initial strength that it required support for many weeks. It was therefore mainly used for external plaster, to give a stone appearance to brick walls. Natural cements became popular, but were of variable quality and this triggered experiments by Louis Vicat in France, aiming to emulate its composition artificially. This was what Joseph Aspdin had in mind when, in 1824, he took out a patent for 'Portland Cement' (so called because it looked like the prestigious Portland stone used on building facades). Around twenty years later, amidst much secrecy, his son William found that by increasing the temperature and limestone content of his father's process he could produce a cement that overcame the problems of rapid setting and low initial strength and 'Ordinary Portland Cement' as we know it was born[3].

In masonry construction (building from blocks, such as stone or bricks), we bond the blocks with mortar—cement mixed with sand and water. An alternative, and the starting point for this chapter in Egypt, is to mix small blocks or stones into the mortar, to create a sludgy liquid that can be poured into a mould: concrete.

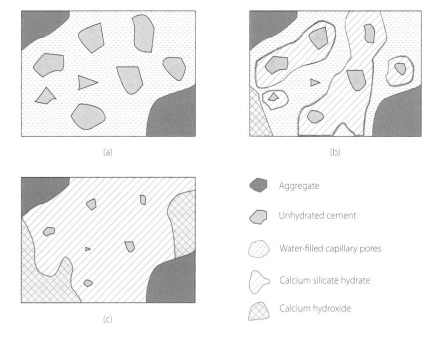

Figure 20.1—**The Portland cement reacts with water to form calcium silicate hydrate (C-S-H) gel which 'grows' out in spike shapes to link in with other particles and aggregate**

Pouring reinforced concrete

King's College Chapel experiencing compression

Concrete must be mixed in precise proportions, as Vitruvius knew: some of the proportions specified in his books are similar to those used today. The small stones (either gravel or crushed stone) and sand should have an even range of sizes so they nest without large gaps and the required chemical reactions can form the microstructure shown in Figure 20.1. The aggregates (small stones and sand) make up 70–85 % of the concrete by mass. They have low embodied emissions (the energy required is for mining, crushing and transportation only), so the figure for embodied emissions in a kilogram of concrete, typically 0.13 kg, is much lower than that for cement, and just over half that of a clay brick[4].

Cement, mortar and concrete are ceramics, so the atoms within their structure are bonded in a different way to those in metals. We discussed in chapter 3 how metals deform by the movement of dislocations, which can move because the atom to one side of the dislocation can form a new bond with atoms to the other side. However in ceramics this shifting is not possible: to use a rather violent variant of our analogy of the Chinese Dragon being pulled up the steps, the shoes of the ceramic dragon are glued to the steps so powerfully that as the force builds up on the man behind the empty step, he can't step forwards and eventually his legs break! Thereafter he can't make any further contribution to the Dragon's pulling power, so the force on the man behind increases and his legs break too, as do all remaining legs, and the Dragon has no remaining strength. This is called 'fast fracture' in the world of ceramics as a result of which all mortars and concretes are strong in compression but weak in tension. Early structures built from masonry bonded by cement were therefore designed to experience compression only, and this led to classic stone arched bridges, and the wonderful design of King's College Chapel. Compression is assured in the Chapel because loads are resisted by a 'line of thrust' in the form of an inverted catenary (the shape that a necklace of beads will adopt if hung loosely between two horizontally separated points) which is entirely encapsulated within the buttresses and roof supports.

However, the advent of Bessemer's steel making process opened up a new opportunity for creating structures with concrete that could withstand both compression and tension—and therefore require less material overall. Steel is strong in both compression and tension, so if a concrete beam will experience bending (as happens in virtually all buildings) thin strong bars of steel (reinforcing bars) can be placed on the lower side of the beam to withstand tension forces, while concrete elsewhere supports the compressive loading. That these two common materials are so compatible is remarkable: they stretch similar amounts when heated (this was where bronze failed the Romans), bond well together and while the steel gives concrete tensile strength, the concrete protects the steel from its main weakness,

Sustainable Materials with both eyes open

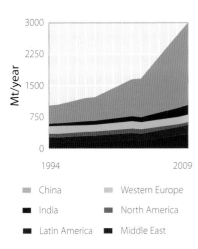

Figure 20.2—**Global cement production over time by region**[6]

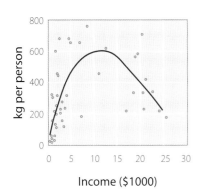

Figure 20.3—**Cement consumption per capita vs. GNP per capita**[7]

corrosion. This composite (mixture of two materials) form of construction is now universal and today nearly all concrete is used in conjunction with steel reinforcing bars. No wonder that with global cement production around 2,800 Mt per year, equivalent to about 23,000 Mt of concrete[5], we found that steel reinforcing bars, with 271 Mt per year, are the largest single application of steel.

In this opening section, we started from the ancient Egyptians and have followed the evolution of cement, from lime based compositions to contemporary Portland cement. We've seen how cement is mainly used to make concrete which in turn is used with reinforcing steel as the world's primary building material. So now we're ready to begin our exploration of the present and future emissions associated with cement. In the next three sections we'll first examine demand for cement, then we'll look at the energy and emissions associated with its production to see whether it can be made more efficiently, and then we'll review opportunities to use less cement in future construction.

Patterns of demand for cement

After Aspdin developed Portland cement in the mid-19th Century it was used in buildings around the UK, despite the initial high cost of the material (due to the cost of energy required to initiate the high temperature reaction). However once William Wilkinson, a builder from Newcastle, patented reinforced concrete in the second half of the century, concrete rapidly overtook other materials, particularly for construction of infrastructure and larger buildings: compared to building with bricks and stones, concrete which can be poured, is relatively cheap, easy to handle, and allows rapid construction. As a result, Figure 20.2 shows that recent global demand for cement has shot up. It was 10 Mt in 1910 and reached 600 Mt by 1970 and is over 2800 Mt today. The colours of Figure 20.2 showing demand by region demonstrate how cement-use relates to economic development: North American and European demand stagnated from the 1970's to 1995, while Chinese demand in particular has expanded at a phenomenal rate. For most countries, the largest end-use of cement is for infrastructure, with domestic housing next and the rest split evenly between other building types.

When we forecast future demand for steel and aluminium in Chapter 4, we noticed that developed countries appear to reach a plateau of stocks per person, after which demand is mainly for replacement goods, and old goods are recycled. There is no recycling route for cement, so no motivation to analyse stocks, however there is a connection between national demand for cement and average national incomes.

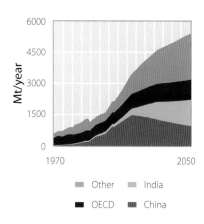

Figure 20.4—**Forecast growth in demand for cement by 2050**[8]

Company	Global share (2003 %)
Lafarge (France)	5.5
Holcim (Switzerland)	5.0
Cemex (Mexico)	4.3
Heidelberg Cement (Germany)	2.5
Italcementi (Italy)	2.1
Taiheiyo (Japan)	1.6

Table 20.1—**World market share of leading cement companies**[9]

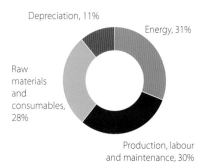

Figure 20.5—**Breakdown of costs in cement production**[10]

Figure 20.3 demonstrates that demand grows as national income grows to around $10–15,000 per person, but then declines, when demand for new buildings and infrastructure has been satisfied. This insight has been used with estimates of regional economic growth rates, income levels and population growth to forecast future demand. It is no surprise that cement use in China and India is expected to drive global demand between now and 2050. Most predictions agree that global cement demand will be between 4,500 Mt and 5,500 Mt by 2050 but it is unclear whether we will have reached 'peak cement' by then, as estimates for the latter half of the century vary substantially.

The raw materials required to make cement are well distributed across the planet, and because it has a low value by weight, relatively little cement is traded internationally: Figure 20.6 shows that the major continents produce most of their own cement. As a result, the industry is quite fragmented: Table 20.1 shows that the largest six cement companies supply only one fifth of global demand.

Figure 20.5 shows a typical breakdown of the costs of cement production. The industry has a high output per person, and has become significantly more productive in the past 30 years, as seen in Figure 20.7. Globally around 800,000 people are employed in making cement. Two thirds of them are in China, although they produce only 40% of the world's cement because small factories using older technology remain common.

Cement with one eye open: energy and emissions now and in the future

The production process for Portland cement has changed little since Aspdin invented it, and is shown in Figure 20.8. Limestone, clay and sand are collected and ground up, then mixed heaed to 1450°C in a kiln which causes chemical reactions that form pellets of clinker. Together with a small amount of gypsum, this is then ground finely to make cement. The hot stage of this process is the source of most emissions, both because energy is required to raise the temperature, and because the chemical reaction which converts limestone to lime releases carbon dioxide. In fact, half of the emissions from cement production are released in this reaction, with a further 40% from burning fuel for heating, and the remaining 10% is split evenly between grinding and transportation[12].

Sustainable Materials with both eyes open

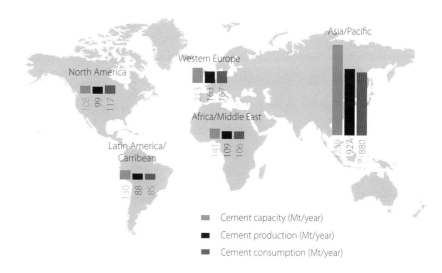

Figure 20.6—**Global cement capacity, production and consumption**[11]

North America
108 99 117

Western Europe
213 163 167

Asia/Pacific
1259 927 880

Africa/Middle East
141 109 106

Latin America/
Carribean
130 88 85

- Cement capacity (Mt/year)
- Cement production (Mt/year)
- Cement consumption (Mt/year)

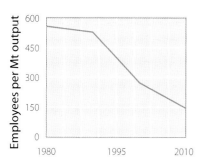

Figure 20.7—**Historical improvements in productivity in cement production**

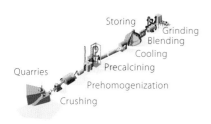

Storing
Grinding
Blending
Cooling
Precalcining
Prehomogenization
Quarries
Crushing

Figure 20.8—**Cement production process**[26]

As with steel and aluminium, we can start our search for future energy efficiency in cement making by calculating the minimum energy for the chemical reaction. The decomposition of calcium carbonate (limestone) into lime and carbon dioxide is the largest of a series of reactions. In total we can predict a minimum theoretical energy requirement of 1.8 GJ/tonne[13] and best practice is already remarkably close to this at 2.9 GJ/tonne, so we cannot expect much further improvement. Cement is so close to its theoretical limits because, in comparison with steel and aluminium, producing cement requires fewer, simpler inputs and demands less purity.

Although best practice in cement production is only 50% over the theoretical limit, the global average is around 4.7–5.5 GJ/tonne, almost double best practice. This wide range is because of extensive use of older, less efficient equipment, especially at cement factories in China and India. Many of these factories use the 'wet' process in which, during preparation, the raw materials are mixed with water which must later be evaporated at high energy cost. Also, older plants do not have the sophisticated heat recovery systems of modern ones in which exhaust gases heat incoming material. Global average energy use should improve rapidly as older plants are replaced, and this is occurring rapidly in China[14].

The cement industry is pursuing two other opportunities for efficiency, both based on substitution—of fuel and of clinker. Cement kilns can burn waste as a substitute for fossil fuel because they operate at a high temperature and the presence of limestone helps to clean the exhaust gases. Substituting waste for fuels reduces emissions, although the magnitude of the reduction depends on the precise exchange. This approach is popular in Europe, and some cement producers claim to have substituted all of their fuel with waste.

Portland cement itself can also be substituted, at least partially with other materials[15]:

- Ground granulated blast furnace slag (GGBS), a by-product of the blast furnace, adds long-term strength and durability to cement at the expense of lower initial strength and slower curing. Current production of GGBS is approximately 200 Mt per year and will increase in line with steel production.

- Pulverised fly ash (PFA) is a waste product from coal power stations that improves concrete workability and long-term strength but decreases initial strength. Current production is around 500 Mt per year.

- Pozzolans arise naturally (for example as volcanic ash) or artificially (for instance in calcinated clay) and can substitute up to half of cement requirements in some applications. During curing they react with water to improve durability and workability, again at the cost of reduced initial strength. At present 150 Mt per year of natural pozzolans are used in cement production. Artificial pozzolans are energy intensive so not widely used and do not provide the same environmental benefits as the other substitutions.

- Limestone can be ground up finely and used as a replacement for Portland cement. This improves workability but reduces strength and durability. Limestone is widely available in large quantities.

Limestone rocks

We've seen that four forms of substitution can offer improved performance and cost reductions, so occur already: on average 10-20 % of cement is replaced this way at present, and this is likely to increase. However with global cement production already greater than 2,850 Mt per year and with annual supplies of GGBS, PFA and pozzolans totalling just 850 Mt, substitution cannot be applied without limit.

For steel and aluminium, recycling is a key energy efficiency strategy, because secondary production requires so much less energy than primary production from ore. However, to reverse the reactions that make cement, the theoretical minimum required energy is around 1GJ/t, so a practical cement recycling process would give little if any energy benefit and, as a result, cement is not recycled at all at present[16]. Instead, concrete is 'recycled' by crushing to make a type of aggregate, which could be used to make new concrete if mixed with new cement. This is not

Sustainable Materials with both eyes open

Crushed concrete

recycling, but is instead 'down-cycling' old concrete as a substitute for aggregate. However the embodied emissions in aggregate are around 25 times less than those of the old concrete and extra cement may be required to bind the wider range of particle sizes in crushed concrete. Crushed old concrete is commonly used for the bases of roads or other infrastructure, and while this is a better destination than landfill sites, it is a waste of such a carbon-intensive product.

We explored carbon capture and storage (CCS) in chapter 10. Not surprisingly, for cement producers CCS is even more attractive than for steel-makers, because of the high and unavoidable process emissions in cement making. Many developments to allow separation of a pure stream of CO_2 from kiln flue gases are underway[17] however, all the concerns we raised in chapter 10 apply equally to sequestering CO_2 from cement production.

If Dr. Davidovits is correct then not only did the Eygptians discover an advanced cement much earlier than previously thought, they also discovered one with low embodied emissions. We don't know what the Pharaohs called their cement but Dr. Davidovits in the 1970s called it a 'geopolymer'. Geopolymers are made from compounds of aluminium and silicon (commonly found in the earth's crust—for example, kaolin clay was found in Eygpt). The compounds harden when mixed with an alkaline solution (such as lime mixed with natron, a salt that doubled as an early form of toothpaste) and strengthen at room temperature. Apart from (possibly) building pyramids, geopolymers have been commercialised on a small-scale but they are expensive and have not yet been tested in large-scale applications where strength is critical[18]. Several other novel cement technologies are in early stages of development with some developers making extravagant claims that their cement absorbs more emissions during its life than emitted during production. However there has yet been little if any independent validation of these claims, and the new cements have not been tested in service or shown to meet standards required in construction[19].

We've anticipated that demand for cement will grow by 75 % by 2050, and looked at five options to reduce emissions associated with conventional cement production. Figure 20.9 shows the build-up of our prediction of how emissions will evolve to 2050? Given the economic advantages of upgrading to the best available technology, coupled with China's ambitious plans, we will bravely assume that global average energy per tonne falls to the level of current best practice, 2.9 GJ/tonne, by 2050. Similarly the economic advantages of substituting GGBS, PFA and pozzolans should drive a steady increase in their uptake to a maximum of 850 Mt/year, and we'll assume that limestone will replace 5 % of the remaining

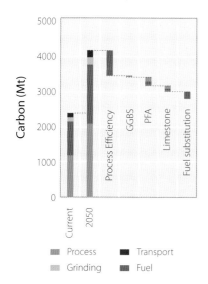

Figure 20.9—**Forecast for emissions reductions in the cement industry**

cement (the level beyond which final performance suffers). We assume that the worldwide fraction of fuel substitution will increase to 17%, the current rate in Europe, and that this will reduce emissions from fuel combustion by the same amount..

In summary, Figure 20.9 shows that if demand grows as anticipated, we can at best hope that absolute emissions from cement production will have grown by only 18% by 2050. This would be an impressive achievement, but our target remains a 50% cut by 2050, so we need to look at cement with both eyes open.

Cement with both eyes open: opportunities to use less cement to provide the same service

Our main work in preparing this book has been to look with both eyes open at the use of steel and aluminium—there has been so little attention given to material efficiency anywhere that we have invested most of our effort in gathering primary evidence about living well with less liquid metal production. So in this section, we'll take inspiration from what we learnt about the two metals, to identify parallel opportunities for using less powdered cement. We've found that this might be possible through using less cement when making concrete, designing structures that require less concrete, substituting other materials, delaying the end of life of concrete structures, and re-using concrete components after their first life.

We can use less cement by improving control of the amount used when mixing concrete. Strength is proportional to the amount of cement in the mix, so lower strength concrete should use less cement. Currently some control is applied, for example to give a lower strength mix for foundations and higher strength for the superstructure, but the concrete equivalent of steel rationalisation tends to favour use of fewer concrete mixes on a site, and hence over-use of cement.

Using less concrete through design has significant potential, and for inspiration we can return to the Pantheon in Rome which has the world's largest unreinforced concrete dome. To build it, the Roman engineers knew they had to minimise weight, so the dome thickness decreases from 6.4 m at the base to 1.2 m at the top, and they even left a 4.1 m radius 'oculus' (opening) at the very top of the dome. A great advantage of concrete is that we can pour into almost any shape, however for simplicity we usually use recto-linear moulds rounded up to the nearest 25mm. If we made optimised moulds we could use up to 40% less concrete in places[20].

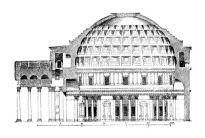

A cross-section of the Pantheon dome

As concrete is only strong in compression, we should really only use it to resist compressive loads. Two strategies can be employed:

- In 'pre-stressing', a tensioned steel cable is used to compress the concrete. By eliminating tension, the full strength of the concrete can be used.

- We can remove concrete from areas in tension either with more advanced moulds, or by introducing pockets of air (or polystyrene) into a standard mould. This is another trick used by the Romans in the Pantheon dome.

Apart from purely structural functions, concrete also serves to protect steel reinforcement from corrosion, indeed a special 'cover' layer of 20–40 mm is specified outside the rebar purely for this purpose. We can reduce this layer either by guaranteeing more accurate placement of bars on site so that designers can cut their assumed margin of error[21], or by using stainless steel or plastic-coated rebar which requires even less cover—however as production of stainless steel leads to greater emissions than production of normal steel, this substitution will only be effective in particular cases.

It's possible to substitute other materials for concrete. The discussion in Chapter 3 showed that masonry, steel and timber are the main contenders:

- Masonry is a good alternative to concrete, being as strong and with lower embodied emissions. However, masonry must be bonded with mortar (made from cement), and cannot be reinforced or moulded into shape.

- Steel is an alternative to concrete in most applications (columns, beams, foundation piles), and unlike concrete it can be recycled. However it is more expensive and more emissions intensive per unit mass or per unit stiffness and must be protected against corrosion.

- Timber gives higher strength and stiffness per unit of embodied energy, however it is not as durable as concrete, so must be shielded against fire and rot. Commercial timber is surprisingly energy intensive because it is dried in kilns.

A few old masonry walls at Machu Picchu

Properly designed and built concrete fails only under exceptional circumstances, for example when it is adjacent to corrosive chemicals in soil or water[22]. Therefore extending the life of concrete structures is an excellent strategy, and as we saw in chapter 16, we inevitably use the same approaches to extend the life of both reinforcing bars and cement.

St Peter's Basilica in Rome was built using reclaimed blocks from the Colosseum

Reusing concrete components is currently rare but would be easier were they to be made in standardised units that could be taken apart and reconfigured—like Lego blocks, Meccano and the Cambridge white bricks we saw in Chapter 15. The key challenge to enabling concrete re-use is to design connections that are strong in use, but can then be released to free the component blocks at the end of life. We have two options to achieve this:

- Chemical connectors, like the lime mortar in Cambridge houses, provide sufficient cohesion but can still be broken. Some work in Japan aims to develop advanced concretes that could be weakened to facilitate easier deconstruction[23].

- Mechanical connections create a physical interface between parts. In the US construction blocks, rather like Lego, are available with this type of connection. Further developments might create composite cement and steel blocks with steel-to-steel interfaces to permit dismantling and reuse.

These options to use less cement have significant future potential and we can also explore reductions in final demand for the services provided by cement. This would raise the same opportunities and issues as we found in chapter 17—but our impression is that the major opportunities for demand reduction will occur in buildings, as infrastructure such as bridges, are already in many cases used more intensely than anticipated in their original design, and are already built for long life.

A concrete highway bridge: has it been made well enough to last?

Outlook

Our exploration of cement in this chapter began with a remarkable theory about building Pyramids, and has taken us on a tour including the Pantheon in Rome and a lighthouse in Devon. We've found that although it will be difficult to improve on current best practice, there are many opportunities for energy efficiency in cement production, due to the wide gap between current best technology and average practice. However, because of the large contribution of process emissions which occur regardless of energy efficiency, we were unable to find sufficient options to meet our target emissions reduction with anticipated demand growth. Instead, we have found a plethora of opportunities for us to live well with less cement.

Cement production is strongly correlated with economic development, and almost half of global production is currently in China. However, this rapid expansion of use is apparently not sufficiently controlled to guarantee long-lasting buildings: we have found evidence that Chinese buildings may only last 20–30 years due to poor quality construction and insufficient maintenance[24]. While we evaluate the opportunities for global reductions in cement requirements for each application, the most urgent priority for future emissions associated with cement is to promote longevity in construction with cement today—to ensure that construction during today's rapid expansion lasts 150 years rather than 30.

Notes

1. Barsoum et al. (2006) describes their analysis of Davidovits' thesis.

2. Yang et al. (2010) describe their research into the use of sticky rice in ancient Chinese construction.

3. This history is based on Stanley (1979) with additions from Francis (1977) and van Oss (2011). The exact discoverer of Portland Cement is somewhat contentious, as several individuals lay claim to it, but the version presented is one generally accepted.

4. From the Hammond and Jones (2008) which is composed of average absolute values for embodied carbon with explanations of the factors considered in them.

5. Estimates concrete produced per tonne of cement varies from 7–9 tonnes as quoted in van Oss and Padovani (2003) so 8 tonnes was assumed.

Cement with one eye open: energy emissions now and in the future

6. Data on historic cement consumption is from Worrell et al. (2001) and from several USGS publications such as USGS (2010)

7. Aïtcin (2000) describes the correlation between cement consumption and development.

8. Forecast taken from Taylor et al. (2006) with different forecasts from Humphreys & Mahasenan (2002) using a range of assumptions.

9. Taken from Baumert et al. (2005)

10. Taken from Lafarge (2007)

11. These numbers are for 1999, from Batelle (2002)

12. Based on sources both from inside and outside the industry such as World Business Council for Sustainable Development (WBCSD, 2005) and Bosoaga et al. (2009). Van Oss (2005) provides further information including a more detailed description of the chemistry of cement.

13. From page 64, 'Cement Chemistry', Taylor, H., 1990

14. Taken from IEA (2007) and similar breakdowns repeated in other sources.

15. Allocation of carbon between products (e.g. steel) and by-products (e.g. slag) leads to splendid arguments because the by-product is made in a carbon-intensive process which operates in order to make something else (steel). Using such by-products as substitutes gives an overall benefit, so who should claim credit? More on this in WBCSD (2009). We could use more substitutes in cement if concrete was supported for longer after pouring, so the lower initial strength which is a consequence of many substitutes would not be a limitation. More on this in van Oss (2005).

16. Page 5 of the WellMet2050 report 'Taking our metal temperature' (Allwood et al., 2011) explains that average global exergy efficiency is about 10%. Therefore the required 30% efficiency to make recovering cement from concrete would be difficult to achieve.

17. Carbon sequestration can be done by either pre- or post-combustion processes, or by introducing an oxy-combustion system, each of which have various levels of capture, and different set-up and running costs. More information can be found in Naranjo et al. (2011) and Barker et al. (2009).

18. Based on information in WBCSD (2009), supported by van Oss (2011).

19. Taken from WBCSD (2009).

Cement with both eyes open: opportunities to use less cement to provide the same service

20. Orr et al. (2010) - This research team have made many exciting and efficient shapes from concrete cast in fabric.

21. Concrete creates an alkaline environment which inhibits corrosion of steel. However this useful effect declines near the surface due to a reaction between the concrete and CO_2 in the air. In order to ensure protection of the reinforcing steel, an additional 'cover layer' of concrete is therefore used. Most modern structural codes of practice allow this cover to be reduced, without affecting performance, provided certain conditions are met. For example, BS EN 1992-1-1:2004 (Eurocode 2) Clause 4.4.1.3 [3] specifies that cover can be reduced by up to 10mm if 'very accurate measurement' is used to verify correct placement of bars.

22. Chlorides, sulphates and silicates can all react adversely with reinforced concrete, but if known during design then appropriate mitigation measures can be taken.

23. Noguchi et al. (2011)

Outlook

24. Hu et al. (2010), states that residential units built in the 1960s and 70s were of such low quality that they only lasted 15 years. In later decades the standard of construction and maintenance has improved bringing the life expectancy up, however current building life is only 30 years in China (Hatayama et al. 2010).

Images

25. Joseph Davidovits, Geopolymer Chemistry and Applications 3rd ed. (2008-2011), Institut Géopolymère, ISBN978 -2-95114820-50

26. IEA and The World Business Council for Sustainable Development, Cement Technology Roadmap 2009

21 Plastic

Plastic waste is in the public eye, but we already know from the labels on packaging that plastic recycling is complicated. Is plastics production as efficient as the production of other materials, and what can we do to use less, recycle more, or use plastics for longer?

Stainless steel teaspoon

Plastic teaspoon

We started the last chapter on a grand scale, with ancient Egyptian construction, so we'll start this one more humbly. In a teacup in fact, and without a storm either, just the gentle swirling of the tea being stirred. Our humbler start reflects the fact that the family of plastics is quite different from our other four materials, with so much variety that it is much more difficult for us to make estimates of future emissions associated with their production because each sub-class of plastic deserves at least a chapter of its own. But the family of plastics sits there on our opening pie chart as one of our five materials of concern, so strengthened by our cup of tea we need to set off, and we'll start not with a toe in the water, but a spoon in the tea.

Most of the world's teaspoons are made from stainless steel or plastic. Stainless steel is 20 times stronger than polystyrene (a plastic typically used for making plastic cutlery) 65 times stiffer, and about 8 times more dense. So, for equivalent strength, we'd expect the plastic teaspoon to be around three times heavier than the stainless steel one and be 20 times larger. But compare the two teaspoons in the photos, and the opposite is true: the plastic teaspoon is lighter and has less volume. Obviously this is mainly because the two spoons are designed for different needs: permanent 'quality' and disposable 'trash'. But take a close look at the second photo, at the back of the plastic teaspoon. The stainless steel teaspoon was cut out of a uniform thickness sheet and then formed to shape, but we can see that the plastic teaspoon has a much more complex geometry. In fact this shape is familiar from chapter 12, because it has been partially optimised. So a crucial difference between producing cutlery from plastic rather than metal is that plastic spoons are injection moulded, squeezed under pressure into a precise mould, allowing very precise control of complex geometry, while the metal spoon was stamped out of a sheet.

Next, take a look at our two family portraits—a diverse family of stainless steel teaspoons, and a diverse family of plastic ones. At the end of their lives, we can recycle all the metal teaspoons and make new ones without difficulty. But at the

Colourful families of teaspoons

end of life of the plastic ones, although they could each individually be recycled, they cannot be recycled together—because the colours (and possibly other 'filler' materials) in the different spoons are all different. In addition, if we had thrown them all into our normal waste bin, they would reach the waste management company mixed in with all other waste. While we have some good technologies to separate out the metals (we have to work harder with stainless steel because it is only weakly magnetic, but it's still possible), but it is much more difficult to separate the plastics in a cost effective manner. Finally, the stainless steel teaspoon is worth more money, so we're much more likely to look after it than the plastic teaspoon which is worth very little. Unfortunately this is also true for many uses of plastic, and small pieces of used plastic have very little monetary value.

We've now set up a rather difficult agenda for our survey of plastics: there are many different types of plastic, most of which can be recycled, but only if perfectly separated from other types; manufacturing with plastic allows us to make very intricate efficient shapes, so in contrast to what we saw with metals, we may not be able to redesign goods to use much less plastic; plastic tends to be discarded in small pieces in mixed waste streams, from which it cannot easily be separated, so post-consumer recycling rates are currently low.

To understand our options for creating a sustainable material future for plastics, we need to look carefully at the different types of plastic, survey current and future uses, explore the efficiency of existing production, and see if we have any options for future material efficiency.

Plastic materials and their production

'Plastics' describes a broad category of materials, the name derives from the Greek *plastikós* meaning 'able to be moulded'. There are two distinct families of plastics—thermoplastics, which can be melted and reformed several times, and thermosets, which cure irreversibly on being heated, mixed or irradiated, so cannot be recycled. Thermosets include the materials used to make electrical fittings, and those that bind composite materials such as glass or carbon fibre composites used to make boats. They are the smaller branch of the family, so we will limit our interest to the larger branch of thermoplastics.

The first thermoplastics were made from natural materials. In 1823, Charles Macintosh of Glasgow experimenting with naphtha, a by-product of natural tar (a resin produced from pine trees) found that it allowed him to join layers of rubber, and so create a waterproof coat—to which he gave his name. In 1845, Thomas Bewley, a Dubliner, set up the Gutta Percha company in London, following a suggestion from Macintosh's brother and a request from the electrical pioneer Michael Faraday, to exploit the properties of the natural latex derived from the sap of the South East Asian Gutta Percha tree. Having invented an extrusion machine to produce insulated electrical cables, they went on to use Gutta Percha to transform the golf ball and initiate root canal fillings in teeth. In 1856, Alexander Parkes from Birmingham patented his invention of 'Parkesine'—the first manufactured thermoplastic, derived from plant cellulose, which itself was a commercial failure, but later developed into celluloid and was the basis of Kodak's films. In 1907, Leo Hendrik Baekeland, made the first (thermosetting) plastic from phenol, a synthetic (i.e. non-natural) polymer, derived from coal tar, and called it Bakelite.

But plastics innovation and production really gathered pace after the first world war, once oil extraction was widely established, and the distillation of oil allowed production of ethylene. After the second world war, production of plastics expanded rapidly, and many new plastics such as polystyrene and polymethylmethacrylate (commonly, and for obvious reasons, known as PMMA) were developed. As the production processes improved, so did the properties of the plastic products they made, and because of their low cost, plastics were used widely. Since then, many new plastics have been developed for use in demanding applications such as healthcare.

Most plastics today are made from oil, but there are many different production routes, which create diverse plastics with their own chemical and physical structure. The main plastics in common use are:

- **PE (Polyethylene, high and low density):** this is the most common and versatile plastic. Its properties can be tailored to many different applications, the most common of which are packaging (e.g. plastic bags and films), bottles and children's toys. It is used in both low-density (LDPE—low density polyethylene) and high-density (HDPE—high density polyethylene) forms, as appropriate to the application. LDPE is used primarily in packaging and film, while HDPE is used for stronger, stiffer products, such as pipework.

- **PP (Polypropylene):** this plastic is tough and flexible, widely used in textiles, stationery, automotive components and also in packaging.

- **PS (Polystyrene):** the properties of polystyrene can be tailored to a number of a different uses. Expanded polystyrene is used as protective packaging, and is extremely light. However, polystyrene can also be moulded into teaspoons, plastic cups and CD cases, for example.

- **PVC (Polyvinylchloride):** PVC is both cheap and versatile. It is used in a wide variety of applications, from pipes and fittings to canoes and garden hoses.

- **ABS (Acrylonitrile butadiene styrene):** this plastic is very tough and easy to mould. It is commonly used for safety helmets, casings for machinery (e.g. power tools), and in children's toys, such as Lego™.

- **PMMA (Polymethylmethacrylate):** PMMA is particularly useful as a tough, transparent plastic. Its first major application was in the canopies of fighter aircraft in the Second World War. Today it is often found in safety spectacles and windows.

- **PA (Polyamide):** the most common use of this plastic is as Nylon, used in a wide variety of clothing. But this tough material is also used in car tires, nylon-fibre ropes, light duty gears and tubing.

- **PET (Polyethylene terephthalate):** this plastic can be processed for very demanding applications. In one of its most common uses as beverage can bottles, it must be strong enough to contain the pressurized liquid.

- **PUR (Polyurethane):** one of the most eye-catching uses of this stretchy material is in Lycra or Spandex. But it is also used in a stronger, stiffer form for gears, bearings and wheels.

The properties of each plastic arise from the chemistry of the different monomers used in their production, but some properties such as strength and stiffness can be influenced through the use of additives, fillers, heat treatment processes and mechanical deformation. Therefore a wide variety of different properties can be produced from a single type of thermoplastic. However, certain general properties explain the choice of particular plastics for certain applications. For example the presence of styrene in the monomer structure in ABS gives a glossy, shiny finish, which is popular for childrens' toys. PVC, PE, PP and PS all exhibit excellent chemical resistance, so PE and PP are used in packaging, and PVC in pipes where chemical corrosion may be a problem. Other key properties which are determined by the chemistry of the plastic include electrical and thermal resistance, resistance to weathering and resistance to humidity[1].

Thermoplastic production, summarised in Figure 21.1, begins with ordinary crude oil. The oil is first distilled to separate out its different components, some of which are treated in a process known as 'steam cracking'. In steam cracking, the oil distillate is mixed with steam and then heated in the absence of oxygen, to create smaller light molecules in the family of olefins, including ethylene and propylene. Olefins are a type of monomer, the fundamental building block from which plastics are made. We can use olefins directly, or we can use further processing to produce a wider range of monomers, such as vinyl chloride, where one of the hydrogen atoms in the ethylene molecule is replaced with a chlorine atom. These monomers are then polymerized, a process in which many copies of a monomer are joined into long chains, polymers, from which plastics are made.

The polymer chains are manufactured into 'resins', similar to the resin of a plant, which are the basic commodity of the plastics industry. These resins are subsequently processed into cylindrical pellets, which are supplied to product manufacturing companies. The pellets are melted and fed into a forming process,

Figure 21.1—**Process chain for thermoplastic production**

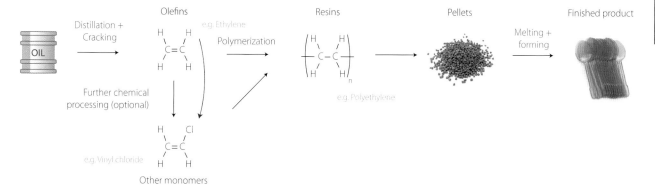

such as extrusion, to produce a finished product. Because the properties of the polymers are mainly determined by their chemistry, this last stage of production is entirely about geometry: so unlike metals, plastics can be formed directly and efficiently into finished shapes, with no need for any further processing. Unlike metals, the energy required to make plastics varies very little between different types, and is around 80 MJ/kg, and as plastics are usually made from oil, their emissions are also very similar at 2-3 kg CO_2/kg.

Our uses of plastic

Globally, current production of plastics is around 230 Mt per year, or around 33 kg per person per year averaged over the world. Of course the consumption of plastic isn't averaged uniformly, and in Europe, Japan or the US our consumption is around 120 kg per person year. We saw in chapter 2 that a family of five in the UK uses around 1 kg of plastic packaging per week to bring their food home from the supermarket, equivalent to 11 kg per person per year (of which around 1 kg was in the carrier bags.) So where's the rest of it?

The two pie charts of Figures 21.2 and 21.3 show the main uses of plastics in Europe and the US, dominated by packaging and uses in building and construction. The figure implies use of around 50 kg of plastic packaging per person per year, five times what we brought home from the supermarket, for other shopping, and all the packaging we didn't see as our goods were shipped into and around the UK prior to arriving in shops. 25 kg of plastics per person are used in building and construction to provide water supply and drainage, lighting, lightweight roofs, cladding and frames for windows, doors and decorative features, electrical trunking and cables, insulation, seals and gaskets.

And all this demand has essentially grown since the Second World War, and continues to grow rapidly. Figure 21.4 shows the history of global production of plastics from 1950 to the present, doubling every 15 years. The International Energy Agency forecasts that by 2050 global demand will be 470 Mt, one further doubling, which if anything seems conservative. Figure 21.5 shows growing demand per person in key regions, with no evidence of a plateau in developed economies, and strong growth, more than 6% per year, in Asia and Eastern Europe. If demand for plastics will double or more in the next 40 years, can we produce plastics four times more efficiently to halve total emissions?

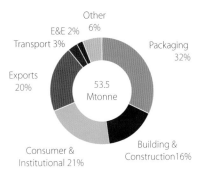

Figure 21.2—**Plastic product categories in Europe**

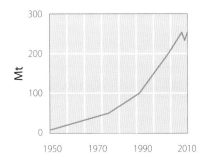

Figure 21.3—**Plastic product categories in the US**

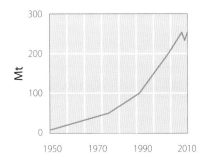

Figure 21.4—**Global growth in plastics demand since 1950**

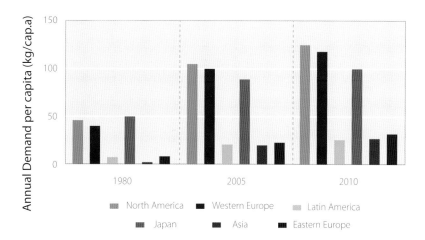

Figure 21.5—**Regional growth in demand for plastics since 1980**

Plastics with one eye open: can we make or recycle plastics more efficiently?

The International Energy Agency[2], in reporting on future energy efficiency options in the plastics industry, estimates that using more efficient steam cracking with higher temperature furnaces, gas turbine integration, advanced distillation columns and combined refrigeration plants could lead to a 15% saving in energy required per unit output of typical plastics. Further efficiency gains will be possible in downstream manufacturing operations as we saw in metals production, but these processes use much less energy than is required to convert oil to basic plastic pellets.

Just as we found in the steel and aluminium industries, there are few remaining opportunities for energy efficiency in plastics production. However, like metals and unlike cement, there is a recycling route for plastics: can we increase the rate of collecting plastics and can we then recycle them more efficiently?

Our opening story with teaspoons demonstrated the difficulty of plastics recycling is, in which different plastic types cannot be mixed. But in fact the story is even worse, because the great variety of additives (to change colours or properties) and fillers (cheaper materials such as chalk which increase strength and hardness) used in commercial plastics tend to degrade the properties of recycled mixed plastic. For a company manufacturing plastic products it is relatively straightforward to recycle plastic scrap generated during production, because the quality of the recycled material is known and it can be separated from other types of plastic. But once plastics have entered general waste streams, it is extremely difficult to separate them with sufficient precision.

Plastic scrap from manufacturing processes is already recycled at a very high rate, as it is automatically segregated without contamination, and can often be recycled back into the same machine that created the scrap. It is unlikely that rates of recycling in this part of the scrap stream can be increased. Therefore increased recycling of plastics depends on two developments: improved separation of plastics from other municipal waste, and improved sorting. Increasing recovery rates is difficult, as plastic waste is often fragmented and diverse. Sorting plastics is also challenging, particularly because many plastics have similar densities and optical characteristics.

Could we improve the recycling technologies themselves? There are four distinct classes of plastic recycling. Primary recycling in which material is directly re-extruded, is simplest, but only possible with a pure waste stream, and therefore only really suitable for recycling process scrap. In secondary (or mechanical) recycling, plastics are ground into small chips or powder, which is then washed, dried and

Plastic Recycling Labels

Plastic products carry labels to identify the type of plastic from which they are made, and indicate whether or not the product can be recycled.

PETE

HDPE

LDPE

PP

V

PS

OTHER

These plastics are widely recycled throughout the EU and the US

These plastic types are hard to recycle, so are sent to landfill or incinerated

Sustainable Materials with both eyes open

converted to resin for re-use at the beginning of the process. This route does not require such a pure scrap source, but contaminants will reduce the quality of the recycled material. In tertiary recycling the old plastic is broken down chemically to produce new feedstock which can be used either to make new plastics, or in other applications. This may occur, for example, in a process called pyrolysis in which unsorted plastic waste is heated in a furnace from which most oxygen has been excluded, to prevent combustion. Plastics recycling by pyrolysis is technically feasible, and has been demonstrated in pilot scale facilities, but to date the energy and financial cost of production has been prohibitively high.

Finally quaternary recycling (energy recovery) aims not to recycle the plastic for use, but to recover the energy embedded in it, through incineration. Burning plastic releases energy, and provided the incineration process is run efficiently so that harmful volatile organic compounds are not released, it is a better option than dumping the plastic waste in landfill. The calorific value (stored energy) of plastic is similar to that of fuel oil, so it can provide a valuable source of energy if burnt in appropriate conditions.

A biodegradable bioplastic bag

Sugar cane—a key feedstock for bioplastics production

Are there any novel technologies that might transform the production of plastics? In the route from oil to plastic, this is unlikely but the area which attracts more attention is the production of plastics from plants, by exact analogy with the production of 'bio-fuel' for energy that we briefly discussed in chapter 9. As we saw earlier in this chapter, the production process for plastic begins with the production of olefins from crude oil. But in fact, one of the most common olefins, ethylene, can be produced from plants such as sugar cane. This bio-ethylene can be used to produce polyethylene which is identical to that produced from crude oil. Bioplastics can also be produced from other plants, and unlike plastics made from crude-oil, can biodegrade. As well as conserving oil supplies, production of bioplastics uses less energy then plastics derived from crude oil. However, just as we saw in considering biofuel earlier, production of plants to make bioplastics requires land, which therefore cannot simultaneously be used to grow food.

So, with one eye open, we've identified a potential 15% cut in energy required per tonne of plastic produced, and two other major possibilities: converting waste plastic back to oil and supplying bio-plastics instead of oil-plastic. The first of these is not yet operating at scale, and the second will be constrained by pressure on land-use. It is therefore very unlikely that we can reach our target 50% absolute cut in emissions for plastics with one eye open. In fact, the most aggressive (i.e. least emitting) forecast constructed by the International Energy Agency assumes emissions from plastics production will more than double from 2005 to 2050, unless CCS is applied both to electricity generation and all other fuel combustion associated with plastic production. We clearly need to look also for options with both eyes open.

Plastics with both eyes open: can we deliver plastic services with less new material?

In our opening foray into the world of teaspoons, we saw that plastic products can already be optimised, because they can fill complex moulds effectively, as part of normal injection moulding processes. Production of plastic parts leads to few yield losses: for example injection moulding is a net shape process, with losses only on the 'runners' through which plastic enters the mould, and with more advanced processing (runnerless moulding), can have no losses at all. So the first two of our strategies from looking at metal with both eyes open offer little benefit, and as the process generates little scrap, there is not much of that to divert, which rules out the approach of chapter 14 also. Our hope for reducing demand for new plastic then relies on keeping products for longer, re-using them at end of life, or of course, on reducing overall demand.

Used PET bottles

If we concentrate on packaging, we've established that in the UK we probably take around 10–20 kg of plastic packaging per person into our houses each year, yet we cause 50 kg of plastic packaging to be made. So approximately 30 kg of plastic packaging per person is required to move goods from factory to factory or shop. This industrial packaging is hidden from our consumer eyes, so unlike consumer packaging, exists solely to protect goods in transit. This industrial packaging is an excellent target for life extension through re-use. Although it has a relatively low monetary value, industrial packaging accounts for around a quarter of all plastic consumption in the UK, so re-use could have a significant impact.

In construction, plastic pipes rarely fail, so ensuring long life and re-use should be feasible—although again, with a low economic value, there is little incentive to dismantle and re-sell old pipe. The difficulty in looking for opportunities to reuse or extend the life of plastic products is that it is cheap and versatile, so used in a plethora of low-value applications. However, a large fraction of plastic use is to make components for use in complex products such as cars. Extending the life of these products, which will also reduce demand for other materials, will help to reduce demand for new plastic production.

If we can't find enough opportunities for re-use and life extension, we must then examine demand reduction. For example, we know we could live with less disposable packaging, because it is a relatively recent invention. This is not a strategy that will be pursued by the plastics industry, but in the absence of other options for emissions saving, demand reduction may be the key policy requirement for cutting emissions in plastics production. At the start of chapter 2, when we looked at domestic plastic waste, we saw that we each use about 1 kg of plastic supermarket bags per year, but more like 7 kg of plastic bottles. So the next time the Prime Minister wants to identify opportunities for saving plastic, we suggest the focus should be on bottles and not bags.

Outlook

Plastics are the most complicated material family of the five we are considering in this book. In our survey of options for change, we have not found enough options to make a 50% cut in emissions while demand doubles. We have four positive suggestions out of the chapter:

- To reduce the variety of plastics in use to simplify recycling and increase recovery rates.

- In recognising the energy benefit of combusting plastic for energy, to work intensively on generating fuel oil from used plastic.

- To replace all possible disposable packaging with long life packaging in continuous re-use and to extend the life of all non-disposable plastic goods.

- To promote life extension for other products, including vehicles, which contain many plastic components, as a part of a general strategy for reducing demand for new materials.

This has been a tough journey, although we've found a few good opportunities to explore, so it's time for another cup of tea.

Notes

Plastic materials and their production

1. Further information on the properties of plastic can be found in Callister (2003).

Plastics with one eye open: can we make or recycle plastics more efficiently?

2. The details of the IEA scenario analysis can be found in their Energy Technology Perspectives report, IEA (2008a)

22 Paper

Paper is a natural product—closely related to trees—so its energy and emissions impact can be surprising: energy is mainly needed to convert trees to a lignin free wet pulp, and then after papermaking to remove excess water by evaporation. Are there other efficiency options, or can we reduce demand for paper?

The British spend their time swapping wordplay jokes that no one understands, hopping on and off red buses, making calls from red telephone boxes, posting their letters in red pillar boxes, and eating their chips from read newspapers. It's the newspapers that concern us here—although of course, Belgian bureaucrats have stopped our material efficiency strategy of eating chips from used newspapers in case the pungent prose in the print is infectious. Presumably now that newspaper sales are slumping, due to the fall in demand for re-use in catering and the rise of electronic alternatives, we'll soon be eating our chips off used eReaders as everybody who bought one last year has to upgrade to this year's eReaders 1.01. After that someone will have to deal with all the chips in the eReaders...

In applying our story to paper, we need to know who's using it, what for, and whether the recent decline of newspaper sales in Europe and the US tells us anything about demand for paper overall. We need to find out what's driving energy use and emissions in making paper, and then we can look at options such as eReaders which might allow us to live well with less paper.

The properties, uses and production of paper

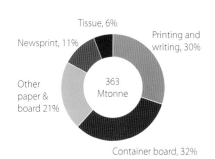

Figure 22.1—**Final uses of paper in 2005**

We'll start with current uses of paper. The pie chart[1] in Figure 22.1 shows that the largest categories of use are container board (corrugated cardboard used in boxes and shipping containers), printing and writing paper (including uncoated papers used in photocopiers, laser printers and books, and coated papers employed in magazines and brochures), newsprint and other types of paper and board employed in packaging. The quality of paper is determined by its optical properties (colour, brightness, whiteness, opacity), resistance to light and ageing, moisture content and 'printability' (smoothness, ink absorption, curl and friction) when used for printing, and by its strength and stiffness when used for packaging, among many other properties.

Figure 22.2—**Magnified picture of conventional office paper**

A paperless office?

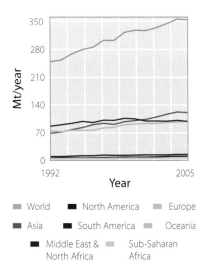

Figure 22.3—**History of paper demand from 1992–2005**

Figure 22.2 shows a sample of conventional office paper in which you can see intertwined wood fibres covered by fillers such as clays and sizing agents. Older papers were made from cotton fibre, or other textiles, while most contemporary paper is made from wood, particularly softwood from conifers (e.g. pine) and hardwood from broad-leafed species (e.g. oak). However, any source of fibre can be used to make paper—and we have samples made from bamboo, hemp, abacá, grasses and even elephant dung (a favourite in the 9 year old boys market segment). To create a smooth surface for printing and to improve optical properties and printability, paper is often 'filled' with kaolin clay, calcium carbonate, titanium dioxide, silica or talc. The strength of the paper is generally determined by the length and origin of the wood fibres (softwood length of 3-7 mm adds strength while hardwood length of 1–2 mm adds bulk and thickness). Cardboard is generally brown because it is mainly made out of unbleached brown wood fibres. Papers for magazines and brochures are coated, generally with kaolin clay and calcium carbonate in order to improve gloss and whiteness. Tissue paper has special strength, water absorbency, appearance and comfort characteristic achieved by controlling pulp quality and additives.

In 1981, when one of the first modern workstation computers known as the Xerox Star was designed to replicate some aspects of paper use, the idea of the 'Paperless Office' was born—and the death of paper has been predicted ever since. In fact the reality has been very different, and to date our enthusiasm for paper has only increased: having a printer in every home, we use more and more paper, as we urgently share important prose and images with each other. Figure 22.3 shows the global history of paper demand from 1992 until 2005[2], with demand broken down by major region. In parallel, Figure 22.4 shows consumption of paper against gross domestic product (GDP) per person in 1995 and 2007 for selected countries[3]. These two images show that demand for paper has steadily grown, with the only modest decline in consumption being in North America, specifically in the US since the last presidential election, mainly due to declining newspaper sales (presumably because there is less need to discuss the behaviour and characteristics of President Bush). Despite this small decline and slow European growth, global demand has increased considerably as a result of high demand growth in Asia. Consumption of paper in Belgium is significantly higher per person than elsewhere in Europe (due to a national commitment to writing annoying directives on chip wrappings and other subversive national traditions), and Figure 22.4 shows that there is some link between wealth and paper consumption. Although growth rates in developed countries vary, their consumption per person is much higher than that observed in developing countries such as China, Brazil and Indonesia. Both

Sustainable Materials with both eyes open

Trees on their way to paper making

figures also show that the paperless office has remained a dream—with economic growth comes demand for more paper.

Although we could make paper from almost any source of fibre, in reality we use trees. Trees and trees and trees, that is. A typical oak tree weighs approximately a quarter of a tonne when chopped down (dry mass)[4]. If it is destined for paper making, the limbs are removed and the trunk is driven to the pulping mill. On average, 24 trees are required to make a tonne of printing and writing paper[5], so the paper consumption of 110 million tonnes of printing and writing paper reported in 2005 required around 2.6 billion (thousand million) trees. Planted at a density of 100,000 trees per square kilometre[6], that requires an annual harvest of 26,400 square kilometres of trees—just less than the total area of Belgium. However, this is for printing and writing paper only. If we assume that all 363 Mt of paper consumed in 2005 was of this type of paper, we would have required nearly 3 Belgiums. Oak trees are usually at least 20 years old when lopped, so in total, at a rate of 3 Belgiums per year, we would cut down 60 Belgiums before the first oak harvest recovers, and this is roughly 1.2% of earth's land area. Paper making requires a lot of trees and a lot of land.

Converting a tree into paper has two main steps. Firstly we need to break down the structure of the tree to extract the cellulose fibres we want to use. In a living tree, cellulose fibres, which are strong in tension, are bound together by lignin, an organic polymer that resists compression. Paper can be manufactured with or without lignin depending on the pulping process used. In mechanical pulping, cellulose fibres are extracted from the wood by pressing and grinding. Paper made in this way is weak and discolours easily when exposed to light due to its high residual lignin content. A stronger paper less prone to discolouration is produced by chemical pulping. In this process the cellulose fibres are extracted and converted into pulp by dissolving the lignin with a chemical/water solution in a high pressure steam cooker. The resulting mass, containing a mix of pulp and black liquor (liquid residues of chemicals and dissolved lignin) is sent for pulp washing where the pulp is separated. The pulp is in some cases dried and transported—high-tree countries like Finland sensibly want to capture the most possible value from their tree harvest, so supply dried pulp to low-tree countries, such as the UK, for rehydrating and paper making. (In fact, in the UK, although we harvest approximately 9 million tonnes of roundwood each year mainly in Scotland, we also import roughly 8.5 million tonnes of pulp and paper[7]). The second stage of the process begins with this pulp, by now relatively pure cellulose fibres in water, mixes into it the fillers and other additives needed to create required properties and then 'lays' the pulp onto a fine mesh. This miraculous process is well worth

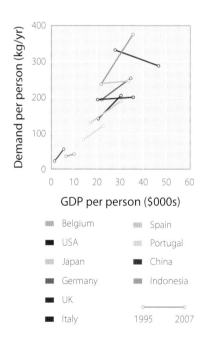

Figure 22.4—**Paper demand vs. GDP per person, 1995-2007**

Wet end of a paper making machine

Dry end of a paper making machine

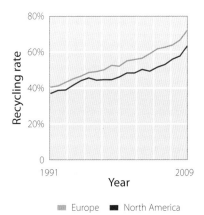

Figure 22.5—**Paper recycling rates in the USA and the EU**

watching if you ever have the chance to visit a paper mill: what appears to be a milky fluid pours onto a moving conveyor of fine mesh; the water drains through and may be squeezed out with a roller, to the point that a wet fibrous sheet can be transferred from the mesh to a hot roller. The remainder of the process is to evaporate excess water from this wet sheet. This must be well controlled so that the moisture content is uniform across the paper, and is achieved by winding the continuous feed of wet paper over a long chain of hot rollers. Eventually a huge roll of paper is wound up, and may then be coated before being cut to final sizes.

Paper recycling is of course widely practised, and we get better at it each year. Figure 22.5 shows estimates of recycling rates in the United States and European Union[8], showing that in the bigger paper-using countries (the richer ones) recycling rates are around 63-73% and improving steadily. When we throw our old newspapers and book drafts into the recycling bin, they're collected into bales, and then sent to a 'pulper' containing water and chemicals. Here, the paper is cut into small pieces and the mixture is heated to help separate the cellulose fibres and form the pulp. The slushy mixture of pulp is then forced through screens with holes of different sizes and shapes to remove contaminants such as glues or other alien materials. Generally the quality of pulp made from recycled papers is lower than that of virgin pulp, because the fibres have been shortened in the recycling process and may have been weakened. Recycling of coated papers is more difficult due to the layer of polymer covering the fibres. Heavy contaminants such as staples are removed from recycled pulp by spinning inside conical cylinders. Glue, old print and adhesives are removed by de-inking in which air and surfactant chemicals are injected into the pulp so that ink particles separate from the pulp and attach to air bubbles which can be removed easily from the mix. The pulp is squeezed dry and residual water is commonly reused.

Energy and emissions in paper making

We have of course created a Sankey diagram[9] to show the global flow of materials through the paper production process to final products, and the diagram also shows current energy requirements per unit of production for the main processes. Making a tonne of paper from recycled old paper uses between 18.7–20.7 GJ while making it from trees requires 15.3–36 GJ, depending on the manufacturing processes used. However, converting this diagram into one showing emissions is difficult—for several reasons in addition to the usual ones related to data availability, not knowing the range between average and best practice, and

Sustainable Materials with both eyes open

understanding the mix of fuels used in generating grid electricity. For paper, our additional challenges are:

- Plant scientists do not yet know the net emissions effects of planting, growing and harvesting a tree, due to the complex effects of soil disruption.

- A substantial fraction of the energy used in paper making, particularly from primary wood, is generated by burning the trimmings from the trees, and the 'black liquor' which is the by-product of pulping.

- Because recycling shortens the fibres, most recycled paper actually has a reasonable fraction of virgin paper to increase its strength or smoothness.

We've therefore found a wide range of estimates for carbon emissions in paper making. Making a tonne of conventional office paper from trees leads to emission of around 0.7–1.2 tonnes of CO_2/tonne of paper, while using recycled pulp, this figure changes to 0.6–0.7 tonnes of CO_2/tonne of paper. However, it is quite possible that some recycled paper has actually led to more emissions than paper from trees—because of the use of biomass (which over its whole cycle does not emit significant CO_2 emissions) in generating energy for primary processes.

Figure 22.6—**Sankey diagram of paper production**

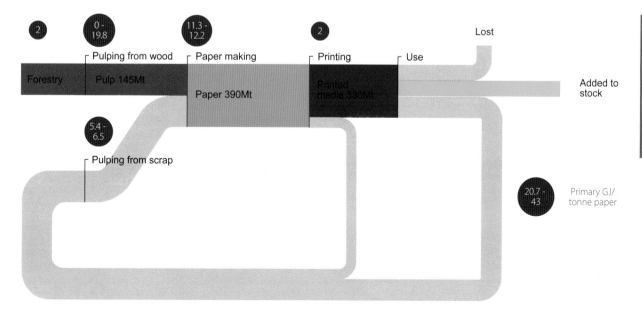

Paper with one eye open

Figure 22.7[10] shows that fuel and electricity purchases accounts for around 11% and 7% of the costs of making paper respectively so, naturally, the pulp and paper industry is highly motivated to adopt every possible energy efficiency measure. Their achievement is clear in Figure 22.8[11]—showing that energy inputs per tonne of paper have improved year on year, but as we have seen with all materials, they appear to be approaching an asymptote. The key steps taken to achieve recent improvements have been the application of bio-refineries to produce fuels, chemicals, power and materials from biomass, adoption of best available technology and the development of new technologies such as black liquor gasification (to produce gas from spent pulping liquor for use in boilers) and new drying technologies (that increase the drying rate). As with all our analysis, don't know to what extent further improvements are possible by raising average to best practice, but assume some improvement remains.

The other strategies being pursued in the industry are to increase the use of biofuel, to pursue CCS, to make better use of waste heat from the process, to produce on-site electricity and heat by combined heat and power (CHP) generation, and to improve the recycling loop.

Primary paper making already makes good use of the biomass from its own waste products and in Europe we have estimates that up to 54% of energy requirements for paper making from pulp are provided in this way[12]. This biomass is combusted to generate heat or electricity. Further substitution of biomass for other fuel forms however raises the same problem we have identified before: it takes a lot of land to create enough biomass to replace fossil fuels. So given other competition for land, it seems this will only make a small contribution. Direct fossil fuel combustion in papermaking is used to provide other energy, so the two candidates for pursuing CCS are to use it directly with furnace exhausts, and to purchase electricity from sources with CCS attached. Given the doubts we've already expressed about CCS, and as the paper industry is not making a significant push in this direction, this doesn't seem a priority.

However, the paper industry has made significant efforts to combine their generation of heat and power. The logic of so-called combined heat and power (CHP) generation is that gas or coal fired power stations create significant waste heat while generating electricity, so potentially the heat could be used as well as the electricity. Potentially this approach applies well in paper making, as most heat is required to cause evaporation in the paper drying process—say at 150–200°C,

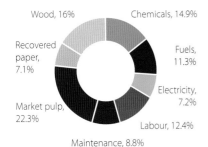

Wood, 16%
Chemicals, 14.9%
Recovered paper, 7.1%
Fuels, 11.3%
Electricity, 7.2%
Market pulp, 22.3%
Labour, 12.4%
Maintenance, 8.8%

Figure 22.7—**Costs in paper making in Europe, 2006**

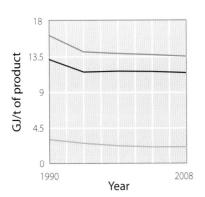

- Total specific primary energy consumption
- Specific fuel consumption
- Specific net bought electricity

Figure 22.8—**History of energy consumption in paper making**

Sustainable Materials with both eyes open

and this is a relatively low temperature compared to the waste heat released by power stations (typically up to 540°C for some condensing power plants) so there's a good match between supply and demand.

Improving the recycling loop for paper has three objectives: increasing the rate of waste paper collection (i.e. avoiding the loss of paper to landfill or incineration); using less energy to pulp recycled paper; improving the yield of recycled pulp by improving the separation of ink and other contaminants from the used paper. The earlier graph on recycling rates showed that we are generally improving collection rates worldwide, but there is a limit: tissue and sanitary paper obviously cannot be recycled, and some paper is kept in archives; 80% recycling rates appear a realistic limit[11]. The yield of recycling, currently limited by paper fibre shortening and the difficulty of separating clean fibres from contaminants, could be improved by replacing the caustic chemicals used in de-inking with less damaging materials and by the design and adoption of inks and adhesives that could be removed more easily.

A survey of forecasts on future paper-making shows that paper demand may be 2.4 times greater by 2050 than in 2008, and over this period it might be possible for the paper industry to reduce its emissions by 40% per unit output if all best practices are applied[12]. This is an incredible reduction but not enough to reach our 50% absolute reduction target by 2050.

Paper with both eyes open

In a crisis we could give up a lot of paper use easily and with little inconvenience: we could rapidly switch from purchasing individual copies of magazines, newspapers and books, to shared use; we know that we could live with less packaging. However, our exploration about a future with both eyes open, aims to look for ways to continue to deliver the services we obtain from paper, while using less of it. We've found four examples of material efficiency for paper: using lighter paper; printing on demand; removing print to allow paper re-use; substituting e-readers for paper. Let's take a look at each in turn.

Most of the paper we use in computer printers and photocopiers has a weight of 80 grams per square metre. This gives it a satisfyingly stiff feel when we turn pages, and is sufficiently opaque that printing on both sides does not create interference. Could we manage with 72 grams per square metre? It's easy to find out: you can purchase 70 gsm paper for use at home, and as far as we can tell it has the same function as 80 gsm, albeit a little less stiff. So, are confident that, if we wanted to, we could save at least 10% of global demand for office paper with lighter weight selection and presumably we could approach that figure in other applications.

A problem for newspaper suppliers is that we buy them in physical form, and if we can't find a particular brand on a particular day, will rapidly switch to an alternative. Despite this, each newspaper lasts for only one day, and then has no value. So the newspaper business must always print too many copies of each day's paper because the commercial risk of running out is far greater than the cost of printing an excess. The same is true of books sold in shops. This over-print is collected and recycled, but that as we've seen has an energy cost. So the idea of 'print on demand' has been around for many years with the hope that we can avoid the excess by printing rapidly whatever the customer really wants. The technology exists for us to do this, even for bound books, but we haven't yet adopted the practice. There are a few possible reasons for this: print-on-demand books are normally slightly more expensive, they have a reputation for lower print quality and readers may be unfamiliar with print-on-demand brands.

In chapter 15 we looked at the opportunity to re-use steel sections in construction without melting them—so how about paper? Most of the paper we discard in offices is undamaged and we discard it only because we don't want to read what's written on it. We were struck by this possibility some time ago, so both Tom Counsell and David Leal have studied for their PhDs in our lab to see if we could find a way to "un-print" used paper[13]. Can we design a front end to a photocopier that would take in yesterday's discarded printing, and clean off the print so that we can then put on today's print? We decided early on to limit ourselves to existing conventional uncoated paper and conventional toner because it would be harder to introduce a system that required either of those to change. We initially examined three options for toner removal:

- rubbing it off with sandpaper worked well, particularly with fine paper moving at high speed across the paper and under light pressure, but although we could remove the print, we couldn't avoid thinning the paper also;

- we found a range of chemical solvents that would remove the toner without damaging the paper, but the safety requirements for the solvents were demanding, and we couldn't imagine installing this approach in an office;

- laser ablation worked to some extent, and removed the print, but the paper under the old print was discoloured in the process, and could still be read.

Sustainable Materials with both eyes open

We've now focused on this last approach, and after searching through a wide range of possible laser settings, can now remove the print effectively and leave the paper undamaged. We're rather proud of this work, so have put a box story below with more detail: potentially using laser ablation to remove print looks like a route that might save some paper in future.

Finally, aren't we about to abandon paper altogether and instead read books, magazines, newspapers and all other documents on electronic screens? This is back to the dream of the paperless office, but has apparently become more of a reality as portable computer screens become lighter and better, light emitting polymers enter the market, and hand-held speciality readers take off. We don't know the answer: sceptics tell us that people buy a new electronic device in addition to all the paper they buy anyway, while enthusiasts tell us that the dip in US paper consumption in Figure 22.3 is not after all because of President Bush's departure, but because of eReaders gaining strength. However, we can look at two aspects of the question: are newspaper sales being affected by e-readers, and what are the environmental consequences of substituting e-readers for newspapers?

Unphotocopying

Unfortunately, designers of toner-print are very good at their job: toner adheres to paper so strongly that it is easier just to get rid of the used sheets of paper than reuse them.

The toner used in typical black and white office printers is a composite material formed by a polymer and a black pigment, commonly a polyester resin and iron oxide respectively. Just like any other opaque material, black toner-print absorbs light, particularly visible light, and specifically, it absorbs more than 95% of green light. If a concentrated green laser beam is fired onto toner, it will raise the temperature. The polymer in the toner will melt, or if the temperature is increased further it will evaporate, detaching the rest of the toner components from the paper. If at the same time the laser energy can be chosen below the ablation or evaporation threshold of paper, paper can be cleaned and re-used instead of being recycled or buried in landfill. We have found that this is possible by using very short pulses (less than a few nanoseconds long) of concentrated green laser light and can remove text from paper without causing any apparent damage to the paper under the print.

The image shows a highly magnified picture of a trial in which we ablated a square in an area of continuous black print. In comparison with Figure 22.2, the revealed paper is close to its original condition.

Toner print layer

Paper area where toner has been removed

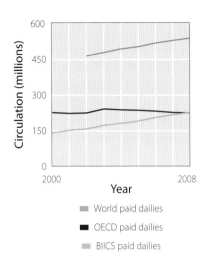

Figure 22.9—**Circulation of newspapers in OECD and developing countries (Brazil, India, Indonesia, China and South Africa)**

Newspaper sales in developed economies are declining. Figure 22.9[14] shows that sales are growing rapidly in developing nations such as Brazil, India, Indonesia, China and South Africa (BIICS), as economic development expands the number of potential buyers. But in OECD member nations such as the US and other European countries, newspapers sales are declining. In parallel, Figure 22.10 shows that the number of people reading newspapers online has grown rapidly[15], so it seems possible that the decline in physical newspaper sales is indeed driven by a substitution of electronic screens for paper (and not just a paucity of factual content as you might suspect). We have not yet seen figures that give evidence about whether electronic reading is changing book print runs.

We have a pretty clear answer to our first question, but unfortunately the second is much more difficult. Comparing the environmental impact of buying books or newspapers as opposed to reading on a screen depends so strongly on your assumptions, that you can easily create any answer you like: how much paper is saved by the electronic screen? How many aspects of the production and disposal of either the screen or the printed paper can be accounted for meaningfully? How do you compare the different environmental impacts of a micro-electronics and paper? All these questions are unanswerable, so although we've found many studies on this topic, we're unsatisfied by their conclusions. Over time, we'll find an answer to the question by watching what happens to paper demand and demand for screens at some meaningful geographical scale—say that of a country. Until that happens, the comparison is theoretical only. However, we can make a few important observations on what happens to electronic waste, at the end of its life. We've seen that paper recycling is effective, and rates are growing. Unfortunately, electronics recycling is not effective, and ought to be a national scandal in developed countries. Recent EU legislation on the take-

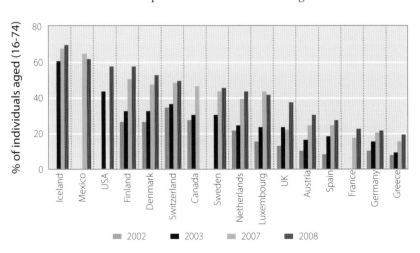

Figure 22.10—**Trends in readership of online newspapers**

Electronics recycling in India[18]

back of electronic goods has reduced the flow of electronic waste to landfill in the EU, but places no burden on manufacturers to deal with their own waste—it is estimated that only one-third of e-waste is treated in line with the EU Waste Electrical and Electronic Equipment (WEEE) directive[15]. Some of the rest is illegally exported to Africa and Asia. In India, some of the poorest people in the country purchase an open bucket of sulphuric acid, and use it in their main living room to extract precious metals from electronic waste. When the acid has lost its strength, it is simply dumped along with the other unwanted material in open ground nearby. The photo is a sombre reminder of this consequence of our enthusiasm for replacing electronic gadgets so frequently, and is unnecessary when companies such as Umicore[16] have the technology to process WEEE safely near to the original point of discard.

So the jury's out on electronic screens replacing paper—we simply don't know if any substitution is really happening, and can't work out the environmental consequences until a measurable shift in national statistics occurs. However, we have seen that we can reduce total paper production without loss of service whether by light-weight paper, print on demand, or un-printing, and let's not forget our great and undervalued libraries as a perfect opportunity for extending the useful life and increasing the service intensity of printed paper.

Outlook

Paper production is already energy efficient, and recycling already operates well but could get better. There are some opportunities to improve efficiency, and there are opportunities for supplying the same service with less total paper production. How does all that add up?

Global paper demand is around 390 million tonnes per year[11] and a survey of forecasts[17] anticipates that demand will have grown by 164% by 2050 compared to 2005. Our survey of potential carbon emissions reduction suggests we might save 40% of emissions per unit of output if we increase global recycling rates to 81%, and apply all possible energy efficiency best practices for the production and recycling of paper and pulp. With demand growing, this isn't enough to reach our target of a 50% absolute cut in emissions. So using less paper through material efficiency or demand reduction is an inevitable requirement for meeting the target, and we've got some exciting opportunities to go and pursue it. We could even make a start by eating our fish chips out of used European Directives!

Notes

The properties, uses and production of paper

1. Forecasts conducted by the RISI (2007).

2. Based on data from the Food and Agriculture Organization of the United Nations (FAO), 2007.

3. Elaborated with data from EIPPCB (2010).

4. Estimated with data from the Technical Association of the Pulp and Paper Industry (TAPPI)—http://www.tappi.org/paperu/all_about_paper/earth_answers/earthAnswers.htm

5. Thompson (1992) refers to a calculation that, based on a mixture of softwoods and hardwoods 40 feet tall and 6-8 inches in diameter, it would take a rough average of 24 trees to produce a ton of printing and writing paper, using the kraft chemical (freesheet) pulping process".

6. Recommended oak planting density across the state of Illinois in the US: 108,000-135,000 trees/km^2.

7. Based on statistics from the forestry commission (2011).

8. Data from American Forest and Paper Association, 2010 and Confederation of European Paper Industries (CEPI), Key Statistics, 2009.

Energy and emissions in paper making

9. Elaborated with data from Paper Task Force (1995), Hekkert, M.P., E. Worrel, 1997, Nilsson et al. (1995), de Beer (1998), Ahmadi et al. (2003).

Paper with one eye open

10. EIPPCB (2010). Reference Document on Best Available Techniques in the Pulp and Paper Industry. European Integrated Pollution Prevention and Control Bureau, Institute for Prospective Technological Studies, European Commission's Joint Research Centre, Seville, Spain.

11. Confederation of European Paper Industries (CEPI), Key Statistics, 2009.

12. Forecast figures from IEA (2008) and Martin et al. (2000).

Paper with both eyes open

13. Key articles on Paper Un-printing: Counsell and Allwood (2006) review 104 patents filed mainly since the mid 1990s that propose technologies to recycle office paper within the office, without destroying the mechanical structure of the paper. Counsell and Allwood (2007) consider how to reduce emissions from cut-size office paper by bypassing stages in its life cycle. The options considered are: incineration, localisation, annual fibre, fibre recycling, un-printing and electronic-paper. Counsell and Allwood (2008) present a feasibility study on the use of an abrasive process to remove toner-print used in laser-printers and photocopiers. Counsell and Allwood (2009) report on experiments that investigate the use of solvents to allow black toner print to be removed from white cut-size office paper. Leal-Ayala et al. (2010). In this article, lasers in the ultraviolet, visible and infrared light spectrums working with pulse widths in the nanosecond range are applied on a range of toner-paper combinations to determine their ability to remove toner. Leal-Ayala et al. (2011) analyse the applicability of ultrafast and long-pulsed ultraviolet, visible and infrared lasers for toner removal. Current work is focused on performing a feasibility study comparing the quality of all proposed solutions, their environmental implications, economical feasibility and commercial potential.

14. Based on research into the evolution of news and the internet (OECD, 2010).

15. As reported by BBC News (Lewis, 2010).

16. Umicore operates an integrated smelter and refinery which is capable of recovering 17 metals (Au, Ag, Pd, Pt, Rh, Ir, Ru, Cu, Pb, Ni, Sn, Bi, In, Se, Te, Sb and As) from distinct e-waste products such as printed circuit boards, ceramic capacitors, integrated circuits and other components contained in small electronic devices such as mobile phones, digital cameras and MP3 players. More info can be obtained from Hagelüken (2006).

Outlook

17. The IEA (2008a) estimate that primary and recycled paper and board production in 2050 will increase by 2.49 times to an overall consumption of 950 Mt (p.503, 164% increase from 2005). This projection is considerably higher than previous IEA projections, where the potential gains from the digital economy and tighter waste policy were overestimated.

Images

18. Photo by Empa

creating a sustainable
material future

PART V

23. Business activity evaluation

Throughout the book we've attempted to examine the business case for each option for change—through some theory and some case studies. In this chapter we'll draw together the lessons we've learnt from this.

24. The influence of policy

Policy makers in many countries recognise the need for action to respond to environmental concerns, but are hampered in their responses by the need to remain popular at the next election. What can they in reality do that would help?

25. The actions of individuals

Sustainability always involves dialogue between the trinity of business, government and individuals (as voters and consumers). So what's the role of individuals in bringing about material efficiency?

23 Business activity evaluation

Throughout the book we've attempted to examine the business case for each option for change—through some theory and some case studies. In this chapter we'll draw together the lessons we've learnt from this.

Our starting motivation in this book has been to find enough options to meet the emissions target we've set into law, and in the scenarios of chapter 19, unlike those in chapter 11, it appears that we do indeed now have enough options. However, in chapter 7 we found that the steel and aluminium industries are already extremely efficient because they pay heavily for energy, so have always had a strong commercial motivation towards using less. In Part IV when we looked at cement, plastic and paper, we found a similar story: all three industries have achieved remarkable energy efficiency already, simply driven by normal commercial concern. So, if we've identified in Part III that there are many options for using less material to deliver the same service, and if materials cost money, why hasn't similar commercial pressure motivated similar efficiency? If no one is investing in material efficiency does that mean that there's no demand for it? We will use this chapter to collect and examine all the issues we identified in case studies throughout the book that explain why companies are not taking up these opportunities. In each case we'll outline the concerns and discuss how they might be addressed.

Problem: the potential cost savings are relatively small

In chapter 6 we found that only a small part of the price of any final product was spent on steel and aluminium, typically 4 to 6%. This small fraction includes indirect demand for steel, for example the steel that goes into trucks used to transport the final product, but excludes any value added to steel inputs, for example through fabrication and assembly. We can estimate that this fraction is in effect equal to the maximum savings we might achieve from yield improvement and designing with less metal.

In demonstrating the relative insignificance of metals purchasing to the total cost of a finished product, we've been looking at the price paid by the final consumer. However, because production chains for products containing metal are typically rather long, the same metal is purchased and sold several times before reaching the final owner. For example, a steel company might sell its products to a stockholder. The stockholder might sell metal to a component manufacturer, who in turn might sell it to a sub-component assembler, and so on. For these earlier purchasers, metal purchasing costs are inevitably a higher fraction of their own sales income.

Figure 23.1 shows data for the sequence of companies adding value to metal in the automotive sector and shows the relative significance of steel purchasing to three companies along the chain: the fabricator, the manufacturer and the consumer. The graph shows that the relative importance of steel purchasing is different for each of the three companies. Metal costs are indeed a small fraction of the final price paid by the consumer, are a larger share for the manufacturer and are a significant share for the fabricator.

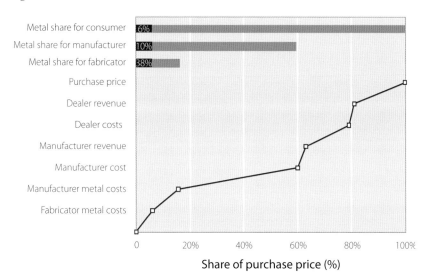

Figure 23.1—**Value added in automotive production**

So why are upstream component suppliers not taking every opportunity to save metal when it forms a substantial share of their costs? The answer inevitably is that using less material incurs other costs, such as higher labour costs, higher tooling costs, or higher costs for higher performance materials. In the UK, if we assume that half of us are currently earning, so divide our GDP by half our population, we have an average income of £50,000 per person per year, or around £30 per hour. Steel sections currently cost around £400 per tonne and aluminium ingots around £1,400 per tonne so one hour of UK labour has the same value as 75 kg of steel or 20 kg of aluminium[1]. If companies are to be motivated to pursue the material efficiency options that we found in Part III of the book, they will want

Sustainable Materials with both eyes open

to save more than 75 kg of steel or 20 kg of aluminium every time they pay for an extra hour of labour.

Solution: Governments could act to stimulate demand for material efficiency, not because of its cost savings but because of its emission savings, in the hope that their stimulus will lead to future reductions in the cost of material efficiency and so release value to both consumers and producers. Developments in equipment and other technologies may allow companies to benefit from material savings with lower additional labour costs, and of course, final consumers can stimulate demand for materially efficient goods through purchasing choices.

Problem: standardisation and optimisation are at loggerheads

Both the steel and the aluminium industry operate at scale: a modern integrated steel plant will easily manufacture more than 1 million tonnes per year and aluminium smelters are approaching 300,000 tonnes per year. By delivering standardised, high volume products, the industries can reap economies of scale in production, handling, storage and transport[2]. However, a consequence of this standardised high volume production is that the efficiency is dedicated to making standard stock products that, as we have seen, are the wrong shape.

Downstream companies can also benefit from economies of scale: producing cars at scale can save a quarter of fabrication costs[3]; in chapter 12 we described the practice of "rationalisation" in the construction sector by which contractors reduce their purchase costs and reduce the difficulty of organising the production site, by substituting standard beams for those originally specified.

However, eventually standardisation reaches a limit, as Henry Ford famously learnt, when his Model T Ford was outclassed by competitors. Consumers have different needs so will pay more for products that serve their particular needs than for standard goods. Steel and aluminium producers, competing in a tough market with standard geometries and composition, have developed an ever wider range of niche alloys to try to gain a competitive advantage[4] but aren't yet applying this competitive instinct to geometries. Producing specialised metal goods, such as optimised beams, has always been more expensive than standardised goods, because more labour is required. However new flexible production technologies may reduce these additional costs, and so stimulate competition to produce semi-finished products made with less metal.

Any innovation that allows material savings through producing semi-finished or stock products nearer to the final required shape are unequivocally worth having, if the cost can be managed. However, our exploration of opportunities to design products with less metal raises a question we cannot yet resolve: does using less metal now to make an optimised component compromise our ability to adapt or reuse the component in future for a changed or different use? As yet we have no clear basis for answering this question—it depends on how certain we are about future requirements. Optimised components are typically more expensive to produce, although they save metal and may have co-benefits, while cheaper standardised components may have a longer service if they can be adapted or re-used.

Solutions: Suppliers of metal components can aim to design more flexible production systems to tailor product geometries efficiently without increasing costs. Customers for components can aim to design families of products around standardised architectures, for instance to use standardised grid spacing in the layout of buildings, or to agree a standardised base architecture for vehicles, so that optimised parts can be produced at sufficient volume to capture the benefits of scale economies and facilitate reuse. Together customers and suppliers can engage in discussions to decide whether the right shapes are being made and explore alternatives.

Problem: the evolution of the industry is path dependent

Some of the strategies that we found in Part III with both eyes open have not already been pursued because they go against industry conventions, or because they require new technology that, if deployed, would devalue existing industry assets. Both the steel and aluminium industry are capital intensive and have long asset cycles, so they can be slow to adapt to change. For example, in the UK we have equipment designed for primary steel making from ore, located in the vicinity of mines that have long since been exhausted. We import 15 Mt of iron ore to feed these primary production plants and at the same time export 7 Mt of scrap because we have inherited our primary assets, and so do not want to switch to secondary steel making. This sort of reticence to change is widespread: by the year 2000 it was claimed that not one traditional primary steel producer anywhere in the world had successfully invested in secondary production, despite the fact that nearly half of North America's steel was produced by Electric Arc Furnaces (EAFs) at the time[5].

The rise of EAF steelmaking in the 1960's occurred with no support from the existing industry and is a classic example of a successful 'disruptive technology'[5]. Possibly this new EAF approach (led by Nucor in the United States) was tolerated by the existing primary industry because its initial production was limited to rebar, a relatively less profitable product (with gross margins of approximately 7%). As EAF steel quality improved, the production method was used for products with tighter quality requirements, first bar (with margins of approximately 12%) and later sheet, so intruding on key markets for conventional producers and indeed causing some bankruptcies. Undoubtedly one of the reasons that EAF became successful was because it could be introduced via independent, profitable production at small scale.

The radical process innovations proposed in chapter 9 do not have this luxury. Implementing novel processes now would only be possible if existing equipment were relocated or replaced. Apart from these physical constraints related to the location of existing assets, development of the new processes also raises concerns about protection of local jobs and the protection of existing intellectual property (patents).

The history of how this industry has developed depends not just on its long-lived assets, but also on industry conventions: earlier in this chapter we mentioned the convention of using standardised rather than customised parts; in chapter 12 we saw that metal savings could be achieved in the production of food cans by addressing cooking conventions; in chapter 13 we saw that metal savings could be achieved in automotive blanking if conventions about tessellation were changed.

Solutions: This inertia which inhibits change could be addressed with government support for new approaches. A simple example at present is the development of the re-used steel market. As far as we can tell this already looks economically attractive, but doesn't occur because without scale, it is too difficult for a willing client commissioning a new building to find suitable supplies of old steel. It would be relatively easy for a national government to stipulate that all new government buildings should contain a fraction of re-used steel—and such a stipulation would force the development of the required supply of steel from deconstruction.

Problem: risk aversion and imperfect information hinder material efficiency

Construction and manufacturing risk is a major driver of design choices, and the risk of product failure carries very high penalties, especially for safety critical parts. Therefore throughout the production chains associated with steel and aluminium, over-specification and over-design is a natural tendency. The strategies of chapters 15 to 16, aiming to make better use of metal after its first use, also carry risk. For example, although we saw that I-beams can be reused with little risk of physical failure, uncertainties over certification introduce legal risks to reuse, and uncertainty over availability of supply can cause delay, which increases costs, and for fabricators creates the risk of damage to their reputation. For other products, such as cars, sellers have an incentive to exaggerate claims of product quality. This decreases the confidence buyers have in product quality and increases the risk of physical failure[6].

Figure 23.2 shows how available knowledge changes between the stages of product life. At the design stage we have perfect information about the original product specification, but little is known about future needs (especially for long lived products). After first use, these future needs are now clear but information on the original design, specification and production may be missing.

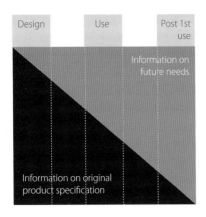

Figure 23.2—**Information availability over the product life cycle**

We saw in chapters 15 and 16 that knowledge about future needs is critical when choosing between strategies for long life design, and that information on product composition is critical for reuse, adaptation and upgrade. As products progress from manufacture to use, through successive reuse to discard, we forget what they were made of, but we begin to understand how they should have been designed. Although, without a crystal ball, we cannot foresee future needs, we can at least improve in remembering what is in our products. We've come across a couple of examples where this better remembering has been imposed: the refurbishment of 55 Baker Street was aided by original calculations and drawings; when installing 'flexible' foundations, developers at Canary Wharf commissioned a close out report from the engineers to document the exact specification of the foundations. Improved information reduces subsequent testing and certification costs and so increases the chances that at the end of its first life a product will be adapted for life extension or reused.

Solutions: Design with excess material is currently promoted by conservative design standards or governmental regulations, particularly when they are written to specify minimum rather than target levels of safety. Collaboration between the full set of companies involved in making a product may allow a more rational selection of a single safety factor, and insurance industries could work with standards bodies to control the tendency to over-specify and to provide certification and buying standards for reuse. Designers can ensure that detailed knowledge about their original intentions survives with their products, to facilitate intelligent adaptation or re-use after first use.

Problem: most companies continue to focus on product sales not service revenue

The steel and aluminium industries make money by selling metal, so are primarily motivated to sell more of it. Similarly component manufacturers, and even final manufacturers of products such as washing machines, are mainly motivated by volume of sales. A switch to a business model based on service more than sales would allow quite different behaviour to become profitable and would internalise the downstream benefits of greater material efficiency. Figure 23.3 shows the relative size of up-front purchase costs and lifetime maintenance costs for two products, a rolling mill and a car.

The relative share of these two costs for these products are opposite: for the long lived rolling mill a lifetime maintenance contract is worth twice as much as the original sale; for the car the value of the initial sale exceeds the lifetime service and maintenance costs. Can we say that rolling mills are long lived because they have a higher service share? Probably not because, as we saw in chapter 16, there are many other reasons for the long life of rolling mills (such as the high value of the core components and fortuitous developments in metallurgical science by which higher strength materials can be rolled in old mill frames), and because the high service share is an outcome of this longer life. We can however, say that, as explored in chapter 16, for long life vehicles to be attractive for car manufacturers, greater profits must be achieved through services than from initial sales.

We've seen in our case studies that there may well be other benefits to offering enhanced services in a longer lasting contract: businesses offering upgrades may be able to develop closer relationships with customers through more regular upgrade of existing products; they may also benefit from more regular cash flows; they may be able to offer their customers a lower total cost of ownership through upgrades.

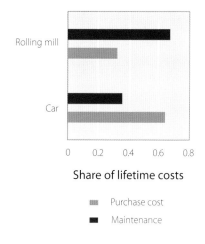

Share of lifetime costs

■ Purchase cost
■ Maintenance

Figure 23.3—**The relative size of purchasing and maintenance costs**

Solutions: Suppliers can investigate options to provide material services rather than materials. We have begun to assess this approach for cars but, due to commercial sensitivity, this sort of analysis is better conducted internally.

Problem: bigger and sooner is better

We have come encountered several examples where excess material is used in order to satisfy customer perceptions of quality. For example, customers demand that cans and car body shells remain rigid in use, and, in the UK, letting agents require office buildings to withstand loads beyond the requirements of building regulations.

We also saw, in chapter 16, that there may be many reasons why consumers do not choose long-lived products: decisions often take into account only a subset of costs; discount rates have a punishing effect on the future benefits of greater durability; short sighted decisions governed by the need for quick payback periods do not allow comparison of options across the longer time spans that would favour more durable products; comparing marginal rather than average costs of two options negates some of the benefits of long life.

Solutions: We need to raise awareness of the emissions and cost implications of these choices and encourage consumers to re-evaluate these preferences.

Opportunity: awareness about embodied emissions is increasing

We're optimists so cannot end a chapter with another problem, so this one's an opportunity. We are all becoming more aware of embodied energy. At present, supermarket chains are competing for 'green credentials', one aspect of which is exploring options to label the 'carbon footprint' of all goods sold. If this occurs, products such as deodorant aerosols or canned drinks, which are sold in aluminium cans, will show significantly higher impacts than those sold in other packaging and this may influence customer purchasing. As part of its waste prevention strategy, the UK government has funded trials of refillable packaging at UK super markets. For example Asda trialled in-store refillable packaging for its own brand fabric softener. This could be a precedent for radical change in the use of metal packaging, reversing the trend away from refillable packaging (for example, as observed for refillable milk bottles (94% of market volume 1974 to 10% 2006), soft drinks (46% 1980 to 10% 1989) and beer containers (33% 1961 to 0.3% 2006))[7].

More broadly, with legislation driving significant reductions in energy used in buildings and vehicles, the embodied energy in their construction and manufacture is a growing fraction of their total impact and developments in certification will increasingly demonstrate this to final purchasers.

We don't yet know when or if the public will radically change its purchasing behaviour due to environmental concern. A much discussed positive example of behaviour change occurred in response to concerns over the Ozone layer, when the public switched to aerosols without CFC propellants as a result of a ban on using CFCs first enforced in the US in 1974. In contrast, despite the fact that every packet clearly tells customers that purchasing carries a significant risk of death, the sale of cigarettes continues. And as we saw, the Easter Island community continued building stone statues cutting down trees until they had no means to continue living.

Taking the opportunity: if customers become more aware of embodied emissions in products, and therefore change their behaviour, this will create a much stronger driver for material efficiency than provided by material cost savings, because it will become part of core marketing messages.

Outlook

In this chapter we have discussed a wide range of opportunities and barriers relating to the material efficiency strategies put forward in Part III. Two things are clear: (1) material efficiency requires a greater level of cooperation between the many companies involved in producing a product made with metal components; (2) some of the changes we have suggested require a radical change in company strategy. A key requirement for many of the strategies we've identified with both eyes open is to create full scale commercial demonstrations to find out how they apply in different sectors and to allow detailed examination of costs and customer responses. That will be the focus of our future work.

Meanwhile, our analysis of costs has shown that material cost savings are only a weak driver of change towards significant material efficiency. Although we've seen that there may be co-benefits and other reasons for companies to change, it is clear from this chapter that change will be instigated much more rapidly if stimulated by other incentives. And in turn that sounds like an invitation to a chapter on policy to promote material efficiency.

Notes

1. This price data was supplied by Steel Business Briefing (SBB,2009) and accessed via UNCTAD (2011)

2. Pratten (1971) examines the source of economies of scale in manufacturing. His analysis includes a case study of the UK primary steel industry in the 1960s

3. Kelkar et al. (2001) provide data on the fabrication costs of five vehicles. On average mass production (say of 200,000 cars per year) saves 26% of production costs compared to medium scale production (around 60,000 cars per year).

4. In his précis of technology shifts in the steel industry, Tomiura (1998) writes "The mass production system is collapsing due to the diversified market requirements"

5. Christiansen (2003) uses the rise of secondary production of steel (referred to as production by mini-mill) as an example of the successful implementation of a disruptive technology.

6. A seminal paper by Akerlof (1970) explains how asymmetric information between buyers and sellers of used cars ultimately causes market collapse because consumers, who lack information on product quality, are only willing to pay the price of an average quality car. Sellers of above average quality cars are unwilling to sell at this price, depressing the average quality (and so price) of used cars brought to market and ultimately causing market collapse.

7. Brook Lyndhurst (2009) conducted an evidence review of refillable packaging pilots. They found that refillable packaging has seen greater success in the US where there is a tendency to shop less frequently and buy in bulk and in Asia Pacific where consumers are well informed about the benefits of reuse/refill

24 The influence of policy

on future material sustainability

Policy makers in many countries recognise the need for action to respond to environmental concerns, but are hampered in their responses by the need to remain popular at the next election. What can they in reality do that would help?

In due course, we anticipate that this book will enter the political mainstream, as material efficiency hits the centre of political debate. "Never was so much owned by so few", "Ask not what your infrastructure can do for you...", "Metal workers of the world unite; you have nothing to lose but your yield losses", and so on. And if the climate scientists are right in their projections on the likelihood and consequences of global warming, or if the other issues we raised in the opening chapter become even more pressing, then without doubt sustainable materials will be a cornerstone of future politics.

But it isn't in the public mind yet and therefore the influence of policy makers is covert rather than overt but certainly real. The absence of border protection combined with the threat of regionally high carbon taxation has driven the European steel industry to invest heavily in research around carbon sequestration. EU regulation on car tailpipe emissions has driven the current rush towards plug-in battery powered electric cars. Failure to regulate or at least failure to apply rules properly, led to the red mud disaster in Hungary. Policy makers determine and enforce the standards and rules which govern materials processing operations, encourage novel developments through taxes, subsidies and investments, enable change by providing infrastructure, information and skills, exemplify good practice through procurement[1] and engage the public and industry through media campaigns and company initiatives.

We saw in the last chapter that several of our options for material efficiency could be stimulated more rapidly through support from governments and the 'policy map' in Figure 24.1 summarises our suggestions for how this might occur. The rest of the chapter is structured around the rows of this table: the four 'E's put forward in the UK sustainable development strategy (encourage, enable, exemplify and engage) to which we've added one further 'E': the rather sterner option to 'enforce' change[2]. In Figure 24.2 we've given general examples of how these five strategies can be applied in future as we become more aware of material efficiency opportunities.

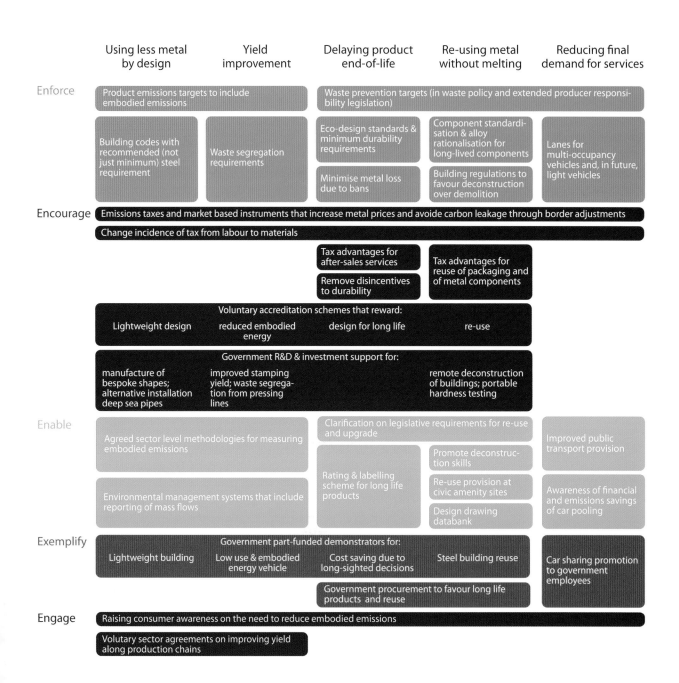

	Using less metal by design	Yield improvement	Delaying product end-of-life	Re-using metal without melting	Reducing final demand for services
Enforce	Product emissions targets to include embodied emissions		Waste prevention targets (in waste policy and extended producer responsibility legislation)		
	Building codes with recommended (not just minimum) steel requirement	Waste segregation requirements	Eco-design standards & minimum durability requirements	Component standardisation & alloy rationalisation for long-lived components	Lanes for multi-occupancy vehicles and, in future, light vehicles
			Minimise metal loss due to bans	Building regulations to favour deconstruction over demolition	
Encourage	Emissions taxes and market based instruments that increase metal prices and avoid carbon leakage through border adjustments				
	Change incidence of tax from labour to materials				
			Tax advantages for after-sales services	Tax advantages for reuse of packaging and of metal components	
			Remove disincentives to durability		
	Voluntary accreditation schemes that reward:				
	Lightweight design	reduced embodied energy	design for long life	re-use	
	Government R&D & investment support for:				
	manufacture of bespoke shapes; alternative installation deep sea pipes	improved stamping yield; waste segregation from pressing lines		remote deconstruction of buildings; portable hardness testing	
Enable	Agreed sector level methodologies for measuring embodied emissions		Clarification on legislative requirements for re-use and upgrade		Improved public transport provision
				Promote deconstruction skills	
	Environmental management systems that include reporting of mass flows		Rating & labelling scheme for long life products	Re-use provision at civic amenity sites	Awareness of financial and emissions savings of car pooling
				Design drawing databank	
Exemplify	Government part-funded demonstrators for:				
	Lightweight building	Low use & embodied energy vehicle	Cost saving due to long-sighted decisions	Steel building reuse	Car sharing promotion to government employees
			Government procurement to favour long life products and reuse		
Engage	Raising consumer awareness on the need to reduce embodied emissions				
	Volutary sector agreements on improving yield along production chains				

Figure 24.1—**Policy map**

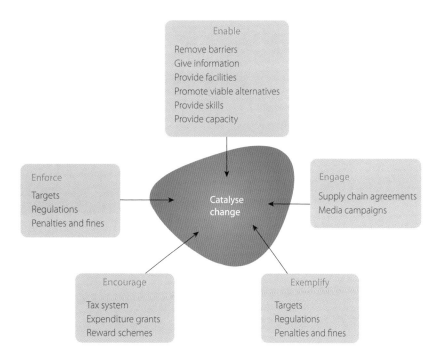

Figure 24.2—**Options for change**

Enforce

Regulations, bans and laws are the least favourite options of policy makers, because they are difficult to specify without creating unintended consequences, and are politically risky. Enforcement is required to ensure the rule of law, for example to ensure that companies do not expose their workers, neighbours, or customers to undue harm. Enforcement has been a powerful strategy to counter some of the specific environmental problems identified in the past century, particularly where a business activity directly threatens human health. So some environmentally harmful products have been banned, and health and safety legislation continues to rule over materials such as asbestos and strong acids that cause immediate harm. However mitigation against climate change is more complex as it acts over long time spans and requires a balance between social, environmental and economic responses. So instead of using enforcement in this area, governments focus more on stimulating change (which is set into law through targets) rather than determining how that change is achieved. The suggestions in Figure 24.1, which arise from our work, aim to remove perverse incentives in emission reduction targets, minimise material inefficiencies due to regulations and enforce greater material efficiency through the rule of law.

Emission reduction targets should take into account embodied emissions

The UK government estimates that 15% of construction emissions are due to the embodied energy in the materials used. By our estimates this varies between 24% for warehouses and 11% for housing. Similarly for vehicles, we find the current embodied emissions share to be in the region of 15% of total life cycle emissions. As a result of these emissions shares, government policy to date has focused on reducing emissions in use, particularly in buildings and cars[3]. However these policies take no account of embodied energy savings so, for example, fail to promote the reuse of structural steel and by measuring emissions when cars are on rollers[4], fail to reflect the true benefits of vehicle weight saving. Current UK government strategy on new homes[5], includes the aspiration that all new dwellings be 'zero carbon' by 2016, but the interpretation of "zero carbon" does not take into account embodied emissions and rather aims at houses that return as much power as they use over the course of a year to the National Grid. As opportunities to reduce emissions in use are exploited, opportunities to reduce embodied emissions will become relatively more important. Even now we can see from our Sankey diagrams that the steel used in construction and in the manufacture of vehicles accounts for half of the output of the steel sector and so roughly half of the sector's emissions.

Waste policy should be directed towards minimising embodied energy losses

Recent UK waste policy, primarily motivated by land shortages, has been successful in diverting waste from landfill, in increasing recycling and in improving treatment of hazardous waste. However the focus on recycling has in effect taken away attention away from options to extend the life of products and components through delayed disposal or re-use. For example, combined targets for recycling and reuse fail to take into account the embodied energy savings of reuse and the process emissions of recycling. Future developments in waste policy should therefore be directed towards products that have high embodied emissions and value all end-of-life options appropriately[6].

Health and safety legislation should not prevent material efficiency

We have no intention to make life riskier by using our materials more intelligently, and there is no need. As we've seen, safety factors tend to multiply along production chains, as each company assesses the cost of its own risks. A result of this, compounded by recent changes in health and safety legislation, is growing material use: a quarter of the weight increase in European vehicles is attributed improvements in crash-worthiness. A separate consequence of recent developments in health and safety legislation has been a drive to avoid the use of manual labour where old buildings are taken down. This has discouraged deconstruction of buildings, favouring remote demolition instead.

Product durability standards could be considered

Governments could stipulate minimum durability, eco-design standards and minimum product guarantees as authorized by the EU EcoDesign Directive. In the past these heavy-handed policies have been voted out in parliament. With greater awareness of the benefits of durability, politicians may be more confident in withstanding opposition from business lobbies that favour short product life to stimulate replacement demand. Alternatively, voluntary codes and standards on durability could be developed within industrial sectors.

Encourage

We saw in our evaluation of business activity in the last chapter, that motivated by cost alone businesses are unlikely to pursue material efficiency aggressively unless they find other benefits from doing so, so there is an important role for policy makers to provide encouragement through these other benefits. Governments have many options to encourage change: they can use the tax system to favour certain behaviours, they can subsidise research and development into technologies that facilitate change and they can develop accreditation schemes that allow companies to advertise the benefits of their work with authority.

We cannot rely on existing policies that price emissions

Existing policies that attempt to put a price on emissions, such as the European Emissions Trading Scheme, are unlikely to encourage material efficiency because as we saw in chapter 6, materials costs are only a small fraction of final consumer prices, and because the policies are structured so that the emissions price has little effect on final prices and hence demand[7]. We saw in the meeting of the UNFCCC in Copenhagen in 2009 how unlikely it is that there will ever be a single global agreement on responses to climate change, so there is unlikely to be a unified global carbon price. So instead of relying on carbon pricing, the tax system could be used to encourage material efficiency.

The tax system should encourage material efficiency

It's a dark secret, but part of the work of the Treasury is to find ways to raise taxes without people noticing. Environmental taxes are intended to have the opposite effect: they are levied precisely so that the drivers of environmental harm cause financial pain. However, with the complexities of the tax system, several disincentives to greater material efficiency linger and should be removed, particularly where tax reductions are offered to encourage more purchasing. For example, in the UK value added tax (known as sales tax in the US) is currently charged at 20% on building refurbishment but is not charged at all for new buildings. 'Capital allowances' which allow some purchases to be depreciated rapidly rather than in line with the incomes they generate, are designed to promote faster replacement purchases. The tax system could also be adapted to encourage material efficiency, for example by charging higher tax rates on disposable products and lower rates for more durable ones.

Material efficiency should be rewarded in voluntary eco-standards

Material efficiency could be rewarded more effectively through certification in voluntary eco-standards that account properly for embodied energy and emissions. We saw in the box story in chapter 15 that the voluntary UK eco-standard BREEAM could follow the lead of the Australian Green Star system and promote best practice in steel production and fabrication and to encourage more efficient use of steel in structural applications.

Enable

We've been dogged throughout the preparation of this book by a shortage of data. Companies are required to release very little data about energy purchases or material flows and this inhibits the adoption of both energy and material efficiency because the real drivers of energy are rather well hidden. Governments could therefore play an important role in enabling future material efficiency, by requiring a greater release of audited data. We have also found areas where the absence of appropriate standards prevents adoption of good practices. For example, the absence of a government standard for re-certifying steel prevents re-use because the risks associated with using old steel (which we believe to be very small) cannot be valued and traded.

Governments should promote meaningful data collection on material efficiency

Much European policy regarding to materials has been developed related to Life Cycle Assessments (LCAs) of the total energy involved in making and using products. However, as we discussed in Chapter 2, this allocation of energy to products is impossible, and also tends to disguise the more important information we'd like to have in the public domain: we could make much more precise suggestions about options for change if we had in the public domain data on energy use at production sites, particularly when related to key processes, provided by the European Environmental Management System (EMAS), as discussed on page 23. A move towards environmental reporting that reveals opportunities to save energy and emissions at national level, rather than promoting blame-shifting at product level, should be encouraged and applied consistently across different sectors. Governments should promote participation in schemes such as EMAS and encourage assessment of metal flows along production chains.

Governments should provide greater clarity on the requirements for reuse

Governments have a role to play in reducing the (small) risks associated with reuse by giving greater clarity on regulations for reuse and by working with insurers to reduce the cost of certifying reused steel. The European Commission is developing "End-of-Waste" criteria under the Waste Framework Directive, with a particular focus on ferrous metals, aluminium, copper, recovered paper and glass. Once completed, these criteria must be interpreted for national application[8].

Exemplify

Government procurement can be used to promote material efficiency. In Europe, public authorities spend 16% of GDP on the purchase of goods and services[9]. Governments could therefore promote material efficiency through their purchasing choices, could fund demonstrator projects to develop experience with reuse including understanding of true costs, inconvenience, project timing and concerns over health and safety, and could report carefully on the experience.

Engage

Initiatives to raise consumer awareness of embodied energy as the next environmental challenge would give businesses a new and positive opportunity for competition. For example, if consumers were more aware of embodied energy, suppliers of more durable goods could more easily advertise their environmental benefits. As well as raising awareness amongst consumers, governments have a role to play in engaging companies in all aspects of materials transformation to encourage collaborative exploration of opportunities to improve material efficiency[10].

Outlook

Many of the recommendations made in this chapter concern removing barriers to material efficiency, but procurement and the development of certification and standards are both positive options that would support its expansion. Government funded pilot studies and the subsequent use of Government purchasing to develop appropriate markets are important opportunities to stimulate constructive change.

Notes

1. The ONS construction statistics annual (ONS, 2010b) includes data on the split of new spending in construction between infrastructure, public, commercial and industrial building works. In 2008 the public sector share (including infrastructure) was 38%.

2. Defra (2005) sets out the UK sustainable development strategy and put forward the four "E"s (encourage, enable, exemplify and engage) as a means of instigating change.

3. For example minimum requirements for operational carbon emissions are imposed through Part L of the building regulations and for cars by specifying fleet average emissions reductions in line with the EU standards for tailpipe emissions (160 gCO2/km in 2008 to 130 gCO$_2$/km by 2015 and 95 gCO$_2$/km by 2020)

4. Tailpipe CO$_2$ emissions are currently determined by running drive cycles (themselves not considered realistic) using static tests on rollers that do not fully take into account the benefits of weight reduction. Certified CO$_2$ figures are calculated using categories that cover a 100 kg range of weights. This means that up to 100-kg in weight can be taken off cars at the top of a weight class before any change in certified CO$_2$ is seen.

5. Defined in the policy statement (DCLG, 2007).

6. The publication of the UK Waste Policy Review (DEFRA, 2011) moves in the right direction – it explicitly makes the link between greenhouse gas emissions and waste and states the aim "to promote resource efficient product design and manufacture and target those streams with high carbon impacts both in terms of embedded carbon (food, metals, plastics, textiles) and direct emissions from landfill (food, paper and card, textiles, wood)".

7. In order to make effective decisions about material choice and product design, manufacturers must face consistent carbon prices so that they can factor in the costs to society they cause both up and downstream. In reality there is no single price of emissions: the average Phase II EUA price has been €20 /tCO$_2$, approximately £15/tCO$_2$; the CCL is levied at 0.47 p/kWh equating to an implied carbon price of £0.09/tCO$_2$; the fuel duty is levied at £0.5819/L equating to an implied carbon price of £220/tCO$_2$ for the use of diesel in cars and £252/tCO$_2$ for the use of petrol. Furthermore there are many reasons why policies that price emissions from energy intensive industries (e.g. the steel and aluminium industry) do not lead to their output prices increasing in line with the emissions associated with production: tax revenues from the Climate Change Levy (CCL) are returned to businesses through cuts in National Insurance contributions; the majority of the CCL can be avoided by industries that negotiate Climate Change Agreements; fears over 'carbon leakage' (this phrase refers to the fact that high taxes on carbon in one country will cause production to shift elsewhere, so lead to national but not global reduction in carbon emitted) result in free allocation of EU ETS emissions permits. As a result of these measures, product manufacturers do not face input prices that properly reflect the embodied emissions in their inputs. Emissions pricing policies are particularly hard to implement regionally; for example, EU policy on carbon pricing currently threatens the survival of energy intensive industries in Europe. In 2011, Tata cut 1,500 jobs in Scunthorpe and Teesside citing EU carbon legislation as one of the reasons for the cut back (BBC News, 2011b). Also, carbon prices cannot effectively encourage material efficiency unless carbon leakage is addressed through border adjustments (that levy a tax on imports) rather than by negotiating agreements that reduce the tax burden within the scheme. The legalities of such border adjustments within WTO trade legislation should be explored.

8. Our discussion with UK steel fabricators about the legalities of reusing steel sections has revealed confusion about current rules on CE marking. For example, do unmarked beams installed prior to the 1991 Construction Products Regulations need CE marking in order to be traded for reuse? Which harmonized standards should be used? How much testing is required in order to validate the properties of the reused steel?

9. In fact some government regulations already favour material efficiency but aren't implemented. In the UK, existing government procurement priorities claim to favour reuse as set out in the recommendations of the OGC (2007).

10. Following the success of the Courtauld Commitment (a UK initiative that reduced food waste by 670,000 tonnes and packaging waste by 52,000 tonnes 2005-2009 by collective action in the food production and retail sector) the UK Waste Policy Review (DEFRA, 2011) recommends further voluntary responsibility deals within the packaging, textiles, paper and hospitality sectors. The analysis in this book suggests that similar initiatives should be instigated in the industries that are the main users of steel and aluminium – construction, vehicles, metal products and machinery and equipment. It is also likely that there will be overlap across these sectors in the lessons learned about particular processes. For example, innovations that reduce the yield losses of stamping and pressing lines will be of interest to both the car and the can industry.

25 The actions of individuals
Lifestyles, behaviour and individual choices

Sustainability always involves dialogue between the trinity of business, government and individuals (as voters and consumers). So what's the role of individuals in bringing about a material efficiency?

All discussions about moves towards a more sustainable future end up caught in a loop with three players: businesses, the government and individuals. Should businesses "take responsibility for their actions" and clean up their act? Should government lead and set rules so that individuals and businesses operate in a more sustainable manner? Should individuals vote with their wallets and ballots to direct businesses and governments to take more sustainable decisions? Always the balance of responsibility between these three is at the centre of discussion about change, and the role of many of the other organisations illustrated in our map of "who's involved" in chapter 6, in research, education, journalism and lobbying for example, is to keep illuminating, probing and pushing to try to support simultaneous action from all three. In our experience, all three parties are willing. The most informed experts on the environmental impacts of steel and aluminium production are within the industry, and have ideas for improvement but can't apply them: if they put costs, up their customers will shift to cheaper producers elsewhere with worse environmental performance. Within government, we have expert scientists informed by the most up to date measurements, giving balanced and accurate opinions to politicians but, even if willing, they cannot put forward policies which decrease the chance that they will be voted back in next time. Meals around the world are shared by concerned individuals, aware of the issues, concerned for their grandchildren, but often unsure about meaningful actions, and short of time to seek out alternatives to mainstream commercial norms.

So having looked at business and policy, this chapter is about you —you as an employee, you as a consumer, you as a voter. What can you do to help bring about the change we've put forward in this book?

Your purchasing decisions: are you buying a…

…building?

- Is there an existing building that meets your needs? Re-using whole buildings is much simpler than arranging deconstruction and new design.

- If no existing building is quite right, tell the design team that both embodied and use phase energy reduction must take priority in all subsequent decisions. If they're not confident about embodied energy, point them towards existing reliable sources of data (such as the ICE database, available online) and re-use as much as possible of previous buildings on the site. Make sure that unwanted old components are extracted carefully and sold for reuse.

- Specify reused steel and plan ahead to allow fabricators time to source steel for reuse. Give the design team time and flexibility to accommodate the material found by the fabricator.

- Alternatively, rather than using standard reused components, you could design an iconic lightweight building and save up to a third of metal.

- Make sure that the building can be disassembled for reuse at the end of its useful life, for example by including a deconstruction plan as part of design.

- Think about what you (or subsequent owners) are likely to want from the building in future: is your business expanding; will you need different access, different ceiling heights or different floor plans in future? Engage the design team in discussions about how the building could be adapted to meet these uncertain future needs.

- In all cases try to eliminate excess loading allowances and materials specified 'to be on the safe side': meet the building regulations without exceeding them. Plan carefully with the contractor to make sure that materials are not over-ordered. Be willing to bear a slightly higher cost and tell the fabricator not to "rationalise" the beams specified. Likewise, insist that the mix and geometry of concrete elements are not greater than necessary. Investigate with the contractor the time, cost and material savings possible by using pre-fabricated components which can be reused later.

- If you choose to use steel or aluminium for aesthetic components (e.g. fixtures and fittings or an aluminium curtain wall) ensure that they are protected against corrosion and will remain attractive over a long life.

- Once it's built be sure to maintain your building. Make sure the building design drawings are kept secure, are updated if you make any modifications and passed on to future owners so that they can modify the building with confidence.

…infrastructure?

- Take a look at our suggestions for buildings; many of them apply to infrastructure too, but even more so as we usually want infrastructure to last as long as possible; use whole-life-costing to aid your decision-making, and make sure you really understand the consequences of purchasing based on lowest initial capital outlay, even if that's your normal practice.

- Consider capacity carefully: can the infrastructure be modular so that capacity can be added incrementally, or removed and used elsewhere as demand changes over time?

- The lifespan of current infrastructure in the UK is far shorter than intended due to poor workmanship during original construction. Negotiate guarantees and terms that ensure contractors are motivated to achieve the quality standards required to guarantee long-life.

- Design condition monitoring from the start, and use it intelligently to inform maintenance.

…industrial equipment?

- As with commercial buildings, make sure you value your options over a long time span; at the least you should compare them over their entire useful life. Be sure to include all costs in your decisions: maintenance costs, operating costs and future replacement costs. Make the case for a more durable product by comparing the average cost of ownership. Ensure you have guarantees in the service contract to provide lifetime operation and upgrade.

- Can you specify a modular design that guarantees longevity for the equipment, as new innovations emerge over the next 50 years?

- If your machine is making metal products, how flexible is it, and how well does it fit the whole production chain from liquid metal to product. When you also consider supplier and customer options? Perhaps the products you are making aren't actually what your customers need? Make sure that the machine can, as part of normal operation, separate out any valuable off-cuts and sell them on, preferably for re-use rather than recycling.

- Design the equipment so it can be turned on and off rapidly, does not consume energy when idle, and has correctly specified variable speed electric motors.

- Don't forget to brag about your sustainable material success —you deserve the credit and you will encourage others to follow your inspirational lead.

…private car?

- Do you really need one? Would a bicycle, sharing with a relative, or membership of a car-sharing scheme be sufficient instead. Lobby your MP for improved public transport connections. Set up a car pool with colleagues at work and offer the neighbour's kids a lift to school on the way.

- If you decide to go ahead and buy a car, buy one with the lowest fuel consumption but also keep an eye out for information on embodied energy — most car manufacturers include some information about this on their websites. Be sure to tell the dealership that you're interested in the embodied emissions. Maybe you could suggest that they display this information?

- Now that you've had the car for a while, are you getting attached to it? All those wonderful memories? Can you keep it for longer and upgrade to a lower emitting engine? Maybe that's something you should suggest to the dealership too, or to the car manufacturer?

- Oh and don't forget to follow the maintenance schedule, it's probably in the glove compartment.

…appliances?

- Buy a size that's appropriate for your needs —you probably don't need to walk in to your fridge. If you later find it's too big or small, swap it with someone else with the reverse problem.

- Try to negotiate a guarantee on your fridge, washing machine or microwave, as part of the purchase contract. A minimum of 25 years would be good.

- If it breaks down, see if you can get someone in to fix it and if not, make sure that you tell the supplier how dissatisfied you are and publicise their response. You shouldn't have to buy two fridges in your lifetime.

…packaged product?

- Negotiate contracts so that the supplier must take back all packaging that comes with your goods: most packaging is used before the final consumer, so motivate your supplier to switch to reusable systems.

- At home, can you use your own packaging to avoid the ever-growing collection of plastic bottles in the garage? Choose products with minimal packaging and make sure you recycle it.

The decisions you make when you no longer want your product

- Could someone restore the product to its original condition or upgrade it to meet new requirements?

- Who might want the product in its current state? Could you sell or give it to them? Be sure to pass on any information you have on the product to help with future maintenance, repair or upgrade.

- Can the product be broken down into its component parts and be re-used? Could you yourself re-use any part of the product? Can you use information from the original design to add value to the components, for example where steel has been certified?

- If it must be abandoned, removed or discarded, allow time for de-construction or disassembly to maximise the value of the components and materials that could be re-used.

Decisions you make at work: are you…

… involved with product design?

- Aside from cost and material properties, be sure to take into account embodied emissions in your material choice and educate clients about their significance. Can you reduce the embodied emissions of the product, while also reducing yield losses in its manufacture? Can you re-design it in some other way to reduce yield losses? Can you use re-used materials as part of the design?

- Are you designing the right product? Is your product design constrained by its final use, or by requirements arising in the journey from production to use, as we saw in cooking food cans and installation for line pipe? Are there any opportunities for change?

- What change in future might make your product obsolete? Can you design your product to adapt to these changes? Maybe design it with upgrades in mind or make it modular? If not, make sure to optimise your product over a suitable life: meet but don't exceed requirements and explore all options to design with less material.

- Use the onion skin model of design to make sure that shorter-lived aesthetic components, or components that may fail, or those likely to be superseded can easily be separated from long-lived structural components.

- Include in the design a plan to disassemble the product at the end of its useful life, so its component parts and materials can be re-used or recycled. Document the product's specification and the materials used for each component, and make sure this is accessible to future owners.

- Engage in development of standards or guidelines to ensure they reflect material efficiency.

- Celebrate the low embodied energy and material efficiency of your designs as part of their branding.

… involved in product manufacture?

- Search tirelessly for opportunities to reduce yield losses within your operations, and along the whole production chain, for example tessellating large and small

Sustainable Materials with both eyes open

parts to improve stamping yield. Take a look at the metal that you're buying. Is it the right shape? Could you tell your supplier what shape you really need and see if they can make it for you? Speak to your customers. Are you delivering what they really need? Can you capture more value by reducing their need to shape components?

- Push for research and development into new manufacturing processes that cut yield losses. Blanking and deep drawing cause the biggest waste of sheet metal for both steel and aluminium and can be replaced already by laser cutting and spinning. How can we cut and shape sheet metal at high speed with low yield losses?

- Segregate metal waste for reuse and recycling. Look for opportunities to cut small blanks from skeletons and perhaps try using solid bonding to add value to your aluminium swarf.

- Explore different service contracts with customers so you can add more value downstream while requiring less metal purchasing upstream.

…working in the steel or aluminium industry?

- Aim to exploit all the efficiencies we've identified, including more efficient processes, better management of heat, and heat recovery from hot products and by-products. Seek opportunities to trade low-grade heat for district heating or to low temperature industries.

- Integrate downstream to extract more value from less liquid metal and work towards selling metal as a service not a commodity.

- Recognise that any overall expansion in primary capacity will deny emissions reduction targets, while aiming to expand secondary production. Support better separation and collection of end-of-life waste streams. Support exploration of carbon capture and storage and novel process development while retaining a realistic view of their likely costs and capabilities.

- Support development of the market for re-use by providing re-certification.

- Aim at greater transparency with energy, emissions and material efficiency data, copying the approach we saw at Alunorf with EMAS certification.

…working in the cement industry?

- Pursue every known efficiency and substitution option while exploring carbon capture and storage and novel cements with realistic expectations.

- Begin development of reusable concrete systems—focus on concrete as a provider of service rather than cement as a commodity.

…working in the paper industry?

- Pursue every known efficiency improvement. Explore alternatives to pulping during recycling to reduce down-cycling.

- Explore options for lighter weight paper and technologies for removing print from paper.

- Promote use of novel inks and dyes that can be removed from used paper more easily.

…working in waste management?

- Support improved separation and collection of aluminium, particularly cans and food packaging and develop plastics separation and recycling to maximise value from all plastic wastes.

- Re-prioritise re-use over recycling.

…working in insurance?

- Collaborate in developing new assessments of risk to allow development of a future market in materially efficient products. For example find new appropriate methods to evaluate and trade risks for re-used structural steel, or for lighter weight designs for buildings and vehicles.

…working in marketing and advertising?

- Provide validated information on embodied energy and life-spans as part of product messages.

- Work towards new customer relationships based on longer term service models requiring a reduced flow of new materials.

…working in education and research?

- Develop teaching about scale in global emissions and opportunities to address environmental problems with both eyes open.

- Clarify, evaluate and validate emissions data, and claims about improvements to processes and products.

- Develop novel technologies, systems and business models to support future material efficiency.

…working in accounting and finance?

- Promote appropriate evaluation methods when making material purchase decisions; raise awareness of the different consequences of decisions based on initial capital outlay and decisions based on whole life costing.

- Invest in companies that use materials efficiently and the technologies that enable them.

…working in retail?

- Work with suppliers to put durability labels on products.

- Explore options for refillable packaging.

- Give priority shelf space to durable and reusable products.

…working in government?

- Turn back to the previous chapter!

Outlook

The logic behind the current pursuit of options with one eye open is that changing consumer or voter behaviour is the most difficult option, so it's better to try to solve everything within existing industries. But as we've seen, there aren't enough options with one eye open, so we need to open both eyes. This chapter has aimed to demonstrate the very broad range of actions that individuals, as private or employed purchasers or through their professional skills, can take to support the development of future material efficiency. When we examined the difference between the Aquatics Centre and the Velodrome at the 2012 London Olympics site, we found that the Velodrome was twice as light per seat. This difference occurred primarily because development of a light solution was a target early in the design process and became an integral part of the project. The most radical changes required to support development of the material efficiency strategies we examined in Part III could be brought about simply by this approach: if purchasers, at the point they are about to agree to a deal, specify the relevant features of material efficiency that we have outlined in this book, they will in many cases be able to achieve them, with little if any additional cost.

With one eye open we cannot achieve our targets for a sustainable material future. And there's no point hoping that someone will innovate and find a new way to make the materials. They can't. We can't boil water without a threshold level of energy, and the same applies to materials. But with both eyes open, we can do it. It requires change, but we're optimistic. It'll be interesting and enjoyable being part of creating the change, and we're all involved.

With one eye open, we cannot get there, and are just "meeting trouble half way" as Joseph Conrad's Captain MacWhirr would say. Instead we should follow his example and set sail, bow first into the storm: "Facing it—always facing it—that's the way to get through… Face it." With both eyes open, we can face it, and plot a path through the storm. We need to think in a different way, we need to recognise a set of options that we've ignored to date, but we've shown that we can do it: we can do enough to set up a sustainable material world for our children at least as good as the one we're enjoying now.

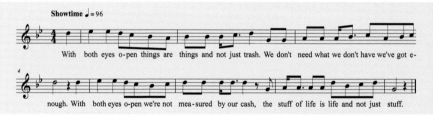

Showtime ♩ = 96

With both eyes o-pen things are things and not just trash. We don't need what we don't have we've got e-nough. With both eyes o-pen we're not mea-sured by our cash, the stuff of life is life and not just stuff.

References

A

Adderley, B., 2011. *Assessing the technical abatement potential in the UK steel sector,* report for the Energy Intensive Industries Strategy Board

Addis W. and Schouten J., 2004. *Principles of design for deconstruction to facilitate reuse and recycling,* London: CIRIA

Ahmadi, A., Williamson, B.H., Theis, T.L. and Powers, S.E., 2003. Life-cycle inventory of toner produced for xerographic processes. *Journal of Cleaner Production,* 11, pp.573-582

Aïtcin, P. C., 2000. Cements of yesterday and today. Concrete of tomorrow. *Cement and Concrete Research,* 30(9), pp1349-1359

Akerlof, G.A., 1970. The market for "lemons": quality uncertainty and the market mechanism, *The Quarterly Journal of Economics,* 84:3, pp.488-500

Allwood, J.M., Laursen, S.E., de Rodriguez, C. M. and Brocken, N.M.P, 2006. *Well dressed: the present and future sustainability of clothing and textiles in the UK.* [online] Cambridge: University of Cambridge Available at: <http://www.lcmp.eng.cam.ac.uk/wellmade/well-dressed> [accessed 27 July 2011]

Allwood, J.M. and Utsunomiya, H., 2006. A survey of flexible forming processes in Japan. *International Journal of Machine Tools and Manufacture,* 46(15), pp.1939-1960

Allwood, J.M., Ashby, M.F., Gutowski, T.G, Worrell, E. (2011) Material Efficiency: a White Paper, *Resources Conservation and Recycling,* 55, 362–381

Allwood, J.M., Cullen, J.M. and Milford R.L., 2010. Options for achieving a 50% cut in industrial carbon emissions by 2050. *Environmental Science and Technology,* 44(6) pp.1888-1894

Allwood, J.M., Cullen, J.M., Carruth, M. A., Milford, R. L., Patel, A. C. H., Moynihan, M., Cooper, D. R., McBrien, M., 2011a. *Going on a metal diet – using less liquid metal to deliver the same service in order to save energy and carbon.* WellMet2050. [online] Cambridge: University of Cambridge Available at <http://www.lcmp.eng.cam.ac.uk/wellmet2/introduction> [accessed 27 July 2011]

Allwood, J.M., Cullen, J.M., McBrien, M., Milford, R. L., Carruth, M. A., Patel, A. C. H., Cooper, D. R., Moynihan, M., 2011b. *Taking our metal temperature – energy and carbon savings by managing heat in steel and aluminium supply chains,* WellMet2050. [online] Cambridge: University of Cambridge Available at <http://www.lcmp.eng.cam.ac.uk/wellmet2/introduction> [accessed 27 July 2011]

Allwood, J.M., Cullen, J.M., Cooper, D. R., McBrien, M., Milford, R. L., Carruth, M. A., Patel, A. C. H., Moynihan, M., 2011c. *Conserving our metal energy – Avoiding melting steel and aluminium scrap to save energy and carbon,* WellMet2050. [online] Cambridge: University of Cambridge Available at <http://www.lcmp.eng.cam.ac.uk/wellmet2/introduction> [accessed 27 July 2011]

Allwood, J.M., Cullen, J.M., Patel, A. C. H., McBrien, M., Milford, R. L., Carruth, M. A., Cooper, D. R., Moynihan, M., 2011d. *Prolonging our metal life – Making the most of our metal services,* WellMet2050. [online] Cambridge: University of Cambridge Available at <http://www.lcmp.eng.cam.ac.uk/wellmet2/introduction> [accessed 27 July 2011]

American Forest and Paper Association, 2010. *Paper and paperboard recovery, Recycling statistics* [online] Available at <http://paperrecycles.org/stat_pages/recovery_rate.html> [accessed 27 July 2011]

Arthur, B, W., 1989 Competing technologies, increasing returns, and lock-in by historical events, *The Economic Journal,* 99, pp.116-131

Arthur, B. W., 1999. Complexity and the economy, *Science, New Series,* 284(5411). pp.107-109

Ashby, M.F., and Jones, D.R.H., 2005. *Engineering materials 1: An introduction to properties, applications and design.* Cambridge, UK: Elsevier Butterworth-Heinemann

Ashby, M. F., 2009. *Materials and the environment – eco-informed material choice.* Burlington: Elsevier

Asolekar, S. R., 2006. Status of management of solid hazardous wastes generated during dismantling of obsolete ships in India. In: *Proceedings of in the International Conference on Dismantling of Obsolete Vessels.* Glasgow, UK, 11-12 September 2006

Avram, O. I. and Xirouchakis, P., 2011. Evaluating the use phase energy requirements of a machine tool system, *Journal of Cleaner Production,* 19 pp.699-711

Aylen, J., 1998. *Trends in the international steel market.* In Ranieri, R. and Aylen, J., eds, 1998. The steel industry in the new millennium Vol 1: Technology and the Market. Cambridge: IOM Communications Ltd

Aylen, J., 2011. Stretch, Paper for: *Managing R&D, Technology and Innovation in the Process Industries,* Manchester 5–6 May 2011

Ayres, R. U., 2006. Turning point – the end of exponential growth? *Technological Forecasting and Social Change,* 73(9) pp.188-1203

B

Barker, D.J., Turner, S.A., Napier-Moore, P.A., Davison, J.E., 2009. CO_2 capture in the cement industry, *Energy Procedia*, 1(1), pp.87-94

Barrett, J., Owen, A., Sakai, M., 2011. *UK consumption emissions by sector and origin*, report to the UK Department for Environment, Food and Rural Affairs (DEFRA) by University of Leeds

Barsoumw, M.W., Ganguly, A. and Hug, G., 2006. Microstructural evidence of reconstituted limestone blocks in the great pyramids of Egypt, *Journal of the American Ceramic Society*, 89(12), pp.3788–3796

Batelle, 2002. *Toward a Sustainable Cement Industry.* World Business Council for Sustainable Development

Baumert, K. A., Herzog, T., Pershing, J., 2005. *Navigating the Numbers: Greenhouse Gas Data and International Climate Policy.* World Resources Institute

BBC News, 2010a, *Villagers despair in Hungary's red wasteland,* [online] 12 October. Available at: <http://www.bbc.co.uk/news/world-europe-11523573> [accessed 27 July 2011]

BBC News, 2010b, *Rio Tinto in $3.1bn Australia iron ore expansion,* [online] 20 October. Available at: <http://www.bbc.co.uk/news/business-11581235> [accessed 27 July 2011]

BBC News, 2011a, *Rio Tinto agrees $2bn land deal with Aboriginals,* [online] 3 June. Available at: <http://www.bbc.co.uk/news/business-13637299> [accessed 27 July 2011]

BBC News, 2011b, *Tata steel to cut 1,500 jobs in Scunthorpe and Teesside,* [online], 20 May. Available at <http://www.bbc.co.uk/news/business-13469088> [accessed 27 July 2011]

BCS, 2007. *U.S. energy requirements for aluminium production, historical perspective, theoretical limits and current practices,* prepared for US Department of Energy [online] Available at <http://www1.eere.energy.gov/industry/aluminum/pdfs/al_theoretical.pdf> [accessed 27 July 2011]

BCSA, 2006. *A century of steel in construction.* London: British Construction Steelwork Association

Bendsøe, M.P., and Sigmund, O., 2003. *Topology Optimization.* Berlin: Springer-Verlag

Bhooplapur, P., Brammer, M.P., and Steeper, M.J., 2008. Upgrading existing plate mill for higher strength steel product, *Ironmaking and Steelmaking* 35(7) pp.491-495

Black, R., 2011. *Polar ice loss quickens, raising seas,* BBC News, [online] 9 March. Available at: <http://www.bbc.co.uk/news/science-environment-12687272> [accessed 27 July 2011]

Boin, U.M.J. and Bertram, M., 2005. Melting standardized aluminum scrap - a mass balance model for Europe, *JOM*, Aug, pp.27-33

Bosoaga, A., Masek, O., Oakey, J.E., 2009. CO_2 Capture Technologies for Cement Industry, *Energy Procedia*, 1(1) pp.133-144

Bouquet, T. and Ousey, B., 2008. *Cold Steel.* London: Hachette Digital

Bowen, A., Forster, P.M., Gouldson, A., Hubacek, K., Martin, R., O'Neill, W., Rap, A. and Rydge, J., 2009. *The implications of the economics slowdown for greenhouse gas emissions and targets,* Centre of Climate Change Economics and Policy, Working Paper No. 11

BP, 2011. *Statistical review of world energy.* [online] London:BP Available at: <http://www.bp.com/sectionbodycopy.do?categoryId=7500&contentId=7068481> [accessed 27 July 2011]

BPF, 2011. *Plastics: recycling and sustainability,* [online] Available at: <http://www.bpf.co.uk/sustainability/plastics_recycling.aspx> [accessed 27 July 2011]

BRE, 2011. *Passivhaus,* [online] Available at <http://www.passivhaus.org.uk/> [accessed 27 July 2011]

Brook Lyndhurst, 2009. *Household waste prevention evidence review: L2 M4-2 retail solutions,* a report for Defra's Waste and Resources Evidence Programme. London: Brook Lyndhurst

Bull, M., Chavali, R. and Mascarin, A., 2008. *Benefit analysis: use of aluminum structures in conjunction with alternative powertrain technologies in automotives,* Aluminium Association. [online] Available at <http://aluminumintransportation.org/main/resources/research-optimizer> [accessed 27 July 2011]

C

Callister, W.D., 2003. *Material science and engineering: an introduction,* Sixth edition. New York: John Wiley & Sons

Canadian Steel Producers Association, 2007. *Benchmarking energy intensity in the Canadian steel industry.* [online] Available at <http://oee.nrcan.gc.ca/industrial/technical-info/benchmarking/benchmarking_guides.cfm> [accessed 27 July 2011]

Car Reg, n.d.. *Environmental site blames DVLA [online]* Available at: <http://www.carreg.co.uk/number_plates/get_news/143>

Carruth, M.A., Allwood, J.M., 2011. The forming of variable cross-section I-beams by hot rolling. To be presented at the *10th International Conference on Technology of Plasticity,* Aachen 28th September

CEMEP, 2011. *Electric Motors and Variable Speed Drives Standards and legal requirements for the energy efficiency of low-voltage three-phase motors, European Committee of Manufacturers of Electrical Machines and Power Electronics.* [online] Available at <http://www.cemep.org/fileadmin/downloads/CEMEP_Motors_and_VSD.pdf> [accessed 27 July 2011]

CEPI, 2009. *Key statistics – European pulp and paper industry.* Brussels: Confederation of European Paper Industries. [online] Available at <http://www.cepi.org/Objects/1/files/KeyStats09_V01.pdf> [accessed 27 July 2011]

CEPI, 2011. *Q&A on the sustainability of the paper industry* [online] Available at: <www.cepi.org> [accessed 27 July 2011]

China Environmental Law, 2008. *Circular economy law of the People's Republic of China.* [online] Available at <http://www.chinaenvironmentallaw.com/wp-content/uploads/2008/09/circular-economy-law-cn-en-final.pdf> [accessed 27 July 2011]

Chester, M.C., Horvath, A., 2009. Environmental assessment of passenger transportation should include infrastructure and supply chains, *Environmental Research Letters*, 4, pp.1-8

Chemical Industry Education Centre, 2011. *Solids in furnace gas turned back into metal*, Sustain-ed [online] Available at <http://www.sustained.org/pages/Materials/MaterialsFrameset.htm>

Christensen, C.M., 2003. *The innovator's dilemma*, New York: Harper Paperbacks

Climate Change Act 2008. London:HMSO

Cole, J., n.d.. *Observations on the London home front in World War Two* [online] Available at <http://www.1900s.org.uk/1942-43-events.htm> [accessed 27 July 2011]

Cooper, T., 2004. Inadequate life? Evidence of consumer attitudes to product obsolescence, *Journal of Consumer Policy*, 27, pp.421-449

Counsell, T. A. M. and Allwood, J.M., 2006. Desktop paper recycling - a survey of novel technologies that might recycle office paper within the office, *Journal of Material Processing Technology* 173(1) pp.111-123

Counsell, T. A. M. and Allwood, J.M., 2007. Reducing climate change gas emissions by cutting out stages in the life cycle of office paper, *Resources, Conservation and Recycling*, 49(4), pp.340-352

Counsell, T.A.M. and Allwood, J.M., 2008. Using abrasives to remove toner-print so that office paper might be reused, *Wear*, 266, pp.782-794

Counsell, T.A.M. and Allwood, J.M., 2009. Using solvents to remove a toner print so that office paper might be reused, *Proceedings of the Royal Society*, A 465, pp.3839-3858

CRU, 2011. *About CRU*, [online] Available at: <http://crugroup.com/AboutCRU/Pages/default.aspx> [accessed 27 July 2011]

Cullen, J.M. and Allwood, J.M. (2010a) The efficient use of energy: tracing the global flow of energy from fuel to service, *Energy Policy*, 38, pp.75-81

Cullen, J.M. and Allwood, J.M. (2010b) Theoretical efficiency limits in energy conversion devices, *Energy* 35(5), pp.2059-2069

Cullen, J.M., Allwood, J.M., Borgstein, E.H., 2011. Reducing energy demand: what are the practical limits?, *Environmental Science and Technology*, 45(4), pp.1711–1718

D

Danloy, G., van der Stel, J., Schmöle, P., 2008. Heat and mass balances in the ULCOS blast furnace, Proceedings of the *4th ULCOS seminar*, 1-2 October 2008

Datamonitor, 2007. *Global automotive manufacturers*, Ref: 0199-2010. New York: Datamonitor

Datamonitor, 2008. *Containers and packaging*, Ref: 0199-2036. New York: Datamonitor

Davis, G. and Hall, J.A., 2006. *Circular Economy Legislation – The International Experience.* [online] Available at: <http://siteresources.worldbank.org/INTEAPREGTOPENVIRONMENT/Resources/CircularEconomy_Legal_IntExperience_ExecSummary_EN.doc> [accessed 27 July 2011]

Davis, J., Geyer, R., Ley, J., He, J., Clift, R., Kwan, A., Sansom, M. and Jackson, T., 2007. Time-dependent material flow analysis of iron and steel in the UK Part 2: Scrap generation and recycling, *Resources Conservation & Recycling*, 51 pp.118–140

DCLG, 2007. *Building a greener future – policy statement.* London: Department for Communities and Local Government

de Beer, J.G., Worrell, E. and Blok, K., 1998. Future technologies for energy-efficient iron and steel making, *Annual Review of Energy and the Environment*, 23, pp.123-205

de Beer, J.G., 1998. Long term energy-efficiency improvements in the paper and board industry, *Energy*, 23(1), pp.21-42

Defra, 2005. *Securing the future – delivering UK sustainable development strategy.* London:HMSO

Defra, 2011. *Government review of waste policy in England.* London: Department for Environment, Food and Rural Affairs. [online] Available at <http://www.defra.gov.uk/publications/files/pb13540-waste-policy-review110614.pdf> [accessed 27 July 2011]

Dennis, M.J. and Kambil, A., 2003. Service management – building profit after the sale, *Supply Chain Management Review*, 7(3) pp.42-48

Denstadli, J.M., 2004. Impacts of videoconferencing on business travel – the Norwegian experience, *Journal of Air Transport Management*, 10, pp.371-376

Devoldere, T., Dewulf, W., Deprez, W., Willems, B., Duflou, J., 2007. Improvement potential for energy consumption in discrete part production machines, *Advances in Life Cycle Engineering for Sustainable Manufacturing Businesses*, Part 3, B5 pp.311-316

Diamond, J.M., 2005. *Collapse – how societies choose to fail or succeed.* New York: Penguin

E

EIPPCB, 2010. *Reference document on best available techniques in the pulp and paper industry.* Seville: European Integrated Pollution Prevention and Control Bureau

EMPAC, 2009. *Cans prevent waste,* [online] Available on: <http://www. empac.eu/index.php/site/section/126> [accessed 27 July 2011]

End-of-life Vehicles Regulations 2003. SI 2003/2635. London: HMSO

Eriksson, O. and Finnveden, G., 2009. Plastic waste as a fuel – CO_2-neutral or not? *Energy and Environmental Science,* 2, pp.907-914

European Nuclear Society, 2011. *Nuclear power plants world-wide* [online] Available at <http://www.euronuclear.org/info/encyclopedia/n/ nuclear-power-plant-world-wide.htm> [accessed 27 July 2011]

EXIOPOL, n.d., *A new environmental accounting framework* [online] Available at <http://www.feem-project.net/exiopol/> [accessed 27 July 2011]

F

FAO, 2007. *FAOSTAT, Food and Agriculture Organisation of the United Nations* [online] Available at <http://faostat.fao.org> [accessed 27 July 2011]

Financial Times, 2010. *Global 500 by sector* [online] Available at: <http:// www.ft.com/reports/ft500-2010> [accessed 27 July 2011]

Fletcher, K., 2008. *Sustainable fashion and textiles – design journeys.* London: Earthscan

Forestry Commission, 2011. *UK wood production and trade (provisional figures)* – 2011 edition, Economics and Statistics, [online] Available at <http://www.forestry.gov.uk/statistics> [accessed 27 July 2011]

Francis, A.K., 1977. *The cement industry 1796-1914 – a history.* North Pomfret: Newton Abbot

French B. F., 1858. *History of the rise and progress of the iron trade of the United States from 1621 to 1857.* New York: Wiley & Halsted

G

Gerst, M. D. and Graedel, T. E., 2008. In-use stocks of metals: status and implications, *Environmental Science & Technology,* 42, pp.7038-7045

Granta Design, 2011. CES 2012 Selector, [online] Available at <http:// www.grantadesign.com/products/ces/> [accessed 27 July 2011]

Greentomatoenergy, 2011. *Case study: PassivHaus renovation in West London* [online] Available at <http://www.greentomatoenergy.com/ about_us/case_studies> [accessed 27 July 2011]

GTAP, 1997. *GTAP 5 Database.* [online] Available at: <https://www. gtap.agecon.purdue.edu/databases/archives.asp> [accessed 27 July 2011]

GTAP, 2011. *Global trade analysis project* [online] Available at: <https:// www.gtap.agecon.purdue.edu/> [accessed 27 July 2011]

Gutowski, T., Murphy, C., Allen, D., Bauer, D., Bras, B., Piwonka, T., Sheng, P., Sutherland, J., Thurston, D., Wolff, E., 2005. Environmentally benign manufacturing - observations from Japan, Europe and the United States, *Journal of Cleaner Production,* 13 pp. 1–17

H

Hagelüken, C., 2006. *Recycling of electronic scrap at Umicore's integrated metals smelter and refinery,* World of Metal – ERZMETALL, 59(3), pp.152-161

Hammond, G. and Jones, C., 2008. *Inventory of carbon and energy, Version 1.6,* University of Bath, Available at <http://www.bath.ac.uk/ mech-eng/sert/embodied/ >* [accessed 27 July 2011]

Hammond, G. and Jones, C., 2011. *Inventory of carbon and energy, Version 2.0,* University of Bath, Available at <http://www.bath.ac.uk/ mech-eng/sert/embodied/ >* [accessed 27 July 2011]

Hatayama, H., Daigo, I., Matsuno, Y. and Adachi, Y., 2009. Assessment of the recycling potential of aluminum in Japan, the United States, *Europe and China, Materials Transactions,* 50(3) pp.650–656

Hatayama, H., Daigo, I., Matsuno, Y. and Adachi, Y., 2010. Outlook of the world steel cycle based on the stock and flow dynamics, *Environmental Science and Technology,* 44(16), pp.6457-6463

Hekkert, M.P., Worrel, E., 1997. *Technology characterization for natural organic materials: Input data for Western European MARKAL,* University of Utrecht, Report no. 98002

Hu, M., Pauliuk, S., Wang, T., Huppes, G., van der Voet, E. and Müller, D.B., 2010. Iron and steel in Chinese residential buildings: A dynamic analysis, Resources, *Conservation and Recycling,* 54 pp.591–600

Humphreys, K. & Mahasenan, M., 2002. *Toward a Sustainable Cement Industry Substudy 8: Climate Change.* World Business Council for Sustainable Development

I

IAI, 2007. *Life cycle assessment of aluminium - inventory data for the primary aluminium industry year 2005.* London: International Aluminium Institute. [online] Available at <http://www.world-aluminium. org/?pg=140> [accessed 27 July 2011]

IAI, 2009. *Global aluminium recycling – a cornerstone of sustainable development.* London: International Aluminium Institute. [online] Available at <http://www.world-aluminium.org/cache/fl0000181.pdf> [accessed 27 July 2011]

IAI, 2011a. *Aluminium fact feature* [online] Available at <http://www.world-aluminium.org/> [accessed 27 July 2011]

IAI, 2011b. *Historical IAI statistics.* [online] Available at <http://www.world-aluminium.org/statistics> [accessed 27 July 2011]

IDES, 2011. *The plastic web* [online] Available at: <http://www.ides.com/> [accessed 27 July 2011]

IEA, 2007. *Tracking industrial energy efficiency and CO_2 emissions.* Paris: International Energy Agency. [online] Available at: <http://www.iea.org/textbase/nppdf/free/2007/tracking_emissions.pdf> [accessed 27 July 2011]

IEA, 2008a. *Energy technology perspectives.* Paris: International Energy Agency. [online] Available at: <http://www.iea.org/w/bookshop/add.aspx?id=330> [accessed 27 July 2011]

IEA, 2008b. *CO_2 capture and storage: a key carbon abatement option.* Paris: International Energy Agency. [online] Available at: <http://www.iea.org/w/bookshop/add.aspx?id=335> [accessed 27 July 2011]

IEA, 2008c. *World energy outlook 2008.* Paris: International Energy Agency. [online] Available at: <http://www.iea.org/textbase/nppdf/free/2008/weo2008.pdf> [accessed 27 July 2011]

IEA, 2009. *Energy technology transitions for industry.* Paris: International Energy Agency. [online] Available at: <http://www.iea.org/textbase/nppdf/free/2009/industry2009.pdf> [accessed 27 July 2011]

IEA, 2010a. *CO_2 emissions from fuel combustion – highlights.* Paris: International Energy Agency. [online] Available at: <http://www.iea.org/co2highlights/co2highlights.pdf> [accessed 27 July 2011]

IEA, 2010b. *Energy technology perspectives.* Paris: International Energy Agency. [online] Available at: <http://www.iea.org/techno/etp/etp10/English.pdf> [accessed 27 July 2011]

IEA, 2010c. *Energy statistics manual.* Paris: International Energy Agency. [online] Available at: <http://epp.eurostat.ec.europa.eu/cache/ITY_PUBLIC/NRG-2004/EN/NRG-2004-EN.PDF> [accessed 27 July 2011]

IEA, 2011. *Energy-Efficiency Policy Opportunities for Electric Motor-Driven Systems – Working Paper*, Paris: International Energy Agency.

IISI, 1998. *Energy use in the steel industry.* Brussels: International Iron and Steel Institute

IMF, 2011. *World Economic Outlook Database, International Monetary Fund* [online] Available at: <http://www.imf.org/external/pubs/ft/weo/2011/01/weodata/index.aspx> [accessed 27 July 2011]

IPCC, 2005. *Carbon dioxide capture and storage.* [online] Available at: <http://www.ipcc.ch/pdf/special-reports/srccs/srccs_wholereport.pdf> [accessed 27 July 2011]

J

Jávor, B. and Hargitai, M., ed. 2011. *The Kolontár report – causes and lesson from the red mud disaster.* Budapest: Budapest University of Technology and Economics [online] Available at <http://lehetmas.hu/wp-content/uploads/2011/05/Kolontar-report.pdf> [accessed 27 July 2011]

K

Kanemoto, K., Lenzen, M., Geschke, A., Moran, D., 2011. *Building Eora: a global multi-region input output model at high country and sector*, 19th International Input–Output Conference, Alexandria, USA, 13–17 June [online] Available at <http://www.iioa.org/files/conference-2/274_20110505091_GlobalMRIO_20110502.pdf> [accessed 27 July 2011]

Kay T. and Essex J., 2009. *Pushing reuse: towards a low-carbon construction industry.* London: BioRegional and Salvo

Kelkar, A., Roth, R., and Clark, J., 2001. Automobile bodies: can aluminium be an economical alternative to steel? *JOM*, August pp.28-32

Kerr, W. and Ryan, C., 2001. Eco-efficiency gains from remanufacturing: a case study of photocopier remanufacturing at Fuji Xerox Australia, *Journal of Cleaner Production*, 9, pp.75–81

Kim, Y. and Worrell, E., 2002. International comparison of CO_2 emission trends in the iron and steel industry, *Energy Policy*, 20, pp.827-838

L

Lafarge, 2007. *Lafarge Annual Report.* Available at: http://www.lafarge.com/28032008-publication_finance-annual_report_2007-uk.pdf

Layard, R., 2006. *Happiness – lessons from a new science.* London: Penguin

Leal-Ayala, D.R., Allwood, J.M. and Counsell T.A.M., 2010. Paper un-printing: using lasers to remove toner-print in order to reuse office paper, Manuscript submitted for publication to Applied Physics A: Materials Science & Processing

Leal-Ayala, D.R., Allwood, J.M., Schmidt, M., and Alexeev, I., 2011. Toner-print removal from paper by long and ultrashort pulsed lasers, Manuscript submitted for publication to *Proceedings of the Royal Society A*

Lewis, A., 2010. *Europe breaking electronic waste export ban*, BBC News, 4 August, [online] Available on <http://www.bbc.co.uk/news/world-europe-10846395> [accessed 27 July 2011]

Lin Wei M., 2011. *Personal communication*, 14 May 2011

Lu, J.L. and Peeta, S., 2009. Analysis of the factors that influence the relationship between business travel and videoconferencing, *Transport Research Part A*, 43, pp.709-721

Luo, Z. and Soria, A., 2008. *Prospective study of the world aluminium industry.* Seville: European Commission [online] Available at <http://ftp.jrc.es/EURdoc/JRC40221.pdf>

M

MacKay, D. J. C., 2008. *Sustainable energy – without the hot air,* Cambridge: UIT. [online] Available at: <http://www.withouthotair.com/>

Margreta, J., 1998. The power of virtual integration: an interview with Dell Computer's Michael Dell, *Harvard Business Review,* March/April

Martin, N., Anglani, N., Einstein, D., Khrushch, M., Worrell, E. and Price, L.K., 2000. *Opportunities to Improve Energy Efficiency and Reduce Greenhouse Gas Emissions in the U.S. Pulp and Paper Industry,* US Department of Energy, Office of Scientific and Technical Information [online] Available at <www.osti.gov/bridge/servlets/purl/790009-AERaSR/native/790009.pdf>

McKinnon, A., 2005. The economic and environmental benefits of increasing maximum truck weight: the British experience, *Transportation Research Part D,* 10 pp.77–95.

McKinsey, 2009. *Greenhouse gas abatement cost curves,* [online] Available at: <http://www.mckinsey.com/en/Client_Service/Sustainability/Latest_thinking/Costcurves.aspx> [accessed 27 July 2011]

Memoli, F. and Ferri, M.B., 2008. *2007- A record year for Consteel®,* Millenium Steel 2008 pp83-88, [online] Available at <http://www.millennium-steel.com/articles/pdf/2008/pp83-88%20MS08.pdf>

Miles, D. and Scott, A., 2005. *Macroeconomics: Understanding the wealth of nations.* 2nd ed. Hoboken: John Wiley and sons

Milford, R.L. and Allwood, J.M. (2010) Assessing the CO_2 impact of current and future rail track, *Transportation Research Part D: Transport and Environment,* 15(2) pp. 61-72

Moinov, S., 1998. *Patterns of privatisation in the world iron and steel industry.* In: Ranieri, R. and Gibellieri, E., 1998. The steel industry in the new millennium, Vol 2: Institutions, privatisation and social dimensions. Cambridge: IOM Communications Ltd

Morgan, C. and Stevenson, F., 2005. *Design and detailing for deconstruction, Design Guides for Scotland (No. 1),* SEDA

Müller, D. B., Wang, T. and Duval, B., 2011. Patterns of iron use in societal evolution, *Environmental Science and Technology,* 45(1) pp. 182-188

N

Naranjo, M., Brownlow, D.T. and Garza, A., 2011. CO_2 capture and sequestration in the cement industry, *Energy Procedia,* 4, pp.2716-2723

Nilsson, L.J. et al, 1995. *Energy efficiency and the pulp and paper industry.* Washington D.C.: American Council for an Energy Efficient Economy

Noguchi, T., Kitagaki, R., Tsujino, M., 2011. Minimizing environmental impact and maximizing performance in concrete recycling, *Structural Concrete,* 12(1), pp36-46

Novelis, 2011. *Markets we serve, packaging, beverage cans.* [online] Available at <http://www.novelis.com/en-us/Pages/Beverage-Cans.aspx> [accessed 27 July 2011]

O

OECD, 2010. *The Evolution of News and the Internet,* Working party on the Information Economy, Directorate for Science, Technology and Industry, DSTI/ICCP/IE(2009)14/FINAL

OGC, 2007. *Sustainability – achieving excellence in construction procurement guide.* London: Office of Government Commerce

Ohno, T., 1988. *Toyota Production System: Beyond Large-scale* Production, Oregon: Productivity Press Inc

ONS, 2010a, *The blue book – United Kingdom National Accounts,* Basingstoke: Palgrave Macmillan [online] Available at <http://www.statistics.gov.uk/downloads/theme_economy/bluebook2010.pdf>

ONS, 2010b. *Construction statistics annual.* London: OPSI [online] Available at: <http://www.statistics.gov.uk/downloads/theme_commerce/CSA-2010/Opening%20page.pdf> [accessed 27 July 2011]

Orr, J.J., Darby, A.P., Ibell, T.J., Evernden, M.C., Otlet, M., 2010. *Concrete structures using fabric formwork,* The Structural Engineer, 89(8), pp.20-26

OSPR, 1998. *OSPAR Convention.* [online] Available at: <http://www.ospar.org/content/content.asp?menu=00340108070000_000000_000000> [accessed 27 July 2011]

P

Paper Task Force, 1995. *Paper task force recommendations for purchasing and using environmentally preferable paper.* New York: Environmental Defense Fund

Parliamentary business, 2006. *Globalisation and the steel industry.* [online] Available at <http://www.publications.parliament.uk/pa/cm200607/cmselect/cmwelaf/ucglobal/uc2602.pdf>

Passivhaus Institut, 2011. [online] Available at <http://www.passiv.de/07_eng/index_e.html> [accessed 27 July 2011]

Passivhaus Trust, 2011. [online] Available at <http://www.passivhaustrust.org.uk/>

Pike, R., Leonard, M., 2011. *China restricts exports of rare earth elements,* Today Programme [podcast] 4 January [online]. Available at <http://news.bbc.co.uk/today/hi/today/newsid_9336000/9336159.stm> [accessed 27 July 2011]

Politics, 2007. *Gordon Brown's speech in full*, 19 November. [online] Available at: <http://www.politics.co.uk/news/2007/11/19/gordon-brown-s-speech-in-full> [accessed 27 July 2011]

Pratten, C.F., 1971. *Economies of scale in manufacturing industry*, Cambridge, UK: Cambridge University Press

Prettenthaler F.E., Steininger K.W., 1999. From ownership to service use lifestyle: the potential of car sharing, *Ecological Economics* 28 pp.443–53

Pudaily, 2007. [online] Available at <http://www.pu366.com> [accessed 27 July 2011]

R

Ramesh, T., Prakash, R., Shukla, K.K., 2010. Life cycle energy analysis of buildings – an overview, *Energy and Buildings*, 42, pp1592-1600

RISI, 2007. *World pulp & recovered paper 15-year forecast*. Bedford, MA: Paperloop, Inc

Rivero, R. and Garfias, M., 2006. Standard chemical exergy of elements updated, *Energy*, 31(15), pp.3310-3326

Roy, J. and Filiatrault, P., 1998. The impact of new business practices and information technologies on business travel demand, *Journal of Air Transport Management*, 4, pp.77-86

S

Saito Y., Utsunomiya H., Tsuji N. and Sakai T., 1999. Novel ultra-high straining process for bulk materials-development of the accumulative roll-bonding (ARB) process, *Acta Materialia*, 47(2), pp.579–583

Secat, 2005. *Sorting the wrought from the cast in automotive aluminium* [online] Available at <http://www.secat.net/answers_view_article.php?article=Sorting_the_Wrought_from_the_Cast_in_Automotive_Aluminum.html> [accessed 27 July 2011]

Seok-Ho L., Hwan-Oh C., Jung-Seok K., Cheul-Kyu L., Yong-Ki K., and Chang-Sik J., 2011. Circulating flow reactor for recycling of carbon fiber from carbon fiber reinforced epoxy composite, *Korean Journal of Chemical Engineering*, 28(1), pp.449-454

Sergeant, 2010. *Top 100 mining companies – what a difference a year makes*, Mineweb, Mining Finanace/Investment [online] Available at :<http://www.mineweb.com/mineweb/view/mineweb/en/page67?oid=95737&sn=Detail> [accessed 27 July 2011]

Smil, V., 2010. *Energy myths and realities*, Washington D.C.: AEI Press

Smith, M.C. and Wang, F.C., 2004. Performance benefits in passive vehicle suspensions employing inerters, *Vehicle System Dynamics*, 42(4), pp.235-257

Solomon, M., Bamossy, G. and Askegaard, S. 1999. *Consumer Behaviour: A European perspective*. London: Prentice Hall International

Spear, S. & Bowen, H.K., 1999. Decoding the DNA of the Toyota production system, *Harvard Business Review*, 77:5 pp.97-106

SSAB, n.d.. *Environmental impact during the production process*, [online] Available at <http://www.ssab.com/Sustainability/Ethical-issuesSustainability/Environment/Environmental-impact-during-the-production-process/> [accessed 27 July 2011]

Stanley, C.C., 1779. *Highlights in the history of concrete*. Slough: Cement and Concrete Association

Steel Business Briefing (SBB), 2009. *European domestic medium section price*, Prices and Indices [online] Available at: <http://www.steelbb.com/steelprices/> [accessed 27 July 2011]

Steel University, 2011. *Blast furnace mass and energy balance*, [online] Available at <http://www.steeluniversity.org/content/html/eng/default.asp?catid=13&pageid=2081272299> [accessed 27 July 2011]

Strömberg, L., Lindgren, G., J Jacoby, J., Giering, R., Anheden, M.,Burchhardt, U., Altmann, H., Kluger, F., Stamatelopoulos, G., 2009. Update on Vattenfall's 30 MWth Oxyfuel Pilot Plant in Schwarze Pumpe, *Energy Procedia*, 1, pp581–589

T

Takano H., Kitazawa K., Goto T., 2008. Incremental forming of nonuniform sheet metal: Possibility of cold recycling process of sheet metal waste, *Journal of Machine Tools & Manufacture*, 48, pp. 477-482

TAPPI, 2001. *All about paper* [online] Available at <http://www.tappi.org/paperu/all_about_paper/earth_answers/earthAnswers.htm> [accessed 27 July 2011]

Tata, 2011a. *The Tata Steel Group Corporate Citizenship Report 2009/2010*. [online] Available at <http://www.tatasteeleurope.com/file_source/StaticFiles/Functions/HSE/CCR-09-10.pdf> [accessed 27 July 2011]

Tata, 2011b. *Tata Steel – at the forefront of low carbon steelmaking* [online]. Available at: <http://www.colorcoatonline.com/en/company/news/tata_steel_low_carbon_steelmaking> [accessed 27 July 2011]

Tata Steel Automotive, 2010. *Personal communication*, Site visit, April

Taylor, H., 1990. *Cement Chemistry*. First edition, London: Academic Press

Taylor, M., Tam C., Gielen, D., 2006. *Energy Efficiency and CO_2 Emissions from the Global Cement Industry*. International Energy Agency

Tekkaya, A. E.; Franzen, V.; Trompeter, M., 2008. Remanufacturing of sheet metal parts (German), Proceedings of the *15th Saxon Conference on Forming Technology*, Dresden, pp. 187-196

Thompson, C., 1992. *Recycled papers - the essential guide.* Cambridge, MA: MIT Press

Tilwankar, A.K., Mahindrakar, A. B., and Asolekar S.R., 2008. Steel recycling resulting from ship dismantling in India: implications for green house gas emissions. In: Proceedings of second *International Conference "Dismantling of Obsolete Vessels"*, 15–16 September, organized by Universities of Glasgow & Strathclyde, Glasgow, UK

Tomiura, A., 1998. *Paradigm shifts in the steel industry*, in Ranieri, R. and Aylen, J., eds 1998. The steel industry in the new millennium Vol 1: Technology and the Market. Cambridge: IOM Communications Ltd

Tribal Energy and Environmental Information Clearinghouse, 2011. *How can we use the energy in biomass?* [online] Available at <http://teeic. anl.gov/er/biomass/restech/uses/howuse/index.cfm> [accessed 27 July 2011]

Tyskend, S. and Finnveden, G., 2010. Comparing energy use and environmental impacts of recycling and waste incineration, *Journal of Environmental Engineering* 136 pp.744-748

U

UK Steel, 2011. *Key statistics.* [online] Available at <http://www.eef.org.uk/NR/rdonlyres/C2F00A49-B277-4015-9EEB-74E3051721D0/19061/KeyStatistics2012.pdf> [accessed 27 July 2011]

UNCTAD, 2011. *UNCTADSTAT*, United Nations Conference on Trade and Development [online] Available at: <http://unctadstat.unctad.org/ReportFolders/reportFolders.aspx> [accessed 27 July 2011]

UNSD, 2008. *Demographic yearbook*, United Nations Statistics Division [online] Available at <http://unstats.un.org/unsd/demographic/products/dyb/dyb2008.htm> [accessed 27 July 2011]

UNDESA, 2009. *World urbanization prospects*, United Nations Department of Economic and Social Affairs [online] Available at <http://esa.un.org/unpd/wup/index.htm> [accessed 27 July 2011]

UNEP, eds., 2011. *Metal stocks and recycling rates*, United Nations Environment Panel [online]. Available at: :<http://www.unep.org/resourcepanel/Portals/24102/PDFs/Metals_Recycling_Rates_110412-1.pdf> [accessed 27 July 2011]

UNPFA, 2010. *State of world population 2010 – from conflict and crisis to renewal, generations of change.* United Nations Population Fund. [online] Available at: <http://www.unfpa.org/swp/index.html> [accessed 27 July 2011]

US DOE, 2004. *Energy use, loss and opportunities analysis – US manufacturing and mining.* Industrial Technologies Program, U.S. Department of Energy. [online] Available at <http://www1.eere.energy.gov/industry/intensiveprocesses/pdfs/energy_use_loss_opportunities_analysis.pdf> [accessed 27 July 2011]

US DOE, 2007. *Improving process heating system performance: a sourcebook for industry*, Second edition [online] United State Department of Energy .Available at: <http://www1.eere.energy.gov/industry/bestpractices/pdfs/process_heating_sourcebook2.pdf> [accessed 27 July 2011]

USEIA, n.d.. *International energy statistics.* United States Energy Information Administration [online] Available on <http://www.eia.gov/emeu/international/electricitygeneration.html>

US Steel, 2011. *History of US Steel* [website] Available at: <http://www.ussteel.com/corp/company/profile/history.asp> [accessed 27 July 2011]

USGS, 2010. *Cement, Mineral commodity summary.* United States Geological Survey [online] Available at <http://minerals.usgs.gov/minerals/pubs/commodity/cement/mcs-2010-cemen.pdf> [accessed 27 July 2011]

USGS, 2011a. *Bauxite and alumina, Mineral commodity summary.* United States Geological Survey [online] Available at <http://minerals.usgs.gov/minerals/pubs/commodity/bauxite/mcs-2011-bauxi.pdf> [accessed 27 July 2011]

USGS, 2011b. *Iron ore, Mineral commodity summary.* United States Geological Survey [online] Available at <http://minerals.usgs.gov/minerals/pubs/commodity/iron_ore/mcs-2011-feore.pdf> [accessed 27 July 2011]

V

van Oss and Padovani, 2003. Cement Manufacture and the Environment Part II: Environmental Challenges and Opportunities, *Journal of Industrial Ecology*, 7:1 pp.93-126

van Oss, 2011. Personal communication, USGS, 2 July 2011

Vattenfall, 2007. *Global climate impact abatement map.* [online] Available at: <http://www.iea.org/work/2007/priority/Nelson.pdf> [accessed 27 July 2011]

Vattenfall, 2011. *The Schwarze Pumpe pilot plant*, [online] Available at: <http://www.vattenfall.com/en/ccs/schwarze-pumpe.htm> [accessed 27 July 2011]

Vitousek P.M., Ehrlich P.R., Ehrlich A.H., Matson P.A., 1986. *Human appropriation of the products of photosynthesis*, BioScience, 36:6 pp.368–73

VW, 2006. *The Golf – Environmental commendation background report.* Wolfsburg: Volkswagen

VW, 2010. *The Polo – Environmental commendation background report.* Wolfsburg: Volkswagen

W

WBCSD, 2005. *The Cement Sustainability Initiative Progress Report.* World Business Council for Sustainable Development. Switzerland: Atar Roto Presse SA

WBCSD, 2009. Cement Technology Roadmap 2009: *Carbon emissions reductions up to 2050.* World Business Council for Sustainable Development. Switzerland: Atar Roto Presse SA

WBCSD, 2010. *Sustainability benefits of concrete*, Cement Industry Initiative, World Business Council for Sustainable Development. [online] Available at: <http://www.wbcsdcement.org/index.php?option=com_content&task=view&id=67&Itemid=136> [accessed 27 July 2011]

Wiedman, T., Wood, R., Lenzen, M., Harris, R., Guan, D. & Minx, J., 2007. *Application of a novel matrix balancing approach to the estimation of UK input-output tables.* In: Sixteenth International Input-Output Conference, 2-6 July, Istanbul Turkey. [online] Available at <http://www.isa.org.usyd.edu.au/publications/documents/Wiedmann_et_al_2007_16th_IIOA_Istanbul_Paper_final.pdf> [accessed 27 July 2011]

Woodcock N. and Norman D., n.d.. *Building stones of Cambridge – a walking tour around the historic city centre*, Department of Earth Sciences, University of Cambridge, [online] Available at <http://www.esc.cam.ac.uk/teaching/geological-sciences/building-stones-of-cambridge> [accessed 27 July 2011]

World Steel Association, n.d.. Statistics archive, [online] Available at: <http://www.worldsteel.org/?action=stats_search> [accessed 27 July 2011]

World Steel Association, 2008. *Fact sheet – steel and energy.* [online] Available at <http://www.worldsteel.org/pictures/programfiles/Fact%20sheet_Energy.pdf> [accessed 27 July 2011]

World Steel Association, 2009. *Yield improvement in the steel industry.* Brussels: World Steel Association

World Steel Association, 2010. *World steel in figures.* Brussels: World Steel Association

World Steel Association, 2011. *Steel's contribution to a low carbon future*, World Steel Association position paper, [online] Available at: <http://www.worldsteel.org/climatechange/?page=2&subpage=1> [accessed 27 July 2011]

Worrell, E., Price, L., Martin, N., Hendriks, C., Ozawa Meida, L., 2001. Carbon Dioxide Emissions from the Global Cement Industry. *Annual Review of Energy and the Environment*, 26, pp.303–29

Worrell, E., Price, L.,Neelis, M., Galitsky, C., and Zhou N., 2008. *World best practice energy intensity values for selected industrial sectors*, eScholarship, University of California, LBNL-62806. Rev. 2, [online] Available at <http://escholarship.org/uc/item/77n9d4sp.pdf> [accessed 27 July 2011]

WRAP, 2010. *Designing out waste – A design team guide for civil engineering, Part 1: Design Guide, Part 2: Technical Solutions*, WRAP, UK

WRAP, 2011. *Total carrier bag use continues to fall.* 25 August. [online] Available at <http://www.wrap.org.uk/media_centre/press_releases/total_carrier_bag.html>

X

Xu, C. and Cang, D., 2010. A brief overview of low CO_2 emission technologies for iron and steel making, *Journal of Iron and Steel Research, International*, 17(3), pp. 1-7

Y

Yang, F., Zhang, B., Ma, G., 2010. Study of Sticky Rice-Lime Mortar Technology for the Restoration of Historical Masonry Construction. *Accounts of Chemical Research*, 43(6), pp.936-944

Yellishetty, M., Ranjith, P.G. and Tharumarajah, A., 2010. Iron ore and steel production trends and material flows in the world: Is this really sustainable?, *Resources, Conservation and Recycling*, 54, pp.1084-1094

Z

Zandi, M., and Zimmerman, W., 2011. *Steel plant CO_2 sequestration using high efficiency micro-algal bioreactor.* METEC

Index

Acknowledgements

Every aspect of this book has involved collaboration, and we have enjoyed tremendous committed support and help from an enormous number of people. We would like to express our warm thanks to:

John Amoore, Karin Arnold, Prof. Mike Ashby, Prof. Shyam R. Asolekar, Roy Aspden, Efthymios Balomenos, Margarita Bambach, Mike Banfi, Prof. John Barrett, Chris Bayliss, Terry Benge, Marlen Bertram, Peter Birkinshaw, Manuel Birkle, Nancy Bocken, Paul Bradley, Mike Brammer, Nigel Brandon, Louis Brimacombe, Clare Broadbent, Emmanuelle Bruneteaux, Chris Burgoyne, David Calder, Simon Cardwell, Heather Carey, Jo Carris, Nick Champion, Andrea Charlson, Barry Clay, Nick Coleman, Grant Colquhoun, Richard Cooper, Steve Court, Polly Curtiss, AnaMaria Danila, John Davenport, Dr. Joseph Davidovits, Prof. Peter Davidson, Richard Dinnis, Prof. David Dornfeld, John Dowling, Kelly Driscoll, Dan Epstein, Jack Fellows, David Fidler, Andrew Fraser, Steve Fricker, Prof. Mark Gallerneault, Rosa Garcia-Pineiro, JoseLuis Gazapo, Bernhard Gillner, Mark Gorgolewski, Staffan Görtz, Prof. Tom Graedel, Bill Grant, Christophe Gras, Allan Griffin, Ellen Grist, Simon Guest, Volkan Güley, Prof. Peter Guthrie, Tomas Gutierrez, Prof. Timothy Gutowski, Christian Hagelueken, Martin Halliwell, Peter Harrington, Judith Hazel, Kirsten Henson, Prof. Gerhard Hirt, Shaun Hobson, Peter Hodgson, Gerald Hohenbichler, Andy Howe, Richard Howells, Len Howlett, Tom Hulls, Roland Hunziker, Jay Jaiswal, Carl Johnson, Aled Jones, Tony Jones, Ulla Juntti, Sarah Kaethner, Andrew Kenny, Holly Knight, Peter Kuhn, Bob Lambrechts, David Leal, Rebecca Lees, Christian Leroy, Ma Linwei, Ming Liu, Peter Lord, Jim Lupton, Kelly Luterell, Prof. David MacKay, Roger Manser, Niall Mansfield, Fabian Marion, Graeme Marshall, Ian Maxwell, Alan McLelland, Hillary McOwat, Alan McRobie, Graham McShane, Christina Meskers, Prof. Cam Middleton, David Moore, Cillian Moynihan, Prof. Daniel Mueller, Daniel Müller, Dr. Omer Music, Sid Nayar, Gunther Newcombe, Anna Nguyem, Duncan Nicholson, Adrian Noake, Sharon Nolan, George Oates, Mayoma Onwochei, Andy Orme, Yukiya Oyachi, Andrew Parker, David Parker, Alan Partridge, Mike Peirce, Matt Pumfrey, Philip Purnell, David Reay, Henk Reimink, Jan Reisener, Chris Romanowski, Mike Russell, Pradip Saha, Geoff Scamens, Thomas Schaden, Patrick Schrynmakers, Prof. Alan Short, Jim Simmons, Kevin Slattery, Emily Sloan, Derick Smart, Andrew Smith, Prof. Malcolm Smith, Martin Smith, Prof. Richard Smith, Greg Southall, Mick Steeper, Michael Stych, Judith Sykes, Katie Symons, Prof. Erman Tekkaya, NeeJoo The, Stefan Thielen, Micahel Trompeter, Robert Tucker, Hendrik vanOss, Tao Wang, Prof. Jeremy Watson, Andrew Weir, Anna Wenlock, Alex West, Glyn Wheeler, Gavin White, Mark White, Ollie Wildman, John Wilkinson, Larry Williams, Pete Winslow, Prof. Ernst Worrell, Masterchef Roseanna Xanthe, Lina Xie, Prof. Liping Xu, and to everyone else we should have named.

To write the book, we've taken a lot of time away from our families, and we'd like to end by expressing our unending appreciation for their loving support.

About the authors

Julian Allwood is a Reader in Engineering at the University of Cambridge where he leads the Low Carbon Materials Processing research group and is a fellow of Gonville and Caius College. He worked for 10 years for the aluminium industry and currently holds an EPSRC Leadership Fellowship which funds the WellMet2050 project. He is joint editor-in-chief of the Journal of Materials Processing Technology, a vice Chairman of the International Academy of Production Engineering (CIRP) and is a lead author for the 5th Assessment Report of the Intergovernmental Panel on Climate Change (IPCC).

Jonathan Cullen is a Research Associate in the Low Carbon Material Processing group at the University of Cambridge and a Research Fellow at Fitzwilliam College. After five years as a Chemical Process Engineer in New Zealand he worked as a consultant and development engineer in Peru, before taking an MPhil in Engineering for Sustainable Development and a PhD on the engineering fundamentals of energy efficiency in Cambridge.

Mark Carruth, Daniel Cooper, Martin McBrien, Rachel Milford, Muiris Moynihan and Alexandra Patel are all currently PhD students in the Low Carbon Materials Processing group as part of the WellMet2050 project, which aims to identify and evaluate all possible means to halve global carbon emissions from the production of steel and aluminium goods. Collectively they hold several degrees in economics, engineering and arts, two husbands and a number of years experience in different design and consultancy roles.

Also published by UIT

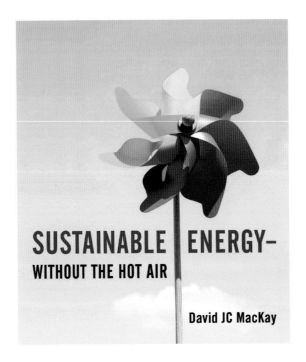

"May be the best technical book about the environment that I've ever read. This is to energy and climate what Freakonomics is to economics." **Cory Doctorow, boingboing.net**

"The book is a tour de force. As a work of popular science it is exemplary. For anyone seeking a deeper understanding of the real problems involved it is the place to start." **The Economist**

"If someone wants an overall view of how energy gets used, where it comes from, and the challenges in switching to new sources, this is the book to read. . . . I was thrilled to see a book that is scientific, numeric, broad, open-minded, and well written on a topic where a lot of narrow, obscure, non-numeric writing confuses the public." **Bill Gates, in blog**

"A must read for everyone who is concerned about global warming. James Atkins is not afraid to challenge everyone and everything when it comes to climate change. And I believe he does so with a lot of insight and comprehension about the problem." **Murielle Ungricht, Greenfudge Blog**

"Climate change is as much about power stations as football is about wearing shorts." **Joint Implementation Quarterly**

"An entertaining and engaging book on the psychology and science of football and climate change." **www.sustainableguernsey.info**

"Read it right away and have to say it is hilarious. The way this difficult topic is presented is also really nice. Great idea!" **Fan from Switzerland**

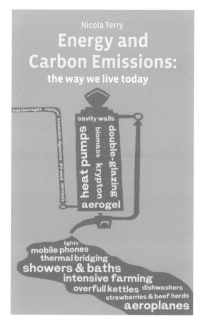

This book is a single comprehensive resource giving you the information you need to understand your carbon emissions and energy consumption. It shows you how you can make practical decisions about your home and the way you live and save money too!

The book also addresses the needs of schools and teachers. It shows how simple experiments and simple calculations can deliver real results about the real world. Pupils get both practical experience (exploring a specific problem) and broader education (learning how to approach things scientifically).

More about this book

This book contains a vision that we want to share—that we need to look for a sustainable materials future with both eyes open. If we look ahead only with one eye open (for efficiencies in existing processes) we won't have much impact, and the impact will anyway be eclipsed by demand growth. So we need to look with both eyes open—for material efficiency and demand reduction.

To share the vision as widely as possible, we're giving the book away for free in PDF format for personal, non-commercial use. You can download it from: *www.withbotheyesopen.com*

Our work towards this book has been funded by the UK government's Engineering and Physical Science and Research Council, and we're carrying on. Our priority now is to develop full scale pilot studies and demonstrators of our strategies 'with both eyes open'—and we'll post updates about them on the website as the work continues.

This book should be cited as: Allwood J.M., Cullen J.M., Carruth M.A., Cooper D.R., McBrien M., Milford R.L., Moynihan M., Patel A.C.H. (2012) *Sustainable Materials: with both eyes open*, UIT Cambridge, England.

More about the publisher

Join our mailing lists: get email newsletters on topics of interest. Receive updates, notifications about author appearances, interviews, podcasts, events, and announcements about new editions. *www.uit.co.uk/subscribe*

How to order: get details of stockists and online bookstores. If you are a bookstore, find out about our distributors, or contact us to discuss your particular requirements. *www.uit.co.uk/order*

Send us a book proposal: if you want to write – even if you have just the kernel of an idea at present –we'd love to hear from you. We pride ourselves on supporting our authors and making the process of book-writing as satisfying and as easy as possible. *www.uit.co.uk/for-authors*

UIT Cambridge Ltd.
PO Box 145
Cambridge
CB4 1GQ
England

Email: book-inquiries@uit.co.uk
Phone: **+44 1223 302 041**